# NEW INTERNATIONAL
# BIBLICAL COMMENTARY

*Old Testament Editors,*
Robert L. Hubbard Jr.
Robert K. Johnston

# EZRA, NEHEMIAH, ESTHER

*Old Testament Series*

# NEW INTERNATIONAL BIBLICAL COMMENTARY

# EZRA, NEHEMIAH, ESTHER

## LESLIE C. ALLEN
## TIMOTHY S. LANIAK

Based on the New International Version

© 2003 by Leslie C. Allen and Timothy S. Laniak
Hendrickson Publishers, Inc.
P. O. Box 3473
Peabody, Massachusetts 01961-3473

First published jointly, 2003, in the United States by
Hendrickson Publishers and in the United Kingdom by the
Paternoster Press, P. O. Box 300, Carlisle, Cumbria CA3 0QS.
All rights reserved.

*Printed in the United States of America*

*First printing — July 2003*

**Library of Congress Cataloging-in-Publication Data**

Allen, Leslie C.
    Ezra, Nehemiah, Esther / Leslie C. Allen. Timothy S. Laniak.
    p. cm. — (New International biblical commentary ; 9)
    Includes bibliographical references and index.
    ISBN 1-56563-218-4 (pbk. : alk. paper) — ISBN 1-56563-593-0
(hardcover : alk. paper)  1. Bible. O.T. Ezra—Commentaries.
2. Bible. O.T. Nehemiah—Commentaries. 3. Bible. O.T.
Esther—Commentaries.  I. Laniak, Timothy S.  II. Title.
III. Series.

    BS1355.53A45 2003
    222'.07—dc21                2003010842

ISBN 1–56563–218–4 (U.S. softcover)
ISBN 1–56563–593–0 (U.S. hardcover)

**British Library Cataloguing in Publication Data**
**A catalogue record for this book is available**
**from the British Library.**

ISBN 0–85364–730–5 (U.K. softcover)

# Table of Contents

*Esther*—Timothy S. Laniak

As an ancient document, the Old Testament often seems something quite foreign to modern men and women. Opening its pages may feel, to the modern reader, like traversing a kind of literary time warp into a whole other world. In that world sisters and brothers marry, long hair mysteriously makes men superhuman, and temple altars daily smell of savory burning flesh and sweet incense. There, desert bushes burn but leave no ashes, water gushes from rocks, and cities fall because people march around them. A different world, indeed!

Even God, the Old Testament's main character, seems a stranger compared to his more familiar New Testament counterpart. Sometimes the divine is portrayed as a loving father and faithful friend, someone who rescues people from their greatest dangers or generously rewards them for heroic deeds. At other times, however, God resembles more a cruel despot, one furious at human failures, raving against enemies, and bloodthirsty for revenge. Thus, skittish about the Old Testament's diverse portrayal of God, some readers carefully select which portions of the text to study, or they avoid the Old Testament altogether.

The purpose of this commentary series is to help readers navigate this strange and sometimes forbidding literary and spiritual terrain. Its goal is to break down the barriers between the ancient and modern worlds so that the power and meaning of these biblical texts become transparent to contemporary readers. How is this to be done? And what sets this series apart from others currently on the market?

This commentary series will bypass several popular approaches to biblical interpretation. It will not follow a *precritical* approach that interprets the text without reference to recent scholarly conversations. Such a commentary contents itself with offering little more than a paraphrase of the text with occasional supplements from archaeology, word studies, and classical theology. It mistakenly believes that there have been few insights into the Bible since Calvin or Luther. Nor will this series pursue an *anticritical* approach whose preoccupation is to defend the Bible against its detractors, especially scholarly ones. Such a commentary has little space left to move beyond showing why the Bible's critics are wrong to explaining what the biblical text means. The result is a paucity of vibrant biblical theology. Again, this series finds inadequate a *critical* approach that seeks to understand the text apart from belief in the meaning it conveys. Though modern readers have been taught to be discerning, they do not want to live in the "desert of criticism" either.

Instead, as its editors, we have sought to align this series with what has been labeled *believing criticism*. This approach marries probing, reflective interpretation of the text to loyal biblical devotion and warm Christian affection. Our contributors tackle the task of interpretation using the full range of critical methodologies and practices. Yet they do so as people of faith who hold the text in the highest regard. The commentators in this series use criticism to bring the message of the biblical texts vividly to life so the minds of modern readers may be illumined and their faith deepened.

The authors in this series combine a firm commitment to modern scholarship with a similar commitment to the Bible's full authority for Christians. They bring to the task the highest technical skills, warm theological commitment, and rich insight from their various communities. In so doing, they hope to enrich the life of the academy as well as the life of the church.

Part of the richness of this commentary series derives from its authors' breadth of experience and ecclesial background. As editors, we have consciously brought together a diverse group of scholars in terms of age, gender, denominational affiliation, and race. We make no claim that they represent the full expression of the people of God, but they do bring fresh, broad perspectives to the interpretive task. But though this series has sought out diversity among its contributors, they also reflect a commitment to a common center. These commentators write as "believing critics"—scholars who desire to speak for church and academy, for academy and church. As editors, we offer this series in devotion to God and for the enrichment of God's people.

Robert L. Hubbard Jr.
Robert K. Johnston
Editors

# Abbreviations

| | |
|---|---|
| AB | Anchor Bible |
| *ANET* | J. B. Pritchard (ed.), *Ancient Near Eastern Texts Relating to the Old Testament*. Princeton: Princeton University Press, 1950; 3d ed., 1969 |
| *Ant.* | Josephus, *Jewish Antiquities* |
| AT | Alpha Text |
| *AUSS* | *Andrews University Seminary Studies* |
| *BA* | *Biblical Archaeology* |
| *BAR* | *Biblical Archaeology Review* |
| *BASOR* | *Bulletin of the American School of Oriental Research* |
| BDB | Brown, F., S. R. Driver, and C. A. Briggs, *A Hebrew and English Lexicon of the Old Testament*. Oxford, 1907 |
| *BEvT* | *Beiträge zur evangelischen Theologie* |
| *BHS* | *Biblia Hebraica Stuttgartensia*. Edited by K. Elliger and W. Rudolph. Stuttgart, 1983 |
| *Bib* | *Biblica* |
| *BibRev* | *Bible Review* |
| BJS | Brown Judaic Studies |
| *BSac* | *Bibliotheca Sacra* |
| BZAW | Beihefte zur Zeitschrift für die alttestmentliche Wissenschaft |
| *CAD* | *The Assyrian Dictionary of the Oriental Institute of the University of Chicago*. Chicago, 1956– |
| *CBQ* | *Catholic Biblical Quarterly* |
| Gk. | Greek |
| HAT | Handbuch zum alten Testament |
| HDR | Harvard Dissertations in Religion |
| Heb. | Hebrew |
| *HR* | *History of Religion* |
| *HTh* | *Ho Theológos* |

| | |
|---|---|
| *IB* | *Interpreter's Bible.* Edited by G. A. Buttrich et al. 12 vols. New York, 1951–1957 |
| IBC | Interpretation: A Bible Commentary for Teaching and Preaching |
| ICC | International Critical Commentary |
| *IDBSup* | *Interpreter's Dictionary of the Bible Supplementary Volume.* Edited by K. Crim. Nashville, 1976 |
| impf. | imperfect |
| impv. | imperative |
| inf. | infinitive |
| *Int* | *Interpretation* |
| ITC | International Theological Commentary |
| *JBL* | *Journal of Biblical Literature* |
| *JES* | *Journal of Ecumenical Studies* |
| *JETS* | *Journal of the Evangelical Theological Society* |
| *JNES* | *Journal of Near Eastern Studies* |
| *JQR* | *Jewish Quarterly Review* |
| *JR* | *Journal of Religion* |
| *JSOT* | *Journal for the Study of the Old Testament* |
| JSOTSup | Journal for the Study of the Old Testament: Supplement Series |
| *JSS* | *Journal of Semitic Studies* |
| *JTS* | *Journal of Theological Studies* |
| KJV | King James Version |
| LCL | Loeb Classical Library |
| LXX | Septuagint |
| mg. | margin |
| MT | Masoretic text |
| NCB | New Century Bible |
| NASB | New American Standard Bible |
| NEB | New English Bible |
| NICOT | New International Commentary on the Old Testament |
| NIV | New International Version |
| NJB | New Jerusalem Bible |
| NJPS | New Jewish Publication Society Bible |
| NRSV | New Revised Standard Version |
| OBO | Orbis biblicus et orientalis |
| OT | Old Testament |
| OTG | Old Testament Guides |
| OTL | Old Testament Library |

| | |
|---|---|
| *PEQ* | *Palestine Exploration Quarterly* |
| perf. | perfect |
| *PRSt* | *Perspectives in Religious Studies* |
| RB | *Revue biblique* |
| REB | Revised English Bible |
| *RevQ* | *Revue de Qumran* |
| *RHA* | *Revue hittite et asianique* |
| RSV | Revised Standard Version |
| SBLDS | Society of Biblical Literature Dissertation Series |
| SBLMS | Society of Biblical Literature Monograph Series |
| SBM | Stuttgarter biblische Monographien |
| sg. | singular |
| SJLA | Studies in Judaism in Late Antiquity |
| *SwJT* | *Southwestern Journal of Theology* |
| TBC | Torch Bible Commentaries |
| TOTC | Tyndale Old Testament Commentaries |
| v./vv. | verse(s) |
| voc. | vocative |
| *VT* | *Vetus Testamentum* |
| WBC | Word Biblical Commentary |
| *WZKM* | *Wiener Zeitschrift für die Kunde des Morganlandes* |
| *ZAW* | *Zeitschrift für die alttestamentliche Wissenschaft* |
| ZBK | Zürcher Bibelkommentare |

## Preface to Ezra-Nehemiah

Writing a commentary is like attending an ongoing seminar, first as a nervous student who is all ears and no mouth and then as a graduate who can cautiously venture to give appraisals of the debate and make a few suggestions. A former colleague of mine, Geoffrey Grogan, used to tell me, "God has set teachers in the church—and many of them have written books." The Holy Spirit's aid in reading the biblical text and taking it to heart comes via the study of lexicons, grammars, commentaries, monographs, essays, and journal articles. My heavy debt to most of them has to be left publicly unpaid, though efforts have been made to credit particular scholars with distinctive interpretations of the text I have used. This series is not meant to furnish detailed discussions of problems, and the commentary of Hugh G. M. Williamson has served as a constant reference point for further information, so that I did not need to reinvent the academic wheel.

I would like to thank doctoral student Sue Fry for diligently unearthing a comprehensive bibliography for me to work with, Alex Pak for her expertise in the word processing office, and Fuller Theological Seminary for funding both facilities and for providing an encouraging environment in which to teach and write.

Leslie C. Allen
September 1998

## *Preface to Esther*

Commenting on a biblical text—verse by verse, chapter by chapter, and book by book—is one of the most enduring and profitable forms of biblical interpretation. It is a process that promotes a unique kind of intimacy with ancient authors, characters, and audiences.

Having already written a thematic study of the book of Esther, I have now had the pleasure of revisiting the unnamed author and his/her script a second time. My admiration continues to grow for Esther herself, a woman whose exceptional journey into leadership has prompted a great deal of personal reflection. This little book devoted to her—like all the others in our canon—is clearly an inexhaustible treasure. It is my hope that the lives of our commentary's readers will be enriched as they consider more fully the implications of this often neglected episode in the history of salvation and the actions of those who mediated that salvation. The extent to which our readers do benefit from the commentary will be a tribute to all those who have contributed to the study of Esther (on whose shoulders I have stood) and, of course, to the inspired account itself.

Tim Laniak
Purim 2003

# *Ezra*

Leslie C. Allen

# Introduction

Ezra-Nehemiah is the OT equivalent of the Acts of the Apostles—it is a book of new beginnings. Acts opens with the outpouring of the Holy Spirit promised by God in Joel 2 (Acts 1:4–5; 2:16–21, 33). The fulfillment of "the word of the LORD spoken by Jeremiah" (Ezra 1:1) launches Ezra-Nehemiah. The book of Acts selectively narrates the early history of the church through the work of Peter, Stephen, Philip, and Paul. Here the re-establishment of the people of God after the exile is presented in a series of phases associated with the names of Sheshbazzar, Zerubbabel, Ezra, and Nehemiah.

## Ezra-Nehemiah as Historical Literature

Twenty-five years ago I taught Ezra-Nehemiah in an academic setting as a window through which to see the history of the postexilic period. That approach was common then, whether one had a minimal or maximal view of the historicity of the book. "What happened?" or "What really happened?" were the questions we tried to answer. We used the evidence of Ezra-Nehemiah to reconstruct history. It is still possible to treat the book like that, and historians continue to do so. But now it is more usual to emphasize the literary nature of Ezra-Nehemiah. We should look primarily at the text, not at something that lies behind it. Of course, in practice one cannot work in watertight compartments, and history has to feature somewhere, since the text's purpose was to talk about the past as relevant to the later time in which the text was written. Yet Ezra-Nehemiah functions primarily as history-related *literature*, and we must listen to the presentation that has been given us. Throughout this commentary, historical concerns will impinge on our exegetical study at two points. First, when the text assumes that we know certain things widely known at the time of writing, we as later readers must learn what is presupposed. Second, when the text deviates from probable historical fact, we need to listen very carefully to the intended message.

## The Structure and Content of Ezra-Nehemiah[1]

Modern readers of the OT think of two books, one called Ezra and the other called Nehemiah. However, the MT, the standard text of the Hebrew Bible, regards it as one literary text—noting, for instance, that Nehemiah 3:32 is the middle verse of the book. The LXX (the earliest Greek translation of the Hebrew Old Testament) also treated Ezra and Nehemiah as a single work. The question arises as to whether its parts add up to a structural whole. We shall see that the answer is yes.

Three parts constitute this whole: (1) Ezra 1–6 is a lengthy report concerning the early returnees from exile; (2) a bridging "After these things" introduces Ezra 7–10, the story of Ezra's return to Judah; and (3) a heading, "The words of Nehemiah son of Hacaliah," introduces Nehemiah 1–13, which is mainly about Nehemiah's return. The three parts tell the story of three missions, and each mission falls into two parts after it is assigned and described. Ezra 1:1–4 announces the first mission, which is found in chapters 1–6. A nucleus of Jewish exiles in Babylonia returned to Judah to rebuild the temple in Jerusalem. They carried this out in two main stages: first, they returned with vessels from the first temple that were officially restored and they prepared to build an altar and laid the temple foundations (1:5–3:13); second, they rebuilt the actual temple (4:4–6:22).

Ezra 7–10 describes the second mission. Here we encounter for the first time the person after whom this first book, Ezra, was eventually named. In 7:1–28a he receives his commission in two parts. First, he is to take valuable supplies and pledges for the temple, along with a new group of returning exiles, back to Jerusalem. Second, he is to implement the adoption of the Torah to regulate the life of the Judean community. The first half of this commission, which Ezra sums up as "to bring honor to the house of the LORD" (7:27), is fulfilled in 7:28b–8:36. The second half, the implementation of the Torah, is described in 9:1–10:44 with reference to the issue of mixed marriages.

Nehemiah 1–13 present the third, or Nehemiah's, mission. Nehemiah 1:1–2:10 announces the mission as the task of rebuilding Jerusalem (2:5). This rebuilding consists of two distinct stages, and at the beginning of each stage Nehemiah claims that God had put the task into his heart (2:12; 7:5). The first stage for Nehemiah on his return is to rebuild the walls, which is accomplished in 2:11–6:19. The second stage is the repopulation of Jerusalem, which necessitates rebuilding houses (7:4). The Hebrew verb "to build" can also have the connotation of building up a community. This second aspect of rebuilding Jerusalem is then accomplished in the course of chapters 7–13. The service of dedicating the walls does not occur until 12:27–43 because it was a celebration held by the citizens of the reoccupied Jerusalem. And so it was a fitting conclusion to both phases of Nehemiah's mission.

The three missions of Ezra-Nehemiah run along parallel lines. An initial section announces each mission, and then two further sections narrate the two stages of its accomplishment. Other common features also underline this parallelism, some common to all three missions and others to two of them. The introductory section in each case founds its mission on both a secular source and a supernatural one. A Persian king—Cyrus in the first case and Artaxerxes in the other two—assigned each mission. Cyrus acknowledged himself as the agent of the God of Israel (Ezra 1:2), and the narrative prefaces his decree with the assertion that "the LORD moved the heart of Cyrus" (1:1) in fulfillment of Jeremiah's prophecy. At the close of this first mission, Ezra 6:14, 22 echo 1:1. In the second mission, the text makes it clear that the commission of Artaxerxes to Ezra is evidence that "the hand of the LORD was on" Ezra (7:6). Moreover, divine inspiration and providence is claimed: "the LORD, the God of our fathers, . . . put . . . into the king's heart" the first half of Ezra's mission (7:27) and "extended his good favor to" Ezra "before the king" (7:28). Ezra 7:27 implies the fulfillment of Isaiah 60:7, where the same Hebrew verb is used in the divine promise "I will adorn my glorious temple." The third mission similarly follows this pattern of being decreed by a Persian king and by the sovereign will of the God of Israel. Nehemiah 1:1–2:8 describes the mission, and 2:18 summarizes the commission as "the gracious hand of my God upon me and what the king had said to me." The claim of divine providence does not in this case accompany an explicit claim that Scripture had been fulfilled. Instead, Nehemiah's prayer appeals to God to fulfill, evidently through his mission, the divine promise in Deuteronomy 30:1–4 that a repentant Israel would return to Jerusalem.

A dominant theme of Ezra-Nehemiah is the opposition that confronted three missions as they struggled to reached their goals. This resistance occurs in five of the six half sections. Neighboring peoples intimidate the Israelites in Ezra 3:3, and then there is much stronger opposition in 4:1–24. In Ezra's mission, the Levites are unwilling to serve in the temple (8:15), there are enemy attacks from which the caravan was delivered (8:31), and then there is minor opposition to the policy on divorce in 10:15. In the first half of Nehemiah's mission, such resistance becomes a recurring theme of the narrative (Neh. 2:10–5:19). The theme of opposition does not appear in Nehemiah 7–13. Another thematic feature of the half sections is the statement of achievement in Ezra 3:3, 10a; 6:14–15; 8:33–34; 10:5 (explained in v. 3); Nehemiah 6:15, and in an expanded form in 11:1–24. Another parallel in Ezra-Nehemiah is the religious celebration that follows most of the mission stages in Ezra 3:3b–5, 10–13; 6:16–22; 8:35; Nehemiah 12:22–43. Such celebration is absent only from the wall building of Nehemiah 2:11–6:19 (clearly the celebration of 12:22–43 was intended to do double duty for both stages).

There are efforts throughout Ezra-Nehemiah to set up normative guidelines for the future, relating either to the temple or to the community, or both—for example, in Ezra 3:6a and 6:18. There are no such prescriptions in either part of Ezra's mission, except perhaps for "never" (NRSV) in 9:12 in relation to mixed marriages. Interestingly, Josephus claimed that a guideline was laid down in the second part of the mission: "So then, having rectified the wrongdoing of the aforementioned men in marrying, Ezra purified the practice relating to this matter, so that it remained fixed for the future" (*Ant.* 11.153). Presumably the "never" of 9:12 influenced his interpretation. The community establishes guidelines in Nehemiah 12:44–13:3, in line with the communal pledge of 9:38–10:39. Nehemiah 13:4–31 was added to give the impression that Nehemiah monitored these guidelines. These verses present him as the servant of the community, ensuring that they were maintained. The focus here is not on the lapses that took place but rather on Nehemiah's prompt realignment of community practice according to the norms, as a model for future generations to follow.

Although the three missions obviously follow this clear structural pattern, each account is distinctive and complex in its own right. As for individual components, the list of early returnees in Ezra 1–6, borrowed from Nehemiah 7, serves in Ezra 2 to make a theological claim that the true people of God were returning to found a new Israel. The leap forward to a later period in 4:6–23 demonstrates that opposition was a recurring experience of God's people, to be endured with patience. Yet the opposition to rebuilding the city walls in Artaxerxes' reign, the theme of 4:7–23, serves also as an introduction to Nehemiah's later, and successful, mission. The king's decree in Ezra 4:21, which held out the possibility that he would permit rebuilding in the future, materialized in Nehemiah 2:1–8. We do not find the basic account of Ezra's reading and teaching the Torah in Ezra 6–10. It appears to have been moved to Nehemiah 8, but 7:10 seems to imply that this reading and teaching occurred as the prelude to Ezra 9. Ezra's prayer in 9:6–15 was a means of winning support for his Torah-based stand and also illustrated how Ezra taught and interpreted the Torah. It is obvious that chapters 8–10 deliberately interrupt the second half of Nehemiah's mission. The theme of repopulating the city is seemingly put on hold from the end of chapter 7 to chapter 11. Here the clue to the insertion is Nehemiah's prayer in chapter 1.[2] The editor has used this prayer as a prescription for the community at large to subsequently take over in spirit. First, according to 1:7, breaking the Torah had occasioned Israel's present plight: "We have not obeyed the commands, decrees and laws you gave your servant Moses." A condition of returning to Jerusalem, to the chosen place for God's name to dwell, was to take the Torah seriously. So the editor moved Ezra's teaching and implementation of the Torah here (Neh. 8). Second, Israel had to return to its God, according to 1:9 ("if you return to me"), and Nehemiah had led the way by his representative prayer of repentance. In Nehemiah 9, a prayer in contemporary use illustrates Israel's return to God. A key verb in this prayer is the Hebrew verb *shuv*, "turn, return," which made it a fitting communal counterpart to Nehemiah's prayer. Moreover, the new prayer's emphasis on the Torah, both as narrative and as that which was to be obeyed, carried forward the message of Nehemiah 8. Third, Israel needed to obey God's commands in the Torah if its exiles were to return to Jerusalem (1:9, "and obey my commands"). So the community's pledge is placed in Nehemiah 10—even though chronologically it must have been made in a later period, after the events of Nehemiah 13—to express communal affirmation of the Torah as a series of contemporary obligations based on it. Step by step, the community fulfilled Nehemiah's presentation in chapter 1, as a spiritual model for each generation to follow in principle. The organic links between chapters 1 and 8–10 show how closely the later chapters were integrated into Nehemiah's own mission, so that we can envision this mission as covering chapters 1–13.

## The Historical Order of Ezra and Nehemiah

Twenty-five years ago, the dominant view was that Nehemiah came to Judah before Ezra. According to this view,

Nehemiah arrived in the twentieth year of Artaxerxes' reign (Neh. 1:1)—in the year 445. Ezra returned not in the seventh year of his reign, 458, but in the seventh year of the reign of Artaxerxes II, or 398. A vocal and influential minority held an intermediate view, which claimed that in Ezra 7:7, and similarly in 7:8, the text should be corrected to read "the thirty-seventh year," referring to the year 428, between the first and second terms of Nehemiah's governorship. The evangelical scholar F. F. Bruce was among those who held this view. These two views were espoused in order to deal with a number of problems arising from the traditional dating of Ezra, which was regarded as a veritable Cinderella. Now academic fashion has changed and, in keeping with the fairy tale's ending, it has remarkably become the majority viewpoint—at least in the English-speaking world of scholarship. This is not the place to review the pros and cons.[3] We have not heard the last of this issue, and the scholarly pendulum may swing again. In principle, the idea that Ezra came after Nehemiah cannot be ruled out. There are enough deviations from a historical order of events in Ezra-Nehemiah to make yet another such deviation a matter of little surprise. The one factor that carries weight for me and topples me from the fence is the issue of Torah hermeneutics. The tradition can hardly be wrong in crediting Ezra with the role of teaching the Torah, whereby he hermeneutically applied the Torah's prescriptions to the issues of his day and trained a corps of instructing Levites to help him. Ezra 9 and Nehemiah 8 are eloquent witnesses to this tradition. However, hermeneutical skill in using the Torah is also displayed in Nehemiah 13:1–3, 4–31, material that must be associated historically with Nehemiah's reforms in his second administration. Even Nehemiah 5, which belongs to his first administration, by its use of Leviticus 25 seems to presuppose prior work done by Ezra. It is difficult to avoid the conclusion that such learning represented the legacy that Ezra left in Judah. In this instance, history and literature seem to be walking a single path.

### The Editing of Ezra-Nehemiah

Since the middle of the last century, it has become customary to regard Chronicles-Ezra-Nehemiah as the product of a homogeneous viewpoint and as the overall work of a single editor. There is, however, a growing tendency to distinguish between Ezra-Nehemiah and Chronicles, while still admitting that the works have much in common and belong to a developing school of thought.[4] More work remains to be done on this issue, but enough evidence of their basic independence has emerged. There are at least five major differences between the two works. (1) Ezra-Nehemiah has an exilic concept of Israel, as exiles from Babylon and their descendants, while Chronicles goes back to a traditional definition of Israel as consisting of twelve tribes, not as an actuality but as an ideal toward which to work. The difference between 1 Chronicles 9:3 and Nehemiah 11:4a speaks volumes. (2) Ezra-Nehemiah has no royal eschatology, unlike Chronicles. (3) Ezra 9 works with the concept of a generational backlog of divine wrath inherited by postexilic Israel, but Chronicles characteristically thinks of each generation as starting fresh with God. (4) Ezra-Nehemiah often uses the typology of a second exodus, whereas Chronicles downplays the exodus in favor of the era of David and Solomon as inaugurating a new work of God on Israel's behalf. (5) While Nehemiah 13:26 cites Solomon in 1 Kings 11 as a bad example, the Chronicler studiously omitted this passage from his history and quietly took a softer line on intermarriage; unlike Ezra-Nehemiah, he never used the Hebrew verb *ma'al*, "to be unfaithful," to refer to mixed marriages.

Ezra 7–Nehemiah 13 appears to be substantially the work of one editor who drew on available documents. The longest of these documents was what is generally called Nehemiah's memoirs because of the refrain "Remember . . . , O my God" that runs through it. We know little about the setting and function of this autobiographical document.[5] This does not greatly matter, since the editor used it secondarily for the account of Nehemiah's work and doubtless regarded the refrain simply as evidence of his spirituality. The editor reproduced the memoirs in Nehemiah 1:1–7:73, most of 12:31–43, and 13:4–31. Evidently the wall-building document of chapter 3 and the list of early immigrants in chapter 7 were already incorporated. The editor used other, community-centered accounts of the repopulation of Jerusalem in 11:1–2 and of the wall dedication ceremony in 12:27–30, and he had access to a list of the new residents of Jerusalem in 11:3a, 4–20. We have already considered the editorial insertion of chapters 8–10. The first of these chapters was an adapted form of part of Ezra's memoirs, the second a contemporary prayer of repentance, and the third a document recording a communal pledge, into which an independent list of names has been inserted. Subsequent compilers added further lists in 11:20–36 and 12:1–26.

For Ezra's mission the basic document was an autobiographical account we call Ezra's memoirs, simply borrowing the term from the counterpart for Nehemiah. The so-called memoirs appear in Ezra 7:27–9:15. Doubtless they already included the preceding letter of King Artaxerxes in 7:11–26 and also parts of the introduction in 7:1–10, adapted to the third person. Ezra 10:1–44 seems to have been adapted in the same way, including the closing list of men with foreign wives. The description of Ezra's commission in the royal letter suggests that his memoirs were rather longer and that the editor provided selected excerpts.

The narrative of Ezra 1–6 appears to be later than the bulk of Ezra 7–Nehemiah 13, since the list in Ezra 2 was evidently taken from Nehemiah 7 in its present literary context.[6] Yet the work was completed earlier than Chronicles because the Chronicler apparently quotes not only from Nehemiah 11 in 1 Chronicles 9, but also from the beginning of Ezra 1 at the end of 2 Chronicles 36. The narrator completed the work by giving an account of earlier settlement in Judah. We can detect certain documents at his disposal: a list of sacred vessels officially returned in Ezra 1:8–11a; the immigrant list re-used in 2:1–3:1; four official letters in 4:6–23; the written messages of Haggai and Zechariah alluded to in 5:1–2; and further official correspondence in 5:3–6:12, including a memorandum of Cyrus' initial decree in 6:3–5. In Ezra 1–6 the narrator took the opportunity to develop his own agenda, particularly in the area of worship.

### The Separatism of Ezra-Nehemiah

Ezra-Nehemiah and the book of Esther make strange bedfellows in this commentary volume, with the latter bordering on an assimilationist attitude to pagan society and the former appealing for a strict religious stand. In fact, Ezra-Nehemiah is written from a more rigorous perspective than Chronicles. Completed substantially about 400, it advocates a separatist community principally made up of Judeans who had returned from exile and their descendants. The Chronicler, writing a little later in the first half of the fourth century, judged that the time had come for a more inclusive policy, now that the community was more settled. He steered a middle course between separatist and assimilationist policies held in Jerusalem. Ezra-Nehemiah, and behind it the individuals Ezra and Nehemiah, adopted a separatist line.[7] It was no accident that Ezra's first supporters were a right-wing religious party, those who "trembled at the words of the God of Israel" (Ezra 9:4; 10:3). Ezra 7–10 emphasizes that the true people of God were Judeans who had returned from Babylonian exile and their families. The elect nation of Israel had by divine providence gone through the narrow tunnel of judgment and emerged in Judah once more. Ezra uses the Torah's ban on intermarriage as an instrument for preserving this understanding of the religious community. For Nehemiah, the specter of assimilation arose on the political front, as he fought in God's name against opponents from neighboring communities and their influence on fellow Judeans. He, too, opposed foreign marriages, especially those contracted for economic and political reasons among the upper classes, and he found scriptural support for his stand. He appealed to such texts as Deuteronomy 7, 23, and 1 Kings 11. Under Nehemiah, the antipathy toward mixed marriages became part of a comprehensive process of establishing a distinctive way of life for the community. In Ezra 1–6 the Israelites rejected overtures from foreign fellow Yahwists (4:1–3), and the exilic nature of the religious community is again emphasized, though at the end this ideal is stretched by welcoming other Judeans who were prepared to adopt the strictness of the core group (6:21).

Clearly there was a selective appeal to Scripture, and Chronicles, though uncompromising in other respects, was less restrictive than Ezra-Nehemiah. The book of Ruth's openness to a Moabite female proselyte who had married into a Judean family, as well as the liberal stand taken by Isaiah 56:3–8, reflect voices singing to a different tune. In our own age it is difficult to sympathize with parts of Ezra-Nehemiah. The work offends modern Christian readers as exclusive and even racist. Yet most of us have religious roots in denominations that began as sects. Such sects broke away from the larger religious community, steering a separatist course and flying from the mast the colors of neglected and necessary truths. Different times require different responses, and it was the judgment of Ezra and Nehemiah and their supporters that a rigorous stand was necessary in times aggravated by political and economic stress. The survival of the weakened community was at stake. Truth had to be zealously guarded and worked out in strict policies, to prevent the community from being swallowed up among the nations. Whenever the church faces threat and persecution, Ezra-Nehemiah is available as an inspiring source exemplifying the conviction and courage the church needs to face its own trials. But there is much more to the work than this issue. Ezra-Nehemiah's commitment to Scripture as a meaningful guide for living and communal worship as a significant part of spiritual life will stimulate every Christian reader. It is part of our own long story. In view of the emphasis on the fulfillment of prophecy, Ezra-Nehemiah must be taken with theological seriousness as marking the inauguration of the eschatological program that continues with the coming of Christ.[8]

### English Versions of the Bible

The NIBC commentary series is based on the widely used NIV. Working with the NIV in detail and comparing it with other English versions, I have found on the one hand that it is an eminently readable version that is good for public reading of the Scriptures and for devotional study. On the other hand, in close study it often lets the reader down, mainly because of its commitment to stylistic variation, which is a feature of modern literary English, and because it sometimes paraphrases to achieve a smoother flow. This issue is part of the unavoidable dilemma that faces all translators as they juggle with losses and gains in their approach to the ancient text. The NIV approach often does not serve the original text well, since Hebrew has a relatively small vocabulary and likes to repeat the same terms for rhetorical effect. For detailed study a more literal version, such as the NRSV, conveys the original better. It stands in a tradition of literal rendering that goes back to the KJV. Other modern versions that I find valuable are the REB, NJB, and NJPS. In the Additional Notes sections, I have taken pains to find at each juncture a rendering in a modern version that best expresses the force of the underlying Hebrew and Aramaic texts.

---

## Notes

---

1. This section is a revised form of conclusions drawn in my essay " 'For He is Good . . .': Worship in Ezra-Nehemiah," *Worship and the Hebrew Bible: Essays in Honor of John T. Willis*, ed. M. P. Graham et al. (JSOTSup 284; Sheffield: JSOT Press, 1999), pp. 15–34.

2. This has been briefly recognized by H. G. M. Williamson and K. D. Tollefson, "Nehemiah as Cultural Revitalization: An Anthropological Perspective," *JSOT* 56 (1992), pp. 41–68, esp. p. 56.

3. See the review of H. G. M. Williamson, *Ezra, Nehemiah* (WBC 16; Waco: Word Books, 1985), pp. xxxix–xliv.

4. See especially S. Japhet, "The Supposed Common Authorship of Chronicles and Ezra-Nehemiah Investigated Anew," *VT* 18 (1968), pp. 330–71; H. G. M. Williamson, *Israel in the Books of Chronicles* (Cambridge: Cambridge University Press, 1977), pp. 1–86. J. Blenkinsopp, *Ezra-Nehemiah: A Commentary* (Philadelphia: Westminster, 1988), esp. pp. 47–54, still works with the notion of the Chronicler as the editor of Ezra-Nehemiah.

5. See the review and suggestion of Williamson, *Ezra, Nehemiah,* pp. xxiv–viii.

6. See in principle Williamson, "The Composition of Ezra i–vi," *JTS* NS 34 (1983), pp. 1–30; not all his suggestions have been adopted.

7. See J. Blenkinsopp, "Interpretation and the Tendency to Sectarianism: An Aspect of Second Temple History," in *Aspects of Judaism in the Graeco-Roman Period* (ed. E. P. Sanders et al.; vol. 1 of *Jewish and Christian Self-Definition;* Philadelphia: Fortress, 1981), pp. 1–26, esp. pp. 1–13.

8. See W. A. Van Gemeren, *Interpreting the Prophetic Word* (Grand Rapids: Zondervan, 1990), pp. 186f., 208f.

## §1 The Long Awaited Signal (Ezra 1:1–4)

This passage launches the first of the three missions narrated in Ezra-Nehemiah. The other two missions will focus on individual leaders, Ezra and Nehemiah, and their God-given work within the restored community. This mission, announced here and carried out in 1:5–6:22, involves restoring the Judeans to their own territory and rebuilding the temple for the worship of God. Throughout the story, the actual return of the people is subordinate to their task of building the sanctuary. Their return is a means of achieving the rebuilding. To be the people of God means to be dedicated to the adoration of God, as a worshiping community. The perspective is that of the Song of Moses in Exodus 15, where the goal of the exodus and of the initial occupation of the land is to bring Israel to the sanctuary graced by God's presence.

**1:1** / It is characteristic of Ezra-Nehemiah to base its missions on both a supernatural and a secular source. When events in human history prove to be of special significance for God's people, they are presented as having been arranged by divine providence. This role of providence is considered so fundamental in the first mission that it is repeated at the end of the account in 6:14, 22, and it frames the passage, serving as an *inclusio*. In the other two missions, divine involvement is simply a theological claim made by the participants (7:27, echoed by the editor in 7:6; Neh. 2:8). This verse, however, confirms that the God of Israel was at work in this crucial historical event, which is hailed as the validation of earlier predictions made by the prophet **Jeremiah.** The divinely given **word** had come true. What passages did the narrator have in mind? The forecast of a seventy-year exile in Jeremiah 25:11–12; 29:10 is often proposed, but the narrative provides its own clue in the phrase "The LORD stirred up the spirit" (NRSV). Jeremiah 51:1, 11 uses the same language in an oracle about the future destruction of Babylon. The latter verse is especially significant, with its statement that "The

LORD has stirred up the spirit of the kings of the Medes" (NRSV). **Cyrus,** king of Anshan and Persia, became king of the Medes by conquest in 549 B.C. before pressing on to capture Babylon in 539. This capture of Babylon made it possible for him to release the Judeans exiled to Babylonia, in the year 538. The narrator probably associated Jeremiah 51 with the even more relevant passages in Second Isaiah, which proclaim that Israel's God "stirred up" (Heb. *he<sup>c</sup>ir*) Cyrus in Isaiah 41:2, 25; 45:13. In these first two cases it was to conquer nations and in the last case to re-build Jerusalem. In Isaiah 44:28, although the verb "stir up" is not used, the divine role given to Cyrus actually includes laying the temple foundations. There was therefore ample material to substantiate the narrative's appeal to prophetic prediction.

The edict of Cyrus is not represented as a directive to the Judean exiles. It is grandly painted on an imperial canvas as infor-mation for all the royal subjects (**you,** v. 3). The whole world must know of this wonderful news. In fact, only the Babylonian Jews are mentioned as returning in the ensuing narrative, definitely not the descendants of the northern kingdom of Israel living else-where in the empire. The narrator seems to have used Cyrus' memorandum, quoted in Aramaic in 6:3–5, as a basis for this edict (here given in Hebrew). The fact that the king **put it in writing** supports this idea, and this is actually the only official document in Ezra-Nehemiah not written in Aramaic. The narrator reserved the stipulation found in 6:5 concerning the return of sacred ves-sels for the narrative of 1:7, where he could associate it with an ex-tant inventory. Because he incorporates a list of returnees from Babylon in chapter 2, he includes the return of exiles in the edict—although simply as builders of the temple. There might also be a side-glance at 7:13, 16.

**1:2–3** / The narrator, perhaps unwittingly, captures the flavor of early Persian policy in attributing Cyrus' military suc-cesses to **the LORD** or Yahweh, **the God of Israel.** It was imperial practice, when a local sanctuary or city was rebuilt, to trace the gift of royal dominion back to the patron deity. Nor should this be re-garded as just a shrewd political move. Polytheism was taken seri-ously and sincerely by the early Persian kings as a supernatural power to be reckoned with. The requirement of Darius that local sacrifices and prayers be offered on behalf of the royal family (6:10), as well as the concern of Artaxerxes to avoid the wrath of Israel's God falling on them (7:23), indicates this concern. Of course, the monotheistic narrator and readers (including us as Christians) must view the issue from a different perspective. The ironic truth is that the God of Israel, and this God alone, was the real power behind the Persian throne and Cyrus' Judean policy, and verse 1 has already used an argument from prophecy to support this claim.

**1:4** / This sentence has a complicated construction in the Hebrew that modern versions have paraphrased, thereby incorporating certain exegetical judgments. The interpretation of the NIV seems to be correct; a more literal version along the same lines appears in the NRSV. The key interpretive question is whether "the people of their place" (NRSV) refers to members of Judean settlements or to their non-Judean neighbors. It is important to note that Cyrus addresses the edict to the non-Judean members of his realm ("you," v. 3), among whom Judeans were settled. Verse 4 explains his purpose in addressing these people—they were to help their Judean neighbors. "The people of their place" is another way of referring to "you." The switch to a third person directive picks up "whatever place" (NRSV) earlier in the sentence. As expected, there is a consistency between the narrator's framing of the edict and his subsequent narrative referring to non-Judean neighbors in verse 6. There, as we shall see, the return from exile is envisioned as a second exodus. That flavor is already evident in verse 4 and appears to be reflected in the statement in the memorandum of chapter 6 that the costs were to be borne by the royal treasury (6:4; compare with the first Exodus, in which Egypt provided resources, Exodus 12:35, 36, 38). In 1:6 that was achieved by diverting local taxes, for which 6:8 may be compared.

## Additional Notes §1

**1:1** / **King of Persia,** used as Cyrus' title twice in this verse and also in 1:2, 8; 3:7; 4:3, 5, designates him as head and founder of the Persian empire, as the Chronicler used it in 2 Chr. 36:20 before citing Ezra 1:1–3a. It was not used by the early kings and reflects later usage in the narrator's period. In 5:13 he is called "king of Babylon," and here his reign is implicitly dated from the capture of Babylon, which enabled him to take over the Babylonian empire. In the pre-539 B.C. Nabonidus Chronicle he is called "the king of Persia" (*ANET,* p. 306), but with reference to his earlier rank as king of a neighboring state. **The word . . .**

**spoken by Jeremiah** is related to the seventy years of Jer. 25 and 29 in 2 Chr. 36:21, but not here, as Williamson, *Ezra, Nehemiah,* pp. 9f., has shown. This is a minor bit of evidence for differentiating the two pieces of literature.

**1:2 / The God of heaven** is a title used in postexilic Jewish literature. It was a common divine title in the Persian empire, and its adoption by Jews may have been an attempt to use a cultural equivalent that would interpret their faith to non-Jews. This acknowledgment of Yahweh may be compared with Cyrus' description of the moon god Sin, in conjunction with the rebuilding of his temple at Ur, as the god who "delivered into my hands the four quarters of the world" (C. J. Gadd and L. Legrain, *Ur Excavations. Texts. 1: Royal Inscriptions* [London: British Museum, 1928], p. 96).

**1:3 /** The Cyrus Cylinder attests that Cyrus returned divine statues to rebuilt temples in the area of Babylonia and repatriated the former inhabitants of associated communities, which may be compared to Cyrus giving permission for Judeans to rebuild **the temple.** (*ANET,* p. 316; cf. A. Kuhrt, "The Cyrus Cylinder and Achaeminid Royal Policy," *JSOT* 25 [1983], pp. 83–97).

**1:4 /** A quite different interpretation is offered in NJPS: "and all who stay behind, wherever he [i.e., any returnee, mentioned in v. 3] may be living, let the people of his place assist him . . ." This rendering takes "the people of his place" as resuming the first phrase, which is related to non-returning Judeans. This interpretation was argued by E. Bickerman, "The Edict of Cyrus in Ezra 1," *Studies in Jewish and Christian History,* Part One (Leiden: Brill, 1976), 72–108, and followed in principle by Williamson, *Ezra, Nehemiah,* pp. 5, 14. The latter uses it as an argument for the independent origin of the edict of vv. 2–4, since it conflicts with v. 6, although he grants that "of Persia" in v. 2 was added by the narrator. For the dependence of the edict on 6:3–5, see B. Halpern, "A Historiographic Commentary on Ezra 1–6: Achronological Narrative and Dual Chronology in Israelite Historiography," in *The Hebrew Bible and Its Interpreters* (ed. W. H. Propp et al.; Winona Lake, Ind.: Eisenbrauns, 1990), pp. 83–93, 122f., and R. de Vaux, *The Bible and the Ancient Near East* (trans. D. McHugh; Garden City, N.Y.: Doubleday, 1971), pp. 94–96. W. Rudolph, *Esra und Nehemia* (HAT 1:20; Tübingen: J. C. B. Mohr [Paul Siebeck], 1949), p. 220, complained that Bickerman's interpretation of "the men of his place" made the phrase superfluous, and indeed Williamson, *Ezra, Nehemiah,* regards it as a gloss or an alternative reading. If possible, a more integrated interpretation of the phrase is preferable on principle. If "the men of his place" is the subject and refers to non-Judeans, the first phrase must relate to the returnees as survivors of the catastrophe of judgment in the year 586, the initial generation of Judeans exiled by Nebuchadnezzar (2:1) together with their families. A theological reference to a remnant is less likely here.

## §2 *Preparations for Implementing the Mission (Ezra 1:5–11)*

Ezra 1:5–3:13 tells the story of the first of the two stages in carrying out the mission of 1:1–4. This section relates the official restitution of temple "vessels" (NRSV) to the returning group (1:7–11).

**1:5–6** / First, however, we find an introductory passage that details the close correspondence between Cyrus' edict and the response it triggered, step by step. The events that follow fulfilled the commands in the divinely inspired proclamation. Having been told to go back to rebuild the temple in verse 3, God's people took steps to do so. Their Gentile neighbors duly helped them, in line with verse 4. But there is more here than a mere repetition in the form of events. The narrator took the opportunity to make a number of theological points. First, the inspiration of verse 1 finds a parallel among the returnees. Those who opted to go back were the ones who responded to divine prompting. All was of **God.** God was the prime mover behind the restoration of the postexilic community. Second, God's **people,** or **Israel,** in verse 3 is now defined as Judean exiles from the three tribes of **Judah, Benjamin,** and Levi, to which **priests and Levites** belonged. Contemporary members of the tribes that had made up the preexilic southern kingdom of Judah constituted the new people of God, as heirs of the earlier community of faith.

Third, there is a typological reference to a second exodus. At the first exodus there was a spoiling of the Egyptians, in which the ancient text revels at several points (Exod. 3:21–22; 11:2; 12:35–36). The Israelites asked their Egyptian neighbors for articles of silver and gold, and received them. The tables were turned, and the victims became the victors by this dramatic means. In verse 6, the addition of **articles** to the command of verse 4 clinches this parallel with the first exodus. Gentile neighbors handed over precious objects, other materials for the temple, and more mundane supplies to the returning Judeans. Biblical typology is the defining of a new act of God in the same terms used for an earlier act. Thus Christ is "the last Adam," head of a new humanity, corresponding to the first Adam (1 Cor. 15:45–49). He is also the "Passover lamb" sacrificed for the church, the counterpart of the first Passover offering for Israel (1 Cor. 5:6–8). This latter parallel is another example of second exodus typology. In the OT, Second Isaiah predicted Israel's return from exile in terms of a new work of God comparable to the ancient exodus (e.g., Isa. 43:19–21; 48:21; 51:9–11; 52:11–12). The same God would again miraculously redeem Israel from oppression and lead them safely to their own land. Our narrator speaks in the same theological vein, but now with the satisfaction of retrospection. He gives a new twist to the typology by applying it to the spoiling of the Egyptians. Other exodus parallels will emerge in verse 11 and in 2:68, and later with reference to Ezra's return in chapter 8.

**1:7** / The royal edict had focused on rebuilding the Jerusalem temple. This purpose comes correspondingly to the fore in Cyrus' restitution of the temple vessels plundered from the first temple. Here the narrator draws on the official memorandum in 6:5 for this detail. He also had at his disposal Tattenai's letter to King Darius, which he incorporated into chapter 5 and which includes further details about the vessels (5:13–15).

**1:8–11a** / In these verses, the narrator reproduces yet another piece of documentation available to him. An **inventory** of the restored vessels was evidently preserved in the temple archives. The official-sounding reference to **Mithredath** and the Persian word used here for **treasurer** suggest that the narrator turned the introduction to the inventory into the narrative of verse 8. Tattenai's letter concurs in its mention of **Sheshbazzar** as the leader of the first group of returnees. This enigmatic figure then fades into obscurity as Zerubbabel, who is known to have been active some twenty years later, takes his place as leader in this story. The inventory proper follows in verses 9–10. The numbers do not add up to the total given in verse 11a, indicating that the text was probably incomplete or corrupted and was simply presented as it was found.

**1:11b** / Whatever the precise numbers may have been, the narrator emphatically states, in the conclusion he has added to round off the section, that Sheshbazzar brought them **all** back—to the last vessel. The restitution closes a long episode of shameful loss. It spelled vindication for the people of God and the triumph of their God. It also supplied continuity in holy worship for the postexilic community. Second Isaiah had envisioned the return of the sacred vessels (Isa. 52:11). Whereas pagan nations had their divine images restored, their counterparts in Judah's case were the vessels of the first temple. They conferred authenticity for the worship that was to be conducted in the second temple. A further allusion to a second exodus appears at the end of this verse. **The exiles** "were brought up" (here the NRSV is more accurate than the NIV's **came up**) **from Babylon to Jerusalem.** The passive verb connotes divine activity. Scripture frequently refers to the exodus in terms of God bringing Israel up from Egypt (e.g., Exod. 32:11; Deut. 20:1). Now the same God was at work again, laying the foundation for a new community of faith, whose members were thereby stamped as bona fide successors to the old community that had once occupied the land.

### Additional Notes §2

**1:6** / For a sensitive discussion of the spoiling of the Egyptians, see B. S. Childs, *The Book of Exodus* (OTL; Philadelphia: Westminster, 1974), pp. 175–77.

**1:7** / There are two traditions about the fate of the temple vessels. According to 2 Kgs. 24:13 (NRSV, REB), all of the golden vessels were cut into pieces. However, Jer. 27:16–22; 28:3–6 speak of the removal of some of the vessels intact to Babylon. The documentation and narrative in Ezra attest the latter tradition, and the Chronicler followed it in 2 Chr. 36:7, 10, 18. See further I. Kalimi and J. D. Purvis, "King Jehoiachin and the Vessels of the Lord's House in Biblical Literature," *CBQ* 56 (1994), pp. 449–57.

**1:8** / **Sheshbazzar the prince of Judah:** In 5:14 he is called "governor," a term used for a range of Persian administrators. **Prince** (Heb. *nasiʾ*) is not itself a royal term. Here the word seems to refer to his role as a prominent member of the Judean community in Babylon, specifically a tribal leader (cf. Num. 1:16, "leaders," translating the same Heb. noun). He was an obvious choice for the Persians to entrust with the responsibility of leading the initial mission. Josephus (*Ant.* 11.13, 92) identified him with Zerubbabel, but (1) while a number of individuals had double names, one was always Hebrew and the other foreign, so the fact that both Zerubbabel and Sheshbazzar are Babylonian names makes this unlikely, and (2) in 5:14–16 he is described as a long-gone figure of the past, distinct from the contemporary governor Zerubbabel mentioned in 5: 2. Some scholars have identified him with the Davidic Shenazzar in 1 Chr. 3:18. It remains a phonetic possibility (see Halpern, "Historiographic Commentary," pp. 91f.), but if so the narrator made nothing of a royal connection and the issue is a historical matter rather than a literary one.

**1:9** / The renderings **pans** (**silver** has no counterpart in the Heb. text) and "knives" (NRSV) reflect the uncertainty of the term. A quite different interpretation is to regard it in a revocalized form as an original marginal comment (wrongly inserted into the text between the numerals) relating to the numbers in v. 9, in the light of the total in v. 11. This form means "to be changed," and the LXX understood it in a similar way. (Rudolph, *Esra und Nehemia,* p. 5; BHS. Here and elsewhere, *BHS* will be used as a conventional way of referring to the edited notes added to the Hebrew text in the *BHS* edition.) With this reading, 1,029 **silver dishes** were intended by the text.

**1:10** / **Matching** or "other" (NRSV): again Rudolph, *Esra und Nehemia,* proposes a similar gloss, revocalized with the sense "to be altered," now querying the number of **silver bowls** (see *BHS*). In 1 Esd. 2:13–14 the individual and total figures agree, and the RSV followed this tradition. (The apocryphal book of 1 Esdras is a Gk. translation of 2 Chr. 35–36, Ezra, and Neh. 8–12, which is independent of the LXX.) However, this tradition represents a secondary harmonization and the NRSV has rightly reverted to the MT. See the discussion in D. Barthélemy, *Critique textuelle de l'Ancien Testament,* vol. 1 (OBO 50; Fribourg: Editions Universitaires; Göttingen: Vandenhoeck & Ruprecht, 1982), pp. 523–25.

**1:11** / For the significance of the temple vessels indicating continuity of worship from the first to the second temples, see P. R. Ackroyd, "The Temple Vessels—A Continuity Theme," *Studies in the Religious Tradition of the Old Testament* (London: SCM, 1987), pp. 46–60.

## §3 The Return of the True People of God (Ezra 2:1–70)

The text now informs us of the composition of the returnees, who duly set out and arrived in Judah and prepared to rebuild the temple. The narrator, writing considerably later than the events of the first mission, drew on this list, which appears again in Nehemiah 7:6–73a. First, Nehemiah found this list in the Jerusalem archives and incorporated it into his memoirs, but the narrator in Ezra did not find it in the archives or the memoirs, since he cited it along with Nehemiah 7:73b–8:1a (= substantially Ezra 3:1). This latter material is part of the next passage in Nehemiah, which is drawn from different material associated with the work of Ezra. Thus the narrator in Ezra knew and used the list in the form in which it currently appears in Nehemiah 7. This fact gives us some insight into how late the narrator was writing the present account. The list supplied a record of early settlers at a certain point in the ongoing history of **the province.** The narrator adapted it for his own story by inserting the major part of verse 68, as the absence of this verse from Nehemiah 7 and its echoing of the mission-linked vocabulary used in chapter 1 indicate. He also summarized Nehemiah 7 in verses 68–69, rounding up most of the figures.

It is noticeable that there is no mention here of Sheshbazzar, who returned in the year 538. Instead, **Zerubbabel** appears, beside **Jeshua,** as the first of the leaders enumerated in the introduction to the list (v. 2). We know of these two men as governor and high priest, respectively, early in the reign of Darius, in 520–515, both from the books of Haggai and Zechariah and from the dependent Ezra 5:1–2. The list here in chapter 2 reflects the membership of the Judean colony at this later, post-Sheshbazzar period. The narrator has merged the early (ch. 1) and later (ch. 2) evidence and presented it as a single return—although the list itself seems to reflect a series of returns in the relatively early period of the postexilic community. We are given a literary, condensed presentation of a protracted history. Its coherence has been achieved by linking later material to the description of the initial wave of migration led by Sheshbazzar.

**2:1–2a** / The concern of the list is to define the restored community as a legitimate continuation of the preexilic people of God who had been exiled but still constitute **the people of Israel** (v. 2b). The list must have appealed to the narrator, who had presented his own similar definition of Israel in general terms in 1:5. Indeed, the list arranges laity, priests, and Levites in the same way. Thus, in the first two chapters of Ezra, the theme of restoration continues. First the vessels plundered by **Nebuchadnezzar** had been handed back (1:7), and now the people deported by the Babylonian king could come back from exile. The people of God essentially consisted of those who had journeyed through judgment—from Judah to exile and then back to Judah.

**2:2b–35** / Verse 2b is a subheading. As is commonly seen elsewhere, here we have the laity of **Israel** distinguished from the temple staff, who are itemized later. The list is a complex collection, formed by the amalgamation of two or three smaller lists. The first list, in verses 3–20, is based on family association— grouped by clan names and supplying the number of those who returned in each clan. There follows a listing by places of residence in verses 21–35. This residential listing subdivides into a group generally introduced by **men** in verses 21–28 and another one in verses 29–35 introduced by "sons" (Heb. *bene*), in the sense of inhabitants, although the NIV has not preserved the division. **Bethlehem** and **Netophah** are in the tribal area of Judah south of Jerusalem, but most of the other towns that can be identified are in Benjamin, while **Lod, Hadid and Ono** in verse 33 are in the far west, outside the province.

**2:36–39** / A list of priestly families follows. There were only four at this stage, but others were to return with Ezra later (8:2–3). A system of twenty-four divisions would be set up eventually—by the time of the Chronicler or a little later (1 Chr. 24:1–19). Although the families were still few, the total number of individuals in these families makes up a tenth of the whole group, whose total is given in verse 64. This ratio is understandable, since the main purpose of the returning exiles was to establish the temple.

**2:40–58** / Verse 40 gives a much smaller list of Levites. Their scarcity must have been one reason why Ezra made a special effort to recruit more to return with him (8:15–20). Their role as assistants to the priests held little attraction to exiled members of the order. The temple **singers** and **gatekeepers** are listed separately from the Levites in verses 41–42. Later in the postexilic period they were both grouped under a Levitical umbrella, as they generally are in Chronicles and indeed in Ezra 3:10; Nehemiah 12:8, 24. The distinct listings are an indication of the relatively early date of this material. **The temple servants** and **descendants of the servants of Solomon,** listed separately by family names in verses 43–57, are grouped together for statistical purposes in verse 58. They were groups of temple workers from preexilic times and were of foreign extraction, as most of their names indicate. They had long been incorporated into the community of faith, and so they are included in the total of verse 64.

**2:59–63** / This sad group of lay and priestly families functions as a telling footnote before the total membership of the gradually increased community is given. Distinguishing people who could not prove the ancestry they claimed underlines the significance of the main list as a census of genuine members who had verifiable links with the preexilic community of **Israel.** First, three non-qualifying lay groups are listed in verses 59–60, according to the exilic communities to which they had belonged in Babylonia. Claimants to a priestly status, who also fall into three family groups, follow in verse 61. Happily the family of **Hakkoz** was eventually accepted, as can be seen by the presence of Meremoth, son of Uriah, son of Hakkoz in Ezra 8:33 and Nehemiah 3:4, 21. This family eventually took its place among the twenty-four divisions (1 Chr. 24:10). But at the time of this list, no member of the three groups was allowed to officiate or to receive priestly rations. A final decision was to be left until the appointment of a high **priest** for the community. He was expected to bring a traditional divining device to ascertain the will of God: **the Urim and Thummim.** Since Jeshua functioned as the high priest during the governorship of Zerubbabel, it is probable that **the governor** was Sheshbazzar, and so this portion of the material is to be dated very early.

**2:64–67** / The **company** is rather the "assembly" (NRSV) in a religious sense, the definitive "assembly of the exiles" of 10:8 and the "assembly of God" of Nehemiah 13:1. The actual total of the individual numbers (29,818) contrasts with the total in verse 64 of **42,360**. Possibly the difference is a reference to women, who have a role in the religious community (10:1; Neh. 8:2). Women feature in the totals of slaves and **singers** in verse 65. The pack animals and riding animals described in verse 67 make a good introduction to the journey of verse 68.

**2:68–69** / Most of verse 68 is a new description that is not taken from Nehemiah 7:70 and was supplied to tie into the narrative context of the mission of chapter 1. In verse 69 the narrator has abbreviated the details of gifts supplied in Nehemiah 7:70–72. The longer listing in Nehemiah 7:70–72 already had a temple concern; this was fittingly adapted in Ezra to the single mission launched by Cyrus' edict. While in Nehemiah 7 the contributions were for the ongoing work of maintaining worship, here they are for building the temple. We are probably to discern a further exodus parallel here. In the wilderness, the Israelites brought **freewill offerings** of precious metals and cloth (Exod. 25:2–7; 35:4–9), while in Numbers 7 tribal **heads** of **families** brought **silver** and **gold** objects. The restored people, or at least some of them, followed this example, willingly faithful to the pattern set out in Scripture.

**2:70** / Verse 70 rounds off the list by echoing the end of verse 1. In the narrative context this sentence marks the conclusion of a single return in an idealistic representation of the birth of the new community.

---

### Additional Notes §3

---

**2:1** / **Province** refers to an administrative district at some level. At least by Zerubbabel's time, from which this introduction dates, Judah, known as Yehud, was evidently an autonomous administrative unit in the Persian imperial system (K. G. Hoglund, *Achaemenid Imperial Administration in Syria-Palestine and the Missions of Ezra and Nehemiah* [SBLDS; Atlanta: Scholars Press, 1992], pp. 26, 75, 86).

**2:2** / **Nehemiah** is not to be equated with the later governor, nor **Bigvai** with the still later one, since Nehemiah himself regarded the list as old (Neh. 7:5). Neh. 7:7 adds in the sixth place another name, "Nahamani," which brings the total number of leaders to twelve. This total reflects an understanding of the new community as a symbolic reconstruction of a twelve-tribe system, as in 6:17; 8:35. We may compare this with the symbolism of twelve disciples in the Gospels. 1 Esd. 5:8 attests this extra name, and the NJB has incorporated it (cf. *BHS*). It is probable that it fell out of the Ezra text through a copyist's error.

**2:5** / In place of **775,** Nehemiah 7:10 has "652." This is the first of many discrepancies between the two sets of numbers, although the names are largely the same. H. L. Allrik plausibly explained the differences in terms of a numerical system of easily overlooked or miscounted strokes and other signs ("The Lists of Zerubbabel [Nehemiah 7 and Ezra 2] and the Hebrew Numerical Notation," *BASOR* 136 [Dec., 1954], pp. 21–27).

**2:21** / The MT has *bene*, "sons," here and in vv. 24–26. Nehemiah 7 has preserved *'anshe*, "men," throughout this section.

**2:35** / The large figure associated with **Senaah** is surprising, and there is as yet no satisfactory explanation for it.

**2:36** / **Jeshua:** The high priest belonged to the clan of **Jedaiah.**

**2:40** / The Levites **Jeshua** and **Kadmiel** are regularly associated with a third, Binnui (8:33; Neh. 10:9; 12:8 [cf. Ezra 3:9 in the NRSV]), while Neh. 8:7; 9:4–5 refer to a similar name, Bani. Moreover, 1 Esd. 5:26, parallel to Ezra 2:40, has "Bannas" in place of Heb. *bene*, "sons." This evidence suggests that here and in the parallel Neh. 7:43 the Levites were originally defined as **the descendants of Jeshua,** namely, **Kadmiel,** Bani/Binnui, and **Hodaviah.** See the comprehensive discussion of Barthélemy, *Critique textuelle*, vol. 1, pp. 525–29.

**2:41–42** / For the eventual incorporation of the **singers** and **gatekeepers** into the Levitical line, see H. Gese, "Zur Geschichte der Kultsänger am zweiten Tempel," *Von Sinai zum Zion: alttestamentliche Beiträge zur biblischen Theologie* (Beiträge zur evangelischen Theologie 64; Munich: Kaiser, 1974), pp. 147–58, summarized by H. G. M. Williamson in *1 and 2 Chronicles* (NCB; Grand Rapids: Eerdmans, 1982), pp. 120f.

**2:63** / The precise meaning of Heb. *tirshata'*, also used in Neh. 7:70; 8:9; 10:1 and loosely translated **governor,** is unknown. See the range of suggested etymologies in Hoglund, *Achaemenid Imperial Administration*, pp. 75, 80. For **the Urim and Thummim,** see Exod. 28:30; Num. 27:21. They were evidently small objects marked with symbols to indicate a yes or no response. The high **priest** carried them in the breastplate attached to the ephod. The ephod is used as a synonym for them in 1 Sam. 23:9–12; 30:7–8. The cultural use of throwing lots as a spiritual aid is illustrated in a non-religious context in Prov. 16:33: "The lot is cast into the lap, but its every decision is from the LORD." An example from the NT appears in Acts 1:23–26. For a discussion of the way they worked, see A. M. Kitz, "The Plural Form of *'ûrîm* and *tummîm*," *JBL* 116 (1997), pp. 401–10. **The most sacred food** refers generally to priestly rations (see Num. 18:1–19).

**2:68** / **The house of the LORD** must refer to the site of the first temple, as also in 3:8. The narrator took the reference to the temple **site** from the documentation in 5:15; 6:7.

**2:69** / In Neh. 7:70, "530" (priestly garments) requires correction to 30, and the 500 refers to silver minas. Rounding up is evident in **5,000 minas of silver,** from 4,700 (500 + 2,200 + 2,000), and in **100 priestly garments,** from 97 (30 + 67). **61,000 drachmas of gold,** standing in place of the expected 41,000 (1,000 + 20,000 + 20,000) may be the estimated monetary value of the "50 bowls" of Neh. 7:70 (Rudolph, *Esra und Nehemia,* p. 26).

**2:70** / The text is slightly different from Neh. 7:73. **In their own towns** seems to be an editorial addition referring to Jerusalem and adjacent towns, made in the light of v. 1. The equivalent in 1 Esd. 5:46, "in Jerusalem and its vicinity" (*added* to the text of Ezra in the NRSV, largely following Rudolph, *Esra und Nehemia,* p. 26), appears to be a secondary and not incorrect interpretation as the domicile of the temple staff and **some** of the laity, i.e., lay officials (cf. Neh. 11:1). According to Neh. 3:26, 31; 11:21, **the temple servants** lived in Jerusalem. The first lay group (NRSV "some of the people") are distinguished from most of the laity, **the rest of the Israelites,** who lived in other towns. The Heb. phrase rendered **some of the other people** is placed not after **the singers,** as in Neh. 7:73 [MT v. 72], but after **the Levites.** This change, not represented in the NIV, presumably reflects their seniority to the lesser temple staff. See the discussions of Williamson, *Ezra, Nehemiah,* pp. 271–73, and Barthélemy, *Critique textuelle,* vol. 1, pp. 530f.

## §4 Making a Start (Ezra 3:1–13)

Here the first of the two implementations of the divine mandate given through Cyrus is completed. A nucleus of the exiled people had come home in order to rebuild the temple. To this end they brought with them Gentile gifts and recovered vessels from the first temple (ch. 1) and then added gifts of their own (2:68–69). Now they were to take the first step of reestablishing the worship of the Jerusalem temple by restoring the sacrificial system on a reconstituted altar (3:1–6) and laying anew the temple foundation (3:7–13).

**3:1–3** / The narrator continued to use his source; here we can see the identification of the new community from Nehemiah 7:73b–8:1a reworked as a fitting introduction to his own story. He returns to the time frame of the beginning of **the seventh month** in verse 6, thus tying the paragraph together. According to Numbers 29:1, the "first day" of this month was a holy day and a time of sacred assembly and sacrifice, and doubtless this was in the narrator's mind. The new sacrifices represent the initial act of worship of **the people,** who **assembled as one man** for this purpose soon after their first return. It is schematically envisioned as taking place in mid-September 538. There is a fitting sense of priority in the story: the community is declared to be first and foremost a worshiping community. The narrator associated a necessary preparatory stage with this act of worship—rebuilding a proper altar on which to offer sacrifice. He also linked with it the names of the later leaders, **Jeshua** and **Zerubbabel,** taking his cue from the list of leaders in 2:2, and dignified them with the patronymics they bear in Haggai 1:1. The high priest is here placed before the governor in recognition of the religious nature of the task. Verses 2–3 function as a flashback. The building of the altar logically precedes the sacrifices in verse 6 and so, implicitly, verse 1. The text reflects a concern to do the sacrificing correctly. For the postexilic community this meant adopting **the Law of Moses,** the

Torah, as the script for their worship. It is hailed as the basis not for building the altar but for the regular **burnt offerings** made each day, morning and evening, as verse 3 elaborates. These verses reflect Numbers 28:2–4. The new altar is carefully built on the "site" (NJPS) of the old altar of burnt offering, a huge structure that had pride of place in Solomon's temple court. Sacred text and sacred tradition are the two religious foundations that provide continuity and authenticity for the contemporary task of worship. Verse 3 translates the intention of verse 2 into satisfying fact. Religious celebration is woven into the implementation of the three missions of Ezra-Nehemiah, and it surfaces here, as well as in verses 4–5. It is the logical conclusion to constructing an altar. Another feature the people encountered in the execution of the missions is the opposition they faced and strove to overcome. It raises its ugly head briefly for the first time here in their intimidation by **the peoples around them.**

**3:4–5** / The narrative jumps to the fifteenth day of the month, following the instructions in Numbers 29:12. In fact, **the required number of burnt offerings prescribed for each day** at the weeklong festival follows Numbers 29:12–38. Again, there is a focus on the scriptural quality of the celebration **(in accordance with what is written).** In line with this desire to be faithful to Scripture, the narrator enumerates in verse 5 the gamut of festival sacrifices covered in Numbers 28:1–29:11. His purpose is to emphasize that the event marked the start of the rhythm of worship in conformity with the Torah. The returning community honored its ritual calendar, now that they had a legitimate altar on which to sacrifice. The **freewill offerings** accord with Numbers 29:39, but their inclusion also traces an arc back to the spontaneous gifts of 2:68 and draws attention to sincere personal spirituality amid the official sacrifices brought on behalf of the people as a whole. Here is a model of true worship flowing up to God both at the official level and at the level of individual contributions. It is no coincidence that the dedication of Solomon's temple took place at the time of **the Feast of Tabernacles** (1 Kgs. 8:2, 65). The echo of that event at the first stage of rebuilding the second temple makes a further claim for continuity with the worship of the first.

**3:6** / A recurring element in Ezra-Nehemiah is the establishment of permanent guidelines for the postexilic community, often in the area of religious institutions. Here is the first such guideline. This second mention of the commencement of the regular **burnt offerings,** morning and evening in line with the Torah (vv. 2–3) is prescriptive in nature. The norms of the community were set in place one by one—norms that were the duty of each generation in turn to maintain. It was a good start, which the building of the altar had made possible. The text is clear, however, that there was still a long way to go in implementing the first mission, for **the foundation of the LORD's temple had not yet been laid.**

**3:7** / The closing statement of verse 6 serves as a headline for the next paragraph. But first, wider preparations for rebuilding the temple are noted, although the opportunity to use these materials was to await chapter 6. Here again we are meant to hear echoes of the first temple in the details relating to its royal building and repair. The hiring of **masons and carpenters** recalls Jehoash's repair work in 2 Kings 12:11–12 and Josiah's in 2 Kings 22:4–6, while the processing of supplies is reminiscent of Solomon's arrangements in 1 Kings 5:8–11. The narrative aims to find continuity between the new work and the older work, bridging the historical chasm of destruction and exile, and paralleling the efforts of the new community with the regular concern of royal patrons. Mention of **Cyrus king of Persia** takes us back to the edict of Ezra 1. There is no precise correspondence here—simply a general reference to Cyrus' authorization that the temple was to be rebuilt.

**3:8–9** / Now the work on the foundation, implicitly announced in verse 6, is begun. The names of **Zerubbabel** and **Jeshua** are again attached to the beginning of the account, as they were in verse 2. Some commentators have supposed that the narrator has moved us down to the reign of Darius, to the period of Haggai's exhortation to work on the temple in the year 520. However, a natural interpretation of **the second year** is that it resumes 2:68, the envisioned arrival of the first returnees in 538. The resumption of the vocabulary of 2:68 suggests that this is in fact the case. In this idealistic account we are now in the year 537, in **the second month,** that is, April/May. Two traditions relating to the temple foundation have been combined. One, appearing in Zechariah 4:9, was that Zerubbabel was responsible for laying it in the later period. The second tradition, in Ezra 5:16, says that Sheshbazzar laid it during Cyrus' reign. There is no reason to doubt either tradition. The attribution of the renewed task to Zerubbabel indicates that the earlier, discontinued work was overlooked after such a lapse of time. The narrator evidently merged the two traditions, taking his cue from 2:2, as in 3:2. Perhaps he was influenced

by the prediction in Isaiah 44:28 that Cyrus would order the laying of the temple foundations. If so, Cyrus' authorization in verse
7 neatly flows into this next section and unites two otherwise disparate passages.

The work on the foundation is attributed to the community
at large. As in verse 2, lay and religious groups are mentioned
separately, headed by their respective leaders. Now there is a
stronger backing. Necessarily, in the flashback of verse 2, two
Jerusalem-based groups took responsibility, but now the whole
community did so, presenting a united front, as in verse 1. We see
here a model of responsibility for later generations to follow—a
united community of faith committed to the temple not only for
worship but also for its maintenance. The appointment of **Levites**
for the work reflects their postexilic role to "supervise the work of
the temple" (1 Chr. 23:4; 2 Chr. 34:12–13), for which a job description is given in 1 Chronicles 23:4–5. The Levites are identified in
terms of the names of Ezra 2:40.

**3:10** / Again there is celebration when the work is done.
The worshiping community gave God the glory. The narrator envisioned a ceremony similar to worship in his own day. While
the temple singers are from the clan of **Asaph,** as in 2:41, they
are nevertheless counted as **Levites** in accord with later practice. The description of the service is like accounts of temple
worship in Chronicles. In both pieces of literature there is an
imaginative reconstruction in terms of a later form of worship.
From 2 Chronicles 5:12 and 7:6 we learn that the priestly trumpeters stood in front of the altar of burnt offering, opposite the
Levitical singers, who faced the altar. The trumpeters sounded a
signal, here presumably for the service to start, while the Levitical
musicians evidently clashed their **cymbals** to announce the start
of the hymn quoted in verse 11. As in the books of Chronicles, the
institution of temple music is credited to **David.** The Davidic standard nicely matches the Mosaic one in verse 2. The authenticity of
temple worship is firmly grounded in the traditions of the Torah
and of the first temple. Another balance is achieved in chapter 3
by the earlier accent on sacrifice and on music and song here—
both were key elements of postexilic worship.

**3:11** / The enthusiastic description continues with reference to a hymn, which is regularly cited as an epitome of vocal
worship in Chronicles, in this form or an even shorter one. We
learn from Jeremiah 33:11 that this hymn was sung before the

exile by those who attended a thanksgiving service, to which grateful worshipers brought their songs and thank offerings after deliverance from personal crisis. In the postexilic era it developed into a standard expression of communal praise for what God had achieved by a new demonstration of power in bringing the people back from exile. So here it is appropriately used to celebrate the restoration of worship after the silence of the exile. That silence is poignantly described in Psalm 137:2 as the time when harps were hung in the branches of poplars beside a Babylonian canal.

The narrator evidently derived the weeping of verses 12–13 from Haggai 2:3, which accounts for its close similarity with verse 12. Haggai refers to dissatisfaction with the new temple's comparative lack of ornamental splendor. The dissatisfaction is here applied to the foundation, although we are not informed what aspect of it sparked the protest. In light of the upbeat nature of Haggai 2:1–9, it is probable that the narrator, in echoing it, wanted to draw attention to the "not yet" character of the restoration to the land. In terms of Psalm 126, the restored fortunes enjoyed thus far by the returned exiles fell short of eschatological expectations. Rather than surpass the glory of Solomon's temple, as Haggai promised it would one day, this second temple showed signs that, initially at least, it was to be decidedly inferior. The congregation's varied vocal responses reflect a generation gap. We may understand the **shout of praise** in general terms as Hallelujah or Amen (1 Chr. 16:36; Rev. 19:4). However, the narrator might have been thinking more precisely of the foundation ceremony envisioned in Zechariah 4:7 and the cry "Grace, grace to it!" (NRSV), paraphrased in the NIV as "God bless it! God bless it!" He himself, while frankly admitting the mixed blessing represented by the new temple, stood firmly on the side of the younger generation, looking hopefully toward the future and patiently grateful for only partially satisfying mercies in the present. The final reference to how far the combined volume of noise carried creates an artistic link with the beginning of chapter 4, where we will find trouble lurking.

## Additional Notes §4

**3:1** / For the narrative sequence of vv. 1–6, see Halpern, "Historiographic Commentary," pp. 97, 127. Continued use of the source left an uneven join between v. 1 and what follows. **Jerusalem** replaces the topographical reference in Neh. 8:1 in order to pick up the thread of the narrative from Ezra 2:68.

**3:2** / **Jozadak,** or Jehozadak, belonged to the Zadokite high priestly line as the son of the last preexilic high priest; he was taken into exile (2 Kgs. 25:18; 1 Chr. 6:14–15). **Zerubbabel** was known as the **son of Shealtiel.** He was evidently his legal son but the natural son of Pedaiah (1 Chr. 3:19). In both respects he was a grandson of the Judean king Jehoiachin. While his Davidic ancestry is regarded as significant in the messianic oracle of Hag. 2:20–23, it lacks overt significance in Ezra 1–6. The **associates** of Zerubbabel were members of the laity (S. Japhet, "Sheshbazzar and Zerubbabel: Against the Background of the Historical and Religious Tendencies of Ezra-Nehemiah," *ZAW* 94 [1982], pp. 66–98, esp. p. 84), presumably the first lay group mentioned in 2:70, who lived in the vicinity of Jerusalem. The description of **Moses** as **the man of God** refers to the divine inspiration of the Pentateuch.

**3:3** / "The peoples of the lands" (NJPS) is a general reference to the inhabitants of Judah and neighboring provinces outside the community of returned exiles (see J. Blenkinsopp, *Ezra-Nehemiah: A Commentary* [OTL; Philadelphia: Westminster, 1988], p. 108). What precisely the causal clause "because they were in dread . . . peoples" (NRSV, paraphrased in the NIV) relates to is not clear. It may refer to an attempt to win God's favor so as to overcome persecution, but comparison with v. 6b and 4:4 suggests rather that, for now, they felt unable to do more than build the altar and could not work on the temple itself.

**3:4** / Why no mention of the Day of Atonement, traditionally held on the tenth day of the seventh month (Num. 29:7)? Perhaps the close involvement of the (as yet unbuilt) temple in the Day of Atonement rituals (see Lev. 16) was a factor, but at any rate the schematic account called not for repentance but for joyful celebration, such as the **Feast of Tabernacles** afforded in the light of Lev. 23:40; Neh. 8:17.

**3:7** / Williamson, *Ezra, Nehemiah,* p. 47, has noted links with 1 Chr. 22:4; 2 Chr. 2:10, 15–16 in the details of **drink, Joppa,** and **Sidon,** and uses it as a plank in his contention that the edition of Ezra 1–6 postdated Chronicles. It is uncertain, however, whether at least two of these parallels are not to be included in his admission of similarities dictated by historical necessity.

**3:8** / For an attribution of this section to Darius' reign, see S. Talmon, *IDBSup,* pp. 322f.; Williamson, *Ezra, Nehemiah,* pp. 43–45, 47. It is more likely that "Zerubbabel's activity is stretched out over the whole length of the first period" (Japhet, "Sheshbazzar and Zerubbabel," p. 94). **Their brothers** posits a parallel and contrast with v. 2. The doubled Heb. *'ahehem,* lit. "his brothers" (fellow priests, associates), is here resumed by the single "their brothers," with the sense of "fellow-Israelites" (REB). The lower limit of **twenty years of age,** also set in 1 Chr. 23:24, 27; 2 Chr. 31:17, seems to reflect the practice in the narrator's period. It is at variance with the limit of thirty years in Num. 4:2–3; 1 Chr. 23:2–3, and was doubtless dictated by the scarcity of Levites.

**3:9** / The NIV has rightly corrected the MT "Judah" to **Hodaviah,** following 2:40 and the reading of the Syriac version here. However, we need to go further and adapt the MT *banayw* **(his sons)** to a name, "Binnui," with the NRSV, REB, and NJB (see *BHS*), as also in 2:40. See the discussion of both cases in Barthélemy, *Critique textuelle,* vol. 1, p. 527. The reference to **the sons of Henadad . . . Levites** poses a problem. In the Heb. this material dangles at the end of the sentence, unattached to what precedes. The NIV and NRSV have integrated it into the sentence by placing it earlier. It evidently originated as a marginal comment relating to the association of **Henadad** with members of this Levitical group in Neh. 3:18; 10:9 (see *BHS*, REB, NJB).

**3:10** / **The foundation of the temple** was a platform or podium, if this feature of Ezekiel's visionary temple in Ezek. 41:8 belonged also to Solomon's temple, whose design was followed for the second temple. See the text and illustrations in *IDBSup,* pp. 543–45. **Took their places:** the NIV, along with the REB and NJB, has rightly followed a different textual tradition of vocalizing the Heb. verb (see *BHS*), which in the MT has suffered assimilation to the form in v. 8. For the trumpeters, see Num. 10:8, 10 and for the whole procedure, see 2 Chr. 5:13; 7:6. J. W. Kleinig, *The Lord's Song* (JSOTSup 156; Sheffield: JSOT Press, 1993), esp. ch. 3, has shed valuable light on postexilic instrumental and vocal music. Though described in general terms, the service corresponds in principle to a traditional ancient Near Eastern practice attested in the Mesopotamian *kalû* ritual—a ceremony of refounding a ruined temple (see D. L. Petersen, *Haggai and Zechariah 1–8* [OTL; Philadelphia: Westminster, 1984], pp. 240–42, with reference to Zech. 4:7).

**3:11** / This snatch of hymn also occurs in 1 Chr. 16:41; 2 Chr. 5:13; 7:3, 6. Psalm 107, in its present redacted form, is an illustration of the later hymnic usage: see Leslie Allen, *Psalms 101–150* (WBC; Waco: Word, 1983), pp. 60–65.

**3:12** / **This temple:** The NIV, along with the REB and NJPS, has wisely ignored the phrasing indicated by the accentuation of the MT. The NRSV has made an effort to keep it, but it posits the historical possibility that the generation who had seen the foundations of the first temple being laid was still living. Heb. *zeh habbayit,* "this is the house," seems to reflect a correct exegetical gloss with the sense "this refers to the (present) temple" (Barthélemy, *Critique textuelle,* vol. 1, pp. 531f.).

## §5 A Temporary and Typical Setback (Ezra 4:1–24)

So far, so good. The return home, the construction of an altar to get worship started, and the laying of the temple foundation had marked the first phase of fulfilling the mission given through Cyrus to rebuild the temple. The second phase, building the temple itself, was to last longer than twenty years. We have to wait until 6:15 to read of its completion. This second phase, with its long delay and fresh start, is narrated in 4:1–6:22. Echoes of 4:1–5 in 6:21–22 reveal that these passages supply a literary framework. The concern of chapter 4 is the delay. Haggai gave internal reasons for it, accusing the community of wrong priorities and mentioning harsh economic conditions (Hag. 1:2–11). Our narrator traced the delay to another factor—external opposition. He painted a picture we know all too well from the later history of Judaism, of a persecuted minority suffering for its spiritual convictions. One of the narrator's aims was to teach the Israelite people a lesson from their early history, as the writer to the Hebrews did in Hebrews 10:32–12:12. They should not be discouraged by setbacks but persevere in commitment to their God.

**4:1–5** / We are still in the year 537, according to the story, although the names of **Zerubbabel** and **Jeshua** are linked with the present incident, as in chapter 3. Mention of **Cyrus** in verse 5 and of **Darius** as a subsequent king there and in verse 24, which resumes the narrative, indicates that the story of a grand initial return is continuing. The sociological language of verse 2a repeats that of 1:3, 5; 2:68 in token of the continuity.

The element of opposition that initially appeared in 3:3 now reappears with a vengeance and is the focus of the entire chapter. The text traces the opposition to a rejected offer of help to rebuild the temple, which triggers a long delay that lasts until the new, successful attempt narrated in chapters 5–6. The opponents are vaguely called the "people of the land" (NRSV) in verse 4, another term for the "peoples of the lands" (NJPS) in 3:3. Verse 1 replaces this general label with the emotive **enemies of Judah and Benjamin,** which prepares readers for the sequel in verses 4–5. It warns them not to take the offer of help at face value, but to judge fair words in light of foul acts that hindered the work of God.

These enemies claimed to be age-old converts to Yahwism and evidently worshiped at the same sacred site as the Judean returnees, for which we may compare the pilgrimage of northerners to Jerusalem in the early exile in Jeremiah 41:5. The narrator, by identifying the newcomers as **the exiles** and **Judah and Benjamin** (v. 1) and **Israel** (v. 3), reaffirmed the dominant message of the earlier chapters—that the people of God had to be defined in exclusive terms and differentiated from self-professed aliens. It is sometimes necessary for a group of believers to stand uncomfortably alone as the trustees of divinely revealed truth. To decide who is "for us" (Mark 9:40) or who "belong to us" (1 John 2:19) is not an easy or necessarily final matter. The exclusivity displayed here is modified to a certain degree in 6:21.

The specific information that those who made the offer were deported by an Assyrian king and the fact that they are differentiated from other such groups mentioned in verse 10 suggest that some documentary evidence or oral tradition lies behind the present story, which has been assembled by the narrator. These people made their offer to the civil authorities. Although the respondents include the high priest **Jeshua,** they reply in political terms and steer clear of direct religious argument. The phrase **our God** is not provocative in the context, but simply a counterpart to **your God** in verse 2. Yet the response contains a deeper meaning; behind the command of **Cyrus** lay the prompting of God (1:1), and these very **heads of the families** were back in Judah to rebuild the **temple** by divine behest (1:5).

The result was intimidation and, claims the narrator, the bribing of Persian officials to obstruct the work over a long period of time—for the rest of the **reign of Cyrus** onward. Verse 5b, resumed with a little extra detail in verse 24, looks forward hopefully and wistfully to chapters 5–6.

**4:6–7** / Reference in verses 6–23 to four letters, sent in much later times, interrupt the narrative here. From a literary perspective, the interruption serves to occupy readers as they wait with the narrator for the delay to end. The content, however, is not irrelevant. No official document from the early period could

be found, but copies of these letters were available in the Jerusalem archives. Although they were written long after the temple
was completed, they illustrate the general point the narrator
makes in verses 4–5. It is clear from 6:14 that he was well aware
that **Artaxerxes** was a later king than Darius, who reigned from
522 to 486, and so he was consciously breaking the time sequence.
**Xerxes,** famous for his unsuccessful attempts to defeat the Greeks,
ruled over the Persian empire from 486 to 465, and **Artaxerxes**
from 465 to 424. By flashing forward in this way, the narrator
shows that opposition to religious ventures was no isolated phenomenon but rather a recurring problem for the people of God,
which they had to endure with patience until the tide turned.
Verses 6–7 refer to the first two letters in passing. The first of these
four letters is mentioned in verse 6 and is defined as **an accusation**
sent to Xerxes. Therefore, it is in parallel to the opposition of
verses 4–5 and is ascribed to the **peoples** of verse 4, further brand-
ing them with the enmity of verse 1. The second letter is not
quoted but is mentioned in verse 7. We are told that it is sent to
**Artaxerxes.** The third letter is also to Artaxerxes, but this list
of senders differs from that of the second letter (vv. 8–16). We
are meant to understand that it was as negative as the others.
The fourth letter (vv. 17–22) is a response from Artaxerxes to the
third letter.

    **4:8–16** / The text of the next letter is found in these
verses. It was from two officials, evidently based in the province of
**Samaria.** They did not write on behalf of the provincial governor.
Rather, they claimed to represent a number of other officials who
worked in the **Trans-Euphrates** satrapy, to which the provinces of
Judah and Samaria belonged. It consisted of territory west of the
Euphrates that had earlier belonged to the Babylonian empire.
What these officials evidently had in common was descent from
colonists from various eastern regions of the empire. They had
been **deported** by the next-to-last Assyrian king, **Ashurbanipal,**
who reigned in the middle of the seventh century. The epithets
**great and honorable** give the impression that they supported the
imperial cause and so acted in good faith in reporting the prospect
of sedition in the neighboring province. They paint an alarmist
picture, quite devoid of historical probability, in lurid hues from
the palette of ethnic prejudice. A recent caravan of returning
Judeans is said, presumably correctly, to have energized the rebuilding of the **walls** of the capital (v. 12). The loyal subjects send-

ing the letter deprecate this activity, interpreting it as a threat to
the empire, a flexing of muscles for independence. The imperial
court is advised to verify the charge that Jerusalem is **rebellious
and wicked** by ascertaining its sinister history from the imperial
**archives** or "annals" (NRSV). What it would learn was that in the
Assyrian period the Judean king Hezekiah had rebelled, while in
the Babylonian period Nebuchadnezzar had destroyed the capital
for rebellion. While this was true, the historical climate was now
completely different—and Judah was in no shape to secede from
the Persian empire. The nightmare of a bid for independence by
withholding imperial taxes or, worse, a takeover of the whole
western satrapy, existed only in the writers' warped minds.

**4:17–23** / A copy of the reply was naturally presented,
along with the letter that prompted it, to the Judean authorities as
warrant for shutting down the wall rebuilding project. It was deposited in the Jerusalem archives, whence the narrator retrieved
it, together with a copy of the original letter (v. 11). The king, taking the scary letter at face value, verified Jerusalem's history of rebellion. He equated this with verification of the present charge
and judged it expedient to **stop** forthwith further rebuilding of
the capital. The narrator deduced that, armed with this imperial
warrant, the local officials procured military backing and enforced the order authorized by Artaxerxes (v. 23). Nehemiah 1:3
may suggest that work done thus far on the walls was destroyed
at this time. Yet all was not lost. The prohibition of work on the city
walls was not permanent, but only to last **until I so order,** wrote
the king (v. 21). We are invited to look ahead at this point to the
mission of Nehemiah, who obtained permission for this very
work later in Artaxerxes' reign (Neh. 2:1–8). A subsidiary role of
this digression in verses 6–23, then, was to give the background to
Nehemiah's mission and to show that it represented an eventual
victory over local opposition.

The switch from temple to city in the digression is not the
big jump it may appear to a modern reader. The holiness of the
temple extended to the city as a whole, making it "holy" as well
(Neh. 11:1). In the Songs of Zion preserved in the Psalter, especially Psalm 48, the temple and capital are bracketed together as a
sacred complex by the believing community. There was thus an
organic relationship between the first and third missions. Nehemiah's mission was the inevitable corollary of the reconstruction
of the temple.

**4:24** / The digression ended, verse 24 returns to the temple project and resumes verse 5 as a bridge to the new and successful attempt of chapters 5–6. The Hebrew draws a parallel between the **stop** of work on the city walls in verse 23 and that on the temple here (NRSV "stopped"). Yet the redeeming **until**, both here and in verse 21, invites readers to look beyond frustrating setback to satisfying resolution.

---

### Additional Notes §5

---

**4:1** / Josephus' identification of the enemies as Samaritans (*Ant.* 11. 84) is an anachronism. The Samaritan schism was a much later phenomenon: see in principle R. J. Coggins, *Samaritans and Jews: The Origins of Samaritanism Reconsidered* (Atlanta: John Knox, 1975). As for the lack of reference to internal factors, "the addressees of Ezra 1–6 were in a situation that did not require Haggai's pointed criticism" (M. A. Throntveit, *Ezra-Nehemiah* [IBC; Louisville: John Knox, 1992], p. 30). In vv. 1–3, the narrator takes a leaf out of Nehemiah's memoirs in using a three-part format: news heard by Judah's enemies, their response, and a counterresponse.

**4:2** / **Seek** is better translated as "worship" (NRSV). **Brought us here:** This deportation is not mentioned in 2 Kgs, although a reference to the northern kingdom in Isa. 7:8 appears to be associated with it. **Esarhaddon** ruled from 681 to 669. His settlement of easterners in Sidon after a Syro-Palestinian campaign (*ANET*, p. 290) makes this claim feasible.

**4:3** / For the literary setting of this incident in the reign of **Cyrus,** see Halpern, "Historiographic Commentary," pp. 103–16.

**4:5** / **Counselors:** The Persian royal "advisers" (NIV) or "counselors" (NRSV) mentioned in 7:14–15, 28; 8:25 may be in view.

**4:6** / **The beginning of** his **reign:** The precise reference is to his "accession year" (NRSV), the period from the end of 486 to April 485, when the first full regnal year began. **Xerxes** inherited an Egyptian revolt, which would have made him particularly sensitive to any suggestion that a neighboring country might cause further difficulties.

**4:7** / **Bishlam, Mithredath:** Or possibly "with the agreement of Mithredath" (REB), a Persian official. The ancient versions variously found in the first Aramaic term a name or a common noun. The final sentence could be interpreted in a number of different ways. The last phrase, "in Aramaic" (NRSV) is widely regarded as originating in a copyist's comment that what follows in 4:8–6:18 is not in Hebrew but in Aramaic, which was used for correspondence by and with the Persian authorities. The NRSV footnote takes it this way, as in Daniel 2:4, while the NIV footnote obscurely seems to imply it. Instead of the actual words in the footnote, "written in Aramaic and translated," the meaning may rather be that it was **written in Aramaic script** and had been translated from Aramaic into Hebrew. Then the copy found in the archives was in Hebrew and used the Aramaic square script rather than the old Hebrew script. A number of Aramaisms in v. 7a suggest that it was originally in Aramaic. The extensive quotation in the following verses from four letters written in Aramaic led the narrator to pen framing and bridging material in that language. Such linguistic attraction also occurs in the Mishnah (see D. C. Snell, "Why Is There Aramaic in the Bible?" *JSOT* 18 [1980], pp. 32–51, esp. p. 34). One expects a return to Hebrew in 6:16, since the letter-related material ends in 6:15. The eventual switch may have been prompted by mention of the Torah at the end of 6:18. Historically, the letters of 4:7–23 would fit well in the years 465–464, when the new king was establishing himself after the assassination of Xerxes and an Egyptian rebellion (Hoglund, *Achaemenid Imperial Administration*, pp. 21f.).

**4:8** / The precise meaning of the Akkadian loan phrase *be'el-te'em* used here and translated **commanding officer** is uncertain. F. Rosenthal, *A Grammar of Biblical Aramaic* (Porta Linguarum Orientalium 5; 6th ed.; Wiesbaden: Harrassowitz Verlag, 1995), p. 62, renders generally "official in charge." The letter itself does not begin until v. 11b. It has two introductions in vv. 8–10. One expects the letter to begin after **as follows,** but v. 9 strangely begins again with "then" (NRSV, omitted in the NIV) and a list of senders, for which the NRSV has supplied a verb, "wrote," in v. 10. Verses 9–10 give fuller particulars about the senders. It is difficult to relate these two verses to the conventions of official Aramaic letters in the Persian period. It was customary to put on the outside of a letter an address specifying sender and addressee. B. Porten has suggested that vv. 9–10, apart from an editorial reference to **Ashurbanipal,** are based on such an expansive external address, while v. 11b preserves the essence of a terse internal address ("The Address Formulae in Aramaic Letters: A New Collation of Cowley 17," *RB* 90 [1983], pp. 396–415). It is also possible that v. 8 was derived from a brief external address and vv. 9–10 as a whole were taken from the beginning of the letter and replaced by the shorter text in v. 11b. But it is difficult to see the point of such editing.

**4:9** / The . . . **officials over the men from Tripolis, Persia:** The footnote gives as alternatives administrative terms, the "officials, magistrates and governors over the men from" Tripolis, which aligns with NRSV "officials." A reference to the Syrian **Tripolis** hardly accords with the following eastern areas.

**4:10** / These deportations are not otherwise known, but **Ashurbanipal's** conquest of Babylon and Elam and destruction of Susa make them feasible, while his deportation of a group to Egypt shows that he continued Assyrian imperial practice (J. M. Myers, *Ezra, Nehemiah* [AB 14; Garden City, N.Y.: Doubleday, 1965], p. 33). **City:** The ancient versions rightly took the Aramaic *qira'* as plural, "cities" (NRSV; Rosenthal, *Biblical Aramaic*, p. 35), so that **Samaria** refers to the province.

**4:12** / **Restoring . . . repairing:** The Aramaic verbs, of which the meaning of the second is uncertain, are strangely perfect. In light of v. 13, possibly an exaggerated claim was made that the work was already done (Barthélemy, *Critique textuelle,* vol. 1, p. 533).

**4:13** / **Revenues,** for which compare BDB, p. 1082, is an uncertain rendering. Rosenthal, *Biblical Aramaic,* p. 63, suggests an Akkadian derivation meaning "certainly," or a Persian one meaning "finally." Thus NJPS translates "and in the end it will hurt the kingdom," which is nicely echoed in v. 22.

**4:14** / A reasonable paraphrase of "eat the king's salt" (REB) is the NIV **are under obligation to the palace.** There is a metaphorical reference to commitment to the court. We may compare a "covenant of salt" in Num. 18:19.

**4:15** / Artaxerxes' **predecessors** are regarded as including kings of the Assyrian and Babylonian empires.

**4:18** / **Translated:** from Aramaic into Persian. If the root meaning of the Aramaic *meparash,* "separate," is involved here, the sense is translation sentence by sentence (D. J. A. Clines, *Ezra, Nehemiah, Esther* [NBC; Grand Rapids: Eerdmans, 1984], p. 81), or in full rather than summarized, and therefore verbatim (Williamson, *Ezra, Nehemiah,* pp. 53, 56).

**4:20** / A reference to the ancient period of David and Solomon is unlikely, since this information would hardly appear in annals of the eastern empires. Unless this is an editorial insertion, this verse refers to Mesopotamian kings, and the implication is that Artaxerxes in turn had to exert strong control over Jerusalem. Thus it is better to translate "However, there have been powerful kings over Jerusalem . . ." (Williamson, *Ezra, Nehemiah,* pp. 53, 64, following K. Galling; similarly NJPS).

**4:24** / **Thus:** lit. "At that time" (NRSV), with a glance past the parenthetical vv. 6–23 back to v. 5.

**5:1–2** / The narrator apparently did not know of any political factors that would have brought about the shift from work stoppage to renewed activity in rebuilding the temple. All he had to illustrate this next stage was the edited text of messages from two postexilic prophets, **Haggai** and **Zechariah** (Hag. 1–2; Zech. 1–8), and copies of the Tattenai correspondence. Verses 1–2 are based on the biblical evidence. Once again prophecy plays a decisive role—not in the fulfillment of an older oracle, as in 1:1, but now by means of immediate access to the divine will through contemporary prophets. The narrator integrated their ministry into his earlier story by associating it with the letter of Tattenai, sent in the same period and also concerned with building the temple. The prophet's records themselves are related only to "the second year of the reign of Darius" (4:24; Hag. 1:1; Zech. 1:1), namely, the year 520 in the case of Haggai and the period 520–518 in Zechariah's case (Zech. 7:1). They say nothing of earlier attempts to fulfill a long-standing mission. The narrator wove the work of these prophets into his larger story. They represented for him the voice of the **God of Israel,** whose people were the postexilic group of returned exiles who claimed continuity with the preexilic religious community. The phrase recalls 1:3; 3:2; 4:3, and it will reappear in 7:15. The civil and religious leaders, **Zerubbabel and Jeshua,** now set in their proper chronological niche in line with the prophetic texts, **set to work to rebuild** the temple, as Haggai 1:12, 14 attest. "Set to work," literally "arose," is the narrator's own phrase. He used it two times before, in 1:5 and 3:2, as the NASV attests for English readers. Each occurrence marks a significant step forward in accomplishing the first mission, first with reference to the return home and then to rebuilding the altar. Now the final phase was being launched. The reference to the help given by the prophets assumes a knowledge of the prophetic material. It recalls not only their effectiveness (Hag. 1:14), but also the challenge they brought to undertake the temple project (Hag. 1:2–11), the assurance they gave of God's will and enabling presence (Hag. 1:13; Zech. 4:9–10; 6:12–13), and the vision they offered of the temple's future splendor (Hag. 2:9; compare Zech. 6:15).

**5:3–5** / **Tattenai** was the **governor** of the overarching province of **Trans-Euphrates**. It formed a Persian satrapy together with Babylon, though by Artaxerxes' time it became a satrapy in its own right (4:11, 17, 20). The chain of command went from Tattenai, probably based in Damascus, to the satrap, his superior, in Babylon, and then to the king. Presumably the letter took this administrative route. **Shethar-Bozenai** was doubtless the secretary who drafted the letter (look at the placement of the name of "Shimshai the secretary" in 4:9, 17 for a comparison). The narrative in verses 3–5 introduces the letter and derives its language from it. The fact that work on the temple was permitted to continue was a reasonable inference from verses 8 and 17, which do not mention any stoppage. But the secular language of the letter is here graced with a spiritual interpretation. The continuation of the work was evidence that **their God**—a term that recalls not only "our God" in 4:3 but also "their God" in Haggai 1:12, 14—was with them in blessing, as Haggai himself had promised (Hag. 1:13). The ground for this claim was that the work now proceeding had been undertaken at the instigation of the prophets. The narrator's vivid phrase, **the eye of their God was watching,** indicates that God was looking out for their interests and keeping a kindly eye on the proceedings to ensure that all went well. The phrase was borrowed from the language of spiritual instruction we find in a group of Psalms (Pss. 32:8 [NRSV]; 33:18; 34:15), though it also appears in Deuteronomy 11:12 and Job 36:7. No date is associated with this letter. Based on 6:15, we know that it belongs somewhere in the period 520–515, and 5:8 suggests a date nearer the end of this period. Unlike the letters of chapter 4, this report reflects no hostility. It is presented in terms of a routine investigation. The absence of any temporary restraining order indicates that Tattenai had no doubt that the necessary bureaucratic confirmation would be forthcoming.

**5:6–10** / The letter was intended to set the scene for the official validation of 6:1–12, celebrated by the narrator in 6:14. But, as verse 5b has implied, it also gives its own validation. Tattenai was confident enough about the outcome not to put a stop to the work. The letter, somewhat like the list in chapter 2, serves as a narrative describing the rebuilding—especially verse 8. We shall see yet another role for the letter in the local report cited in verses 11–16. The narrative heading of verse 6 was evidently taken from the address or opening section of the letter. It allowed the narrator to shorten the beginning of the letter in verse 7b. The title **great God** is used as a mark of polite respect. We learn from verse 8 that the authorities' start on the work in verse 2 was matched by good **progress.** The narrator had already extracted information concerning the official authorization and the bureaucratic inquiry for local names to nail down responsibility in verses 3–4. He presumably omitted the actual names, which must have been included in the letter (**for your information,** v. 10). They may have coincided to a certain extent with the list of leaders in 2:2.

5:11–17 / Another purpose of the letter emerges here. The report of the history of the temple project serves for the reader as a flashback to the narrative of the Cyrus-backed mission in chapter 1. We are reminded that the present rebuilding is the long-awaited fulfillment of that mission. Chapter 6 will bring its own reminder of the first chapter, but even now the narrator draws an arc of literary coherence, spanning the lapse of a score of years. The council of "elders" was evidently unable to produce a copy of Cyrus' edict, which was to be unearthed in chapter 6 and eventually added to the Jerusalem archives as part of Darius' letter. If they had been able to find this, an appeal to the Persian court would have been less necessary. Instead, they gave an oral account. The divine title used by Tattenai in verse 8, "the great God," is capped by the elders' **God of heaven and earth,** an expansion of the more conventional "God of heaven" (see 1:2), which serves to express indirectly the importance of the temple project. The **answer** they give is phrased in such a way as to remove any inkling that the project was a novel one, conceived recently by the Judeans for political ends. Rather, this temple was associated with a long religious tradition going back to the **great king** we know as Solomon, who reigned in the tenth century. However, the powerful God in whose honor it had been built had abandoned in displeasure both a recent generation and the original temple.

The theme of divine abandonment of people and temple was a common one in Mesopotamia. A later king often rebuilt a ruined temple and restored its divine image by the will of the local god. So the story runs here, with **Cyrus,** the new **king of Babylon,** in the role of the later king. In this case, sacred "vessels " (NRSV) had to replace the image, since such images were no feature of orthodox Yahwism. The vessels provided continuity between the old divine dwelling place and the rebuilt one—a continuity that was enhanced by its being built on the same **site** (v. 15). The elders knew of a tradition that at an earlier time **Sheshbazzar,** whom the reader met in 1:8, 11, had been authorized to do the rebuilding and install the vessels, and he had actually begun the project. Their claim that the project had been progressing ever since conflicts with the narrator's own view, expressed in 4:5, 24 and based on the evidence of Haggai's text (Hag. 1:2, 4, 9). The discrepancy is a small indication that he was citing an independent document. It was clearly an exaggerated, diplomatic attempt to claim that the original **decree** had not lapsed, and the present work was covered by the original authorization. To have openly admitted the stoppage of 4:24 would have weakened their case. Tattenai took the elders' version at face value, but he felt it necessary to obtain official verification of Cyrus' decree. He left it to the king to decide whether its validity should be extended to the present. He himself clearly had no objection to the work, which augured well for the outcome—but we readers hold our breath, hoping with the elders for a royal yes.

---

## Additional Notes §6

---

**5:1** / **Iddo** was the family name, mentioned in Neh. 12:16. **In the name ... over them:** There is no relative pronoun **who** in the Aramaic text. It is better construed as a separate clause: "In the name . . . Israel (they prophesied) to them." The NEB and REB reflect this interpretation.

**5:3** / **Rebuild** is better translated "build" (NRSV) here and in v. 9, although "rebuild" is satisfactory in vv. 11, 13, 15, 17. The elders' historically weighted report will argue that this is no new project, as Tattenai seems to assume. 1 Esdras 6:9, where Tattenai reports that "a new house" was being built, reveals a good exegetical instinct. **Structure:** In the Aramaic papyri, the term *ʾushsharnaʾ* is used of material employed in the construction of a building, boat, and altar, and evidently refers to woodwork. Here it could refer to the horizontal beams of wood inserted in the stone walls, to the wooden linings of interior walls, or to rafters to support the roof (compare v. 8; 6:4; 1 Kgs. 6:15–16, 36).

**5:4** / The NIV footnote should read, "We said to them, 'What are the names ... building?' " The NIV corresponds to the Aramaic text except for the initial first plural verb. This oddity is best explained by the narrator's own borrowing of the verb from v. 9 without adjusting it to the third person (Barthélemy, *Critique textuelle,* vol. 1, p. 534).

**5:6** / **Officials,** or more specifically "inspectors" (REB) or investigators, were a standard feature of Persian administration. See B. Porten, *Archives from Elephantine: The Life of an Ancient Jewish Military Colony* (Berkeley: University of California Press, 1968), pp. 53f.

**5:7** / **Cordial greetings** is lit. "all peace" (NRSV). This phrase appears to be a discreet abbreviation of a common type of pagan greeting, "May all the gods seek the welfare (or peace) of my lord abundantly at all times" (J. A. Fitzmyer, "The Syntax of *kl, kl'* in the Aramaic Texts from Egypt and Biblical Aramaic," *Bib* 38 [1957], pp. 170–84, esp. pp. 178–82).

**5:8** / **District** is rather "province" (NRSV). After **Judah,** we should restore to the Aramaic text on the evidence of 1 Esd. 6:8, "and we found the elders of the Jews in the city of Jerusalem building (the temple)" (see *BHS*). This was the source of the narrator's reference to "the elders of the Jews" in v. 5, instead of his usual "family heads," and it paves the way for "these elders" (NJB, compare NRSV "those elders") in v. 9, loosely rendered "the elders" in the NIV. Mention of Jerusalem is expected as the location of the temple. One or two lines were probably omitted by error from the text. Surprisingly there is no reference to Zerubbabel as the local governor, who features in Darius' reply, in 6:7, together with the council of elders. Presumably he was included in the "leaders" of v. 10. **The people are building it** is lit. "it is being built" (NRSV). The precise meaning of the Aramaic *gelal* is not known, and the NIV rendering **large** is a common one. It relates the term to the root meaning "roll": the stones had to be moved by rolling because they were massive. The Akkadian *galalu,* itself of uncertain meaning, refers to stone treated in a special way (*CAD* 5:11). In line with the LXX "chosen" here, H. G. M. Williamson, "*'eben gelal* (Ezra 5:8, 6:4) Again," *BASOR* 280 (1990), pp. 83–88, has argued that the term refers to specially selected stone.

**5:12** / For the ancient Near Eastern theme of divine abandonment, see D. I. Block, *The Gods of the Nations* (Evangelical Theological Society Monograph 2; Jackson: Evangelical Theological Society, 1988), pp. 129–61; D. Bodi, *The Book of Ezekiel and the Poem of Erra* (OBO 104; Freiburg Schweitz: Universitätsverlag; Göttingen: Vandenhoeck & Ruprecht, 1991), pp. 191–218. **Nebuchadnezzar** belonged to the group of tribes living in southern Babylonia called **Chaldean.** His father inaugurated a new dynasty, distinct from the line of old Babylonian kings.

**5:15** / **Take . . . site:** The order is illogical but understandable. The temple had to be rebuilt before the vessels could be installed.

This chapter draws to a triumphant close the accomplishment of the first mission given by God through the Persian king Cyrus in 1:1–4. Stage one was realized by chapter 3. Now stage two is brought to a satisfying finale in the completion of the temple-building project. The temple represented the heart of Israel's spiritual life as the sign of God's presence with the people, the focus of their worship and the source of divine blessing. Now, in principle, the postexilic community stood on a par with the preexilic one. The dynamic role of the temple in the OT may be measured by its multiplicity of metaphorical uses in the NT. There it is related to Christ (John 2:21), the church at large (Eph. 2:21–22), the local church (1 Cor. 3:16), and the individual Christian (1 Cor. 6:19). The concept of the temple radiates through NT theology and spirituality. In passages such as Ezra 6 we find the literal basis that helps us understand such metaphors, the hearth of meaning from which later fires were lit.

**6:1–2** / This narrative and the memorandum set out in verses 3–5 were evidently derived from Darius' reply to Tattenai's query. The narrator accordingly omitted the address and opening formulas, and then shifted abruptly in verses 6–12 to quote the continuation of the letter. The crucial evidence of Cyrus' edict turned up not in **Babylon,** as Tattenai had reasonably supposed (5:17), but in the summer residence of the Persian kings, **Ecbatana.** The narrator exercised restraint, letting the record speak for itself. He reserved his jubilation for the worship of verses 16–22, where the community's joy would express his own.

**6:3–5** / The **memorandum** has the narrative role of reminding readers of the edict of Cyrus supplied in chapter 1, which was actually based on the present text. At long last, after about twenty years, the mission of rebuilding the temple was to be accomplished in its entirety. The details of its construction should probably be taken as intimating its close correspondence, and therefore continuity, with the old temple of 5:11, just as the restoration of the original vessels "each to its place" (NRSV) does. Their return served to confirm the testimony of the Judean elders in 5:13–15. Readers are left with no doubt that, in basic format and in ongoing function, the second temple had the same value as the first. It was an essential part of the narrator's agenda that the postexilic community was an authentic representation of the Israel of God.

**6:6–12** / The text continues with the actual letter, with its direct address to Tattenai and his "inspectors" (REB). The edict of Cyrus was allowed to stand, and Tattenai's policy of noninterference (5:5) was approved, with the added ruling that the investigation was not to be continued. There is a happy contrast with the experience of 4:24, where a (later) royal command stopped the Jerusalem building program (4:21, 23). Not only was an administrative stoppage prohibited, but the possibility of a stoppage for economic reasons was removed. The earlier decree of Cyrus was formally renewed, precisely in the area of the financial aid promised in verse 4. This was spelled out as a fiscal responsibility of the **Trans-Euphrates** province. Doubtless this would entail, at least in part, remission of taxes normally paid by Judah to the authorities in the larger province to which it belonged. Such financial support of local cults was a feature of Persian policy. The ongoing cost of daily sacrifices (but evidently not those of festivals) was also to be met. This ruling is akin to Artaxerxes' exemption of temple staff from taxation (7:24). The request for prayer to accompany daily sacrifice (v. 10) must have reminded the postexilic community of Jeremiah's advice to the exiles of his day to pray for Babylon (Jer. 29:7), while in turn Christian readers recall 1 Timothy 2:1–2. The temple was both a "house of sacrifice" (2 Chr. 7:12, NRSV) and a "house of prayer" (Isa. 56:7). The edict is enforced by a penalty clause affecting the person and property of offenders.

**6:13–15** / The narrator deduced, from Tattenai's letter and from Darius' reply with its generous updating of Cyrus' decree, the positive sequel in verse 13 and the continuation of the good work of 5:8b. He reminded his readers of the initial stimulus of **Haggai** and **Zechariah,** which he had related in 5:1–2. He probably learned from a temple inscription the date of the red-letter day when work on the temple was **completed.** Alternatively, he might have calculated it with the aid of Zechariah 1:12 as the end of a seventy-year period from 586, when Jerusalem fell and the old temple was destroyed. The narrator recapitulated the opening of his story, the proclamation of **Cyrus** at God's behest (1:1), speaking of Cyrus' **decree** in line with 5:17; 6:3. He could now refer to the extra decree of **Darius,** with verses 8 and 11–12 in view. He even referred to the future king **Artaxerxes,** assuring his readers that he was not always as hostile as he was in 4:7–23. He could be thinking of the next phase in the ongoing story, Artaxerxes' embellishment of the temple mentioned in 7:27. But we have seen that he had Nehemiah's mission in mind in referring to a subsequent "decree" of Artaxerxes in 4:21b. So in a context full of recapitulation, it is more likely that he neatly tied this loose end. He jumped to the final phase of the saga, Nehemiah's building work to restore the holy city as the corollary of the new temple.

**6:16–22** / Communal religious services are a regular feature of Ezra-Nehemiah in narrating the execution of its missions. We noticed the celebrations that attended the fulfillment of the first part of this mission in 3:3–5, 10–13. Here, too, worship is a fitting climax, now that the temple was built. Another recurring feature in these narratives is the establishment of norms for the community to follow, as here in verse 18. We saw in 3:6 that, after the building of a legitimate altar, the regular offerings were introduced in line with the Torah. Here the narrator noted the appointment of temple staff in the categories he knew in his own period, tracing them back to the Torah. The reference is a general one, to such passages as Exodus 29 and Leviticus 8 concerning the ordination of priests, and to Numbers 3, 8, and 18 concerning the ordination and duties of Levites.

In the twin celebrations of verses 16–22, one specific and the other seasonal, the keynote is **joy,** sounded at beginning and at the end. This joy expresses the fervor of the community's gratitude to God. In the temple they had a symbolic center that covered them with an aura defining them as the people of God. So it is not surprising that **Israel** occurs twice in verses 16–17, and **the God of Israel** twice in verses 21–22. In verse 16, **Israel** stands for all the returned **exiles** in their religious and lay groupings. As in 2:1–2, continuity with preexilic Israel had taken an exilic detour. Historically the returnees comprised only three tribes—Judah, Benjamin, and Levi—but for the narrator they were the essential representatives of the traditional **twelve tribes,** as verse 17 maintains. Later the editor of Chronicles was to qualify this narrow definition, and verse 21 seems to make a move in that direction.

The narrator's fingerprints are all over this section, even though verses 16–18 are in Aramaic and verses 19–22 are in Hebrew. He described the **dedication** of the temple on the lines of religious practice in his own day and also with an eye to the great dedicatory service for Solomon's temple (1 Kgs. 8:62–63). The reference to "all Israel" there presumably prompted its appearance here in verse 17, with the claim that the community of returned exiles was its current counterpart. Most of the sacrifices were offered as grateful expressions of inaugural worship. Other sacrifices represented **a sin offering** or "purification offering" (REB, NJPS). The temple required decontamination from the people's sin. The reference to exile in verse 16 suggests that their sin was domicile in the unclean land of exile. Now they could make a fresh start at worship in a new and purified temple. With their exilic contamination removed, they were heirs of the preexilic Israel of twelve tribes who had worshiped at Solomon's temple.

The resumption of worship is typified by the celebration of the traditional **Passover** and the associated festival of **Unleavened Bread** in the following month. The Passover commemorated the exodus from Egyptian oppression, and the account is meant to remind readers of the second exodus theme in chapter 1. Now the community could celebrate its liberation from Babylonian exile. Verse 20 reflects conditions familiar to the narrator from his own experience of temple worship, including the Levites' slaughtering the Passover lambs for each family, which does not accord with the Torah (see Exod. 12:6; Deut. 16:2). The account of the celebration in verse 22 catches the excitement of this first festival in the precincts of the rebuilt temple. Verse 21 mentions converts who joined the community of returned exiles, using language that occurs in Ezra-Nehemiah only here and in Nehemiah 10:28. Their inclusion echoes a provision in Exodus 12:48 that aliens who had been circumcised could celebrate the Passover with Israel, though here no mention is made of circumcision. In this section, which wraps up the second phase of the mission, the language and motifs recall its beginning in 4:1–4. There a claim from other communities to worship the same God as the exiles cut no ice with them, but here individuals who were prepared to make a fresh start and throw in their lot with the exiles were welcomed into the worshiping community. It is not specified whether nonexiled Judeans were involved or some of the Yahweh-worshiping aliens of 4:2 or both; we shall revisit this issue in connection with chapter 8. They functioned like Rahab in the first occupation of the land long before (Josh. 2:9–14). The idealism of having the experience of foreign exile as a qualification for membership was tempered by the practicality of gaining adherents who espoused the community's own uncompromising stand for orthodoxy. Nonetheless, there still stood out against the rest a group of former exiles who regarded themselves as a faithful minority.

Verse 22 contains a last echo of the opening of chapter 1. There God inspired Cyrus to launch the first mission. Here Darius, it is claimed, had been supernaturally led to support its completion. The same providential hand is seen to have been at work, bending imperial power to the divine will. All was of God. This conviction made the festival held in the temple precincts a very special one.

---

## Additional Notes §7

---

**6:1–2** / The NIV appears to interpret **Babylon** as the whole area of the center of the Persian empire, including **Ecbatana.** It is more likely that it refers to the city, which was the administrative headquarters of the satrapy of Babylon and Trans-Euphrates and so a reasonable place to expect a copy of Cyrus' decree to be filed. It is better therefore to begin v. 2 with "But" (NRSV). The search proved fruitless until it was extended elsewhere. Ecbatana, the capital of the earlier Median empire, was used as a summer residence because it was in a mountainous region and had a more temperate climate. Cyrus left Babylon in the spring of 538, and it is feasible to assume that he issued the edict from Ecbatana and so it was recorded there. "Memorandum" evidently refers to a brief record of an oral decision written on a leather or papyrus **scroll,** instructing the royal treasury about the expenses for rebuilding the Jerusalem temple. This memorandum was addressed (v. 5) to the treasurer as administratively responsible (Bickerman, "The Edict of Cyrus," 274).

**6:3** / **And let its foundations be laid:** This meaning for the Heb. verb is doubtful. It should probably be rendered "retained" (NJB; see Williamson, *Ezra, Nehemiah,* p. 71; Barthélemy, *Critique textuelle,* vol. 1, p. 535). The verb primarily means "carry," and in the Aramaic papyri it refers to providing for an aged parent. In this context a sense of solicitous preservation is plausible. The significance of the requirement was that costs should be kept down by following the ground plan of the old temple. The NRSV, "where . . . burnt offerings are brought" (similarly REB), presupposes a repointing of the Aramaic noun following the paraphrase of the clause in 1 Esd. 6:24, "with perpetual fire." However, the Aramaic form would literally mean "*its* burnt offerings," which does not match "sacrifices" in the previous clause. A reference to **foundations** aptly introduces the next item about the temple's dimensions. The dimensions of **ninety feet high and ninety feet wide,** or "sixty cubits" (NIV mg.), are strange for two reasons. (1) The length is missing and (2) the other dimensions do not match those of Solomon's temple, "sixty cubits long, twenty wide and thirty high" (1 Kgs. 6:2). The width given here would have meant enlarging the old foundation to three times its size. This contradicts the previous clause as understood above and hardly accords with the disappointment expressed in 3:12. Correspondence with the size of the first temple is expected. The Syriac version has twenty cubits for the width. All ancient authorities support the MT there, which indicates that it is a very old reading. A primitive error may be explained in terms of a copyist's eye slipping ("cubits [thirty, its length cubits] sixty"; see *BHS*), with subsequent assimilation of the final number to the remaining earlier one.

**6:4** / The detail of wall construction accords with 1 Kgs. 6:36; 7:12, although it applies only to the walls of the temple court there; it may have been an earthquake precaution. Knowledge of the first temple presupposes Cyrus' access to local information. Possibly his decree was drawn up in response to a Jewish petition, as Williamson, *Ezra, Nehemiah*, p. 80, suggests. Inside knowledge depending on a Jewish informant in Darius' case is reflected in the technical details of v. 11, the **pleasing sacrifices** in v. 10 (compare Lev. 1:9), and the reference to God's **name** dwelling in the temple in v. 12 (compare Deut. 12:11). **One:** The MT has *hadat*, "new," but *hadaʾ*, "one," is presupposed by the LXX and is generally read. 1 Esdras 6:25 has a conflated reading, "one course of new wood."

**6:5** / **They are to be deposited:** lit. "you [sg.] shall put them" (NRSV).

**6:9** / Unless the title **the God of heaven** merely copies that in 5:12 and shortens the longer one in 5:11, its use by Darius may reflect an assumption of Yahweh's kinship with Ahuramazda, the creator god of the Persians, who is often named in the inscriptions of Darius. He would have regarded Yahweh as a lesser deity, but the theological similarity may have encouraged Persian support. For worship of Ahuramazda by the Persian monarchy, see M. Boyce, *Zoroastrians: Their Religious Beliefs and Practices* (London: Routledge & Kegan Paul, 1979), ch. 5. For Darius' support of local cults in general, see de Vaux, *The Bible and the Ancient Near East*, pp. 74–79.

**6:10** / According to Herodotus (1.132), it was a Persian custom to pray for the king whenever a sacrifice was offered. On the Cyrus Cylinder, Cyrus expressed a wish that the gods whose worship he had restored should speak daily to the gods Marduk and Nebo on behalf of himself and his son Cambyses (*ANET*, p. 316).

**6:11–12** / A penalty clause was characteristic of ancient Near Eastern laws and treaties. In Darius' inscriptions the curses refer to his successors, but here to aliens **(any king or people)**. Halpern, "Historiographic Commentary," p. 120, suspects editorial modification here, with local opponents in mind. **Changes, change:** better "disobeys, defy" (NJB; see Williamson, *Ezra, Nehemiah*, p. 72). **Lifted up and impaled on it:** This meaning for the second verb, though widely held, is uncertain; an alternative is "fastened erect to it and flogged" (REB). **Pile of rubble:** this is again an uncertain term, possibly "dunghill" (NRSV). The phrase **caused his Name to dwell** is characteristic of Deuteronomy and probably refers to the sanctuary as the divinely authorized place for God to be named in worship, in light of Exod. 20:24.

**6:15** / **Adar** ran from mid-February to mid-March. The year was 515.

**6:17** / For the role of the **sin offering** in decontaminating the sanctuary from the effects of human sin, see Exod. 29:36; Lev. 16:19; Ezek. 43:19–26. For the uncleanness of an alien land, see Amos 7:17 and also Ezek. 4:13; Hos. 9:3.

**6:18** / In Chronicles, the complex organization developed in the postexilic period is attributed to David (1 Chr. 23–26), with which we may compare the attribution of temple music to David in Ezra 3:10. Williamson, "History," *It Is Written: Scripture Citing Scripture,* ed. D. A. Carson and H. G. M. Williamson (Cambridge: Cambridge University Press, 1988), pp. 25–38, esp. p. 36 n. 2, has made the valuable suggestion that the correspondence with the Torah qualifies **the service of God.**

**6:19** / The **Passover** was celebrated in the evening of Nisan 14 (Exod. 12:2; Lev. 23:5), followed by the week-long festival of **Unleavened Bread** (Exod. 12:17–20; Lev. 23:6–8).

**6:20** / **The Levites:** This phrase in the second sentence is not present in the Heb. (compare the NRSV), although it is clear from the end of the verse that a reference to them must be intended. One of a number of suggested solutions is to reconstrue the present text as "The priests purified themselves, and the Levites were all clean together and slaughtered . . ." (Williamson, *Ezra, Nehemiah,* p. 72, following C. F. Keil). Another possibility is to insert extra material attested in 1 Esd. 7:11 after the first sentence, "Not all the returned exiles were purified, but the Levites were all purified together (and slaughtered . . . )." This material could easily have dropped out due to a similar ending (Barthélemy, *Critique textuelle,* vol. 1, p. 537).

**6:21–22** / H. C. M. Vogt, *Studie zur nachexilischen Gemeinde in Esra-Nehemia* (Weil: Dietrich Coelde Verlag, 1966), pp. 51–53, has set out seven parallels, both matching and contrasting, between 4:1–4 and these verses. Thus "the people of the land" (4:4, NRSV) is matched by a synonym "the nations of the land" (6:21, NRSV). A negative attitude is taken in both places to the general population, as "enemies" there and as marked by "unclean practices" here. A less obvious parallel in modern versions, but one that is preserved in the literal KJV, is that "the people of the land weakened the hands of the people of Judah" (4:4) in the matter of building the temple, while in 6:22 the king was caused to "strengthen their hands." As in 4:2, **seek** means "worship" (NRSV). In the context, **the king of Assyria** refers to the king of Persia, specifically Darius. The actual Assyrian king mentioned in 4:2 was at the back of the narrator's mind; **Assyria** is now used as a generic term for the empire that eventually succeeded it, still in the business of sending colonists to Palestine.

## §8 Ezra's Commission (Ezra 7:1–28a)

Chapter 7 introduces us to the person and mission of Ezra. His mission is the second of the three presented in Ezra-Nehemiah. It has two parts: first to take back to Jerusalem valuable supplies and pledges for the temple, along with a fresh group of returning exiles; and second to implement the adoption of the Torah to regulate the life of the Judean community. We notice, looking over the chapter, that it falls into three sections. First, verses 1–10 give a preview of the journey of chapters 7–8, interspersed with a formal introduction to Ezra and statements of his qualifications. There follows in verses 11–26 the report of a letter of the Persian king Artaxerxes, setting out Ezra's commission. Finally, Ezra's response of praise to God comes in verses 27–28a, along with a narrative introduction to his journey in verse 28b—both of which are written in the first person. The mixture of styles reminds us of chapter 6, with its narrative, decree, and letter. The autobiographical style of verses 27–28 continues until the end of chapter 9. It signifies the use of a literary source generally called the Memoirs of Ezra. Artaxerxes' letter was evidently quoted in this document, and the person who edited the memoirs cited it from there. Some elements of the introduction in verses 1–10 probably came from there too; the editor changed them into the third person and amplified them. For instance, the date given for the start of the journey in verse 9 has a ring of authenticity as the scheduled date, which had to be deferred because of an unexpected delay (8:31).

**7:1–10** / Verses 1a, 6a, and 8a provide a narrative skeleton. The phrase **After these things** bridges a gap of nearly sixty years since the completion of the temple in the year 515, related in chapter 6. Now, assuming that **Artaxerxes** is Artaxerxes I, as in 4:7–23 and 6:14, we are brought down to the year 458. The genealogy of verses 1b–5 is an editorial amplification, roughly wedged between the imperial dating and Ezra's journey. The genealogy is clearly related to the linear genealogy of the Jerusalem high priesthood at the beginning of 1 Chronicles 6. Apparently the same document from the temple archives was used in both writings. The descending genealogy preserved in Chronicles is here turned into an ascending one so as to focus on ancestry rather than descent. In its present form it is even more selective than the prototype, skipping six names in the middle. Whereas 1 Chronicles 6:14 continues the listing to Jehozadak, the exiled son of the last high priest before the exile, this list begins with his father **Seraiah.** We recall from Ezra 3:2, 8; 5:2 that Jehozadak was the father of Jeshua, the first high priest after the exile. By starting with Seraiah, this genealogy associates Ezra with a collateral line through another, unnamed son of Seraiah. So Ezra is invested with impressive priestly credentials, as a cousin of the contemporary high priestly family. Knowledge of this relationship presumably came from an oral tradition. The genealogy functions as an editorial commentary on the simple designation of Ezra as **priest** in Artaxerxes' letter in verses 12 and 21. The editor will revert to this title in narrating Ezra's religious work in 10:10, 16. Ezra's priestly credentials are not irrelevant to his teaching of the Torah, as Nehemiah 8:2 will show, but here their function is evidently to introduce his temple-related work, in which chapters 7 and 8 will major. Overall, the genealogy underlines his intrinsic religious authority within the Judean community. Although from a Persian perspective Ezra was sent as an imperial administrator, he was no mere collaborator but rather, by breeding and rank, supremely qualified for his work in and for Judah.

Within the priesthood Ezra functioned as a "scribe" (NRSV, v. 6), a designation that is here associated with the Torah. This label and its application pave the way for a portrayal of him in the letter as "the scribe of the law of the God of heaven" (NRSV) in verse 12, and also in verse 21. This description seems to be referring to Ezra's authoritative role in the community of Jewish exiles in Babylonia. One of the traditional functions of the priesthood was to put into writing, preserve, and communicate the legal traditions of Israel (as Deut. 33:10; Hos. 4:6; Mal. 2:4–9 imply). The exile evidently provided the opportunity for priests to study and work on these traditions, and Ezra was apparently an acknowledged expert in the enterprise. Accordingly he was judged to be the right person for having the Torah implemented in Jewish communities in the west, as Artaxerxes was to order (vv. 25–26). The editor filled out the designation with an insider's language of faith, both here and in verse 10. The wording of verse 6b probably goes back to Ezra's own introduction. It supplies information not mentioned elsewhere, that Ezra had himself solicited the office of special commissioner with the particular tasks outlined in Artaxerxes' letter, rather like Nehemiah in Nehemiah 2:8. Both Ezra and Nehemiah traced royal assent to divine blessing **(the hand of the LORD his God)**, as Ezra was to do later in verse 28 and 8:18, 31. This testimony dovetails with the statement about the first mission in 1:1, that behind Cyrus' authorization of it lay the will of God. Verse 27 provides an even closer parallel to the inspiration of Cyrus.

In verse 9, the success of the journey is credited to the same divine source, as 8:31 will repeat. Everywhere Ezra found welcome signs that not only Artaxerxes but also God had sent him on this mission. Both the commissioning and the stages of its implementation were marked by success in which he saw God's **gracious hand,** or active presence, for good. Verse 10 returns to Ezra's expertise, first broached in verse 6. Now the editor celebrates the strength of will and breadth of vision that Ezra brought to his work. No wonder he had approached the king for permission and embarked on an arduous four-month journey. It was consistent with his enthusiastic commitment to interpreting **(study)**, practicing, and teaching the Torah. Now he had the opportunity to minister to the community of faith in the homeland. There could be no better qualifications for such a task than Ezra's.

**7:11–20** / The editor used the announcement of Artaxerxes' letter to reemphasize Ezra's double role as **priest** and "scribe" (NRSV), explaining the latter in terms of an understanding of the Torah as the revelation of the divine will for the life of **Israel.** The reader can sense by now the editor's spiritual devotion to the Torah, as ardent as that of Psalms 19 and 119 and of the aged Elizabeth and Zechariah in Luke 1:6.

The official document, which is written in Aramaic, defines Ezra in terms of his credentials within the Jewish community— both at the beginning and in the transitional verse 21. It may be assumed that the Jewish coloring of the letter indicates Ezra's influence. According to verse 6, he had initiated the mission. There is no good reason to deny the essential authenticity of the letter, although the editor might have supplied some Jewish details. The main part of the letter falls into verses 13–20 and 21–26. At the outset, Artaxerxes gives permission for Ezra to lead a group of Jewish volunteers back to the homeland. Ezra was to augment the community of returned exiles. There may be a reference in 4:12 to this group of newcomers and to the dynamism they brought to the existing community. Artaxerxes then assigns Ezra a basic role involving the Torah, which lays a foundation for another Torah-related responsibility to be assigned at the end, in verses 25–26. Here in verse 14 Ezra is ordered to carry out an investigation among the community in Judah. His role was to be like that of Persian "inspectors" (REB, 5:6; 6:6) sent to conduct inquiries. In this case the Torah was to be the standard by which to assess deficiencies. There is an allusion to this investigative role later on, in 10:16. The task involved a hermeneutical application of the Torah, for which Ezra's background stood him in good stead.

After these brief statements of two of Ezra's responsibilities, verses 15–20 describe a third at greater length—his duties relating to the temple. First, he was to be responsible for taking to Jerusalem donations of money given by the Persian court and by "officials" (8:25) of the satrapy of **Babylon,** and also gifts from the community of exilic Jews. Both were to be used toward the cost of animal sacrifices and their accompanying offerings. The disposal of surplus funds was confined to religious use but otherwise left to the discretion of Ezra and his "colleagues" (NRSV) in the Jerusalem priesthood. Second, he was to **deliver** new "vessels" (NRSV) for temple use. Both the amount of the money and details of the vessels are specified later in the narrative, in 8:26–27. Third, Ezra was authorized to apply for extra temple funding from imperial funds (v. 20).

**7:21–26** / The third responsibility explains this letter within a letter addressed to the treasury officials of the **Trans-Euphrates** satrapy, who were to supply the required funding in cash and kind, up to specified generous limits. The inserted letter corresponds with Ezra's delivery of the royal instructions as described in 8:36; presumably he was given copies addressed to particular officials. Scrupulous regard for local religious traditions was motivated by a desire to propitiate the Judean God, whose power over the Persian royal family could be demonstrated both positively, via prayer (6:10), and negatively, as seen in the curse invoked in 6:12. Besides direct funding, temple staff were to be exempted from any form of taxation, so as to encourage the maintenance of regular worship.

The close of the letter in verse 25 returns to the mandate of verse 14 and extends it. Not only Judah was to be Ezra's bailiwick but also Jewish communities throughout the satrapy. In addition to being an inspector taking his cue from the Torah, he was to introduce a judicial system based on it. This mandate raises questions we cannot answer with certainty, not least because the following narrative of Ezra's mission leaves out any account of its institution. It presupposes Jewish groups outside the province of Judah, of which we know only the neighboring "(men of) Lod, Hadid and Ono" in Nehemiah 7:37 (= Ezra 2:33). The verb **know** refers to recognizing the Torah in one's lifestyle. Both Jews committed to the Torah as well as others who had abandoned their traditional faith and practice for assimilation to a pagan way of life were brought within the sweep of Ezra's jurisdiction. The royal letter appropriately concludes with a penalty clause (v. 26), like Darius' letter in 6:11–12. Here it backs up verse 25. The relevance of verses 25–26 to the account of the implementation of the second mission is that the third of the four punishments is echoed in 10:8, and thereby the view of intermarriage as an infringement of the Torah receives support.

**7:27–28a** / Now Ezra's own voice breaks in, although the editor has in fact been quoting him for most of the chapter. The doxology traces Artaxerxes' patronage not to his own endeavors, as in verse 6, but ultimately to providential grace. Once again God inspired a Persian king for the temple's sake, as in the first mission. This focus on the temple aspect of the commission paves the way for its implementation in chapter 8, the narrative of which actually begins in verse 28b. The honoring of the temple appears to deliberately echo the divine promise in Isaiah 60:7, "I will adorn my glorious temple," where the same Hebrew verb is used.

This eschatological prophecy about adorning the temple with lavish sacrifices had now come true, it is claimed. Artaxerxes was the very agent of God in providing so liberally for the temple sacrifices mentioned in verses 17 and 22. Then Ezra praises God for the fact that the Persian authorities selected him as special commissioner. He credits it to God's "steadfast love" (NRSV), that covenant love shown to past generations of believers (**our fathers**) and now revealed afresh. "The steadfast love of the LORD never ceases" (Lam. 3:22, NRSV).

## Additional Notes §8

**7:1** / See the introduction for the vexed issue of the chronology of Ezra.

**7:3** / The genealogy in 1 Chr. 6:3b–15 lists six more names between **Meraioth** and **Azariah**. Some of those extra names appear to have been inserted at some stage from a separate, overlapping list, which helped to fill a long gap between **Zadok** and **Shallum**. Then **Ahitub** and **Zadok**, repeated in the Chronicles list, refer to the same individuals who lived in the time of David (2 Sam. 8:17). In the inserted list other priestly names from the same period were associated with them, Ahimaaz and Azariah (2 Sam. 15:27; 1 Kgs. 4:2) and Johanan, if he is the same person as the Jonathan of 2 Sam. 15:27. In Ezra 7 the editor abbreviated the list for convenience in a narrative setting, exploiting the tendency of Israelite genealogies to be selective. Accidental omission of the names is unlikely, since there would have been a jump from the Amariah of 1 Chr. 6:7 to the same name in 1 Chr. 6:11, and Azariah's name, attested in both 1 Chr. 6:11 and Ezra 7:3, would have been lost too. So the Ezra form of the list presupposes the fuller list in Chronicles, but probably antedates its use by the Chronicler. For a comprehensive study of extant priestly genealogies, see J. R. Bartlett, "Zadok and His Successors in Jerusalem," *JTS* NS 19 (1968), pp. 1–18, esp. pp. 1–6.

**7:6** / In Nehemiah, the NIV renders Ezra's designation as "scribe" (Neh. 8:1, 4, 9, 13; 12:36), but in Ezra 6 it paraphrases **teacher.** Earlier scholarship argued that in the letter in vv. 12 and 21, "scribe of the Law of the God of heaven" was a title relating to Ezra's previous role in the Persian administration before being posted to Judah, virtually "secretary of state for Jewish affairs." Williamson, *Ezra, Nehemiah,* p. 100, still finds value in this interpretation, citing Neh. 11:24 in support, though he relates the designation to Ezra's official status in Jerusalem. But see the discussion of Hoglund, *Achaemenid Imperial Administration,* pp. 227f. Here the designation, like the preceding one of **priest** in vv. 12 and 21, is taken as a description of Ezra's standing within the community of Jewish exiles, rather like "the prince of Judah" predicated of Sheshbazzar in 1:8. For the exilic development of the late form of the Torah and of priestly expertise in it, see M. Fishbane, *Biblical Interpretation in Ancient Israel* (Oxford: Clarendon, 1985), pp. 113, 263–65.

**7:7** / In Ezra's own introduction the text would have read "We came up," referring to both himself and his fellow exiles (Williamson, *Ezra, Nehemiah,* pp. 90, 93). This gave a smooth continuation between the original first sg. references of vv. 6 and 8–9. The editor replaced "We" with a definition of Ezra's companions, taken from v. 13 and amplified with the vocabulary of v. 24. This added a greater specificity than that of 8:1–20, by mentioning **singers, gatekeepers.**

**7:9** / **He had begun:** The NIV has correctly revocalized the noun in the MT as a verb (see *BHS*), but a better rendering would be "fixed" (REB).

**7:12** / For the authenticity of the letter, see D. R. Daniels, "The Composition of Ezra-Nehemiah," in *Ernten, was man sät* (ed. D. R. Daniels et al.; Neukirchen-Vluyn: Neukirchener Verlag, 1991), pp. 311–28, esp. pp. 315–17. In the year 458 the Persians were trying to cope with a revolt in Egypt, which was exacerbated by Greek military support. The political aim may have been to keep the neighboring province of Judah firmly on the Persian side by granting cultic concessions and a measure of local autonomy based on native traditions. There are parallels in the Persian treatment of the satrapy of Egypt at earlier periods, in Cambyses' restoration of worship in the sanctuary of the god Neith, and in Darius' order that the ancient Egyptian laws be codified (see J. Blenkinsopp, "The Mission of Udjahorresnet and Those of Ezra and Nehemiah," *JBL* 106 [1987], pp. 409–21, esp. pp. 410–13). The Persian kings regularly styled themselves **king of kings.** On **the God of heaven,** see the additional note on 6:9. 1 Esdras 8:9 and the Syriac version rendered **Greetings,** which suits the context. The meaning of the Aramaic *gemir* is uncertain. The best suggestion is that it is used in the sense of the rabbinic Heb. *wegomar* "et cetera"; thus the NJPS translates "and so forth." The term replaces conventional introductory greetings.

**7:14** / **Seven advisers** (or "counselors," NRSV) made up the royal privy council, mentioned in Esth. 1:14 and Xenophon, *Anabasis* 1.6.4–5. The implication is that Ezra had Persian backing at the highest level. Probably the meaning of **which is in your hand** is not to be taken literally, but either as "which is at your disposal" (L. H. Brockington, *Ezra, Nehemiah and Esther* [NCB; London: Oliphants, 1969], p. 80) or as "of which you have the mastery" (Clines, *Ezra, Nehemiah, Esther,* p. 103). There is no suggestion that Ezra brought a version of the Torah not already available in Judah. Verse 25 indicates that it was already known or could be known by Jews in the satrapy. Ezra's skill and mandate lay in hermeneutical interpretation and systematic application to the life of the community. In vv. 6, 10, and 11 the editor had the completed Pentateuch in view, and there is little reason to suppose that the version Ezra used was substantially less. See the discussion of Williamson, *Ezra, Nehemiah,* pp. xxxvii–ix.

**7:17** / This verse seems to envision a celebratory sacrificial service on arrival, like that in 8:35. Routine sacrifices are covered in vv. 20–23. For **grain** and **drink offerings** accompanying animal sacrifices, see Num. 15:4–13.

**7:22** / The detailing of items that follows indicates that **a hundred talents of silver** was intended for the purchase of sacrificial animals. This amount, weighing about 7,500 pounds, is unreasonably large. Perhaps minas were originally specified, which are a sixtieth of the weight (Clines, *Ezra, Nehemiah, Esther,* p. 104), or the following series of hundreds caused textual assimilation (Williamson, *Ezra, Nehemiah,*

p. 103). **Salt without limit:** The comparatively small amount used meant that it was not necessary to prescribe a limit.

**7:24  /  Priests ... other workers:** This range of categories is the same as in Neh. 7:39–60 (= Ezra 2:36–58), where the workers are described as the "servants of Solomon."

**7:26  /  The law of your God ... king:** In principle, both traditional Jewish law and imperial law were binding on the communities. The latter was already in force, but now the former was to be officially added, presumably especially in the area of religion. **Banishment** is more probably "capital punishment" (NJPS). An Aramaic form of a Persian word with this meaning is used here: see Rosenthal, *Biblical Aramaic,* pp. 20, 33, 63. **Imprisonment** was a Persian punishment.

## §9 Bringing Glory to the Temple
## (Ezra 7:28b–8:36)

Ezra was given two mandates in chapter 7. The first was to lead a party of immigrants back to the homeland and to take along the sacred contributions of the Persian court, the Babylon satrapy, and Jews remaining in exile, and deliver them to the temple authorities in Jerusalem. This first assignment is accomplished here. Apart from the conclusion in verses 35–36, this section comes from the Ezra memoirs and falls into three parts: 7:28b–8:20; 21–30; and 31–34. Each part has a double theme. The first part lists the members of the party that accompanied Ezra and tells of the search for a missing element. The second part details preparations for the people's journey and for transporting the temple contributions. The third describes their safe arrival and arrangements for handing over the contributions in Jerusalem. Throughout, there is testimony to the strength of God's **(gracious) hand**—helping prior to the journey (7:28), providing Levites (8:18), protecting the enterprise (v. 22), and enabling the successful completion of the journey (v. 31). Ezra envisioned himself as fulfilling the divine will and found each step of faith honored by God.

**7:28b–8:14** / Ezra had just relived, in the outburst of praise in 7:27–28a, his sense of God's involvement in the generous commission of Artaxerxes. Now he records that this conviction gave him encouragement to get started. He had a record of the party of volunteers available, which he incorporated into his narrative. For the sake of the story line, he omits the Levites for the time being—until verses 18–20. The record falls into a pattern after the first three cases. It supplies the name of the clan to which each group belonged, the name of the patriarchal family head together with his father's name, and the number of male members of the extended family who returned with him. Pride of place is given to two priestly groups. This is not surprising, since a priest was leading the party; it was also warranted by the religious nature of Ezra's mission. This whole account is dominated by the temple ("house"), which will feature in verses 17, 25, 29–30, 33, and also 36, although the phrase **temple servants** in verses 17 and 20 is a paraphrase that imports the term. Ezra's summary of the royal commission as bringing honor to the temple in 7:27 set the agenda for this chapter. The account of the first mission was similar: the destination of the returning exiles was the temple, to hand over contributions (2:68). This religious phenomenon of exiles returning precious items reappears in the brief reference to a group of immigrants in Zechariah 6:10.

The first group of priests belonged to Ezra's own clan of **Phineas,** Aaron's grandson through Eleazar (7:5); they were naturally drawn to their relative's project. The second group traced their heritage from **Ithamar,** another son of Aaron. **Gershom** and **Daniel** were evidently family heads, since verse 24 mentions twelve priests belonging to the party. We are not told how many priests returned with Ezra. In the list of Nehemiah 7/Ezra 2, they made up a tenth of the immigrants. In that list a Davidic group was not singled out, although Zerubbabel's leadership bore implicit witness to its representation. Here explicit mention attests the continuing honor paid to the preexilic royal line. Later the Chronicler would reflect such honor by tracing it down to his own era (1 Chr. 3), seemingly with an eschatological interest, but Ezra-Nehemiah as a whole displays no such interest. **Hattush** (v. 2) is given a position separate from the rest of the laity, who are significantly grouped under twelve family names. This symbolic number, which will reappear in a priestly and Levitical context in verse 24 and also in a sacrificial setting in verse 35, reveals a claim for a representative role for the party as reflecting the totality of the true Israel with its tradition of twelve tribes. Here was a microcosm of the authentic people of God returning to the land. The numbers of males add up to about 1,500, to which those given in verses 19–20 need to be added, and the lack of numbers in verse 2a also needs to be taken into account. With women and children, there would have been a total of about 5,000 in the returning party.

Many of the clans of the earlier list in Nehemiah 7/Ezra 2 naturally reappear here—eleven of them. Relatives were to be reunited. The new clan of **Joab** (v. 9) represents a later subdivision of the large clan of "Pahath-Moab" (see Neh. 7:11 = Ezra 2:6). In the case of the clan of **Adonikam** (v. 13), no relatives were left behind in Babylon.

**8:15–20** / The assembling of the party resumes and develops 7:28b. That Ezra **found no Levites** worried him. The tiny
number of Levites, compared with priests, in Nehemiah 7:43 (=
Ezra 2:40) had been bad enough. Ezra's determination to recruit
some Levites would delay the starting time by nearly two weeks,
according to 7:9 and 8:31. They were needed for temple duties:
this is the explanation given in verse 17. In verse 16, Ezra sent an
impressive delegation to find Levites—**leaders** and **men of learning.** The latter seem to have been priestly instructors in the Torah.
It is significant that in Nehemiah 8:7, 9, which belong to the Ezra
memoirs, this term appears twice as a verbal form ("instructed,"
"instructing") that describes the Levites as hermeneutical interpreters of the Torah. Ezra needed Levites to be trained for such a
task. He sent fellow experts in the Torah to offer them a new job
opportunity and so persuade them to come. A third, more immediate, reason for the indispensability of Levites will emerge in
verses 24–30.

There was a settlement of Levites and other former temple
workers at **Casiphia,** whose location is unknown. Evidently a
sanctuary of some kind was based there, perhaps adumbrating
the much later Jewish institution of the synagogue. The delegation netted 38 Levites and **220 temple servants**—not a bad total at
such short notice. The latter formed a subordinate group, also featuring in Nehemiah 7:46–60 (= Ezra 2:45–48). Here their origins
are traced back to the period of David, like the institution of
temple music in Ezra 3:10; Nehemiah 12:24, and in Chronicles
generally. Ezra was not displeased with this result, and he interpreted it as a further sign that God was behind the project.

**8:21–23** / An essential part of Ezra's preparations for the
long trek to Judah was prayer, reinforced by the self-deprivation
of fasting, which in the Bible regularly accompanies prayer offered at a time of crisis. What made the situation especially critical
was Ezra's strong conviction that he should not request an armed
escort from the Persian authorities, along with his other requests
in 7:6. This refusal contrasts with Nehemiah's acceptance of an escort, following normal practice for a Persian administrator (Neh.
2:9). Ezra regarded secular guards as embarrassingly inconsistent
with his testimony to **the king** himself—a prerequisite of divine
favor was commitment to God. Seeking human help would have
implied forsaking God. How did he know that to "seek" (NRSV)
God necessitated taking such an extreme stand at this time? The

phrase **a safe journey** gives us a clue—literally a "straight way," one with no complications. It appears to echo the language of Isaiah 40:3, which promised that God would take the exiled people back to their homeland. This promise was supplemented in Isaiah 52:12 by one of a new exodus under divine protection: "the LORD will go before you, the God of Israel will be your rear guard." Ezra evidently regarded the journey as a partial fulfillment of prophecy relating to the return of the people of God. The need for Levites to carry the religious vessels, which will be the concern of verses 24–30, fits this interpretation. It accords with the call of Second Isaiah to those "who carry the vessels of the LORD," to leave Babylon "and be pure" (Isa. 52:11). In the wilderness journey centuries before, the Levitical division of Merari had been responsible for transporting the tabernacle (Num. 4:29–33). Ezra cast the latest additions to the party in that ancient role from the Torah. He might have wished for Levites from the division of Kohath, who were specifically responsible for vessels (Num. 4:4–20; 10:17, 21), but he gladly accepted the Levites who were available. He was a student of both the Torah and the prophets, in accord with the later description of a scribe in Sir. 38:24–39:11. We noticed an echo of Isaiah 60:7 in 7:27. To ask for a bodyguard did not fit the prophetic pattern, and Ezra judged that it would have meant incurring God's **great anger.** To seek God meant both to seek the divine will in the Scriptures and then with ardent prayer to "seek from him" (NRSV, v. 21) the "safe journey" promised to Israel in returning from exile. Ezra anticipates verse 31 by gratefully commenting with hindsight that the party's prayers were answered.

**8:24–30** / Ezra now made arrangements to transport the temple contributions given in accord with 7:15–16, to protect them against theft or other loss. The Torah directed that priests had charge of sacred objects and actually handled them, while Levites carried them without physical contact (Num. 3:6–4:33). So Ezra chose **twelve** of the **priests** and an equal number of Levites for this special task. The list of the contributions, which consisted of both ingots and articles of precious metal, was derived from the record eventually deposited at the temple (v. 34). In a charge to the religious guards (vv. 28–29), Ezra spoke of the sacred trust assigned to them. Both the conveyors and what they conveyed were covered with an aura of holiness during the interim period before they reached the holy temple. This was both an assurance of divine protection and a challenge to honesty in protecting other people's offerings to God. They were playing a vital role in the ongoing spiritual history of Israel in thus serving **the God of** their **fathers.**

**8:31–34** / Very little is told about the journey itself, which was a long trek of three and a half months according to the arrival date already given in 7:9. It was over 900 miles if, as is likely, the route via north Syria was taken. Verses 31–32 endorse the early notice of answered prayer in verse 23. Attacks were fended off, and this too is interpreted in terms of the presence of their own God, who came to the rescue (see additional note). We would like to read of Wells Fargo-type adventures, but instead we are told of God's loyalty to the covenant relationship **(our God).** "The righteous cry out, and the LORD hears them; he delivers them from all their troubles" (Ps. 34:17). Here again we encounter the factor of enemy oppression that was to dog all three missions of Ezra-Nehemiah. Yet it was overcome in each case so that God's work went forward. The **three days** of rest and reorientation correspond to the same period of preliminary organization in verse 15. The focus of the narrative is on delivery of the contributions, which is related with the same eye to detail as the arrangements of verses 24–30. **Meremoth,** evidently the temple treasurer, formally received and checked them in the presence of others, presumably members of his staff. Scrupulous accounting has always been one of the obligations of holy stewardship.

**8:35–36** / We hear an echo of the religious celebrations that followed the completion of the two phases of the first mission in chapters 3 and 6. It was time to celebrate again. A switch to third-person narrative appears to indicate that the editor was responsible for bringing the episode to a close. These verses were a natural deduction from the royal mandates in 7:17, 21–23, with a side-glance at Nehemiah 2:9. The sacrificing is also an act of thanksgiving for the safety of the journey. It is a religious counterpart to the literary tribute paid to divine help earlier in the text. The **sin offering** got rid of the uncleanness of exile, as was suggested in 6:17, and it is even more obviously in view here. The last clause in verse 35 draws attention to the quality of the other sacrifices in that they took the form of **a burnt offering.** As thank offerings, they might have been partial sacrifices in which the meat was returned to the sacrificer for a sacred meal with his family— the "fellowship offering" of Leviticus 3:3–4; 7:11–15. Instead, as in Psalm 66:13–15, whole ("burnt") offerings were brought as a measure of the immigrants' utter gratitude and praise. The delivery of the royal warrants mentioned in verse 36 had doubtless taken place during the journey south. Here it introduces the financial **assistance** duly given for the temple and so for the benefit of **the people.** The first phase of Ezra's mission was now over.

---

## Additional Notes §9

---

**8:1** / For the presence of the list in the Ezra memoirs, see Williamson, *Ezra, Nehemiah*, pp. 108f.

**8:2** / In the later development of the priestly divisions attested in 1 Chr. 24, the divisions branched off from two groups—a major one descended from Aaron's son Eleazar and a smaller group descended from his brother **Ithamar.** This is the earliest mention of the latter group in the postexilic history of the priesthood. Aaronic lineage evidently played a crucial role from Ezra's period. Ezek. 44:15 simply specified Zadokite ancestry.

**8:3** / The NIV has rightly adjusted the verse division of the MT. **Shechaniah** is the clan name of the family led by **Hattush.** In 1 Chr. 3:22 his position is four generations after Zerubbabel, if the genealogy is continuous at this point.

**8:5** / The NIV has rightly restored **Zattu,** attested in the LXX and 1 Esd. 8:32. The clan name recurs in Neh. 7:13 (= Ezra 2:8). The pattern of the list shows that a name is required; it was lost by assimilation to "the descendants of Shechaniah" in v. 3. By the same token, in v. 3 the name of Zechariah's father was lost at an early stage.

**8:10** / **Bani** has correctly been restored with the LXX and 1 Esd. 8:36. This clan name is found in the form "Binnui" in Neh. 7:15 (= "Bani" in Ezra 2:10).

**8:14** / The pattern of the list suggests that **and Zaccur** was originally "the son of Zaccur" (NJB), as 1 Esd. 8:40 attests (see *BHS*), and as the following "with him" in the MT implies. The NIV has changed this to **with them** with some ancient support, which looks like a correction made to cope with the textual alteration. There was ancient uncertainty whether the name was "Zaccur" or "Zab(b)ud" (REB, NJB).

**8:15** / A series of canals ran from the Euphrates and Tigris to irrigate and provide transportation for the Babylonian heartland. The Jewish exiles were settled near some of these canals (see Ps. 137:1; Ezek. 3:15). This one chosen for the rendezvous is called "the Ahava Canal," for short, in vv. 21, 31.

**8:16** / The names look suspiciously repetitious, but the appositional nouns indicate two separate groups (Blenkinsopp, *Ezra-Nehemiah*, p. 165).

**8:17** / The NIV has failed to represent a recurring element. The NJB gives a more literal rendering, "a place called Casiphia . . . the place called Casiphia." The repetition of "place" seems significant. In the OT it can connote a sanctuary (see BDB, p. 880), especially in the phrase "the place the LORD your God will choose" in Deut. 12:5 and elsewhere. **And his kinsmen the temple servants:** The NIV has restored "and," easily lost in the Heb., and revocalized "his brother" in the MT—both on the evidence of 1 Esd. 8:48 and the Vulgate, or Jerome's Latin translation of the OT (see *BHS*). But one expects a reference to Levites in **kinsmen.** Iddo was probably a Levite, and Levites were Ezra's primary concern. The text of 1 Esd. also has "and" between the two terms, again easily lost. Then the two groups mentioned in the listing of vv. 18–20 are introduced here.

**8:18** / The clan of **Mahli** was part of the division of Merari (Num. 3:33; 1 Chr. 6:19), which was one of the three Levitical divisions (1 Chr. 6:16).

**8:19** / The **his** refers back to **Hashabiah,** as comparison with v. 18 suggests, where "Sherebiah's" is an elucidation of "his" (NRSV).

**8:20** / **All were registered by name:** The names were supplied in the original list. The attribution to **David,** found only here in the case of the **temple servants,** may have been suggested by analogy with the parallel group "the descendants of the servants of Solomon" in Neh. 7:57–60 (= Ezra 2:55–58).

**8:21** / For the influence of Second Isaiah, see K. Koch, "Ezra and the Origins of Judaism," *JSS* 19 (1974), pp. 173–97, esp. pp. 187f., and Blenkinsopp, *Ezra-Nehemiah,* p. 168. **Children** is better translated "dependents" (REB, NJB), including wives.

**8:24** / The NIV, unlike the NRSV, has rightly added "and" to the MT (on the evidence of 1 Esd. 8:54), so that the translation **together with** makes it clear that the Levites are a separate group. Verse 30 implies this, and the actual names refer back to the Levites of vv. 18–19.

**8:25** / **Offering** echoes a term often used in Exod. 25 and 35 for contributions to the tabernacle.

**8:26** / The unreasonably heavy weight of the **silver** and **gold** is as problematic as the amount in 7:22 (see Williamson, *Ezra, Nehemiah,* p. 119). 1 Esdras 8:56 interpreted the phrase as **silver articles weighing 100 talents,** but the MT is to be understood as "one hundred silver vessels worth . . . talents" (NRSV). The parallel structure of v. 27 indicates that the number has not been preserved, unless the term of **talents** is to be revocalized as a dual, "two talents" (REB, NJB).

**8:31** / The word **protected** connotes a lack of anticipated hostility. A more careful translation is "delivered" (NRSV) or "saved" (REB,

NJPS), implying that attacks did occur. Similarly in v. 22, "protect" means literally "help from" with the sense of "help in defending against."

**8:33** / **We weighed out** is lit. a passive form, "were weighed" (NRSV), but there is no reason to doubt that Ezra's memoirs are still being cited at this point (see R. A. Bowman, "The Book of Ezra and the Book of Nehemiah," *IB* 3:549–819, p. 642).

**8:34** / **At that time** is better taken with v. 35, as the NRSV does. Otherwise the Heb. of the next sentence is abrupt. The phrase fittingly introduces a separate topic broached by the editor.

**8:35** / **Seventy-seven:** Since the other numbers are divisible by twelve, the reading "seventy-two" of 1 Esd. 8:66 is preferable. Josephus, *Ant.* 11.137, supports it. The NJB reads thus and has widespread scholarly support, including Barthélemy, *Critique textuelle,* vol. 1, p. 543, where, following Rudolph, *Esra und Nehemia,* the reading of the MT is explained as due to internal assimilation. **All this** cannot include the **sin offering,** which was only a partial offering, not a whole offering (Lev. 4:8–10, 26). The comment draws special attention to the earlier **burnt offerings.**

**8:36** / **Satraps:** The satrapy of **Trans-Euphrates** had only one satrap, so the term refers generally to satrapal officials.

The mission assigned to Ezra had two parts. While we have seen the first part carried out in chapter 8, the second part remained to be done. In 9:1–10:44, we shall read how the Judean community, complying with Artaxerxes' decree in 7:14, 25–26, accepted the Torah. Comparison with the latter passage shows that the editor's presentation of Ezra's work was highly selective, and that here the issue of intermarriage with the local population was the focus of his concern. To that end the story of reform jumps from the fifth month, when the exiles with Ezra arrived in Jerusalem according to 7:9, to the ninth month mentioned in 10:9. In the gap, we expect that Ezra would have taught The Torah to the people. This is just what we read in Nehemiah 8, dated in the seventh month. It is most likely that this chapter, more precisely starting from Nehemiah 7:73b, was originally part of the Ezra memoirs—and the editor moved it to its new position for good reasons. Readers are still meant to presuppose from 7:10 that Ezra read the Torah and applied it hermeneutically to the current situation. Ezra's "counsel" in 10:3 seems to refer back to this displaced ingredient. So verses 1–2 here in chapter 9 are actually the first-fruits of his labors, when some of the community's **leaders** reported evidence that a Torah prohibition was being ignored. The account goes on to tell how Ezra persuaded the rest of the people to support his assessment. He worked slowly and in a roundabout way to let his teaching seep into their minds and consciences. He preferred not to parade his authority as a Persian administrator, functioning rather as a Judean religious leader, only too aware that he was a newcomer and did not belong to the established Jewish hierarchy.

**9:1–2** / The hermeneutical sophistication of **the leaders'** report is a clue that the speakers were siding with Ezra and echoing lessons already learned from their teacher. Basically the complaint is of marriage to women from outside the community. It is branded as **unfaithfulness,** a term that as a noun or a verb reverberates through the account. It is an accusation here, acknowledged by a larger group in verse 4; then a community spokesperson in 10:2 cites it as the reason for Ezra's continued grieving in 10:6. Finally it is Ezra's accusation directed to the whole people in 10:10. This key term, used in the priestly books of Leviticus and Numbers, has two meanings. It is used as a general theological term for infidelity to the God of the covenant in Leviticus 26:40 (NIV "treachery"), where it is linked with a need for confession. This covenantal infidelity comes to the fore in its uses in Ezra 9–10 and motivates Ezra's calls for confession in 10:1, 11. However, the term also had a precise religious meaning— violating that which was holy, which required a specific offering (Lev. 5:14–16). This offering will duly be made in Ezra 10:19. The concept of holiness pervades these two chapters, which took it beyond the temple sphere and applied it figuratively to the lifestyle of the community. This application features strongly in the report, in the references to separation and **the holy race.** The appeal to holiness is implicitly based on Deuteronomy 7:6, where Israel is called "a people holy to the LORD." This holy status is an aspect of the theological particularism that characterizes the OT. In Deuteronomy 7 this special relationship with God is stated as the reason why Israelites should not intermarry with the traditional seven ethnic groups they found in the promised land. In the leaders' report here in verse 1, these groups listed in Deuteronomy 7:1 are represented by the first four names, **Canaanites . . . Jebusites.** They no longer existed as ethnic entities in the postexilic period; the mixed local populations living around the immigrant community are regarded as their virtual equivalents.

The next pair, **Ammonites, Moabites,** still existed, but their importance lies in recalling Deuteronomy 23:3, where neither they nor their descendants are permitted to join the "assembly of the LORD." Ezra will cite Deuteronomy 23, as well as Deuteronomy 7, in the course of his prayer in verses 10–12. The next reference, to **Egyptians,** echoes Deuteronomy 23:7–8, where their immediate descendants were prohibited from joining the assembly, while the last group, **Amorites,** is another of the seven nations listed in Deuteronomy 7:1. The lesson learned from Deuteronomy 7 was that intermarriage with neighboring "peoples of the lands" (NRSV, v. 2, also v. 11) was wrong according to the Torah. These references to Deuteronomy 23 set up an analogy to show that alien spouses and their children could not be accepted as members of

the religious assembly. It is likely that this hermeneutic was facilitated by the similarities with Deuteronomy 23:2, "No one born of
a forbidden marriage nor any of his descendants may enter the assembly of the LORD," which was interpreted as referring to mixed
marriages. The logical, drastic conclusion to be drawn was that
they must be expelled. There can be no doubt that the hermeneutic was derived from the teaching of Ezra, who was to work these
very texts into his prayer. This thinking marks a development
consistent with the representation of the community's earlier history in Ezra 1–6 as made up of returned exiles. In fact, this definition will feature in verse 4 and 10:6, 8, 16. Outsiders belonging to
"the peoples of the lands" had no place in the new Israel, as the
narratives of 4:1–4 and 6:21 had made clear, using similar language. The latter verse mentioned proselytes who had renounced
such tainted practices. Here, however, conversion was not envisioned as an option, and racial purity was pursued on religious
grounds. If one seeks to harmonize 6:21 and chapters 9–10, the
reference in 6:21 could only be to nonexiled Judeans who renounced pagan assimilation, so that the crossing of racial lines
was not a factor. It is clear from Deuteronomy 7:4 that religion was
the basic ground of the exclusion. There was a fear of reverse conversion, of seduction from worshiping Israel's God only. This
nightmare evidently loomed large for the early, fragile community of returned exiles. They felt overwhelmed by an established,
culturally heterogeneous population, in a setting where religion
played a large role in culture. Consequently only marriage inside
the community was expedient and indeed necessary—so strong
was the scent of spiritual danger. The NT issues a similar warning,
"Do not be yoked together with unbelievers" (2 Cor. 6:14). However, the NT does not urge automatic divorce from unbelieving
spouses (see 1 Cor. 7:12–16; 1 Pet. 3:1–2). In the latter passages
there is no trace of a threat that Christian partners might lose their
own faith, and herein lies the difference with the underlying tone
of Ezra 9–10. The struggling postexilic community feared for their
spiritual survival, and they found appropriate Scriptures to fit the
current need. Evidence in the book of Malachi, from about the
same period, suggests that the problem was more complex than
presented here. The prophet deplored Judean males divorcing their
wives and marrying into non-Judean, non-Yahwistic families—
which they did presumably for economic betterment (Mal.
2:10–16). In Malachi, too, it was a case of offending holiness:
"Judah has profaned what is holy to the LORD" (Mal. 2:11, NJPS).

With his use of Deuteronomy 23, Ezra was able to provide chapter
and verse for this conviction.

   A negative term characteristic of Deuteronomy, **detestable
practices,** reinforces the references to Deuteronomy 7 and 23, describing the pagan religion of the local population; Deuteronomy
17:2–5 is a typical example. Malachi 2:11 went further and actually
applied the term to Jewish intermarriage. The holy community
was not to be contaminated in this way. Rather, its members must
keep **themselves separate.** The phraseology is priestly: in 8:24 it
described the religious group segregated ("set apart") by Ezra and
so called "holy" (NRSV) in 8:28. Since the people as a whole had a
holy status, segregated from other peoples, they had to live accordingly (Lev. 20:24, 26). The Christian hears an echo of this
teaching in 2 Corinthians 6:17, a quotation from Isaiah 52:11
applied to the church in relation to pagan society. This priestly
doctrine is here applied to the issue of intermarriage. Prophetic
endorsement of the Torah is obtained by calling the community
"holy seed" (NRSV; NIV **holy race**), a phrase that refers to the
postexilic remnant in Isaiah 6:13. Different biblical traditions were
combined and powerfully brought to bear on the contemporary
problem of mixed marriages. The impulse behind this hermeneutical barrage was spiritual expediency, created by the sense of
being a weak and threatened community. The note of opposition
sounded repeatedly in Ezra-Nehemiah is a testimony to this conviction. The community was endangered, and they had to take a
firm stand against fraternization. The fact that leading members
had succumbed only increased the sense of urgency. It was advisable to make a definitive ruling and to apply it to the whole
community.

   **9:3–5** / The leaders' formal report told Ezra nothing
new, but it gave him the opportunity to move beyond teaching to
enforcement. The report was evidently presented in the outer
court of the temple, and he chose to make a public demonstration
there, according to 10:1. While this action undoubtedly expressed
his own spiritual convictions, his intention was to draw support
extending beyond the particular leaders already on his side. Ezra
engaged in ritual mourning that reflected extreme crisis. In the
context it was meant to indicate repentance, like the grieving rites
advocated in Joel 2:12. He was acting on behalf of the community
and implicitly urging them to follow his example. His silent performance was a dramatic version of the confession he was to make

in his prayer. The first support he attracted was from a like-minded group committed to strict observance of the Torah. This circle of sympathizers will be mentioned in the same breath as Ezra in Shecaniah's speech in 10:3. They were a religious group who received prophetic commendation a little before Ezra's time, in Isaiah 66:2, 5, where they are presented as a fringe group regarded as too extreme by others in the community. They found a soulmate in the strict Ezra, and they welcomed as timely his selection of texts from the Torah against intermarriage. Ezra broke his silence at the time of **the evening sacrifice** offered nearby in the inner court of the temple—an appropriate time to approach God in prayer, as Acts 3:1 attests. His posture for prayer, kneeling with head bowed and arms outstretched, expressed through body language his submission to God and ardent entreaty.

**9:6–9** / Ezra engaged in a prayer of confession, somewhat like the cries of lament voiced in the course of 3:10–13. It is, by its hortatory nature, incomplete, and it is continued by the community's formal confession in 10:7–14 and by the individual sacrifices of 10:19. This first half of the prayer does not specifically mention intermarriage, but its general theological terms presuppose its wrongfulness in the sight of God. The report of verses 1–2 had made clear Ezra's teaching on the issue. Now something had to be done about it, and repentance was to pave the way for reform. The prayer begins by confessing present **guilt.** The community as a whole—not just particular individuals—was contaminated. In terms of Joshua 7:11, *Israel* had sinned. The prayer moves to a statement of solidarity with guilty generations who lived before the exile. Ominously, that past **guilt** had resulted in deserved, dire punishment from God in the form of exile. Yet the postexilic community had seen evidence of divine grace unexpectedly following on the heels of punishment. This pairing of punished guilt and compassionate grace functions as a stimulus against continuing in present guilt. For the people to continue would show both ingratitude and disregard of the grim warning of history. It would add to an enormous mountain of sins piled up before the exile (vv. 6–7)—and the danger was that it would collapse and bury them all, as verse 14 will intimate. In verses 8–9, the switch from direct petition to third-person statements about God indicates the horizontal direction of the prayer. It was a message for the increasing number of bystanders (v. 4; 10:1) to take to heart, identifying with the references to **we, us,** and **our.** Ezra uttered his prayer first out of his own heart in intercession (**my God,** twice in v. 6), and then in self-identification with the community (**our God,** v. 8 and thereafter).

The narrator presents the postexilic period with deliberate ambivalence. It had a negative side. The shock waves of foreign invasions and the fall of Jerusalem continued to reverberate in the community's present experience (**as it is today,** v. 7). Political independence (**our kings**) had given way to the control of **foreign kings,** which meant political and economic **bondage.** These things were evidence of the continuing judgment of God. This was not a God to be provoked by further sinning. Yet the storm clouds had a silver lining in postexilic experience. The long period of deserved oppression at the hands of Assyrian and Babylonian **kings** had been succeeded by a comparatively **brief moment** of God's surprising grace in the postexilic era. Evidence of a **new** lease on **life** lay all around Ezra and the bystanders as they stood in the grounds of the rebuilt temple, which was a symbol of their firm "foothold" (REB) in the land. God's grace, providentially mediated through the Persian empire, had restored them from exile as a **remnant** surviving judgment. They lived secure, ordered lives in their province and were free to worship according to their own traditions. All this had boosted the morale of the community, but such blessing carried an obligation to respect the will of so gracious a God, who had gone the extra mile for them.

**9:10–15** / Ezra poignantly returns in the second half of the prayer to the direct petitioning of the opening. The prayer remains horizontal in spirit, as indicated by the use of questions—especially the first one, which is a call for a response and a change of heart. Ezra comes to the point. He specifies the people's present guilt in terms of mixed marriages, and he interprets this as breaking the Torah. The Torah is represented by a medley of allusions, principally from Deuteronomy 7:1–3 and 23:6. Verse 13 briefly recapitulates the communal history of divine punishment set out in verses 7–9. Then Ezra spells out the fatal consequences of persisting in present guilt, with an allusion to Deuteronomy 7:4. The survival of the community was at stake. If on the social plane there was a threat of assimilation, on the theological plane there was a threat of divine extermination. The prayer ends as it began, with general confession. The prayer does not include a petition for forgiveness. The next step lay not with God but with the people, who needed to identify themselves with the prayer's perspective and realize they had abandoned the Torah and were guilty of unfaithfulness, in the hope that God's fatal anger might be averted. This human step is not spelled out but is left for members of the community to deduce for themselves, in chapter 10.

The latter half of the prayer polarizes different uses of **this.** In verses 10 and 13 it refers to divine grace, while in verse 15 ("because of this," NRSV) it stands for human guilt. The polarization updates the contrast in the first half of the prayer, between past guilt—leading to punishment—and present grace. The message is to stay with grace by dealing with the present guilt and distancing themselves from it. The grim alternative was divine anger that would leave no survivors. "It is no doubt a weakness of modern spirituality that it regards a real fear of God's wrath which does not immediately lead to assurance of God's forgiveness as somewhat fanatical" (Clines, *Ezra, Nehemiah, Esther*, p. 122). The letter to the Hebrews stands alongside Ezra's prayer, delivering warnings that believers disregard at their peril.

---

## Additional Notes §10

**9:1** / The placement of Ezra's reading of the Torah in Nehemiah 8 will be further discussed below. For a summary of scholarly discussion, see Williamson, *Ezra, Nehemiah*, pp. 127f., 282–86. Perhaps **the leaders** function in the local role of the Torah-based "magistrates and judges" of 7:25, here consulting with Ezra. **Like those . . . Amorites:** The NIV and the similar NJPS and REB rightly do not identify **the neighboring peoples** with the ancient ethnic groups, as the NRSV and NJB do. Instead, they intend to draw an analogy between them and regard them as comparable counterparts. The list of the first four ancient nations, headed by **Canaanites,** follows a widespread tradition different from that of Deut. 7:1 (see T. Ishida, "The Structure of the Lists of Pre-Israelite Nations," *Bib* 60 [1979], pp. 461–90). It may represent a deliberate approximation of the order in Exod. 34:11 and so constitute an appeal to Exod. 34:11–16—a further Torah passage opposed to mixed marriages. **Amorites:** 1 Esdras 8:69 reads "Edomites" with Deut. 23:7 in view, but this is an easier and therefore secondary reading that ignores the difference in order. There is evidence that **Amorites** was used to mean Arabs in the postexilic period (Ishida, "Structure," p. 488). The term was displaced from its position in Deut. 7:1 to align it with the three other surviving groups, Ammonites, Mobabites, and Egyptians.

**9:2** / For the particular cultic offense of **unfaithfulness,** see esp. Lev. 5:15, where the NIV renders the Heb. as "violation." The term will also be used of intermarriage in Neh. 13:27. J. Milgrom, *Cult and Conscience* (SJLA 18; Leiden: Brill, 1976), pp. 16–35, 71–73, has helpfully defined the cultic sense of the Heb. term *maʿal*, and also Ezra's hermeneutic in terms of a fusion of priestly and Deuteronomic concepts. Good analyses of the hermeneutic have been made by Fishbane, *Biblical Interpretation*, pp. 114–23, and by Williamson, *Ezra, Nehemiah*, pp. 130–32.

**9:3** / For these procedures of ritual mourning, see 2 Kgs. 19:1; Job 1:20; 2:12–13.

**9:4** / The Heb. impf. verb translated **gathered** indicates the gradual growth of the crowd. The Syriac version gives a correct paraphrase of **until the evening sacrifice,** "until the ninth hour," that is, 3:00 P.M. One wonders whether the custom of praying at traditional times of temple sacrifice grew up during the exile, as a substitute for sacrificing.

**9:8** / **A firm place** is, lit., a tent peg or nail. The NRSV and NJPS capture the metaphor well with "stake."

**9:9** / The Heb. term for **a wall of protection** is metaphorical, as the NIV recognizes. In Ps. 80:12; Isa. 5:5 it describes the enclosure of a vineyard and refers to (a reversal of) God's protective care for the covenant people and their land.

**9:11** / Although there are some echoes of the texts of the **prophets,** most are from the Pentateuch. The term refers loosely to scriptural revelation. Moses is regarded as a prophet in Deut. 18:15; 34:10; Hos. 12:13.

**9:12** / The translation **friendship,** or "good relations," (NJB) is better than "prosperity" (NRSV) here and in Deut. 23:6. The linguistic basis for the rendering is noted by D. R. Hillers, "A Note on Some Treaty Terminology in the OT," *BASOR* 176 (1964), pp. 46–47.

**9:15** / **You are righteous** is a typical formula of confession in the OT. Exod. 9:27 spells out the implication, "The LORD is in the right, and I and my people are in the wrong." A forensic flavor continues with **stand** here—the sense is to win one's case.

The story continues so smoothly from chapter 9 that, although it switches to third-person references to Ezra, this must be an editorial change made to the Ezra memoirs. He is labeled **Ezra the priest** in verses 10 and 16, for he was engaging in priestly work as he instructed the people about their uncleanness and pointed to the remedy, along the lines of Leviticus 10:10–11. In this way he discharged the second half of his mission, teaching the Torah and making it the basis of communal life.

**10:1–4** / In his Gandhi-like campaign of social persuasion, Ezra had already won the allegiance of some of the provincial leaders and of a right-wing religious group (9:1, 4). Now his public stance attracted support from other people in Jerusalem. A man from the lay clan of Elam acted as their spokesperson in backing the earlier teaching of Ezra and the policy of his support group. He admitted that marriage to **women** from "the peoples of the land" (NRSV) constituted a serious breach of the covenant, and he advocated a communal "pledge" (REB) to expel the wives and children of the illicit unions. Dealing with the offense opened a window of **hope** for the community to survive despite the fact that they had offended God. They would regularize the situation and restore compliance to the Torah. As before, the prohibition of mixed marriages for the holy community in Deuteronomy 7:1–6 was in view, and the radical solution was inspired by Deuteronomy 23:2–7, as an interpretive corollary of its ban on neighboring aliens belonging to the religious community. **Shecaniah,** in the name of the **crowd,** encouraged Ezra to do his duty by initiating such a pledge.

**10:5–17** / Assured by this mandate from the people in Jerusalem that he was not running ahead of the community he served, Ezra administered the pledge, in the form of an **oath,** to religious and lay leaders in the city. Then he was able to let matters take their natural course, since the pledge obliged the provincial

administration (**officials and elders,** v. 14) to convene a national
assembly to enforce divorce proceedings. But on the religious
front Ezra continued his intercession in a nearby **room** (v. 6) inside
the temple area, presumably praying that the divine anger of
Deuteronomy 7 would be averted from the community. Verses 2
and 14 show widespread public awareness of the severity of the
situation. Nevertheless, the summons of the officials for conven-
ing the religious **assembly of the exiles** further underlined the crisis. Only **three days'** notice was provided, and noncompliance
would mean automatic expulsion from the community and confiscation of property. The males from the province duly arrived
for the special meeting. They met in a **square** near the temple, presumably between the temple and the Water Gate to the south,
where Ezra's reading of the Torah took place (Neh. 8:1). The
weather could hardly have provided a more fitting backdrop for
the grim occasion. It was December, in the season of the early
rains, and up in Jerusalem it was cold and miserable at the open-
air meeting. Ezra addressed his "shivering" (REB) congregation.
He began with a digest of his prayer, concentrating on past and
present **guilt** and defining the latter in terms of intermarriage. In
verse 11 he turned to what should be done, although the reference to **the God of your fathers** harked ominously back to the
divine judgment on preexilic sin (9:7). He issued a call for **confession** and reform, interpreting the latter step as the divine **will.**
Separation from "the peoples of the land" (NRSV) necessitated separation from **foreign wives,** in order to maintain the exclusive status of a community made up, in principle, of returned exiles and
their families. The assembly gave its enthusiastic support to Ezra's
call, but it also made practical proposals about the details of the execution. Ezra seems to have been more of a strategist than a tacti-
cian. The theological goal of averting the divine **anger** (v. 14)
threatened in 9:14 reveals the strong influence of Ezra's teaching
from the Torah. Opposition did raise its head (v. 15), but it was
minor enough to be overruled. The fact that the role of opposition
is a persistent motif in Ezra-Nehemiah suggests that it should be
regarded as a negative factor here. Doubtless these men advocated a liberal stand and condemned Ezra's harsh and innovative
measure as too extreme, perhaps citing other OT texts that permitted intermarriage.

Following the assembly's sensible proposals, the matter
was not resolved but was delegated to a commission. Ezra set up
this commission, which consisted of **family heads** representing

the various clans. Their names were originally recorded but have been dropped, as in 5:10 and 8:20. They met in Jerusalem and examined cases for three months, presumably liaising with local officials who accompanied accused men from all over the province, as verse 14 stipulated, to establish the truth.

**10:18–44**  /  This list of men with **foreign** wives was probably included in the Ezra memoirs. The requirements of verse 19 applied not only to the priestly group but also to the rest; there was no reason to single out one group. References to these requirements must have been dropped in other sections for stylistic reasons to avoid repetition. There were offending members from the four priestly clans mentioned in the oldest provincial list in Nehemiah 7:39–42 (= Ezra 2:36–39), including the high priestly clan, here traced through the well-known **Jeshua.** Seventeen priests were offenders; in fact, they were subject to a separate, strict law concerning marriage (Lev. 21:7, 13–14, see also Ezek. 44:22). Since numbers of male clan members are attached to the Nehemiah 7/Ezra 2 lists, we can roughly ascertain how comparatively small the proportion of offenders actually was. Indeed, the ratio is small in each part of this list. For Ezra it was a matter of principle, of nipping in the bud a limited problem and making an example of just over a hundred offenders, to prevent others from being tempted to go down the same path. The individual commitments and sacrifices of verse 19 remind us of the sin offerings in 6:17 and 8:35. Here the **guilt offering** reflects Leviticus 5:14–16 as the means of gaining divine forgiveness. The guilt offering sacrificed to God accompanied reparation at the human level, which in this case meant resolving the problem of mixed marriages by divorce. The reference to the offenders' **guilt** echoes the term used in Ezra's prayer on behalf of the community, in 9:6–7, 13, and 15, and in his summary in 10:10. With their guilt removed, the offenders were restored to the community and, implicitly, the related anger of God no longer loomed over it.

Lists of other members of the temple staff and of laymen follow the list of priests. The closing comment in verse 44 mentions that **children** were involved in the process (the exact involvement of the children is unclear; see additional note). The purpose of this verse seems to be to correct the sole mention of wives in verse 19, following the expulsion of wives and children proposed in verse 3 and indeed the logic of Deuteronomy 23 in chapter 9. The rams of verse 19 were not the only sacrifice offenders had to make on behalf of the holy community—nor were the wives. With the wives went the children of the now illicit unions. An empathetic reading of the story leads us to the challenge Jesus posed to his followers in Mark 10:29–30 (also Matt. 19:29–30; Luke 18:29–30) as a biblical parallel, to the call that sometimes comes to believers to leave children and other family members for the sake of Jesus and the gospel.

---

### Additional Notes §11

**10:1** / For discussion of the widely held view that this chapter was an adaptation of the Ezra memoirs, see Williamson, *Ezra, Nehemiah,* pp. 145–48. It is not obvious why the shift to the third person was made. Daniels, "Composition," p. 322, suggests that it was to ease transition to the first-person Nehemiah memoirs, so as not to confuse Ezra's "I" with Nehemiah's. "The people" (NRSV for **they**), as another weeping group, seem to be a separate group from **the crowd,** and must therefore refer to Ezra's supporters in 9:4.

**10:2** / For the clan of **Elam,** see Neh. 7:12 = Ezra 2:7; 8:7. Verse 26 discloses that **Shecaniah** had a foreign stepmother, if **Jehiel** refers to the same person.

**10:3** / **Now** is lit. "And now," which idiomatically introduces the main point of a statement. But the same Heb. phrase in v. 2 ("But even now," NRSV for "But . . . still") is chronological, referring to confession as an urgent opportunity. The Heb. verb *hotsiʾ,* **send away,** appears as part of the vocabulary of divorce in Deut. 24:2 (NIV "leaves"). The MT vocalized **my lord** as a divine term, "the Lord," but the pairing with Ezra's support group points to a human reference, which is implied in 1 Esd. 8:94. **Fear** is lit. "tremble at" (NRSV), as in 9:4.

**10:5** / The flow of the narrative suggests that "leaders" (NKJV) qualifies not only **priests** and **Levites,** but **all Israel** (Brockington, *Ezra, Nehemiah, and Esther,* p. 93). The Judean community will not meet until v. 9.

**10:6** / **While he was there** seems to be a paraphrase of "where he spent the night" (NRSV). It represents a correction of the MT "and he went," in agreement with 1 Esd. 9:2 and the Syriac version. Accidental assimilation to the previous verb occurred in the MT.

**10:8** / The word **forfeit** refers to the fact that the items would be dedicated to temple use. Movable property seems to be in view. Compare the paraphrase in 1 Esd. 9:4, "their livestock would be seized for sacrifice." **Expelled** appears to be a modification of earlier capital punishment, expressed in terms of being "cut off from the community of Israel"

(Exod. 12:19; compare Ezek. 13:9). Literally, the term used here is "be separated," in a negative sense. The term recurs in the desirable sense, "separate oneself," in 9:1; 10:11. The penalty for not attending the assembly convened for such separation was to be separated from membership of the community, like the foreign wives and the children of mixed marriages (compare the use of the verb in Isa. 56:3). For this concept of excommunication, see W. Horbury, "Extirpation and Excommunication," *VT* 35 (1985), pp. 13–38.

**10:9** / For the restriction to **men**, compare Exod. 23:17, reinforced in 34:23; Deut. 16:16.

**10:11** / **Now** is lit. "And now," with the same role as in v. 3, above. **Make confession**, or "give thanks" (NJB), is a call for a doxology of judgment, a praising acknowledgment that God was in the right. The expression also occurs in Josh. 7:19.

**10:14** / **Until . . . is turned away** is better translated, with the LXX, "in order to avert . . ." (NJPS).

**10:15** / It is possible that **Meshullam** and **Shabbethai** were the Torah teachers of Ezra 8:16 and Neh. 8:7, but there can be no certainty about this.

**10:16** / The rendering **selected** involves a slight, necessary change of the ungrammatical MT, in accord with 1 Esd. 9:16 (see *BHS*).

**10:19** / **As a guilt offering:** The vocalization in the MT as an adj., ʾashemim, "(being) guilty," does not fit very well. The REB, implicitly following the LXX, has revocalized it as a plural noun, "(as) guilt offerings," understanding a carryover of the verb in the preceding clause. The NRSV and NJB ("their guilt offering") have revocalized to ʾshamam, which nicely accords with the style of the underlying Lev. 5:15. The sin was unintentional (Lev. 5:15) in that the marriages were contracted before their illicit nature was realized. The Torah text applied to the entire community, not just priests.

**10:24** / As in the list of Neh. 7/Ezra 2, these subordinate temple groups were not yet amalgamated into the clans of Levites.

**10:31** / **From the descendants of Harim:** The MT lacks the preposition, which, however, is widely attested (see *BHS*).

**10:34** / The clan name **Bani** has already occurred in v. 29, where its placement in a cluster of clan names is in agreement with Ezra 2:7–11. By the same token, since **Hashum** is followed by "Bezai" in Neh. 7:22–23, that may have been the original name here, though no textual evidence for it has survived (Barthélemy, *Critique textuelle*, vol. 1, pp. 528f.).

**10:38** / **From the descendants of Binnui:** The MT, retained in the NJPS, has "and Bani and Binnui." The NIV, together with other modern versions, has reconstructed the text, claiming the support of the LXX and 1 Esd. 9:34. Barthélemy, *Critique textuelle*, vol. 1, p. 529, has pointed out that the alleged counterpart in 1 Esd. corresponds to the beginning of v. 34, while the actual counterpart is of no help. The LXX reads "the sons of Banoui and the sons of (Semei)." The LXX has the same Gk. name in v. 29 for the MT Bani, while in Neh. 7:15 and Ezra 2:10 Bani and Binnui are alternative forms of the same name. There seems to have been no separate clan name Binnui, but the very large number of personal names in the context suggests that more than one was involved. The new clan may start in v. 40 rather than here.

**10:40 / Macnadebai:** This odd-looking name (to non-Scots!) is suspicious. 1 Esdras 9:34 found here a new clan: "from the sons of Ezora," which may represent *mibbene 'azzûr* (see *BHS*). Then the reference is to a clan that may have fallen out of Ezra 2:16 but was preserved in 1 Esd. 5:15 (see Williamson, *Ezra, Nehemiah,* pp. 22, 25). Since in 1 Esd. some of the names in the context bear little relation to those in the MT, it may be better to postulate a form closer to its consonants. Thus the NJB prefers "of the sons of Zaccai," which relates to the clan name in Neh. 7:14/Ezra 2:9. Here an Aramaic form of the name "Daccai," may have been intended (Clines, *Ezra, Nehemiah, Esther,* p. 132).

**10:44 / And some of them . . . wives:** The NIV has wisely resisted the adoption of 1 Esd. 9:36, as the NRSV (and other modern versions) have done, "and they sent them away with their children." This is clearly a secondary correction of a difficult text, making it say what one would like it to say in the context. Although the Heb. verb is difficult, the MT may be taken to mean "but there were among them wives (with whom) they had had children" (Barthélemy, *Critique textuelle,* vol. 1, p. 547), which is similar to the interpretation in the NIV.

# *Nehemiah*

Leslie C. Allen

## §1 The Background to Nehemiah's Mission (Neh. 1:1–11)

The two missions in Ezra 1–6 and 7–10 were launched by the decree of a Persian king, behind which lay the sovereign will of the God of Israel, disclosed in Scripture and providence. The third and last mission, spread over 1:1–2:8 and summarized in 2:18a, also follows this pattern. The focus on Nehemiah in 1:1–10 corresponds to the description of Ezra's qualifications by birth and training in Ezra 7:1–7. The narrative here reveals Nehemiah's strong convictions, which laid a spiritual foundation for his mission.

**1:1a** / The editor supplied a brief heading that takes its cue from Nehemiah's memoirs, which supply the substantial framework of Nehemiah 1–13. This heading implies that these chapters form a single structural block. The heading rescues from anonymity the autobiographical narrative that will follow. It identifies Nehemiah—not an uncommon postexilic name—by his patronymic, a tradition known to the editor. The heading takes a form found in the titles of some prophetic and wisdom first-person texts (compare Jer. 1:1; Prov. 30:1; and Eccl. 1:1).

**1:1b–4** / There was no need to specify the king for readers of Ezra 7–Nehemiah 13 because the story continued on from Ezra's mission set in Artaxerxes' reign (Ezra 7:1), specifically in his seventh year (Ezra 7:7–8). The event that triggered the new mission, by making a strong emotional impact on Nehemiah, was his hearing bad news about **Jerusalem,** brought or at least mediated by his brother **Hanani,** who will reappear in the story in 7:2. The sorry plight of the Judeans is explained in terms of damage inflicted on the **wall** and **gates** of the city. This damage can hardly refer to the catastrophe of 587, when the Babylonians destroyed Jerusalem. Nehemiah's shocked reaction indicates that it must be the result of a recent disaster. It is probably linked with the frustrated attempt to rebuild the wall of Jerusalem in Artaxerxes' reign that is narrated in Ezra 4:8–23. The implication is that the military "force" that compelled the Judeans to stop at the end of that account was violent enough to destroy the repair work they had already done. Alternatively, if the incident of Ezra 4:23 should be placed at the outset of the king's reign, making it ancient history by Nehemiah's period, an attack from the south by Arabs may be presupposed, taking advantage of Artaxerxes' decree against rebuilding. At any rate, the mission of Nehemiah is the satisfying ending to the sad story of Ezra 4:23. Nehemiah's family links with Jerusalem, described in his response to the king in 2:3, explain his concern. Yet the religious statement about Jerusalem in verse 9 suggests that this concern probably went deeper; later in this book it is depicted as no less than "the holy city" (11:1, 18), a place of venerable mystique that tugged at every Judean's heartstrings.

Nehemiah's open reactions of grief were like those of Ezra in Ezra 9:3–4 and 10:6. He engaged in cultural forms of mourning, so shocked was he by the news of the destruction of Jerusalem's defenses. Shock waves run through the text: the motif of destruction in verse 3b will be repeated in 2:3, 13, 17, as the problem that Nehemiah eventually solved. A need does not always constitute a call to remedy it, but it did for Nehemiah. He tested his conviction that he should regard it as a call by the success or otherwise of pushing open a door of opportunity at his disposal, according to verse 11. In due course he was gratified to find that the door did swing open, confirming his sense of call (2:8b).

**1:5–10** / Some scholarly doubts have been expressed over the authenticity of the prayer in verses 5–11a. This prayer lays a meaningful foundation for Nehemiah's mission, defined in 2:5 as the rebuilding of Jerusalem. This prayer was certainly important for the editor in formulating his adaptation of the mission in later chapters, and this could imply that he added both the prayer and the adaptation. But the objections that scholars have raised regarding the authenticity of the prayer are not compelling. The existing prayer seems to have provided a springboard for editorial development, so that the present version of the mission finds its logical basis in the prayer, as we shall observe in chapter 8. It is a penitential prayer that reflects the sorry plight of the Judeans mentioned in verse 3. It is expressed in liturgical language derived from sacred texts, especially Deuteronomy. This private prayer forms a bridge between Nehemiah's response of grief and his audience with Artaxerxes in chapter 2. It summarizes from later recollection his praying over that period, as he moved slowly through the grieving process toward a creative decision.

Repentance is the keynote of the prayer. God's normative relationship with the covenant people is mentioned tantalizingly as being beyond their reach, as in Daniel 9:4. Although their God was **great and awesome,** they had disobeyed **his commands.** That divine greatness made human guilt more reprehensible. So they were in dire need of a prayer of confession, which Nehemiah now proceeded to offer on their behalf. He included himself and his family in that confession—we can almost hear an amen from Hanani at this point. It is a general confession, uttered with sincerity. The crux of the prayer occurs in the composite quotation of verses 8–9. As a divine **instruction,** or "word that you commanded" (NRSV), it put the focus on the need for the people to **return** to God in repentance—but only as a trigger for God to act on their behalf. The ruined wall symbolized a relationship in ruins and was a symptom of it. Was Nehemiah aware that Second Isaiah often used the ruined Jerusalem as an emblem for the exiled people, for example, in Isaiah 49:14? The quotation here fuses three promises from the Torah relating to restoration from exile. It is mainly derived from Deuteronomy 30:1–4, but it also echoes Deuteronomy 4:27 and the alternative "if . . . , but if" of Deuteronomy 4:25–31. Nehemiah knew that beyond the conditional presentation of the covenant at the core of Deuteronomy, whereby blatant disobedience meant dismissal from the land, at the fringes of the book lay promises of divine acceptance beyond rejection, if only the people repented and made a fresh commitment to God. The prayer also echoes a third text from the Torah, Leviticus 26:14–45, which is another statement of "if . . . but if" alternatives. Nehemiah borrows the distinctive term **unfaithful** from this text, which corresponds to the noun rendered "treachery" in the NIV in Leviticus 26:40. The message of all three texts was that God was prepared to take the word of repentance for the deed of obedience, the profession of conscience in place of the performance of conduct.

The old texts had envisioned a return to the land, explicitly or implicitly. Nehemiah stipulated the people's return to Jerusalem, challenging the bad news of its destruction with an expression of divine purpose to which he laid claim. In Deuteronomy, the temple was **the place . . . chosen as a dwelling for** God's **Name** (e.g., Deut. 12:5, 11). Here, however, it appears to be the city of Jerusalem that is chosen by God, corresponding to texts like 1 Kings

8:44; 11:13 and the Zion tradition expressed in the Psalms, such as Psalm 132:13, and reaffirmed in Zechariah 1:17; 2:12. Jerusalem had been the prey of hostile nations, but the true ending of exile would mean that God's people would take control and regain the capital. There was a need for the walls to be rebuilt and for Jerusalem to be repopulated. This was, in fact, to be the double mission of Nehemiah. He was no innovator of such a hope. Second Isaiah had expressed this hope nearly a century before, as a twofold divine promise to Jerusalem: "your walls are ever before me. Your sons hasten back, and those who laid you waste depart from you" (Isa. 49:16–17). Full restoration from exile would not occur until these steps had been taken. Until then the exile was to continue, despite the work of restoration already accomplished. Psalms 85 and 126 poignantly state the tension of a return undertaken but not consummated with expected divine blessing, and this tension underlies Nehemiah's prayer. As Zechariah had intimated about sixty years before, the condition for full restoration was a spiritual return to God in repentance (Zech. 1:2–6). Nehemiah strove to meet this condition representatively in his prayer.

In verse 10 Nehemiah ventured to argue that God was committed to the covenant people as a master to his servants (the "Lord" of v. 11), and so God was obliged to help them. Comparison with Deuteronomy 9:26 reveals a reference here to the exodus from Egypt. The exodus constituted a proof of divine commitment. The argument is driven home by the principle of theological contemporization, which the OT sometimes employs (e.g., Amos 2:10). The bond forged between God and Israel by the exodus covered not only the first generation of Israelites who came out of Egypt, but every generation in turn down to the present. Similarly, but with human commitment rather than divine commitment in view, the Mishnah declared that at the Passover festival "in every generation a man must so regard himself as if he came forth himself out of Egypt" (*Pesah.* 10.4).

**1:11** / Nehemiah turned to a smaller but crucial request that he was making, evidently along with a group of like-minded people—probably his brothers, in light of verse 2 and 5:14. He asked God to crown with **success** an approach he was planning to make to King Artaxerxes. This request looks forward to chapter 2, specifically to 2:5, 8. But Nehemiah offered this prayer day after day over a period of months, that each **today** might provide the opportunity for the mission he proposed to materialize, so that he could be the agent of God's will for national renewal as revealed in the Torah. Yet the decision would lie not with the king, who was just a **man,** but with God, who was ultimately in control, as 2:8 will attest. So God's **favor** was what was really required. In terms of Hebrews 4:16, he needed grace to help in time of need.

---

### Additional Notes §1

---

**1:1** / **Kislev** was the month from mid-November to mid-December. To place it in **the twentieth year** creates tension with the later narrative of 2:1, set in Nisan, or mid-March to mid-April, of the same year. It appears to be a slip on the editor's part: he failed to adjust the year to the nineteenth. We may compare the retention of the verbal form of Ezra 5:9 in 5:4. There is widespread scholarly agreement in the light of evidence from the Elephantine papyri that Nehemiah functioned in the reign of Artaxerxes I (465–424), so that **the twentieth year** (in 2:1) was 445. Williamson, *Ezra, Nehemiah,* p. 168, gives a survey of the evidence. **Susa,** the capital of the earlier state of Elam, was made the main royal residence and the administrative capital of the Persian empire by Darius I, while Ecbatana was the summer residence (Ezra 6:2).

**1:2** / **Hanani . . . came from Judah:** The rendering is uncertain. The NIV follows the Masoretic accentuation. But it is more natural to take **men** and **from Judah** closely together, as in the NJPS, "some men of Judah." This implies that the Judeans first contacted Hanani in Susa, and he brought them along to tell his brother about conditions in the province. We cannot ascertain whether they represented an official delegation sent to persuade Nehemiah to intervene, or a casual meeting with an expatriate, as Josephus (*Ant.* 11. 159–60) took it, although with some imaginative rewriting. Does **the Jewish remnant that survived the exile** refer to returned exiles? The NIV probably interprets the similar reference in v. 3 in this way, by rendering "there" (NRSV) as **back.** It is likely that the editor took it that way, in line with Ezra 9:8, 13–15. The Nehemiah memoirs generally do not discriminate between returnees from exile and non-exiled Judeans. As governor of the province of Judah (5:14), he would have been responsible for all Judeans there. It is probable that the original reference was to all Judeans descended from survivors of the exile of 587, whether returnees or not, as Vogt, *Studie,* pp. 44f., has argued.

**1:3** / Here and in 2:17 **disgrace** is an objective term referring to humiliation at the hands of enemies (see BDB, p. 358). Compare Lam. 5:1–2. **The wall . . . fire:** For the supposition of an Arab raid, see M. Smith, *Palestinian Parties and Politics That Shaped the Old Testament* (2d ed.; London: SCM, 1987), p. 97.

**1:4** / See the notes on Ezra 1:2; 6:9 on **the God of heaven.** Here and in v. 5 it connotes the God who reigns over the whole world.

**1:5** / U. Kellermann, *Nehemia: Quellen, Überlieferung und Geschichte* (BZAW 102; Berlin: Töpelmann, 1967), p. 9 n. 16, has summarized scholarly doubts about the authenticity of the prayer. Williamson, *Ezra, Nehemiah,* has discussed them on pp. 167–68, 173–74. He has also conveniently listed the prayer's many links with Deut. (p. 172) and characterized it as Nehemiah's summary of prolonged prayer (p. 168). Clines has explored its nature as a literary reconstruction in "The Nehemiah Memoir: The Perils of Autobiography," in *What Does Eve Do to Help? And Other Readerly Questions to the Old Testament* (JSOTSup 94; Sheffield: JSOT Press, 1990), pp. 124–64, esp. pp. 129–32. **O LORD:** The divine name that underlies this translation is not characteristic of Nehemiah's prayers; it occurs in the memoirs only in 5:13. Dependence on the language of Deut 7:7, 21 explains its presence (Clines, *Ezra, Nehemiah, Esther,* p. 138).

**1:6** / Prayer involved not only words but also body language **(and your eyes open),** including the fasting of v. 4 in this case.

**1:7** / Here and in v. 8 the reference to **your servant Moses** is to Moses' role as a covenant mediator. Elsewhere in the prayer the term **servant(s)** refers to heirs of the covenant relationship, with its commands and promises.

**1:8** / **If you are unfaithful:** In Ezra 9–10, and also in Neh. 13:27, the Heb. verb *maʿal* or the associated noun refers specifically to intermarriage as a covenant violation, but here it is used generally of breach of covenant, as in Lev. 26:40.

**1:11** / The NIV rightly sees a divine reference in **favor** here, like the NRSV, rather than a reference to the king, as in the REB, NJB, and NJPS. Two important codices of the LXX read *eunouchos,* "eunuch," as an error for *oinochoos,* **cupbearer.** Some scholars think that Nehemiah was a eunuch, but this is unlikely (see Williamson, *Ezra, Nehemiah,* pp. 174f.).

## §2 *The Assignment of the Mission (Neh. 2:1–10)*

**2:1–3** / For some reason, Nehemiah had to wait four months after receiving the bad news about Jerusalem, before his chance came to present his case to the king. Verse 1 describes the procedure for serving the **wine:** servants **brought** it into the royal presence and Nehemiah poured it, probably after sampling it to check for poison. Evidently he had hidden his grief while on duty, but this time it showed—perhaps on purpose—and attracted the king's attention. His concerned question about Nehemiah's unhappiness launches the first of three interchanges in verses 2–8. Each question Artaxerxes asks is more specific as the dialogue continues, and his courtier gives answers ever more germane to the mission he wanted to fulfill. His reaction of acute anxiety seems to reflect the fact that the destruction had been officially sanctioned, or at least that the authorities had turned a blind eye in compliance with Artaxerxes' own decree (Ezra 4:21). Yet a redeeming feature, readers will remember, was that the king had not made a permanent ruling but had left open the possibility of rebuilding the city. However, Nehemiah had to tread very warily and choose his words with care. He was diplomatic in making no political reference to Jerusalem at this stage. Rather, he confined his response to a personal concern related to its destruction—the emotive issue of family graves in its vicinity.

**2:4–8** / The king's concern for his high-ranking courtier extended to a desire to relieve his unhappiness. Nehemiah realized that the interview had reached a crucial stage. So he mentally offered a quick prayer that presumably repeated the petition made day after day in the preceding months (1:11), as the servant of two masters and seeking **favor** from both. He repeated his family connections with the **city in Judah**—still unnamed, though hardly beyond the royal ken—as motivation for his desire to rebuild it. As he recalled the pause before the king's answer, a detail of the scene imprinted itself again on his mind—the presence of

**the queen** at the king's side. Artaxerxes' last question, about the anticipated length of absence from the court, implied that his mind was quite open to the proposed mission. Nehemiah therefore volunteered specific requests, for **letters** of **safe-conduct** and authorization of lumber supplies, probably from Lebanon. It is clear that both prayer and planning had occupied Nehemiah's mind over recent months. The delay had been put to good use.

Of the three building projects mentioned **(the gates of the citadel, the city wall,** and **the residence),** the second is singled out as the focus of the following chapters. Such narrative selectivity is also found in a comparison between the powers initially entrusted to Ezra and the actual account of his mission. A further tension between this introduction to Nehemiah's mission and its outworking is that he was appointed governor in this same year, according to 5:14, and held the office for twelve consecutive years. Here, however, a relatively short commission is envisioned, and the narrative concentrates on its accomplishment. We do not know at what point he became governor, although his intervention in 5:7–13 implies that he was already governor at that time.

Nehemiah interpreted the royal assent to his requests as an answer to his prayer for success in his negotiations with the king. Using the same language of blessing as we read in Ezra 7:9, he assigned it to the providential intervention of his higher master **(my God).**

**2:9–10** / The commissioning account concludes with a short description of his journey to and through Syria and Samaria. The overall narrative about rebuilding the city wall is split into a series of progressive stages, each concluding with a report describing how his opponents reacted when they **heard** the news. Opposition, a regular feature of the first two missions, continued to raise its ugly head in the third, but it was equally unavailing. Verse 10 is the first instance of this sectional finale. Nehemiah probably took the northerly route through upper Mesopotamia and north Syria, traveling down to Damascus, the capital of the satrapy of **Trans-Euphrates,** and further south, presenting the royal documents at the capital of each of the provinces that made up the satrapy. He noted with grim satisfaction that **the letters** were backed by the imposing presence of an imperial escort. Ezra, it will be remembered, had dispensed with one because of special spiritual convictions (Ezra 8:21–23). Nehemiah found no reason to break with normal practice. Undoubtedly he would have regarded it as further evidence of divine favor displayed through earthly means (see v. 18). With hindsight sharpened by subsequent skirmishes, he recalled with relish that his eventual opponents were kept at bay by his Persian bodyguard. The juxtaposition of the Persian bodyguard and his later enemies in verses 9–10 is significant. Probably **Sanballat** was already governor of the province of Samaria at this time. **Tobiah** is probably a Samarian official subordinate to him, as the word order in 4:7 suggests. Looking back later over a period of conflict, Nehemiah traced it to this initial stage and gave it a basically religious interpretation (**Israelites,** as in 1:6), as a battle between spiritual truth and error. The clashes with neighboring political authorities encountered in the first mission and the mixed marriages that marked the second will be climactically combined in this final mission. Nehemiah's appointment to make Jerusalem well defended and self-sufficient must have meant a shift in the political balance of power between Judah and the neighboring regions, while his subsequent religious measures broke up close involvement by marriage and friendship with leading Judean families (6:17–18; 13:4, 28). So, commented Nehemiah, anticipating verse 19—as God's human answer to bad news about Jerusalem (1:3), he was himself bad news to them. It is significant that, as in the prayer of chapter 1, Nehemiah closely linked the fortunes of Jerusalem and the covenant people.

## Additional Notes §2

**2:1** / The term **before,** lacking in the original, is correctly added in translation to bring out the pluperfect force the verb must have in the context.

**2:3** / For the courteous introduction **May the king live forever** in addressing a king, see 1 Kgs. 1:31 and Dan. 2:4; 3:9.

**2:6** / **So I set a time** is more probably "when I told him how long I should be" (REB, similarly NJB). Ezra 4:21 already envisioned the king's change of mind. Evidently his earlier ban was an emergency ruling at the troubled start of his reign, when insurrection was feared in the outlying areas of the empire. According to Hoglund, *Achaemenid Imperial Administration,* pp. 166–205, 224, following Pierre Briant, the strengthening of Jerusalem's defenses marked its establishment as a center for collecting and storing increased imperial revenues to finance a chain of garrisons being built across the Levant to prevent the continued intrusion of Hellenic influence into the eastern Mediterranean.

**2:8** / **The citadel by the temple** must have been somewhere on the northern side of the city, which was otherwise vulnerable to attack. It indicates Jerusalem's strategic importance to the imperial authorities. Although the wall was primarily constructed of stone, **timber . . . for the city wall** fits with Ezra 5:8. **The residence I will occupy** seems to refer to rebuilding an existing residence.

**2:10** / Kellermann, *Nehemia,* pp. 4f., observed the structural role of the opposition notices as a conclusion to each stage. Throntveit, *Ezra-Nehemiah,* p. 10, has a useful list of the seven notices. For **Sanballat** and **Tobiah,** see Williamson, *Ezra, Nehemiah,* pp. 182–84. The latter had Ammonite ancestry, ch. 13 implies, but in view of his Yahwistic name (and his son's, 6:18) was half Judean. We do not know whether he was the ancestor of the prominent Tobiad family in the Transjordan in the third and second centuries. Sanballat was also a Yahwist, according to the names he gave his two sons. **Disturbed:** There is wordplay between the Heb. verb *raʿ,* "feel bad," and the noun *raʿ,* "trouble," in v. 3 and the related forms for "sad(ness)" in 2:1–3, while **welfare,** or "good," echoes the "gracious" or good "hand" of God in v. 8.

## §3 Nehemiah's Private and Public Measures (Neh. 2:11–20)

**2:11–15 / Jerusalem** at last! One might have expected Nehemiah to seek the public support of verses 17–18 from the outset. As verses 12 and 16 clearly state at key points, he chose instead to make a private inspection of the wall under the awkward cover of darkness, mounted and escorted by a few of his staff walking with him. An emotional factor cannot be discounted: this was a matter that had weighed obsessively on his mind for months, and he needed to come to terms right away, and relatively undisturbed, with the reality. A suspicion verified in 6:17–19 also evidently colored his action—that there was a close affinity of interests between high-ranking people in Judah and outsiders who were to oppose his mission. Moreover, he had to get correct information about the state of the wall, firsthand knowledge for his presentation at the coming meeting. In an insecure environment he needed to find the solid ground of truth as soon as possible. Only then could he disclose what he believed to be the God-given task of rebuilding the city wall. Nehemiah displays this same sense of conviction in 7:5, when he calls the people to register by families. The rebuilding and registering are the two aspects of his overall mission.

Nehemiah wrote for people familiar with the topography of Jerusalem. While we cannot identify all the places mentioned in his tour of the wall, his general movements are clear enough. He left the city at the derelict **Valley Gate,** about halfway along the western side of the wall. He proceeded south outside the wall, past **the Dung Gate** 500 yards away (3:13), which must have led down to the city dump in the Valley of Hinnom to the southwest. Then he went around the southern tip of the wall. Before he had gone very far, his progress in trying to follow the line of the east wall was impeded. The obstacle was evidently the debris of collapsed terraces under the ruined wall, left unrepaired since the

Babylonian destruction of the city. He could not continue riding, since there was no room for his **mount** to pass through the debris. He proceeded on foot down the slope into the Kidron **valley** on the east, trying to make his way north to survey the extent of the damage suffered by this southern part of the east wall. Apparently he did not continue much further. He retraced his steps, re-entering the city by the same gate he had exited earlier. He did not visit the parts of the wall around the temple area in the northern sector of the city. Perhaps he had already managed to inspect them inconspicuously during the **three** rest **days** of verse 11.

**2:16–18** / Now it was time to call a meeting of the **officials** and other leaders in the city. Nehemiah shared with them his sense of divine calling and his mission. Identifying with them by first plural references, he appealed to them to **rebuild the wall** with him and put right a situation so degrading to the community. He was here recapitulating the data of 1:3, and he continued re-telling the story to 2:8, testifying to God's providential goodness and reporting the mandate he had been given. As in 2:8, he again gave priority to **the gracious hand of my God.** He wanted them to catch his vision in turn. And he succeeded. The leadership, abandoning the complacency or resignation over a situation they had long lived with, took up the wording of his appeal with an enthusiasm of their own.

**2:19–20** / Opposition dogged every step of Nehemiah's progress, but he was able to meet the challenge. His opponents from verse 10 soon **heard** of the preparatory meeting through the grapevine of their Jerusalem contacts. Now the two Samarian enemies were joined by **Geshem the Arab**, king of Qedar and head of a powerful confederation of Arab groups massed around the eastern side of the Dead Sea and to the south of Judah, who were linked to Persia by alliance. The opponents **ridiculed** the spiritual nature of the meeting and suggested that their sinister political purpose was to rebel against the empire—the old trick of Ezra 4:12–16. In response to their challenge, Nehemiah disputed their right to interfere. First, however, he redefined the issue in spiritual terms, claiming divine support. This reinforced the theme of verse 18 and was meant for the ears of his new supporters, as a pastoral antidote to the intimidating circle of secular opposition. Their role as **servants** of God made them eligible for supernatural help, as Nehemiah had argued in his prayer in 1:10. He deliberately repeated the words of the pledge they had just made in verse 18. Then, drawing a virtual line in the sand, he declared Jerusalem's independence over against its neighbors' meddling. He had no need to repeat his imperial credentials, which had already been presented.

## Additional Notes §3

**2:13** / For a map of postexilic Jerusalem in Nehemiah's period, see Y. Aharoni et al., eds., *The Macmillan Bible Atlas* (3d ed.; New York: Macmillan, 1993), p. 129, map 169.

**2:14** / Archaeological excavation has discovered massive ruins in this area (Myers, *Ezra, Nehemiah*, p. 105).

**2:16** / **The Jews** refers to the inhabitants of the province of Judah in Nehemiah's memoirs in 1:2; 4:1–2, 12; 13:23. But Japhet, "Sheshbazzar and Zerubbabel," p. 87 n. 48, has plausibly argued that in other parts of the memoirs it refers to a stratum of leadership, here and in 5:1, 17; 6:6, and is the equivalent of heads of families elsewhere in Ezra-Nehemiah. The phrase **any others . . . work** refers to building the wall. But more probably in this list of leaders this particular category, lit. "the doer(s) of work," refers to civil administrators (Bowman, "Ezra and Nehemiah," p. 680). The last two terms are rendered in NJPS "the prefects and the rest of the officials."

**2:18** / Since v. 20 implies that the work of rebuilding had not started yet, a more feasible rendering of **they began this good work** is "So they encouraged themselves for the good cause" (F. C. Fensham, *The Books of Ezra and Nehemiah* [NICOT; Grand Rapids: Eerdmans, 1982], p. 168). Compare the NRSV, "So they committed themselves to the common good."

**2:19** / **"What is this you are doing?"** is a formula of accusation (compare Judg. 8:1).

**2:20** / **Share** or "stake" (REB) refers to political association, as in 1 Kgs. 12:16; **claim** refers to a legal right relating to Jerusalem, such as Judean citizenship conferred; and **historic right** to traditional prerogatives, probably here a right to worship, which was repudiated in Ezra 4:3.

## §4 Details of the Wall Building (Neh. 3:1–32)

Here, by contrast, is a list of those who had a "share," a "claim," and a "historic right" in Jerusalem (2:20), and who proudly exercised their privileges by rebuilding its wall. Nehemiah evidently persuaded them that the "welfare of the Israelites" (2:10) was at stake. This section seems to have originated as a separate list found in the temple archives: it gives pride of place to the **high priest** (v. 1). Instead of first-person references to Nehemiah, he is probably mentioned in the third person in verse 5. Chapter 3 describes the complete rebuilding of the wall, including the gates, and so it does not fit the sequence of the rest of the narrative, in which the wall was built in separate stages (4:6–7) and the gates were not fully restored until the last stage, in 7:1, as 6:1 emphasizes. Nevertheless, this section roughly corresponds to the pattern in Nehemiah's autobiographical story, in which each phase of progress on the walls is followed by opposition—here in 4:1–5, whereas it previously occurred in 2:19–20. Nehemiah evidently found this document and inserted it into his narrative as a convenient summary, although it was not an exact fit, instead of writing his own report of a particular phase. For this procedure we may compare 7:5 and the narrator's use of the same list in Ezra 2. The opening verbs **went to work and rebuilt** follow on nicely from the same Hebrew verbs used in 2:20, rendered "will start rebuilding."

The official document describes the work done on each part of the city wall and preserves for posterity the names of those heading each work party. It begins and ends at the **Sheep Gate** on the north part of the wall and takes the reader on a counterclockwise tour of the mile and a half-long wall surrounding Jerusalem. It moves from the north wall (vv. 1–5) to the west wall (vv. 6–13), then continues to the short southern stretch of wall (vv. 14–15) and to the east wall (vv. 16–31), before ending at the eastern stretch of the north wall (v. 32).

The work on the wall was a remarkable feat of organization, diplomacy, and cooperation. The wall was divided into forty sections, each with its own work party, although in three or four cases the same work party repaired two sections. People with houses, shops, or places of work near parts of the wall worked on these sections in many cases, out of self-interest. Different sectors of the Jerusalem population were represented in the communal project, from **priests** and other temple staff to laity such as **merchants** and guild members. Judeans from a number of towns in the province, such as **Jericho** (v. 2), came to the city and took responsibility for certain sections. In a number of cases they were grouped under the leadership of officers in charge of administrative regions in the province, who were officially assigned to the project, as verse 17 **(for his district)** seems to indicate.

**3:1–5** / The first section to be rebuilt evidently featured in a representative ceremony of consecration (NRSV), which corresponds to the service of dedication for the entire wall in 12:27–44. The gates of verses 1 and 3 required complete rebuilding. The first four work parties had to deal with extensive damage, as the recurring verb **rebuilt,** rather than **repaired,** seems to indicate. The only note of noncooperation in the list is struck in verse 5, concerning the **nobles** of **Tekoa.** Their townspeople made up for it by tackling two sections (v. 27).

**3:6–15** / Verses 6–13 describe the repair work on the west wall and its gates, and verses 14–15 report on the south wall and gates.

**3:16–31** / Meanwhile, work was progressing on the east wall. The fact that the east wall required twice as many work parties as the west wall seems to indicate that much more work was necessary. In fact, much of the east wall was built further to the west than the preexilic wall. Although one would have expected the verb "rebuilt" to be used instead of "repaired," there are two reasons for why "repaired" may have been the better description. First, the recurring phrase "next to him/them" in verses 2–12 is changed to "After him" (NRSV; the NIV is erratic here) in verses 16–21. It was no longer a case of repairing adjoining sections of the old wall, but of following a consecutive guideline for a new one. Second, the topographical sections are now defined in terms of existing adjacent structures. Probably only the southern half of the east wall had to be rebuilt from scratch on a more westerly line; the text simply continues in the same style even when the old line of the wall was resumed. Groups of **Levites** were involved from verse 17, probably as far as verse 20.

**3:32** / The listing concludes with work on the eastern stretch of the north wall, which brings the reader back to the starting point, the **Sheep Gate.**

---

### Additional Notes §4

---

**3:1** / Myers, *Ezra, Nehemiah,* p. 118, has reproduced a detailed map of the walls and gates, although not all of the locations can be identified with certainty. The map seems to be correct in placing the postexilic city on the eastern hill of Jerusalem, instead of including the western hill that was incorporated into the city in late preexilic times. See the discussion of H. G. M. Williamson, "Nehemiah's Walls Revisited," *PEQ* 116 (1984), pp. 81–88.

**3:3** / The **beams** were for the gatehouse, which was roofed (v. 15) and supplied with double front and back doors.

**3:5** / The Heb. word for **nobles** is different from that used in Nehemiah's memoirs, for instance in 2:16. This phenomenon reinforces the idea that ch. 3 is from an independent source. The NJPS is more probably correct with its rendering "the work of their lord," with reference to Nehemiah, than **the work under their supervisors.** Compare the similar description of Ezra in Ezra 10:3. Nehemiah's authority in organizing the project, although resisted here, is clear.

**3:6** / **The Jeshanah Gate:** The mg. "Old" is better, but better still is "the gate of the old city (or wall)" (see Clines, *Ezra, Nehemiah, Esther,* p. 152). From the eighth century, the city was extended westward and a new wall was built around the expansion. This development was abandoned after the exile, and these workers followed the line of the old wall.

**3:7** / **Places under the authority of the governor:** The Heb. phrase lacks "places" and qualifies **Mizpah,** "namely, the seat of the satrap" (Clines, *Ezra, Nehemiah, Esther,* p. 153). This was his official residence when he visited the province, as he did in Ezra 5:3, 8. Mizpah had once been the administrative center for Judah (2 Kgs. 25:23; Jer. 40:5–10).

**3:8** / **One of the goldsmiths** is lit. "the goldsmiths," which may refer to both father and son (Barthélemy, *Critique textuelle,* vol. 1, pp. 551f., following Rashi). The rendering **They restored** postulates a second Heb. root *ʿazab,* which may be preferable to finding here the well-established first root with the sense of the mg. "They left out part of." It is uncertain whether this verb, meaning "abandon," can be used in the sense of "leave out, omit" (Blenkinsopp, *Ezra-Nehemiah,* p. 230).

**3:9** / **Half-district:** Chapter 3 mentions five administrative districts of the province, each with its headquarters at an urban center. In three cases these are divided into two subdistricts (vv. 9/12, 17/18; compare v. 16), and in two cases they function as a single area (vv. 14–15). In v. 19 a "ruler" of a city appears to be in view, if the text is correct.

**3:11** / **Another section:** While one work party tackled two sections in at least three cases (vv. 4/21, 5/27, 18/24; and also perhaps in vv. 4/ 30), three other instances, here and in vv. 19–20, refer only to a second section. This seems to indicate that some material has dropped out of the list in its present form.

**3:12** / **Daughters:** There were probably no sons. Presumably sons, though they are not mentioned, generally helped the individuals responsible for sections in their role as heads of families.

**3:16** / **Beyond him** is lit. "after him" (NRSV). Williamson, *Ezra, Nehemiah,* p. 200, observed the significance of the change in prepositional phrase after this point. For the destruction of the terraces on the southeast side of the city, see K. M. Kenyon, *IDBSup*, p. 208.

**3:18** / **Their countrymen** were more probably "their kin" (NRSV), referring to fellow Levites. Verses 17–18 mention Levites who were secular administrators, somewhat as the Chronicler envisioned in 1 Chr. 26:29–30, 32.

**3:20** / The uncertain term **zealously,** if the interpretation is correct, means that **Baruch,** not to be outdone by Ezer in v. 19, also **repaired another section.** But see the discussion of Williamson, *Ezra, Nehemiah,* p. 198.

**3:21** / **Meremoth** was evidently a priest in light of Ezra 8:33; Neh. 7:63 (= Ezra 2:61), where the descendants of Hakkoz are described as priests.

**3:22** / **The priests from the surrounding region** were from the area around Jerusalem, as in 12:28. They were evidently differentiated from priests who lived in the city (v. 1).

**3:25** / Topographically, **palace** must refer to David's palace rather than to Solomon's to the north, which was south of the temple area.

**3:26** / **The Water Gate:** We are not told whether a corresponding gate was built in the new wall to the west.

**3:27** / The existing **wall of Ophel** was an internal east-west wall that divided the city of David to the south (v. 15) from the temple hill to the north.

**3:30** / The Heb. indicates that **living quarters** refers to a room in the temple precincts.

**3:31** / In view of v. 26, **the house of the temple servants,** shared with **the merchants,** was used just when they were on temple duty. The unidentified **Inspection Gate** was probably one of the temple gates (see Myers' map, *Ezra, Nehemiah,* p. 118) and not in the city wall, so that a new stretch of city wall is not implied at this point. There was evidently a shopping area inside the north wall, catering to visitors to the temple.

## §5 Hurdles to Get Over (Neh. 4:1–23)

This section deals with a cluster of obstacles that had to be overcome. It is closely tied into the pattern of opposition we have already observed. Strictly speaking, verses 1–5 round off chapter 3: progress in wall building was countered by enemy opposition triggered by news of it **(heard)**, which in turn was checked by a response from Nehemiah. Verses 6–9 reproduce this pattern of chess-like moves on a smaller scale. Verses 10–23 loosely continue the theme of overcoming obstacles. The structure of the passage follows a series of problems and their solutions. Nehemiah counters three negative statements in verses 10–12, the second spoken by Judah's foes and the third enemy related, by three positive statements (vv. 14, 19–20, 22) and appropriate actions. He translated his spiritual vision into practical details of resourceful management and unsparing effort.

**4:1–5** / The chapter is the story of a war of nerves—a sort of phony war in which Judah's neighbors had their hands tied by his imperial authorization, but then freely resorted to what turned out to be mere intimidation. Here ridicule is the one-upmanship ploy they chose. Presumably we are to envision Samaria's Judean supporters reporting this demoralizing reaction. **Sanballat,** the governor of Samaria, takes the major role in this account of opposition. His anger indicates an intensification of the reaction in 2:19. He used a military parade of local troops as an occasion to make a political speech directed against Judah's enterprise. His barrage of questions dismisses the Judean workers as "pathetic" (NJB) and as underestimating the size of their task. They had no magic wand to wave over the debris and turn it into a rebuilt wall. **Tobiah**'s supporting quip pokes fun at poor workmanship. The opposition presumably made these remarks at a preliminary stage of the building. In the present context, doubtless deliberately, the remarks fall flat. Nehemiah, writing these memoirs, had the last laugh.

Nehemiah's response took seriously the religious expectation of the third question, **Will they offer sacrifices?** although he opted for prayer rather than sacrifice. The prayer is in the style of a communal lament, like those found in the Psalms (e.g. Ps. 79), which combine lamenting and praying. Israel objected to the ridicule and consequent loss of face. The lament typically appeals to God to providentially intervene with merited punishment, to prove beyond all doubt that right lay on the side of those who were praying. The prayer Nehemiah prayed as representative of the covenant community took the Samarian ridicule with absolute seriousness—not only as a weapon of demoralization, but also as an indication of hostility to God's own work and will. So he claimed divine help. Judah's enemies heard the ridicule, but then God heard the call of Nehemiah. The battle lines were implacably drawn.

**4:6–9** / This next report on the wall, given in verse 6 and expanded in verse 7, reflects the real progress thus far and enables readers to imagine the earlier stage to which Sanballat was actually responding in verses 1–2. Verse 6 describes it as a significant advance on the previous one, which is credited to **the people** that worked "with a will" (REB). As usual, news of it was soon heard beyond the province, and it occasioned a show of hostility. This incident of opposition involved not only Samaria **(Sanballat, Tobiah),** but also an encircling group of neighbors, including for the first time the province of **Ashdod** to the west and **the Ammonites** to the east. An allied coalition on all four sides drew up plans for a military attack on Jerusalem, so threatened did they feel by the fortification project. Here, of course, we have Judah's side of the story—and they took both religious and practical measures. They **prayed** another communal lament, which must have sounded like Psalm 83. But, as if identifying with Oliver Cromwell's reputed counsel to "put trust in God, my boys, and keep your powder dry," Nehemiah also arranged for a twenty-four-hour lookout.

**4:10–12** / These verses report three negative statements, which will find responses in the following verses. First, there was an internal problem of discouragement. The Judean workers on the wall were singing a short dirge as they worked, consisting of two lines of poetry. Of the two groups engaged in the work, **the laborers** ("the burden bearers," NRSV) were physically flagging, while the builders **(we, that is, the people in Judah)** felt overwhelmed by their task (see vv. 17, 18). Second, there were rumors of an impending surprise attack on Jerusalem. This is the longest of the three statements and the crucial one, which the other two served to aggravate. Third, there was a message from outlying areas of Judah, urging workers to evacuate the endangered city and return home for their own good. Those who sent the message, living **near** Judah's enemies, obviously had independent information about the attack that motivated their message.

**4:13–15** / Nehemiah responded to the three statements in order of importance. His answer to the main threat emanating from the enemy side was to call a military assembly of the people, grouped by **families** and equipped with offensive weapons. The place of assembly was evidently behind a low stretch of wall, from which the massed people could be easily seen. It was a brazen show of force that spies could easily observe and report. Any surprise attack, a surprise no longer, would find an armed militia waiting. By engaging in this performance, the people adopted the comforting role of soldiers rather than defenseless citizens. Nehemiah gave a battle speech, preparing them mentally for an actual encounter. Having grouped them in families, he was able to appeal to their family loyalties. He continued to boost popular morale, using the traditional language of holy war, with which the book of Deuteronomy is replete. As the antidote to fear of an invading army, he reminded them of a **great and awesome** God (Deut. 7:21) who was their ally. Verse 15 begins with the structural element that hitherto prefaced a vehement response from Judah's enemies (**When . . . heard,** e.g., 4:1, 7). In this case, strikingly, it tails off as information disappointingly received. Nehemiah wove into the report his interpretive testimony of praise to God, whom he credited with providentially overruling the enemy plans. Now the people could get back to their normal **work** on the wall.

**4:16–21** / Military precautions continued to be taken, including setting up an alarm system and dealing with the demoralization of the work song quoted in verse 10, which was not conducive to good esprit de corps. The two groups of workers in verse 10, "burden bearers" (NRSV) and builders, are mentioned again in verses 17–18. Both groups were armed, as their work allowed. Nehemiah assigned **half** of his retinue to the workforce, doubtless to help different work parties in turn and thus raise morale. He supplied the **other half** with offensive and defensive weapons and made a permanent armed force, while **officers** were evidently deployed to mobilize the workers into extra troops as necessary. In a public speech, Nehemiah reassuringly explained that in case of an attack he himself, presumably on constant patrol as he supervised the work, would respond to it and a trumpeter accompanying him would sound the alarm. Then the mobilized people, and evidently the permanent force, would converge on the isolated working party to defend it. In closing, Nehemiah assures them that their divine ally would support them and fight on their side (v. 14). The result of Nehemiah's measures from verse 16 onward was that the workers were able to work long days with high morale and a bolstered sense of the spiritual nature of their task.

**4:22–23** / One by one, Nehemiah covered all the issues raised in verses 10–12. Finally, he dealt with the temptation to desert—to slip off home after a day's work—in response to the insidious, if well meaning, appeal of verse 12. In view of the emergency, he ordered that from now on nobody was to leave Jerusalem for the night and that the workers were to do sentry duty overnight, presumably by shifts. He himself, along with his family and retinue, tried to be good role models of constant alertness. They slept in their work clothes with their weapons at the ready. Nehemiah was acting in the conscientious spirit of Uriah in 2 Samuel 11:8–13.

---

### Additional Notes §5

**4:1** / The progress in **rebuilding the wall** is put in general terms, rather than the specific ones of v. 7, in order to accommodate the document inserted in ch. 3.

**4:2** / The **associates** are apparently fellow officials, including Tobiah (v. 3), rather than allies. The interpretation of **Will they restore their wall?** is uncertain (see the discussion of Williamson, *Ezra, Nehemiah*, pp. 213f.). Most scholars envision a second Heb. root, ʿazab, meaning "restore," as in 3:8, because unless the text is emended, the first root meaning "forsake" (NJB "Are they going to give up?") lacks the sarcasm of the other questions. The literal "Will they restore for themselves?" may have the derogatory connotation "Is this a do-it-yourself job?" instead of employing professional masons (Clines, *Ezra, Nehemiah, Esther*, p. 159). The question **Will they offer sacrifices?** could refer to dedicatory sacrifices once the wall was completed (12:43). The question then expresses doubt as to whether this stage would ever be reached. It is more likely that it refers to an attempt to pressure God to bless the work, in order to avoid inevitable failure.

**4:4** / The prayer is not, like the negative "Remember . . ." petitions of 6:14; 13:29, a prayer contemporary with the memoirs. It is, rather, a vivid flashback to the occasion recalled in the story, as in 6:9 and in line with the narrative of v. 9, below. The Heb. *buzah* and *bizzah* (MT 3:34), **despised, plunder** represent wordplay, a dynamic feature of Israelite speech, to link crime and punishment.

**4:5** / The parallelism in Ps. 85:2 with **Do not cover up their guilt** indicates that forgiveness is in mind, here deprecated as inappropriate.

**4:6** / Often the human will is intended by this term **heart,** as often in English.

**4:10** / **The people in Judah** is lit. "Judah," in the sense of "the people of Judah who were building the wall" (vv. 16–17). The two lines of Heb. poetry (MT v. 4) have a 3+2 meter associated with mourning (see *BHS*). The REB and NJPS use a poetic layout and try to reproduce the meter.

**4:12** / The sentence **Wherever you turn, they will attack us** is very difficult. The best suggestion is "from all sides, 'You must return to us'" (Williamson, *Ezra, Nehemiah,* pp. 220–22, who explains the Heb. construction in the MT [v. 6]). Compare NJPS. **Ten times** is idiomatic for a large number (see Gen. 31:7; Num. 14:22; Job 19:3).

**4:13** / **Some of** is unnecessarily added in the translation. The people listed in v. 14 seem to indicate a general assembly. The Heb. verb **I stationed** (MT v. 7) is repeated resumptively later in the sentence (NIV **posting;** see NJPS). The same repetition of a Heb. verb occurs in v. 2 (MT 3:34).

**4:16** / As in 2:9, **the officers** refers to military officers.

**4:21** / The phrase **with half the men holding spears** is very difficult in the context (see Williamson, *Ezra, Nehemiah,* p. 223). It is best omitted and regarded as a marginal correction of the similar clause in v. 16 that was wrongly inserted into the text at this point (MT v. 15): see *BHS* and NJB.

**4:23** / **Even when he went for water** is a desperate attempt to make sense of one Heb. word, *hammayim* "the water" (MT v. 17). A conjectural emendation widely advocated is *hēmînû* "they kept in their right hand." Then the consonants *hmym* were originally *hmynw* and the Heb. letters *nw* and *m* were confused, as has happened elsewhere. The NRSV, REB, and NJB have adopted this emendation.

We seem to move into a different world in this chapter. Gone is the battle zone of chapter 4. In its place is a seemingly unrelated area of social tension, where one would scarcely think that rebuilding the wall was a top priority. The recurring pattern, from chapter 2 onward, of progress on the wall, the response of enemy opposition, and Nehemiah's counterresponse, is put on hold. The enemy response of 6:1 appears to target the progress of chapter 4, as if chapter 5 did not exist. The blatant digression of 5:14–18, in which Nehemiah discusses his conduct over the course of a twelve-year governorship, increases our sense that the previous story is now interrupted. It is clear that chapter 5 as a whole belongs to Nehemiah's memoirs, but it is difficult to connect the chapter with the surrounding narrative. However, verse 16 supplies a clue that 5:1–13 is still inside the wall-building time frame—the 52 days of 6:15. Nehemiah informs us in passing in 5:16 that he did not exploit an opportunity that presented itself to **acquire land,** but instead concentrated on the **wall** project. This information ties the wall theme together with the material in 5:1–13 and takes us into the heart of that passage, to a detail about Nehemiah's provision of loans in verse 10. So we are assured that the bulk of the chapter is chronologically on track, despite its novel theme. Here is a new and different obstacle, in the wake of those narrated in 4:10–23.

**5:1–5** / In 4:10 we heard a cry of demoralization over the rebuilding of the wall. Now we hear another cry from the people—this time of protest. Unchecked, it would soon throw another wrench into the smooth-running machine portrayed in chapter 3 and bring it to a halt. This problem challenged the unity of the people and threatened to divide it into two opposing groups—the oppressed and their oppressors. The ideal of the chapter is the expression of communal brotherhood, which emerges from a term used in verse 5, "brothers" (NJB and NJPS, in place of **countrymen**). Nehemiah borrowed the term from the cry of v. 5 and gave it pride of place in the narrative of verse 1 **(their Jewish brothers)**.

Three reported statements tell the story of the crisis. These remind us of the three negative statements, each from a different quarter, in 4:10–12. Here, however, the reported speech is a device to gradually unwrap a complex problem, moving from a basic generality to more and more detailed information. The problem concerned getting sufficient **grain** to feed large families. Verse 3 indicates that a recent **famine** was to blame. The barley harvest was in April/May, and the wheat harvest in May/June. The setting of this narrative appears to be August or September, according to 6:15. Shortages due to failure of these crops earlier in the year meant that farmers had to pledge their land and houses in order to obtain loans to purchase the now expensive grain they needed to feed their families and also to sow next year's crop. The annual imperial tax was also generally paid in grain, and this obligation again necessitated the pledging of land as collateral against loans, with consequent fear of losing it if the loans could not be repaid on time. Another grim prospect was that dependent children would be forced into debt slavery. This had already happened in some cases. The debtors felt **powerless.** There was no legal redress because all of this hardship had resulted from a series of legal expedients. They appealed instead to a humanitarian principle, that as fellow members of the community they were the same **flesh and blood** as their creditors, who were their "brothers." There was unfairness in the present crisis, a lack of family spirit. Paul appealed to this motive in tackling a lesser evidence of disunity in 1 Corinthians 11:17–22, 33–34. In essence it corresponds to the practice of the Torah not only to prescribe legal rulings but also to counsel charity and benevolence toward the poor in the community (e.g., Exod. 23:10–11; Deut. 15:7–11; 24:19–22). Indeed, Torah texts that deal with pledges advocate a humane approach.

**5:6–13**  /  In reacting to the protest and its detailed charges, Nehemiah used the provincial power vested in him. Perhaps he was already governor, since in verse 16, when he is describing how he was a better governor than previous governors, he mentions the building of the wall. Ironically the formula **When . . . heard,** hitherto an external response to progress made on the wall (including an angry response in 4:1), here constitutes an internal response to an implicit barrier to progress. The echoing of the formula does indicate a certain awareness of, and continuity with, the context. After due deliberation, like that shown in the night ride of 2:11–16 before the encounter of 2:17, Nehemiah met with the wealthy creditors. He made their practice of loaning money against pledges a matter of accusation. The suffering it was causing in the present situation was inappropriate for a community of "brothers" (NJPS, for **countrymen** again). Then he **called** a **meeting** of the full assembly of citizens (see v. 13) and virtually put the lenders on trial before them. They had to answer to the people for their behavior. He addressed the worst case of debt slavery that occurred when a loan could not be repaid as arranged, and he argued that it was a scandal insofar as **brothers** were involved. He adduced as a parallel a current program, otherwise unknown to us, of buying back Judeans from foreign slavery, arguing that local debt slavery was inconsistent with it. The creditors could have argued in reply the utter legality of the practice, but they tacitly acknowledged the force of Nehemiah's humanitarian argument—and doubtless his vehemence backed by political power.

He went on to define their practice as **not right** or "good" (NRSV). In Paul's terms it was permissible but not beneficial (1 Cor. 10:23). It was something a foreign nation would judge to be inhumane behavior, Nehemiah claimed, and it was also an immoral course of action that did not spring from a proper reverence for God. Here Nehemiah may have had Leviticus 25 in view, especially verses 39–43, and the appeal to "fear your God." If so, he was reapplying its jubilee ruling about releasing debt slaves to the present emergency. "Let us give up," he demanded, "this taking of pledges for debt" (REB). He deliberately included himself and his family in the demand, admitting that he too—evidently a person of wealth—had lent **money and grain** in return for pledges. Nehemiah's demand must have been intended only for the period of wall building and recuperation from it. Otherwise, in the future, few would have been prepared to lend without collateral property as a safeguard against defaulting. A different, permanent solution was adopted later, in 10:31. For now, pledges of productive property were to be returned and no further interest of **money** or produce was to be exacted.

The creditors agreed to these concessions, making the loans unsecured and also free of interest. To ratify the agreement and ensure it would be honored, Nehemiah made them take a religious **oath**. Going further, he laid on them his own solemn curse, with a symbolic enactment and an explanatory statement. The **assembly** endorsed the sanction and turned their satisfaction at this solution into divine praise. God, they acknowledged, had been at work through Nehemiah, resolving the crisis.

**5:14–18** / Nehemiah correlated this event with his general policy during his **twelve years** as **governor** of the Persian province, which we now hear about for the first time. Contemporary readers of the memoirs, of course, would have been fully aware of this fact. As verse 16 will make clear, what he particularly had in mind was his refusal to exploit the people by acquiring **land** when he made loans during the emergency and debts were unpaid (v. 10). Nor did he permit his family or staff to do so. Instead, he served their interests by devoting his energies and those of his retinue to rebuilding the **wall** of Jerusalem, as 4:16 had stated. The reference to 4:16 gives the impression that verses 14–19 were meant as a generalizing conclusion to 4:10–5:13, while verses 14 and 16 repeat the denial of 4:23 in other areas. In verse 16, Nehemiah claimed that his specific lack of exploitation in the case of land was consistent with his habitual refusal to make use of the statutory **food** allowance for himself and his family at the governor's residence. He contrasted his policy with that of **earlier governors** of the province of Judah, who had, he claimed, taxed **the people** heavily for this purpose and let their staff abuse their bureaucratic power. What motivated him was the same "fear" of God (NRSV) that he had urged his fellow creditors to respect in verse 9. He had a higher master to report to, like Jehoshaphat's judges in 2 Chronicles 19:6–7 and the slave owners in Ephesians 6:9. He spelled out what it meant to forgo the food allowance. The expenses of hospitality that went with the job were enormously high, as he regularly wined and dined both local dignitaries and **officials** and foreign visitors on imperial business. No Scrooge, he entertained well, out of his own (obviously deep) pocket. He did so out of consideration for the burdens of Persian taxation that the **people** carried (v. 4). There is a parallel here with Paul, who refused to exercise the apostolic right of financial support on a regular basis (1 Cor. 9:3–6, 12).

**5:19** / This is the first of the **Remember** petitions that appear as a refrain in Nehemiah's memoirs. Here it is of a personal and positive nature, as in 13:22, rather than negative and related to other people, such as we will find in 6:14. This one seems to reflect Nehemiah's attempt to defend himself against subsequent criticisms of his administration. Verses 14–18, as well as 4:10–5:13, gave him an opportunity to plead his integrity over against those who were maligning his character. The editor retained these petitions from the memoirs, which he used as the source of information about Nehemiah's achievements on behalf of God's **people.**

---

## Additional Notes §6

---

**5:1** / For a defense of ch. 5 in its present setting, see Williamson, *Ezra, Nehemiah,* pp. 235f. Throntveit, *Ezra-Nehemiah,* pp. 61, 123f., regards it as originally following ch. 13 on the grounds of content and style, but that chapter's chronological setting of Nehemiah's second term of office does not favor his view. **The men and their wives** would be better translated as "the people and especially their wives" (Vogt, *Studie,* p. 111; compare the NRSV). Wives were left to run the smallholdings while their husbands were working on the Jerusalem project. "The people" connotes "the common people" (REB) by being differentiated from the oppressing upper class. The representation of the oppressed as "the (real) people" is reminiscent of the use of the phrase "my (= God's) people" in prophetic literature, for example in Isa. 3:12, 15. As in 2:16, **their Jewish brothers,** or "(their brother) Jews" (NJPS), must refer to a social stratum here and in v. 17. They are broadly identified with "nobles and officials" in vv. 7 and 12, but differentiated from the latter in v. 17 and from both in 2:16.

**5:3** / For the pledge as a token of the debtor's intention to pay off a debt, see Exod. 22:26–27; Deut. 24:10–13.

**5:4** / Herodotus (3.19) tells us that the satrapy that included the province of Judah had to provide 350 talents annually. According to Hoglund, *Achaemenid Imperial Administration,* pp. 212–14, the intensification of the Persian military presence in the west in the middle of the fifth century meant higher taxation than before.

**5:5** / For the connotation of the Heb. term for "flesh" in **flesh and blood,** compare Judg. 9:2; 2 Sam. 5:1. **We have to subject our sons and daughters to slavery** was imminent rather than actual in most cases. The Heb. construction here means that they were on the point of doing so (Williamson, *Ezra, Nehemiah,* pp. 231, 238; compare NJB "we shall have to sell . . ."). For debt slavery, see Exod. 21:2–11; Deut. 15:12–18; 2 Kgs. 4:1. The Heb. verb may have a sexual connotation when it occurs again in the next sentence (**enslaved;** NRSV "ravished"), as it has in Esth. 7:8. Sexual cohabitation with female debt slaves is regulated in Exod. 21:8–11.

**5:7** / Rather than **You are exacting usury from,** the Heb. verb has the basic meaning of loaning against pledges (Rudolph, *Esra und Nehemia,* p. 130; Clines, *Ezra, Nehemiah, Esther,* p. 168), as the NIV seems to acknowledge by its translation "are lending" in v. 10. Taking interest was illegal (Exod. 22:25; Lev. 25:36–37; Deut. 23:19–20)—whether in the form of advance interest, by loaning a sum minus contracted interest, or of accrued interest, by repaying the amount of the loan with added interest. Yet it was frequently practiced, as such texts as Ps. 15:5; Prov. 28:8 imply. In this case interest played a minor role according to v. 11, and the major concerns were loss of pledges and debt slavery.

**5:8** / For foreign slave trading, esp. in prisoners of war, see Ezek. 27:13; Joel 3:3–7. The redemption of Israelite slaves from foreigners is advocated in Lev. 25:47–48. **Only for them to be sold back to us:** Nehemiah's complaint that another, internal program to free Judean slaves would need to be instituted objects to the notion of Judean enslavement. We may compare the tone of Lev. 25:39–43, itself based on the concept of brotherhood ("your brother," Lev. 25:39, NJB), to which Nehemiah might implicitly have been appealing.

**5:11** / The precise sense of the Heb. term for **the hundredth part,** lit. "a hundred," is uncertain. If the text is correct, it may refer to one percent, presumably calculated monthly and so twelve percent per annum, or it may refer more generally to a percentage. A verb such as "remit," or "abandon," (NJPS) is to be understood in the second clause, as the response in v. 12 implies. It is not likely that Nehemiah was counseling the cancellation of debts, as Williamson, *Ezra, Nehemiah,* p. 241, has urged. It is strange that the text does not mention the release of the few debt slaves, and the failure to do so seems to indicate that it was more a threat hanging over debtors' heads than a reality.

**5:13** / **The folds of my robe:** This lay across the breast and normally served as a pocket, so that it was like turning one's pockets out. See Exod. 4:6–7; Prov. 21:14. For **Amen** in affirming response to a curse, see Num. 5:22; Deut. 27:15–26. **The people** can hardly refer to the victims of v. 1, or to the assembly from whom it is distinguished as a separate subject. So it must refer to the creditors, who make the promise in v. 12.

The keyword of this chapter is intimidation. Of the major English versions, only the NJPS is consistent in its fivefold rendering of the same Hebrew verb for intimidation. It occurs regularly at the conclusion of paragraphs, in verses 9, 13–14, 16, and 19. The first main section, consisting of verses 1–14, is divided into two parallel subsections describing different attempts to intimidate, in verses 1–9 and 10–14. Then verses 15–16 record a great reversal of the multinational intimidation of verses 1–9. Finally, verses 17–19 constitute a postscript that amplifies Tobiah's attempts to intimidate Nehemiah in verses 10–14. So the chapter has a consecutively parallel ABA'B' format.

A verses 1–9
   B verses 10–14
A' verses 15–16
   B' verses 17–19

**6:1–9** / The structural pattern in the wall building story that occurred repeatedly in chapters 2 and 4 and was interrupted by chapter 5 is now resumed. It is a threefold pattern, first reporting progress on the wall, then a response from Judah's enemies when they hear of it, and finally a counterresponse from Nehemiah. The response from Judah's enemies comes in verse 1, which literally begins "When it was heard by . . ." They are reacting to the work on the wall recorded in 4:15–18, 21 in the course of defensive measures. Here we see that they are close to completion, lacking only the crucial supply of **doors** for the gateways. The nuance that **I had rebuilt the wall** does not deny or dismiss the contributions of a host of individual workers, which 4:15 and 18 **(each)** had recently celebrated. The first-person statement reflects, rather, Nehemiah's role as organizer and inspirer of the wall project and introduces the point of the chapter—a new focus on Nehemiah himself. His indispensable role in the project motivated a series of threats against him. "Strike the kingpin, and the rest will fall in quick succession" was now the motto of the opposition. Judah's neighbors evidently regarded building the wall as the first stage of political and economic resurgence for the province under Nehemiah's leadership. This uneasiness over future implications of a shift in the balance of regional power will be reflected in the misinterpretation of verses 6–7.

The coalition of 4:7 is in view in verse 1, with **Sanballat** and **Geshem** as the ringleaders. Sanballat's subordinate **Tobiah** is mentioned initially, but not in verses 2 or 5–6. Nehemiah was suspicious of the invitation to a meeting of regional leaders. There was an enclave of Judean settlements (Lod, Ono, and Hadid) in the far west on the coast (7:37 = Ezra 2:33), and **the plain of Ono** was called after one of the towns. The area was under Sidonian control and was not part of the province of Judah. When the coalition proposed a conference on this neutral ground outside his province, Nehemiah smelled antagonism. He refused to go. In response to this and three other invitations, he alleged that he needed to be present for the important **project** of rebuilding the wall of Jerusalem. In verse 9 Nehemiah interprets their intentions as to somehow deflect him from his assigned work, and here in his refusal he implicitly challenges them by alluding to their real purpose.

The **fifth** invitation (v. 5) reveals that the conference proposal was not simply a goodwill gesture. Now in exasperation, and to coerce Nehemiah, the invitation **(in an unsealed letter)** blatantly cited rumors of his sinister intentions, which required immediate discussion at the local level—or else **this report** would **get back** to the Persian king. These words revived the old accusation of rebellion reported to Artaxerxes earlier in the reign and taken seriously by him at that time (Ezra 4:12–16, 19, 22). The suspicion that Nehemiah would rebel from the empire by making himself king had been expressed at the very start of the building project, in 2:19. Here his enemies claimed that it was to be an imminent event, and they alleged that they had detailed information. He retorted with a flat denial: the rumors were "a figment of your imagination" (NJB), rather than reported from elsewhere. He interpreted the letter (v. 9) as an intimidation attempt to prevent the completion of the **work** by demoralizing the workers. If the translation is correct, his recourse was to turn to God in prayer, as in 4:4–5. This time he prayed for personal assurance as he exercised leadership in the face of intimidation.

6:10–14 / If the letter envisioned prophets who supported Nehemiah, this next section tells of **prophets** who opposed
him and who, he claimed, were on Samaria's payroll. Again the
theme is intimidation, as verses 13–14 state. This time it was not an
external stratagem but an internal attempt to **discredit** Nehemiah. He realized eventually that it was the direct doing of **Tobiah,** who had close connections with Judah, as Nehemiah would
explain in verses 17–19. So Tobiah's name occurs first in verses 12
and 14, although his master **Sanballat** stood behind him. Nehemiah was invited to the home of **Shemaiah,** presumably to receive
a divine message from this person, whom we are later told was a
prophet. He delivered a frightening prophetic oracle, which superficially reads like the warning Agabus gave Paul in Acts 21:11.
Shemaiah had a solution for Nehemiah to escape the threat of
assassination—to retreat with him inside the temple. Nehemiah
refused on two grounds. First, it was inappropriate for him as a
high-ranking official with his own armed bodyguard (4:23) to
slink away in cowardly panic. Second, and more importantly, it
would be sacrilegious for him as a layperson to enter the temple
building, and he refused to commit such a **sin.** At first Nehemiah
had assumed that **God** had given Shemaiah this message. Testing
the prophetic spirit (1 John 4:1), he came to a different conclusion.
Its incongruity made him aware that Shemaiah was no well-
wisher, but an enemy agent. It was an attempt at entrapment, a
scare tactic and a put-up job.

Verses 10–14 close with another **Remember** petition. While
it is like the first one in 5:19, this time it is negative in tone, directed
against his two adversaries—the go-between and his boss. Nehemiah appeals to God to vindicate him by providentially punishing
these Samarian officials and the local **prophets,** who had evidently played the same sort of game as their colleague Shemaiah.
By this means justice would be done—such justice as the widow
persistently pleaded for in the parable of Luke 18:1–8.

6:15–16 / Nehemiah could now proudly announce the
completion of **the wall,** presumably including the doors (v. 1; 7:1).
It was a red-letter day, probably in early October 445. The extensive repair work, probably begun but not completed at an earlier
period (Ezra 4:12), had taken only two months **(fifty-two days),**
and so they must have started in mid-July, assuming a six-day
work week. A lot had happened since the day in Susa less than six

months before, when Nehemiah had received his mission from the Persian king (2:1–6).

This passage marks the last cycle of the literary pattern that begins with progress on the wall. There is now no room for the third element, Nehemiah's counterresponse, because these verses highlight the second element, the enemy response. This time the enemy reaction to the news was an overwhelming sense of defeat. It was their turn to be "intimidated" (NJPS for **afraid**), after attempting to intimidate the Judean workers and Nehemiah (vv. 9, 13–14). It was also their turn to experience the loss of face they had tried to inflict on Judah (4:14–15). Here was the happy experience of Psalm 126:2 all over again: "Then it was said among the nations, 'The LORD has done great things for them.'" How could anyone deny divine enabling in this amazingly rapid achievement against such odds?

**6:17–19** / This postscript to verses 10–14 gives general information about Tobiah's meddling in Judean affairs. It continues the intimidation theme of the chapter, and so the implication is that this information related to a time before the completion of the wall. It begins with a loose time reference, **in those days**, like 13:15, 23. Tobiah had high-level contacts in Judah, and **letters** back and forth were evidently the source of Samaria's constant access to information about Jerusalem. Tobiah's Judean contacts were members of a family network by marriage and were his sworn political supporters. They lost no opportunity to commend him to Nehemiah and to report back Nehemiah's stated views. Tobiah sent **letters** of a different character directly to Nehemiah—hostile letters meant to intimidate. We have not heard the last of Tobiah. Nehemiah was later to confiscate his apartment in the very precincts of the temple, given to him by a priestly member of the pro-Tobiah party (13:4–8). That report in chapter 13 provides literary closure for this unsettled postscript, although Nehemiah still wanted a final resolution through a providential verdict from God (v. 14).

---

## Additional Notes §7

---

**6:2** / **One of the villages:** The MT has a place name, "Hak-kephirim" (REB), which BDB, p. 499, wrongly identified with Kephirah in

7:29 (= Ezra 2:25). The LXX and Vulgate, as well as the eastern tradition for public reading of the MT, imply a different vocalization, *hakkepārîm,* "the villages," which the NIV and NRSV have followed. For **the plain of Ono,** see *Macmillan Bible Atlas,* p. 129, map 170.

**6:5** / **Aide:** This is not a reference to Tobiah. Although the NRSV fairly renders "servant," the Heb. term here implies a lesser rank than that used for Tobiah in 2:10, 19 (NIV "official").

**6:6** / The Arabic form for **Geshem,** "Gashmu," is used. He evidently confirmed the rumor, claiming solid evidence for it.

**6:7** / For the prophetic role in king-making, compare 1 Sam. 9–10; 1 Kgs. 11:29–39; 2 Kgs. 9:1–13 and, in recent postexilic times, Hag. 2:21–23; Zech. 6:10–13. There may have been an extreme nationalistic group in Jerusalem that advocated his kingship, but Nehemiah denies this possibility in v. 8.

**6:9** / The interpretation of v. 9b is uncertain and depends on the Heb. verb rendered **strengthen. But I prayed** is not in the original, nor is "O God" (NRSV). If the verbal form is intended as an impv., a rather abrupt prayer is implied, vividly recalled in the narrative, like the one in 4:4–5. But one does expect a voc. "O my God," as in v. 14, like "O our God" in 4:4. The objection that this verb does not occur elsewhere in Nehemiah's prayers is less compelling than the fact that nowhere else in the OT is it used with a divine subject. The alternative is to construe the verb as an inf. absolute, here equivalent to a first-person sg. perf., as the ancient versions took it (see *BHS*). Then the sense is, "But my morale rose even higher" (NJB). It is difficult to make a clear-cut decision. It is interesting that the revisers of the NEB switched from the second interpretation ("So I applied myself to it with greater energy") to the first in the REB ("Strengthen me for the work, was my prayer").

**6:10** / **Shut in:** The reason for this confinement is not given, but it explains why Shemaiah did not visit Nehemiah. For other suggested explanations, see Williamson, *Ezra, Nehemiah,* p. 249. It is feasible that Shemaiah was on the temple staff and had a house in the precincts. **Let us . . . they are coming to kill you:** The message is given as a three-line poem, with a 3+2, 3+2, 3 meter, the dirge rhythm used in 4:10. *BHS,* REB, NJB, and NJPS give a poetic layout.

**6:11** / **To save his life:** The RSV and NJPS rendering "and live" is a possible and, at first sight, more obvious translation, referring as it does to the risk of being killed for trespassing in the sanctuary (Num. 18:7). But as Fensham, *Ezra and Nehemiah,* p. 205, observed, according to v. 13 the plot was intended to discredit Nehemiah rather than kill him. Verse 10 mentions the aim of killing him, but the plot may have been designed to drive a wedge between Nehemiah and the priesthood (K. D. Tollefson and H. G. M. Williamson, "Nehemiah as Cultural Revitalization: An Anthropological Perspective," *JSOT* 56 [1992], pp. 41–68, esp. p. 54).

**6:12** / "[A] true prophetic word cannot override what is known on other grounds to be right" (P. R. Ackroyd, *I & II Chronicles, Ezra, Nehemiah* (TBC; London: SCM, 1973), p. 289).

**6:15** / **Twenty-fifth of Elul:** For the date, see Williamson, *Ezra, Nehemiah,* p. 260.

**6:16** / **Enemies** refer to the leaders, and **nations** to their followers. The rendering **were afraid** corresponds to the accentuation of the MT and also to the ancient versions. It has been urged that the Heb. term should be taken from the verb "see" ("saw," REB, NJB). In favor of this is the parallelism of "enemies" and "nations," while seeing and hearing would match. However, the key role of the verb "fear" in the chapter tips the scales in favor of the former option.

**6:18** / **Arah** was the name of a Judean family in 7:10 (= Ezra 2:5). **Meshullam son of Berekiah** was an energetic wall builder (3:4, 30).

## §8 Preparations for Consolidating the City (Neh. 7:1–73a)

Was Nehemiah's mission complete with the rebuilding of the wall? Did that satisfy his ambition to rebuild Jerusalem (2:5)? At the very least, security measures were required. In this section we read of such measures and also initial steps taken to increase the number of residents in Jerusalem. Since the Hebrew verb "to build" can connote community building, the definition of Nehemiah's mission in 2:5 implied the repopulation of the city.

**7:1–3** / The memoirs of Nehemiah continue. This discussion of Jerusalem's security marks a transition in the narrative and might be regarded as rounding off the account of wall building. However, there seems to be a new beginning after the completion of the wall, the story of which was interwoven with intimidation in the scenes of chapter 6. The wall's completion in 6:15 included the provision of **doors** for the gatehouses. This last detail had been taken care of by then, in the light of 6:1. The question of doors broached the issue of security and of appointing personnel. The mention of personnel leads into the larger concern of the repopulation of Jerusalem. Temple **gatekeepers** were used temporarily, because of their experience. Since there were not enough of them to cover both temple and city gates, they were supplemented with other members of the temple staff until a corps of secular gatekeepers could be established. In another emergency situation Nehemiah ordered Levites to guard certain city gates (13:22), although in that case it was to resolve a religious problem. Laypeople were to be coopted at the end of verse 3.

It was also necessary to appoint officials responsible for overall security. Nehemiah chose as executive mayor his **brother Hanani,** who had been associated with the project since it was a gleam in Nehemiah's eye (1:2). The military officer in charge of the **citadel** near the temple (2:8) was to assist him. Nehemiah selected this **commander** based on two outstanding qualities:

trustworthiness, a virtue conspicuous by its absence in 6:10–19, and a reverence for God that shaped his moral decisions. Nehemiah had shown how important he thought practical piety was in 5:9, 15. The two officials were responsible for the security of the gates, and they were given instructions for the daily procedures. Nehemiah also ordered them to enlist vigilantes from the small pool of city residents—some to guard gates **near** their homes and others to defend **posts** assigned to them on a roster.

**7:4–5** / These expedients were obviously makeshift and indicated a serious problem. Jerusalem as yet functioned as an administrative and religious center for the provincial community, rather than as the metropolis it had been in preexilic times. Then its streets rang with "the sounds of joy and gladness, the voices of bride and bridegroom" (Jer. 33:11). The prophetic hope that "the city streets will be filled with boys and girls playing" (Zech. 8:5) was still a dream. Even with the postexilic capital reduced to the eastern hill (having lost its western suburb), it must have had the air of a ghost town after most of the wall builders left Jerusalem and went home. An extensive house building project had not been implemented, such as will be implied by the repopulation program of 11:1, for which 7:5 was preparing. Nehemiah claimed, as in 2:12, that his **God** had **put** the idea **into** his mind. These two statements of divine guidance, in 2:12 and here, introduce the execution of the two halves of his mission. By way of preparation, Nehemiah organized the **registration** of the population of the province by family groupings, and he called a national assembly to this end. Finding in the archives an old record of immigrants who had settled in Judah greatly facilitated this task. This record was about seventy-five years old. It simplified Nehemiah's administrative work by providing him with a ready-made list of clans and local communities where immigrants had settled.

**7:6–69** / We have seen this list before. The narrator of Ezra 1–6, finding it in its present literary place, reused its evidence of early settlement in Judah to illustrate his story of the return from exile sparked by the decree of Cyrus (see the comments and notes on Ezra 2, above). Now, as readers of the canonical Ezra-Nehemiah, we encounter the list not only as a source for Ezra 2 but also as a repetition that defines the Judean community as a continuation of the preexilic people of God, brought through the trauma of exile. We shall see in coming chapters that this basic theological truth created a challenge that demanded a dynamic response. For Nehemiah, however, burdened with details of administration, the list was a convenient document. He put it to practical use and eventually incorporated into his memoirs, like the wall builders' list in chapter 3. He used the list to determine the population of a renewed Jerusalem. The population of the eschatological city of God in Ezekiel's vision included representatives from all of the tribes of Israel, as the names of its gates attest (Ezek. 48:19, 31–34; compare 45:6). Similarly here, the people in the city would represent each clan and local community as a microcosm of the total community that made up **Israel** (v. 7).

**7:70–73** / A catalogue of donations made for the ongoing work of the temple at some date, or over a certain period, supplemented the list. The narrator of Ezra 1–6 simplified it and adapted it to his own literary content in Ezra 2:68–69. A statement recapitulating the renewed settlement in the land rounded off the amplified list—combining the opening in verse 6 ("they returned to Jerusalem and Judah, each to his own town") with the categories listed in verses 7b–60.

We await the implementation of the repopulation project, and a long wait it will be, as it does not begin until chapter 11. Not before chapter 12 do we find the ceremony dedicating the city wall that we might have expected after chapter 6. Another agenda intervenes to ensure that the people of God were properly prepared for the privilege that would be theirs.

---

### Additional Notes §8

**7:1** / **The gatekeepers and the singers and the Levites:** The two latter groups might seem to be strange choices to guard the city gates. They are frequently regarded as a later gloss (see the REB and NJB), which misunderstood lay gatekeepers as temple ones and included the two other groups of the three mentioned in vv. 43–45. If the gatekeepers were actually temple officers temporarily drafted to secular duties, assistance from other temple staff is feasible.

**7:2** / The rendering **along with,** rather than "that is" in the mg., is doubtless correct in view of "them" in v. 3, which seems to indicate that two individuals are mentioned here. It is less likely that the new gatekeepers were addressed, or a combination of them and Hanani, since they are mentioned in the third person. Hanani apparently had a role corresponding to that of the ruler of Mizpah (3:19), rather than to that of the two rulers of the district of Jerusalem (3:9, 12). **A man of integrity** is, rather, "trustworthy" (REB, NJB, NJPS).

**7:3** / The instructions for operating the gates are by no means clear. It appears at first that there are orders about morning opening and evening closing each day, implying that they stayed closed all night. But the phrase rendered **until the sun is hot** more naturally refers to the heat of noon than to a morning rise in temperature. Evidently the gates were open for only half of the day, perhaps because there were not enough gatekeepers to keep them open for longer periods. Another possible rendering is "during the heat of the day" (REB), implying that the gates had to be closed at this siesta time, when security would be lax (compare 2 Sam. 4:5–7, esp. in the REB or NJB). But Clines, *Ezra, Nehemiah, Esther*, p. 178, gives reasons why this is a less likely rendering. **While the gatekeepers are still on duty:** This order seems to indicate that the gates did not stay open after the guards left their posts. The REB, "while the gatekeepers are standing at ease," again refers to a siesta—but this is not an obvious meaning for the verb.

**7:4** / Although Nehemiah says that **the houses had not yet been rebuilt,** there were, of course, some that had been—as verse 3 and the evidence in chapter 3 indicate. The clause envisions a new project yet to be undertaken by Nehemiah. Sir. 49:13 credits him with rebuilding ruined houses, while Josephus (*Ant.* 11:18) claims that he did so at his own expense, as part of the repopulation program.

**7:7** / **The men of Israel:** The lay immigrants who later returned with Ezra (Ezra 8:3–14) belonged to some of the same clans mentioned in the following verses. This fact illustrates the continuing validity of the old list.

**7:68** / This verse is restored from Ezra 2:66. It fell out of the MT because of the numeral "200" in the Heb. of v. 67. A copyist's eye slipped to the same word seven words later. In light of Ezra 2:65–66, "45" belongs in this verse and "245" in v. 67 should be "200" (see Williamson, *Ezra, Nehemiah*, p. 28).

**7:70** / **530 garments for priests:** The MT (v. 69) has "30 garments for priests and 500," omitting what the latter numeral refers to. The narrator of Ezra 1–6 in Ezra 2:69 read, or took it as a reference to, "minas of silver" (see the note there), which is widely supposed to have fallen out of the text here.

**7:73** / **Along with certain of the people and the rest of the Israelites** is, more probably, "along with the rest of the people, and so all Israel." See the discussion of Williamson, *Ezra, Nehemiah*, pp. 271–73, who substantially follows A. H. J. Gunneweg. The phrase rendered "certain of the people" seems to refer to laypeople, as distinct from religious groups. In Ezra 2:70 the narrator interpreted "certain of the people" as lay officials living in the Jerusalem area, and Neh. 11:1 may reflect the same perspective. The following "and so all Israel" (compare the NRSV) sums up the various groups into a larger whole. The NIV has not represented the strange order of terms, reproduced in the NRSV, which may reflect textual disarray.

## §9 Back to Basics (Neh. 7:73b–8:18)

Nehemiah's work of repopulating Jerusalem is put on hold until chapter 11. The editor has put chapters 8–10 together and placed them here in pursuit of a different but related agenda. This chapter presents the first two of a series of readings from the Torah. At first sight, the topic of the Torah seems irrelevant to Nehemiah's practical measures. In fact this material develops chapter 1, where Nehemiah's prayer traced Judah's plight and Jerusalem's sorry state back to breaking the Torah, its "commands, decrees and laws" (1:7). So his mission, sincere and inspired though it was, was just a Band-Aid. Judah needed to learn the Torah in order to avoid its curses, enjoy its promises, and reclaim Jerusalem for the people of God.

We saw in the discussion of Ezra 9, above, that Nehemiah 7:73b–8:18 originally belonged to Ezra's memoirs. **The seventh month** fits historically between the fifth month of Ezra 7:9 and the ninth month of Ezra 10:9. In its new position here, the material acquires its own literary logic as the story progresses from Elul, the sixth month, in 6:15 to a seventh month in 7:73b (although it is now a different year). As in Ezra 10, the first-person references of Ezra's memoirs have been editorially changed to the third person. Another consideration in this case was to avoid confusion with the "I" of Nehemiah's memoirs, last encountered in 7:5 and to be resumed in 12:31. The editor here transferred Ezra's public reading of the Torah. The purpose was to teach the spiritual lesson that a regard for God's word leading to repentance and reform must precede the solemn integration of the covenant people into the holy city, Jerusalem (11:1, 18). It was the message of chapter 1 painted on a larger canvas. It was a model for later generations to emulate. Who may dwell on God's holy hill, representatively as well as by pilgrimage? Those who walk blamelessly (Ps. 15:1–2)—because their delight is in the law of the Lord (Ps. 1:2). "Sinners in Zion" were a veritable contradiction in terms (Isa. 33:14–15).

The first of two days of reading and teaching the Torah is described in 7:73b–8:12, and verses 13–18 describe the second day that leads into a week of readings. A pattern of coming together (REB "assembled," vv. 1, 13), taking the Torah to heart, and **joy** marks both sections.

**7:73b–8:8** / The Israelites celebrated a minor festival, the feast of Trumpets (Lev. 23:24–25; Num. 29:1–6), on **the first day of the seventh month.** It was a holiday and a time of sacred assembly. The community judged it a convenient time to invite Ezra to lead a service of instruction from the Torah. One can almost hear a fanfare of trumpets accompanying the grand description of the Torah at the end of verse 1. The editor honored Ezra here, and elsewhere, with the title **the scribe** (vv. 1, 4, 9, 13) to highlight his role as Torah teacher, as in Ezra 7:6. He also called him **the priest** at the start of each section (vv. 2, 9) to emphasize his religious role, as in Ezra 10:10, 16. Custody and communication of the Torah were traditional parts of the ministry of the priesthood (Mal. 2:1–9). They held the meeting in an open **square** near the **Water Gate** on the east side of the city, a little down the slope and inside the line of the old wall that Nehemiah discarded (3:26). Not only did the adult males of the community attend the meeting, as in Ezra 10:9, but also their wives and children old enough to **understand.** Verse 3 summarizes Ezra's six-hour reading of the Torah, and then verses 4–8 describe it in more detail. Persons identified by name but not by their social status or their role on this occasion flanked him on the specially made **platform.** They were probably representatives of the people who had invited Ezra—perhaps members of the religious party of Ezra 9:4; 10:3. The preliminary liturgical rites when Ezra ceremonially unrolled the scroll (vv. 5–6) probably reflect ancient religious practice: Ezra's benediction and the response of the people, standing in respect, with words of self-identification and acts that expressed pleading and submission. They provided a worshipful, appreciative setting for Ezra's reading and for its explanation by thirteen **Levites** he had trained who circulated among those assembled. We have seen an example of the Torah hermeneutic taught by Ezra in Ezra 9, with reference to mixed marriages.

**8:9–12** / There is a triple refrain in verses 9–11 concerning the holiness of **This day** as a festival day and the obligation not to grieve. The monthly New Moon festival and the longer festivals were to be days of rejoicing, according to Numbers 10:10, while Deuteronomy stipulates that joyful celebration was to be a regular feature of the festivals (Deut. 12:7, 12, 18; 14:26; 16:11, 14). The tension between the people's **weeping** and the leaders' exhortation to rejoice is reminiscent of Ezra 3:12–13, where official rejoicing mingled with lamenting dissatisfaction. Here, however, the grief was evidently due to the content of the reading, which prompted a healthy recognition of falling short of its standards, like King Josiah's response to the reading of the Torah in 2 Kings 22:11–13. Yet the sacred duty of the day as devoted to the joyful worship of God made tears inappropriate. Rejoicing over the Lord is described as a source of protection, the people's "stronghold" (NJB). Such a positive attitude supplied a stimulus to comply with the moral will of God in the future, and so gave protection against the divine wrath for disobedience that had loomed in Ezra 9. The special, party-like fare that expressed their joy and the generous sharing with those who had no food are both reminiscent of Deuteronomy 12:18–19 and 14:26–27. The end of verse 12 resumes verse 8: it was not simply the holiday that sparked communal joy, but the appreciation of the reading and exposition of the Torah.

**8:13–18** / Most of the people went home, but the temple clergy and the community elders reassembled for a **second day** of Torah study with Ezra. The Festival of Tabernacles (or Booths) was due to be celebrated two weeks later in the month, from the fifteenth day, and so they paid special attention to celebrating it in line with the Torah **(as it is written).** The section focuses on how a careful study of the Torah can explain the festival, rather than on the festival itself. It had been celebrated before, according to Ezra 3:4, while Ezra 3:5–6 implies its regular celebration. The issue was not whether it should be celebrated, but rather how. In Ezra 3:4 the focus was on sacrificing, in line with Numbers 29. Here the account of Leviticus 23:39–43 is in view, particularly its prescription to commemorate the wilderness period after the exodus by camping in booths (vv. 42–43), which the postexilic community had evidently not practiced. From this passage, the people extrapolated instructions for making the shanty structures. Leviticus 23:40 mentions fruit and branches, which the people were presumably to carry, as in later tradition. The people here reinterpreted these as materials for the booths, with necessary adaptation according to availability. The eventual rejoicing in verse 17 also marks an implementation of Leviticus 23:40. However, the fact that verse 16 describes booths placed on top of or near the houses of Jerusalem residents and in the open squares of the city recalls the centralized venue of worship prescribed in Deuteronomy 31:11, although the phrase "before the LORD" in Leviticus 23:40 also presupposes it.

Certainly the prescription in Deuteronomy 31:10–12, that the Torah was to be read at this festival every seven years, motivated Ezra's reading from it (v. 8). He integrated two Torah texts about the festival (Lev. 23 and Deut. 31). The duration of the festival as **seven days,** plus a closing celebration on the **eighth** day in verse 18, reverts to Leviticus 23 (vv. 34–36, 39). Numbers 29:12–38 also specifies this duration, but since the sacrificial emphasis of that passage is not mirrored here and the context does depend on Leviticus 23, it is the latter text that is in view here. They held the festival in verses 16–18, presumably from the fifteenth day. Verse 17 brings the character of the worshipers, as essentially returned exiles, to the reader's notice. This echoes 7:6 and the portrayal of the people in Ezra 1–6 (2:1; 3:8; 6:16) and 7–10 (8:35; 9:4; 10:6, 8, 16). A typological parallel is drawn between these celebrants and the Israelites who entered the land under **Joshua.** The general link between them was that they were both brought home at last by an exodus and were enjoying the keeping of a divine promise. But Ezra's role as Torah reader added an extra precision to the parallel. The text implicitly invites the reader to compare Moses' injunction in Deuteronomy 31:10–13, that the Torah was to be read aloud at the Feast of Tabernacles every seven years, and to recall that this injunction was given in the context of the appointment of Joshua as Moses' successor (Deut. 31:7–8, 14–29). It was assumed that Joshua carried it out (Josh. 1:8; 8:34–35), and Ezra's introduction of Torah reading to the postexilic celebration of the festival constituted a special parallel with Joshua. Mention of his reading the Torah in verse 18 flows naturally from this Torah-related parallel in verse 17.

---

### Additional Notes §9

**7:73b** / **The seventh month:** Nehemiah's memoirs used names for the months (1:2; 2:1; 6:15), while Ezra's used numbers (Ezra 7:9; 8:31; 10:9, 16–17, as in Neh. 7:73b; 8:2, 14). **The Israelites had settled in their towns** must originally have referred to the party of immigrants who traveled with Ezra and arrived in Jerusalem in Ezra 8:32. Here it echoes and provides a neat link with 7:73a, which referred to immigrants long before Ezra's and Nehemiah's time—the phenomenon still applied at this late period. This designation identifies the contemporary community as those who had returned from exile (compare 7:6; 8:17). The movement of material to Neh. 8 to make a literary point is paralleled in the narrative of Ezra 1–6, where the chronologically later account of Zerubbabel and Jeshua in Ezra 2:1–4:5, 24 was put back into the earlier period of Cyrus and Sheshbazzar. The position of Neh. 8 after Ezra 10 that is reflected in 1 Esd. simply corresponds to the excerpting of material relating to Ezra from the Nehemiah narrative, as the use of Neh. 7:73a in 1 Esd. 9:37 shows.

**8:1** / Although the Heb. verb for **assembled** here (and in v. 13) is different from that used in 7:5, the editorial intention may have been to equate this assembly with Nehemiah's, as a step toward the repopulation of Jerusalem.

**8:3** / **He read it** could also be "he read from it" (NRSV), implying extracts chosen beforehand.

**8:6** / In terms of benedictions in the Talmud, this one would have taken the form "Blessed are you, LORD (O great God), who give the Torah to your people Israel" (*Ber.* 11b).

**8:7** / **The Levites:** The MT has "and the Levites" after the names (see the NRSV), but 1 Esd. 9:48 and the Vulgate attest a text without the conjunction. This is preferable, since most of the names can be identified with Levites elsewhere, in 9:4–5; 10:9–13; 11:16. **Standing:** The point is that they "remained in their places" (REB), while the Levites moved from group to group.

**8:8** / **They read:** It is not clear who the subjects of this and the other verbs are—probably Ezra for the reading and the Levites for the other verbs, perhaps in the former case also members of the platform party, relieving Ezra in his long stint. The Heb. verb translated **making it clear** is of uncertain meaning. The term also occurs in the Aramaic of Ezra 4:18, but it does not necessarily have the same meaning here. The NJB and NJPS side with the NIV mg., which relates to translation into Aramaic. See further Williamson, *Ezra, Nehemiah*, pp. 278f.

**8:9** / **Nehemiah the governor:** The LXX attests only the name, and 1 Esd. 9:49 only a transliteration of the Heb. noun for governor, while the MT seems to conflate both readings. Together with **and,** the whole phrase looks like a combination of alternative notes that has been incorporated into the text (see *BHS*). The notes were each trying to integrate the account into the context. There seems to be no role for the secular official in this religious setting. As Williamson, *Ezra, Nehemiah*, p. 279, has observed, while the Heb. sg. verb rendered **said** is syntactically possible before a multiple subject, the sg. verb in v. 10 refers naturally to Ezra. This in turn suggests that the other sg. subject in v. 9 was not there originally. In fact v. 9, minus the initial reference, has the same summarizing role as

v. 3 and is subsequently explained by Ezra's statement in v. 10 and the Levites' in v. 11.

**8:10 / Nehemiah** has been supplied in the NIV for attempted clarity: contrast the NRSV. Josephus (*Ant.* 6.156) took the word translated **strength** here as "a security and a safeguard" that they would not sin again, although he related it to the weeping of v. 9, which is a religious truism and not the point here.

**8:12 / The words that had been made known to them** refers to the words of the Torah (v. 9), rather than to the advice of vv. 9–11. There is a reference to the Torah at the end of each subsection, in vv. 8, 12, 15, and 18.

**8:13 / The heads of all the families** is lit. "the heads of families of all the people."

**8:14 /** One would expect a reference to the Day of Atonement, to be held on the tenth of the seventh month according to Lev. 23:26–32. The present account, concentrating on the theme of the Torah, is highly selective. It would be unwise to assume that Ezra's Torah contained no reference to the Day of Atonement.

**8:15 / Proclaim:** The source seems to be the general proclamation of the festivals commanded in Lev. 23:4, 37, although a different Heb. verb is used (Williamson, *Ezra, Nehemiah,* p. 295). The proclamation in v. 15 was Ezra's hermeneutical version of that commanded in the Torah. Fishbane, *Biblical Interpretation,* pp. 109–12, has done a valuable study of vv. 13–15, which Williamson has qualified in "History," pp. 29–31.

**8:16 / The Gate of Ephraim:** See 12:39 for its general location on the other side of the city, on the north part of the west wall. It is not mentioned in ch. 3 and may have lain outside the future line of Nehemiah's wall (Williamson, *Ezra, Nehemiah,* p. 375).

**8:17 / From the days . . . this:** Behind the rhetoric there seems to lie a combination of two claims. First, these people possessed a renewed capacity to appreciate the land—in contrast to centuries of preexilic celebrations by those who knew no other home. Second, it was the first postexilic celebration that approximated the ancient one, with booths and Torah readings.

## §10 Restoring Right Relations with God (Neh. 9:1–37)

This chapter follows in the wake of 7:73b–8:12 and 8:13–18. The people "assembled" (REB) once more for a third public reading of the Torah and a communal response. This time their response is one of repentant confession. As soon as the festivals of joy ended (8:12, 17), it was appropriate to act on the instinct to respond to the Torah with lament in 8:9. Set in the new literary jigsaw that chapters 8–10 constitute in their present setting, Nehemiah 9 seems to be of composite origin. Verses 1–5 fit best after Ezra 10:9–15, which is dated on the twentieth day of the ninth month, while the appended prayer of verses 6–37 was probably an independent one used in contemporary worship. In the new editorial context, **the twenty-fourth day** of verse 1 slots neatly after the twenty-second day implied in 8:18. Like chapter 8, this chapter works out at a communal level the ideal that Nehemiah expressed in chapter 1. In his private prayer, he representatively confessed the sins of the community of exiles as a prerequisite for their taking up residence in Jerusalem. This was not enough. Now the whole community prays such a prayer after him, as a necessary preliminary to occupying Jerusalem in chapter 11. Their repossession of Jerusalem would mark a significant step forward in regaining the land, which is a major theme of the prayer in Nehemiah 9.

The prayer also seems to echo the divine condition of repentance laid down in Nehemiah's own prayer in 1:9, "if you return to me." This verb occurs a number of times and now functions as an echo. Verse 26 speaks of God sending the prophets **in order to turn** their contemporaries **back to you.** Verse 28 mentions that ancestors who were punished "turned and cried to you" (NRSV). Verse 29 gives the purpose of God's prophetic warnings—to encourage the hearers **to return to your law.** Finally, in verse 35, the preexilic people of God did not **turn from their evil ways.** The prayer is an account of Israel sinning and then confessing that sin. References to (re)turning in repentance—the direction God wanted them to take—multiply toward the end of the prayer.

The third of the above references to returning to God, in verse 29, recognized the Torah as expressing the divine will. This, too, had been a concern of Nehemiah's prayer in the first chapter, as we noticed in connection with chapter 8. Contemporary Israel had broken the terms of the Torah given by God to Moses (1:7), but the Torah also provided a divine promise for them to claim (1:8–9). In this prayer, too, the Torah is much in evidence, with its commands and its promise of the land. An organic link was thus forged between the Torah reading of verse 3 and the prayer. The prayer represents the Torah as given by God in verses 13–14, and as spurned by Israel in verses 16, 26, 29, and 34. Moreover, much of the content of the prayer is devoted to telling stories from the Torah, from the creation narrative of Genesis 1 in verse 6 to Israel eating, being filled, and growing fat in Deuteronomy 32:15 (NRSV) in verse 25. The prayer, then, lays out the importance of the Torah for Israel. Divinely inspired, it was an integral part of their history.

**9:1–5** / Mourning rites indicated repentance, as in Joel 1:13–14 and 2:12–14. The wording of verse 2a originally related to the specific sin of mixed marriages in Ezra 9–10. Here those **of Israelite descent** separate themselves from the **foreigners;** the rites take on a more general flavor and refer to the distinctiveness the people of God should maintain, which will be explained in chapters 10 and 13. Verse 2b serves as an inverse summary for the prayer, the confession of contemporary **sins** corresponding to verses 33–37 and of ancestral **wickedness** corresponding to verses 16–30. The details of the service commence in verse 3, a three-hour reading from the Torah, followed by three hours of confession concluded with praise. The **loud voices** (v. 4) with which the Levites cried to the Lord recall the loud voices heard in the lamenting of Ezra 3:12 and the confession of Ezra 10:12. Here the Levites were engaging in confession on the people's behalf. In verse 5, an overlapping group of Levites summoned the people to concluding **praise** of the God who transcends all praise.

**9:6–15** / The prayer here returns to the confession of verse 4, giving detail for what was summarized there. Sometimes prophetic oracles make the people's sins more glaring and reprehensible by prefacing them with God's initial grace and so providing extra warrant for punishment in the sin of ingratitude. An example of this is found in Amos 2:9–16. This saga of sin and punishment adopts the same approach in retelling God's goodness. This goodness shines out in the creation of the living world, which ever inspires heavenly praise (e.g., Job 38:7), and in the keeping of the promise of **the land** made to **Abraham.** The prayer finds further divine goodness in Israel's deliverance from **Egypt,** the gift of the **good** Torah, and provision in the wilderness on the way to the promised land. God's positive response to Israel's **cry** (v. 9) as they suffered offered a ray of hope for the Levites crying on behalf of the people ("cried," v. 4, NRSV; Heb. *za'aq* in both cases).

**9:16–25** / The rest of the Torah's story, as presented in the prayer, does not (yet) follow the prophetic pattern of sin (shockingly following divine grace) and punishment, although it could have found in the Torah suitable material for such a sequence. Instead, Israel's sinning in the wilderness was met by the divine grace of Numbers 14:18a (in the amplified form of Exod. 34:6). Along with it went the continued blessings of God's presence and material provision and the ultimate gift of **the land** of Israel, as well stocked as Deuteronomy 6:11 had promised. All this was evidence of God's **great compassion** (v. 19) despite Israel's "great blasphemies" (NRSV, v. 18) on the one hand, and God's **great goodness** (v. 25) on the other.

**9:26–31** / Verses 6–25 presented kaleidoscopic pictures of divine grace: common grace, prevenient grace, and forgiving grace. Against this background, Israel's sins in verse 26 are all the more shocking—especially since God went the extra mile in providing **prophets** to urge repentance. Punishment achieved what their warnings could not, and the subsequent cry of repentance achieved what an earlier cry had in verse 9. Again God demonstrated **great compassion** in delivering the Israelites from their **enemies,** once more despite "great blasphemies" (NRSV, v. 26) on Israel's part. This cycle of sin, punishment, confession, and restoration relates in general to the period of the judges, the **deliverers** of verse 27. This revolving wheel of Israel's experience summarized the period in Judges 2:10–19, where it went around not merely once but in a succession of cycles. Here a second main cycle follows in verse 28 with a final reference to further spins of the wheel. Verse 29 initiates a third cycle. Now we are in the period of the classical **prophets,** who heralded the exile from the eighth century on. Sinning resulted in punishment, but even there grace was evident, for they survived the catastrophes of national destruction and exile. This was no less than God's

**great mercy,** which translates the same Hebrew phrase as that rendered "great compassion" in verse 19. Sin abounded, but grace superabounded.

**9:32–37** / A major shift in the prayer comes in verse 32 with "And now" (NJPS)—a word that customarily introduces the main point. The third cycle, in verses 29–31, was left incomplete. The expected cry for help and divine response, parallel with verses 27b and 28b, went unspoken. Now in these verses we find the present generation's petition, confession, and descriptive lament, bringing the third cycle to a positive conclusion. **Our, us, we** replace "their, them, they." Their pleas, both explicit and implicit, are emboldened by the propositional theology of grace formulated in verse 17 and found in an abbreviated form in verse 31b, and also by the "great compassion" or "mercy" mentioned in verse 19 and again in verse 31a. God's pervasive grace serves to uncover the notion of sin as "utterly sinful" (Rom. 7:13), as it does in verse 35, which repeats God's **great goodness** from verse 25. It also holds out hope that, as before in verses 27–28, the cycle might come to a satisfying conclusion of divine rescue and rest in answer to prayer. In particular, hope took the shape of a full restoration of the gift of the land promised in verse 8 and initially presented to Israel in verses 22–25. Grace would then happily come around full circle.

With spiritual audacity God is addressed as one **who keeps his covenant of love,** the love of verse 17 that refused to let loved ones go and the covenant of verse 8 that promised the land. Yet sin could not be swept under the rug: **we did wrong** (v. 33) and **our sins** were to blame (v. 37). In the context of this general confession God is declared to be **awesome** and **just** in subjecting the people to imperial domination lasting from the eighth century to the present, which had undermined Israel's social structures. Long ago, while they were "in their time of distress" (v. 27; NIV "when they were oppressed"), God had responded to their cry with "great compassion." God's people were crying out once more, now **in great distress** (v. 37), with the wish that God would answer their prayer in the same dynamic way. As in Psalm 106:44 God "took note of their distress when he heard their cry," so the postexilic community poignantly brought to the divine notice their **hardship** in terms of political and economic enslavement in order to elicit sympathy. They had no claim but God's own proven quality of mercy that seasons justice.

## Additional Notes §10

**9:1** / For the literary background of ch. 9, see Williamson's discussion in *Ezra, Nehemiah,* pp. 308–9. He has also suggested that the prayer originated in Judah during the exilic period ("Laments at the Destroyed Temple," *BibRev* 6 [1990], pp. 12–17, 44, esp. pp. 14–16).

**9:2** / **Those of Israelite descent** are lit. "the seed of Israel" (KJV), which together with the notion of separation harks back to Ezra 9:1 and intermarriage as the basic problem, to be resolved by the divorce proceedings of Ezra 10. There is no linguistic ground for the pluperfect **had separated themselves.** The rendering seems to be an attempt to juggle literary and chronological factors, inasmuch as the fulfillment of Ezra's injunction in Ezra 10:11 was in view in the source material. But in fact the specific issue of mixed marriages was not carried over into its new setting.

**9:3** / **They stood where they were and read:** In this condensed account of the service, the general subject "they" refers to the people who stood to listen, as in 8:5b, and to the Levites who read.

**9:4** / **Standing on the stairs were the Levites:** The NIV has misconstrued or heavily paraphrased the original, which means "(Jeshua . . .) stood on the stairs of the Levites" (NRSV). The overlap of names with v. 5, 8:7, and 10:9–13 indicates that Levites are in view. We are not told where the stairs were. Perhaps they led up to the portico of the temple.

**9:5** / Concluding calls to praise, marking the close of the service, seem to be intended here. Blenkinsopp, *Ezra-Nehemiah,* p. 296, has compared the doxologies that close the first four books of the Psalms, Ps. 41:13; 72:18–19; 89:52; 106:48. **Blessed be** is lit. "and let them bless" with an indefinite subject, "let people bless." In **who is from everlasting to everlasting,** "who is" is wrongly supplied (see the NRSV). The people are to praise God forever. The phrase is also used hyperbolically in benedictions of God in 1 Chr. 29:10; Ps. 41:13; 106:48.

**9:6** / The NRSV ("And Ezra said") has unwisely adopted the LXX addition, which was an attempt to integrate ch. 9 more closely with ch. 8, where Ezra officiates. The LXX added the same words in 8:15 for a similar reason. The LXX did recognize that the prayer begins here in v.6, rather than in v. 5b, where the NIV starts it. Compare, apart from the NRSV, the REB and NJPS. The prayer is written in rhythmical prose: see the layouts in the REB and NJB. The opening **You alone are the LORD** is similar to that of Hezekiah's prayer in 2 Kgs. 19:15. The sense must be "You, Yahweh, are the only (God)" (Clines, *Ezra, Nehemiah, Esther,* p. 193).

**9:7** / **Chose Abram:** Only here is Abraham's election mentioned. It is an inference from Deut. 4:37; 10:15.

**9:8** / **Righteous** here has the sense of being faithful to the covenant, doing what was right in view of the covenant relationship. The reference to **Canaanites . . . Girgashites** is to Gen. 15:6, 18–21, and here to vv. 22–25. The geographical list from Genesis is replaced by a more common stereotyped one of three major groups and three minor ones (see Ishida, "Structure," pp. 463–78, 481–85).

**9:13** / The giving of the Torah (Exod. 19–23) is put before the provision of manna and water (Exod. 16–17) in order to give prominence to the Torah, a major topic in the prayer.

**9:14** / **Your holy Sabbath:** Since this is mentioned separately from the gift of the Torah, the distinct episode of Exod. 16:23–30 is in view (M. Gilbert, "La place de la Loi dans la prière de Néhémie 9," in *De la Tôrah au Messie* [ed. J. Doré et al.; Paris: Desclée, 1981], pp. 307–16, esp. p. 311). Gilbert also suggested that the renewed mention of the Torah material refers to the collection of laws in Lev. and Deut., in light of Lev. 26:46 and Num. 36:13.

**9:16** / **Became arrogant:** The same Heb. word is used of the Israelites as in v. 10 of the Egyptians. They put themselves in the enemy camp.

**9:17** / **In their rebellion:** The LXX and a minority reading of the MT attest "in Egypt" (after **slavery**), representing an extra consonant (Heb. *bmtsrym* rather than *bmrym:* see *BHS*). It has been adopted by the NRSV and NJB and by Barthélemy, *Critique textuelle,* vol. 1, p. 568. The textual basis at this point is Num. 14:4, which specifically mentions Egypt. The phrase **a forgiving God**, found neither in the formula of Num. 14:18a nor in that of Exod. 34:6, may depend on Num. 14:19–20 (Bowman, "Ezra and Nehemiah," p. 750). It is echoed in Dan. 9:9.

**9:18** / **Blasphemies:** This refers to despising or rejecting God in favor of the golden calf in Exod. 32:8.

**9:20** / **Your good Spirit to instruct them** is the prophetic "spirit" (NRSV, better in an OT context than NIV's capitalization) of Num. 11:17, 25, 29. The spirit is again associated with prophecy in v. 30, below (see also Zech. 7:12).

**9:22** / For the linguistic basis of the possible rendering **even the remotest frontiers,** see Williamson, *Ezra, Nehemiah,* p. 305.

**9:26** / **Killed your prophets:** One would expect this sin to feature in one of the later cycles (see 1 Kgs. 19:10, 14; 2 Chr. 24:19–21; Jer. 2:30; 26:20–23). The cycles seem to be partly literary compositions, partly in historical sequence. Just as in the recapitulation of vv. 13–14, in v. 20a prophetic revelation replaced that of the Torah, so one prompted mention of the other here. The Torah and prophetic warnings are similarly paired in v. 34. Here, unlike v. 18, **blasphemies** refer to acts of contempt for God's prophetic word.

**9:27** / **When they were oppressed** is lit. "in their time of distress." The NIV translation tried to catch the Heb. wordplay with the preceding word, but in so doing lost the link with v. 37, where the same Heb. noun is deliberately used.

**9:28** / **They cried out to you again** is possible, but a preferable rendering is "they turned and cried to you" (NRSV), with the intentional use of a keyword of the prayer which signifies repentance.

**9:29** / For the Torah as the source of life, see Lev. 18:5, echoed positively in Ezek. 20:11, 13, 21; Luke 10:25–28. Physical life is the product of God's creation (v. 6), and spiritual life of revelation (vv. 13–14).

**9:31** / The NRSV's more accurate translation shows that this verse echoes the wilderness experience of God's grace: "Nevertheless, in your great mercies you did not make an end of them or forsake them, for you are a gracious and merciful God." The repetition held out hope that the people of God would once more enjoy the full occupation of the land (vv. 22–25).

**9:32** / For the three cycles and the different treatment of the third cycle, see Williamson, *Ezra, Nehemiah,* pp. 315, 317, who develops the insight of Gilbert, "La place de la Loi," pp. 312f. In the Pentateuch, the Heb. term for **hardship** describes oppression in Egypt and adversity in the wilderness (Exod. 18:8; Num. 20:14), and so here it fittingly refers to a period before full enjoyment of the land.

**9:37** / Conscription for forced labor and requisition of property are in view with **our bodies and our cattle.**

## §11 A Communal Pledge of Obedience (Neh. 9:38–10:39)

Before Jerusalem could be repopulated in line with Nehemiah's plan in 7:4–5, the last part of the program laid down in chapter 1 had to be implemented. The community had started to take the Torah into account in the readings and responses of chapter 8, but they had to go further. Their prayer of repentance in chapter 9 must logically lead to wholehearted obedience to God's commands. The divine condition for a return to Jerusalem, "if you return to me and obey my commands" (1:9) is here met in principle. Chapter 10 contains a pledge of obedience to God's will as revealed in the Torah. The editorial introduction **In view of all this** marks a transition from returning to God, in chapter 9, to obeying God's commands by turning from their evil ways (9:35) to follow the Torah (10:29). The pledge corresponds to Israel's "we will" at Mount Sinai, agreeing to the terms of the covenant revealed in Exodus 20–23: "we will obey" (Exod. 24:7). It translates old obligations into a contemporary form. By this expedient God's revelation in the Torah is applied to the actual life of the community and challenges it to change in specific areas of shortcoming.

The pledge has six clauses, and the new introduction before the fourth clause in verse 32 divides it into two halves. While all the stipulations relate to the Torah, those in the second group also refer to the temple, as does the closing affirmation. Jerusalem, to which they were to come, was no less than "the holy city" (11:1, 18), the home of the temple. To reoccupy Jerusalem meant deciding to live as a temple-centered community.

The editor who inserted Nehemiah 8–10 into the story of Nehemiah's mission used a document evidently preserved in the temple archives. The specific stipulations of the pledge reveal its association with Nehemiah's work. One of the stipulations relates to his economic reforms in chapter 5, and the remaining five relate to the religious reforms of his second term as governor recorded in chapter 13. This close affinity with chapter 13 suggests that the communal pledge was sworn after the events recorded there; it was the community's adoption of a codified version of Nehemiah's ad hoc measures. However, in the ideal presentation offered in the current arrangement of texts, which would serve as a model for the community thereafter, the pledge is put earlier, as a final step in a threefold program of reorientation. As part of this scenario, the people of God were to move from pact to act, as by their performance they lived out the pledge, step by step, in 12:44–13:31. This sequence, though not chronological, reflects good spiritual logic.

**9:38** / The **binding agreement** was a pledge made by the whole people, a promise of obedience to the Torah, as 10:29 will explain. The **writing** and addition of personal **seals** were proof of its authenticity and represented an objective reminder of their obligation to live up to it. While lay and religious representatives of the community evidently added their names to the document, the rest made a solemn verbal promise (10:29).

**10:1–27** / This list of names interrupts the introductory sentence in 9:38 and 10:28–29 and gives a different order for the three groups than that in 9:38. It was not part of the pledge itself but a separate document that the editor inserted to illustrate the groups in 9:38.

**10:28–29** / **The rest of the people** was originally the sequel to the civil leaders and religious representatives mentioned in 9:38. The editor has enumerated different groups to emphasize the comprehensiveness of those who committed themselves to the pledge and to tie it into the preceding context: the social divisions recall the groupings of the old immigrant community in 7:39–56. It was a **separated** community, as 9:2 stated and as verses 30–31 will further explain. It embraced women as well as men, and children old enough to **understand** and relate meaningfully to the pledge, as seen in the Torah reading of 8:2–3. Chapters 7–10 convey a sense of continuity, with the fresh start in chapter 7 leading into the second half of Nehemiah's mission.

**10:30–31a** / After the general preamble, the first two of six specific stipulations follow. The two applications of Torah material considered here have already been defined in terms of separation in 9:2 and would be implemented in chapter 13. The first relates to mixed marriages, already a problem in Ezra 9–10. Here the reference is to Deuteronomy 7:3, which prohibited marriages to the **sons** or **daughters** of the nations of Canaan, which were traditionally defined as seven in number (Deut. 7:1). Verse 30 follows the intention of the Torah more closely by defining the particular nations more comprehensively as "the peoples of the land" (NRSV)— that is, all non-Judean groups in the area. This ruling makes sense in terms of Nehemiah's opposition to local intermarriage with women from Ashdod in 13:23. This text interprets the old law in a way that is relevant to a contemporary threat to the community. The second clause in verse 31 relates to observing **the Sabbath** by abstaining from work. But what did the word "work" in the old laws mean? Here again we find a more comprehensive definition. The law had long been interpreted as a prohibition against selling on the Sabbath (Amos 8:5). Now the commandment was extended to prohibit buying. There is also a reminder that any **holy day**, such as New Moon days and festivals, was defined as a Sabbath for this purpose. The specific question of buying arose from the practice of non-Judeans bringing their wares to Jerusalem to sell at a Saturday market, which Nehemiah addressed in 13:18–22.

**10:31b** / The third clause of the pledge integrates two separate laws relating to the **seventh year** and endorses both of them. Exodus 23:10–11 stipulated an agricultural fallow year for the sake of the poor, while Deuteronomy 15:1–11 made an economic ruling for the remission of **debts.** The second ruling was intended to stop the recurrence of the problem encountered in Nehemiah 5. Both were measures to improve the lot of the poor.

**10:32–33** / The fourth stipulation concerns an annual temple tax. Since this temple tax is being instituted, we can assume that the Persian financial support mentioned in Ezra 6:9–10; 7:21–24 was temporary or insufficient, perhaps blocked by the satrapy treasurer. Exodus 30:11–16 set a precedent in the Torah for this new prescription, stipulating a tax of half a shekel for the sanctuary at the time of a census. Here this becomes an annual tax to meet contemporary needs. "For the service of the Tent of Meeting" in Exodus 30:16 now becomes **for the service of the house of our God.** Verse 33 carefully defines how the funds are used to maintain the ongoing routine of temple worship.

**10:34** / The fifth clause is an example of a facilitating law that creates the means of carrying out a command in the Torah. Leviticus 6:12–13, which is **the Law** referred to here, stipulates that the **altar** fire should be kept burning with wood added every morning. To that end, the people drew up an annual roster by lots for **families** to provide firewood. According to 13:31, Nehemiah organized this wood offering.

**10:35–39** / The sixth and last stipulation comprises a series of three promises to support the temple staff in order to maintain worship. A number of separate laws on the subject were collected and defined as cumulative rather than alternative. The support of temple staff was a recurring problem in early postexilic times, as the earnestness of Malachi 3:8–12 implies. Nehemiah 12:44–47; 13:10–13, 31 will demonstrate the governor's efforts to remedy this problem. The first two of the three pledges here relate to the support of **priests.** Verses 35–36 reaffirm the old law of **firstfruits.** People brought a token amount for the use of priests acknowledging that the whole harvest belonged to God as landlord and consequently releasing the rest for human use. The explicit inclusion of the **fruit** of trees redefines the categories. The same principle of giving applied to the **firstborn** of humans and animals. Parents paid a fee to the sanctuary for the priests to redeem firstborn male children, and this redemption is taken for granted. The firstlings of animals were either handed over or redeemed. A further priestly perquisite was the **first** of certain agricultural products or food processed from crops.

Tithes of **crops** (v. 37), later defined as **grain, new wine and oil** (v. 39), were a tenth of the crops given to support Levites. Verses 38–39 give instructions for the collection of tithes. Instead of bringing them to the temple, the people were to hand them in at local collection centers to Levites working under the direction of a **priest,** since priests benefited in part. The old ruling that Levites tithed their tithes, giving them to the priests, was retained. The Levites were to deposit them in the temple **storerooms.** Verse 39a, a later addition to the text as its dropping of the "we" references of the pledge shows, clarifies the foregoing in a number of particulars. Both laity and Levites had to pay the tithes, the former presumably through the system set up in verse 37b. Verse 39 specifies the items on which tithes were paid and clarifies that the storage facilities are at the temple. It may be implied that, apart from the Levites, other temple staff on duty received a share of the donations.

The pledge closes with a general statement of intent concerning commitment to the temple, summing up the drift of the last three stipulations. The temple stood at the center of the community's life and was the focus of many of the Torah's rulings. The obligation to support it corresponds to Nehemiah's exasperated question in 13:11, "Why is the house of God neglected?" It was a good note to end on, as God's people turned their faces toward Jerusalem.

---

## Additional Notes §11

---

**10:1–27** / The text of the introductory clause in v. 1 (MT v. 2) is uncertain (see the NRSV and *BHS*), but the NIV gives the general sense. For this list of names, see the long discussion in Williamson, *Ezra, Nehemiah,* pp. 325–30. Williamson follows S. Mowinckel's verdict that the list is not authentic but a literary composition drawn from other lists of names elsewhere in Ezra-Nehemiah. It brings together in spirit at this climactic ceremony those who had featured elsewhere, in order to illustrate the support of the whole community. Of the twenty-one **priests** in vv. 2–8, fifteen appear in 12:1–7, 12–21, allowing for minor variations. Since the names were from an earlier period, on a literal understanding of the list they function here as family names rather as individual heads of families. **Seraiah** (v. 2), for instance, refers to the high priestly family. Other names recur in different parts of Ezra-Nehemiah that refer to priests.

The seventeen **Levites** in vv. 9–13 are divided into three leaders and fourteen **associates** (with a strange repetition of **Shebaniah** and **Hodiah** in vv. 10 and 12–13). There is considerable overlap with Levitical names in 8:7; 9:4–5; 11:17; 12:8–9, 24. Of the forty-four lay leaders in vv. 14–27, the first eighteen in vv. 14–19a have a very close affinity with early immigrants in 7:8–24 (= Ezra 2:3–19) and so, again, must function as family names if they are to be taken literally. Of the remaining twenty-six names, at least eight appear randomly in the list of builders in ch. 3. Three or four are also found in 8:4, while three or four towns listed in ch. 7 reappear here as personal names. Myers' lists in *Ezra, Nehemiah,* pp. 234–41, are useful for comparing all the evidence. Much of it favors a literary origin for the present list. However, we must also take unique names into account. **Zedekiah** (v. 1), who does not seem to have been a priest (see the NRSV), is not known elsewhere. He may have been a civil leader or the official who wrote out the document, like Shimshai, the letter writer of Ezra 4:8. **Obadiah** (v. 5) occurs only here as a priest. Of the Levites' names, those new to us are **Rehob** (v. 11), **Zaccur** (v. 12, an Asaphite name in 12:35), and **Beninu** (v. 13), unless it is a corruption of the Levitical name "Kenani" in 9:4 (*BHS*, NJB). Of the laypeople after v. 19a, there are ten or so who do not feature in other lists in Ezra-Nehemiah. The overall evidence of literary dependence on those lists is very strong and suggests that this list as a whole was not intended to be a historical record. The unique names leave loose ends that preclude a clear-cut solution.

**10:28–29** / Before the list in 10:1–27 and the itemizing categories in 10:28 were inserted, this material continued in 9:38: "and (we) the rest of the people, join . . . and bind . . . oath." The following infinitives define the general thrust of the pledge, entered into by all who made it. The addition of the list of names broke this continuity. The addition, and also the new material in v. 28, encouraged the switch to the third person. In **and all who separated themselves from the neighboring peoples,** the conjunction is probably explicative, "namely all" (Vogt, *Studie,* p. 143). Compare 9:16, where in place of the NRSV "they and our ancestors" the NIV rightly has "they, our forefathers." Here the REB takes it in this way and the evident intention to echo 9:2 clinches this interpretation. Ezra 6:21 (written at a later date) used similar language, doubtless inspired by this usage, but it applied to new adherents to the community. Unlike the separation from "all foreigners" in 9:2, here it is from "the peoples of the lands" (NRSV), a phrase that echoes the language of the similar Ezra 9:1. **For the sake of** is lit. "to," as the positive purpose of the separation. **A curse and an oath** describes a verbal oath to keep the pledge, accompanied by self-imposed sanctions if it was broken (compare Deut. 29:12).

**10:30** / The hermeneutical principles of interpreting the Torah developed in this and the rest of the stipulations have been analyzed by Clines, "Nehemiah 10 as an Example of Early Jewish Biblical Exegesis," *JSOT* 21 (1981), pp. 111–17. My comments and notes reflect his analysis.

**10:31** / See Exod. 20:8–10; 34:21; Deut. 5:12–14 for **Sabbath** regulations. For the extension to **any holy day,** see Num. 28:18, 26; 29:1, and so on.

**10:32** / The change from half a shekel to **a third** may reflect the use of a heavier shekel (see Bowman, "Ezra and Nehemiah," p. 764).

**10:33** / For the **bread,** see Exod. 25:30; Lev. 24:5–9. For the daily or **regular grain offerings and burnt offerings** and the less frequent **offerings,** see Num. 28–29. The **holy offerings** were sacrifices that must be fellowship offerings (compare the list in Num. 29:39 and also Lev. 19:5, 8; 2 Chr. 29:33). They were normally voluntary, but here they are public sacrifices, as in Lev. 23:19. **Sin offerings** were made publicly each month and on festival days (Num. 28:11–29:38). The temple **duties** or "work" (NRSV) is a comprehensive term: "anything else that had to be done" (REB).

**10:35** / For **firstfruits,** see Exod. 23:19; Num. 18:13.

**10:36** / For **firstborn of our sons,** see Exod. 13:13; 34:20; Num. 18:15–16. **Our cattle:** Unclean animals were treated differently from clean ones (see Num. 18:15–18). The clause **As it is also written in the Law** in the original (MT v. 37) qualifies "our cattle" (see the NRSV) and seems to be aware of this distinction by using this generic term taken over from Num. 18:15 (NIV "animal"), before it mentions the treatment of clean animals. The specific terms **herds** and **flocks** come from Deut. 12:21.

**10:37** / See Lev. 23:10; Num. 15:20–21; 18:12, and *IDBSup,* pp. 336f. **Grain offerings,** lit. "contributions" (NRSV), is absent from the LXX and is of uncertain meaning here. See Williamson, *Ezra, Nehemiah,* p. 338, for some possible explanations. It may have originated as a marginal note rightly explaining "a tithe of our crops" in v. 37b in terms of the explicit "contributions" of v. 39, but was then inserted into the text at an inappropriate point. The category of **the fruit of all our trees** was covered in the firstfruits of v. 35. Here it refers to fruit products and is defined by the following "new wine and oil" (see the NRSV). For **tithes,** see Num. 18:21, 24–32; Deut. 14:22–29.

## §12 Moving into the Holy City (Neh. 11:1–12:26)

At last the time was ripe for the editor to pick up, from 7:4–5, the story of the repopulation of Jerusalem. First, the ideals in Nehemiah's prayer had to be realized on a communal level: the new focus on the Torah as determinative for the life of the community in chapter 8, the prayer of repentance in chapter 9, and the pledge of commitment to the Torah and the temple in chapter 10. Now 11:1–2 gives the procedure for allocating settlers in Jerusalem, and verses 3–24 list the new settlers with their pedigrees. Finally, verses 25–36 list certain postexilic settlements outside Jerusalem. The geographical widening at the end of the chapter reflects the importance of the promise of the land in the prayer of chapter 9. The people regarded the communal move to Jerusalem as a significant step toward their independent control of the promised land. It was an earnest of their eventual reoccupation of the whole land. Yet, as chapters 8–10 affirmed, it could materialize only if the people maintained obedience to God by following the way of life outlined in the Torah, including worship at the temple. The editor would have agreed with the Chronicler, in 1 Chronicles 28:8, that a spiritual agenda had to be followed in order to "possess this good land and pass it on as an inheritance." The fate and fortune of Jerusalem symbolized those of the covenant people, as in the messages of Second Isaiah. Building Jerusalem, not merely with stones but with people, was an omen laden with hope for the fulfillment of God's ancient promises to Israel.

The listings of temple staff in 12:1–26 are a later supplement to the record of those who moved to Jerusalem in 11:10–23. This text again reminds us that moving to the capital meant coming to the home of the temple, but it now presents a bigger picture. The rebuilt temple, with its staff of priests and Levites, had existed since early in the history of the postexilic community, when Zerubbabel had been governor and Jeshua high priest (7:7). This larger perspective bridges the list in chapter 11 and the wall dedication ceremony in 12:27–43, in which priests and Levites were to play a major part. It announces their participation as a salute to their vital contribution over the years to the postexilic community and to the work of God.

The bulk of the list is in 12:12–26, which attempts to present lists of the priests, Levites, and gatekeepers in office in Nehemiah's period. The editor used this evidence to deduce a list of priests and Levites officiating in the earliest days of the second temple in 12:1–9.

**11:1–2** / The editor did not continue at this point with Nehemiah's memoirs, which we last encountered in the citation of the list of earlier immigrants as a basis for drafting Judeans into Jerusalem (7:5–73a). He drew instead on a source that presented **the people** as initiating the relocation. Before citing the new source, the editor resumptively repeated in verse 1a the gist of 7:73a, concerning the lay and religious leaders already living in Jerusalem. The narrative in verses 1b–2 quotes from this new source, introducing the list of those who moved there. We do not know whether the casting of **lots** replaced the drafting scheme proposed by Nehemiah to repopulate the city or somehow complemented it. Throwing lots was regarded as a valid means of discerning God's will (Prov. 16:33; compare Acts 1:24–26). The description of Jerusalem as **the holy city** here and in verse 18 reflects the presence of the temple. It evokes in principle the old Zion tradition (see Ps. 46:4), and in particular Second Isaiah's promises that echoed it (Isa. 48:2; 52:1). The idea of the holy city suggests reestablishing continuity with the sacred past and moving forward with God to a divinely given hope. The blessing (**commended;** NJPS "gave their blessing to") of the new citizens was an appreciative, prayerful wish that God would bless them for their sacrificial move and help them settle down. Somewhat strangely, they are called volunteers. Unless this is a euphemism referring to an after-the-fact acceptance or a separate group is in view, it means that there was some leeway—perhaps families could decide which members of an extended family chosen by lot actually went.

**11:3–9** / The heading of the list refers to the heads of families in the province who moved with their families and **settled** in the capital. Verses 4b–9 list the lay heads. But first, in an aside, the editor relates the present list to the one found by Nehemiah by recalling the categories of 7:7b–60. Although he was citing a new source, he endeavored to integrate it with the old one, both here and in verse 1a. The list includes family heads of the tribes of **Judah** and **Benjamin.** In the tribe of Judah two family heads are mentioned, but only the males of the first family are enumerated. The heads represented two of the traditional tribal clans of Judah, **Perez** and **Shelah.** The extensive genealogical information that these lists contain shows the authentic membership of the new citizens in the community of Israel. If this ancestry was necessary for returning to the land (7:61–65 = Ezra 2:59–63), it was equally so for returning to Jerusalem. For the tribe of Benjamin, **Sallu,** the head of an extended family, represents all of the Benjaminites. Verse 8 enumerates that family's manpower.

**11:10–20** / Now follows the list of temple staff who moved to Jerusalem instead of commuting when they were on duty. The priestly list is uneven. Verses 11–14 supply one family name and the names of two family heads: **Seraiah, Adaiah,** and **Amashsai.** The second and third names are linked respectively with the clans of **Pashhur** and **Immer** that featured in 7:40–41. The first is the name of the last preexilic high priest mentioned in Ezra 7:1 and is traced back to **Ahitub,** high priest in David's reign. In verse 10, if the text is correct, there are brief references to two other family names, of which the first, **Jedaiah,** also appeared as a clan name in 7:39.

The list mentions three **Levites** who were family heads. The first, **Shemaiah,** is honored by a long genealogy. We met the second and third before as contemporaries of Ezra in Ezra 8:33; 10:15; Nehemiah 8:7. Their **outside work** may relate to the administration of tithes and other supplies mentioned in 10:32–39. Included in the Levitical ranks are three family heads of singers, **Mattaniah, Bakbukiah,** and **Abda.** The first and third are linked with two choirs named after traditional founders of religious music and song in David's time, **Asaph** and **Jeduthun.** Finally, the list mentions the family names of two temple **gatekeepers,** who were cited as returnees in the old list in 7:45. The original list ended at verse 20, since only representative families relocated to Jerusalem.

**11:21–24** / These verses form a later supplement to the list, adding a series of footnotes. The first gives information about another category of sanctuary personnel, the **temple servants,** who already lived in Jerusalem according to 3:26. Presumably the editor's mention of them in his aside in verse 3 inspired this addition. The second footnote names the missing **chief officer** for the Levites, corresponding to that of the priests in verse 14. If **the king** in verse 23 is Persian, as he must be in verse 24, the point is that the singers came under imperial direction, perhaps being responsible for daily prayers for the royal family (Ezra 6:10). We may compare the sung prayers for Israelite kings in Psalms 20 and 21. A lay royal agent, a member of the tribe of **Judah** from the clan of **Zerah,** maintained the liaison with the imperial authorities in this and other matters.

**11:25–36** / This supplementary list of Judean settlements picks up and develops verse 20. It was probably an earlier addition to the list of newcomers than was verses 21–24. This is a provocative list. Jerusalem was capital of the kingdom of Judah with its two tribes, and earlier of all of Israel with its twelve tribes. As capital it carried tribal associations, as Psalm 122:4 affirms. Jerusalem and the promised land went together, as the prayer in chapter 9 implicitly reminded us. This list exploits those associations. It does not match the contemporary Persian province of Judah. Of the settlements that are mentioned, only those in verses 29 (after **En Rimmon**)–33 were inside the province. Just one of the settlements, **Zanoah,** coincides with those listed in the wall building document of chapter 3. Of the twenty settlements listed in 7:26–38 (= Ezra 2:21–35), only eight feature here. Obviously this is not a standard or complete list. Its division into the old tribal territories of **Judah** and Benjamin corresponds to the same two tribal groups of the lay newcomers to Jerusalem in 11:3b–9, and this correspondence is likely the reason for the inclusion of the present list. Verse 30 gives southern and northern boundaries of the tribal territory of Judah by way of summary. The settlements in verse 25 up to "En Rimmon" in verse 29, over half of the Judean ones, were south of the Persian province, in an area under Edomite control. As for the settlements in the tribal land of Benjamin, the first five in verses 34–35 lay in the coastal area west of the province. Many of these communities may have been preexilic ones that were never exiled. The importance of the list for the editor who included it was that it, like the Jerusalem list, provided an earnest of a renewed spiritual reality that did not yet exist of recreated tribal territories in a promised land that lay beyond the limitations of the Persian province of Judah.

**12:1–9** / The temple was finished in the year 520 during the governorship of **Zerubbabel,** when **Jeshua** was high priest. This section traces worship back to that time by means of a list of **priests and Levites** who officiated then. The priestly list in verses 1–7 has been extrapolated from the subsequent one in verses 12–21, which relates to a later period when Joiakim was high priest. The compiler responsible for the present list took the family names listed there and used them by themselves to represent the groups extant then. We may compare how 7:39–42 (= Ezra 2:36–39) lists only family names. However, the list of priests who returned in chapter 7 knew of only four priestly families. Their numbers grew, and they had been extensively subdivided by Joiakim's period of office according to 12:12–21. This later subdividing was read back into Jeshua's period. The main point was the establishment of worship in the earliest period and its continuity since then. Verses 1–7 attempt to tell in list form what Ezra 3:1–6 told as narrative.

The list of later leading **Levites** in verses 24–25a gives no separate family names. So in the corresponding list envisioned for Jeshua's period in verses 8–9, the compiler chose to largely repeat the same names—with a summary of the function of the singers in verse 24. Verse 23 calls the named Levites "family heads," but they were more probably family names. The compiler responsible for verses 8–9 took them as such, as comparison with the list of returning Levites in 7:43 indicates.

**12:10–11** / Someone subsequently supplied a checklist of the high-priestly succession in the postexilic period, which enables us to get our general chronological bearings. The names cover the high priests mentioned in verses 1, 12, 22–23, and 26. This list found in the archives continues the earlier one preserved in 1 Chronicles 6:4–14 that closed with Jehozadak father of **Jeshua.** This list also presents succession to office by genealogical descent.

**12:12–21** / The purpose of this list was to supplement the list of priests who moved into Jerusalem in 11:10–14. Unfortunately there was no available list of **heads of priestly families** in Nehemiah's period, which coincided with Eliashib holding the office of high priest (3:1) and perhaps overlapped with Joiada (see 13:28). Therefore an extant list of priests under a recent high priest, **Joiakim,** appears in its place as an alternative. It lists twenty-one current family heads with their family affiliations. The list of family names evidently came from the same source as the priestly component of the signatories to the pledge in chapter 10 (vv. 2–8): it reproduces fourteen of its twenty-one names. The last six families here, from **Joiarib** to **Jedaiah** (vv. 19–21), were added at some stage to update the list, as their introduction by "and" (NJB) in verse 19 confirms.

**12:22–25** / Verse 22, as a whole or in part, is a later anno-tation. It tantalizingly hints at further information available in temple records about **Levites** and **priests** that covered a long pe-riod after Joiakim's period of office. Verse 23 speaks of **recorded** information about priests and Levites who officiated up to the pe-riod a generation or two after Nehemiah. It seems to refer to the following list of Levites in verses 24–25a. This list is in a different style from the previous priestly one and highlights one of their duties, their ministry of song. It mentions three—originally four (see the additional note) **heads**, and three singers: **Mattaniah, Bakbukiah, Obadiah.** Comparison with verses 8–9 and 11:17 shows that these are meant to be singers, not gatekeepers. The singers are described as performing in antiphonal choirs. This de-scription nicely paves the way for the references to the two choirs that had an important role in the wall dedication ceremony de-scribed in the next section (vv. 31, 38, 40). The text draws attention to their divine warrant—they perpetuated an institution that went back to **David**, who was inspired to found it **(man of God)**. The four leaders also appear in the list of Levitical signatories to the pledge in 10:9–13, and the first two are listed as returning with Ezra (Ezra 8:18–19), while two of the three singers were among the Levites who moved to Jerusalem in 11:15–17. Details of the **gatekeepers** follow in verse 25 in the form of family names, as comparison with 7:45 (= Ezra 2:42) shows.

**12:26** / By way of summary, a general date for the fore-going body of information from verse 12 on is given as **the days of Joiakim** as high priest. It takes its cue from the major list that began in verse 13, rather than from the dating of verse 23. His-tory had moved on since **the time of Jeshua** (v. 1), but still temple ministry faithfully continued. This statement expresses the purpose of this supplementary section: to try to give infor-mation about temple personnel in **Nehemiah**'s period and to categorize their ministry as ongoing. It loosely equates the pe-riod of Joiakim with that of Nehemiah and also of **Ezra.** The jux-taposition of the two leaders reflects the literary phenomena of the book of Nehemiah, in which they are associated by means of Ezra's appearance in chapter 8. Ezra's secondary position corre-sponds to this minor role.

## Additional Notes §12

**11:1** / For the differences between this account and Nehemiah's memoirs, see Williamson, *Ezra, Nehemiah,* p. 345.

**11:3** / **Leaders** translates a different Heb. word than that found in v. 1 and is lit. "heads" (NJPS), a shorthand reference to heads of families or "chiefs," as in 1 Chr. 5:7; 7:3; 8:28. The term **Levites** must here include the singers and gatekeepers of 7:44–45, as it generally does in Chronicles. The following list includes singers (v. 17) but not gatekeepers, who are listed separately (v. 19). The difference indicates a later hand (Williamson, *Ezra, Nehemiah,* p. 348).

**11:5** / For **Shelah,** contrast "the Shilonite" (NRSV), someone from Shiloh. The NIV has implicitly and correctly revocalized the Heb. word (see *BHS,* REB, and NJB), although not in 1 Chr. 9:5 (compare Num. 26:20). The Chronicler cited and updated vv. 3–11 in 1 Chr. 9:2–17.

**11:6** / The NRSV has "valiant warriors" for **able men** here and in v. 14, clarifying the military connotation. This military language, also found in "chief officer" in vv. 9 and 14 (compare 2 Kgs. 25:19), suggests that the list was originally compiled to record the militia that could be mobilized to defend the city.

**11:9** / The Heb. for **over the Second District of the city** must grammatically mean "second in command of the city" (NJB and NJPS; compare the NRSV and REB).

**11:10** / The related text in 1 Chr. 9:10 has two independent names for **Jedaiah; the son of Joiarib,** "Jedaiah; Jehoiarib," which helps explain the NIV's strange semicolon after Jedaiah here. The Chronicles text is supported by 12:6, 19, where Jehoiarib and Jedaiah are placed in the same generation, and by 1 Chr. 24:7, 17, where, together with **Jakin,** they are the names of three priestly divisions. The omission of **son of** would give a total of six priestly extended families.

**11:11** / The title **supervisor in the house of God** here refers to the high priest in relation to his administrative function (Bartlett, "Zadok," pp. 12f.). The same Heb. phrase occurs in 2 Chr. 31:13 (NIV "official in charge of the temple of God") with reference to the high priest of 2 Chr. 31:10.

**11:22** / **Uzzi** belonged to a later generation than Mattaniah in v. 17, but the number of generations indicates that he was contemporary with Zechariah, who took part in the wall dedication ceremony in 12:35. This suggests that Mattaniah belonged to an earlier period. **Service** refers to music and song.

**11:25** / **Villages** refer to unwalled communities (Lev. 25:31). **Kiriath Arba** is another name for Hebron. For most of the places mentioned in the following list, see the *Macmillan Bible Atlas*, p. 129, map 170. They fall into four distinct geographical clusters—in the Negev to the south, in the Shephelah to the west, in the mountains north and northwest of Jerusalem, and on the coastal plain in the far west. Since eleven of the Judean settlements are also found in the list of tribal towns in Josh. 15:20–62, the list has been credited to imaginary idealization. But in that case one would have expected close conformity with the list of Benjaminite towns in Josh. 18:21–28, which is not the case. Y. Aharoni, *The Land of the Bible: A Historical Geography* (2d ed.; tr. A. F. Rainey; Philadelphia: Westminster, 1979), pp. 409f., 416, has contended that the list presents nonexiled settlements, but the coastal ones at least were occupied after the exile.

**11:30** / **Were living** is lit. "camped" (NRSV), which may imply that they lived in many cases among non-Judean neighbors rather than as independent communities. A typological comparison with the wilderness period is sometimes suggested but is unlikely. If there is a typological allusion, it is to the period when the patriarchs shared Palestine with native groups (see Gen. 26:17; 33:18).

**11:36** / The move may have been occasioned by the fact that preexilic Levitical settlements were no longer located in the province, which consisted of Benjamin and the northern part of Judah. If so, the passage closes with a sober realization of the "not yet" character of its territorial hope.

**12:1–21** / In comparing the list of the four priestly families in 7:42 (= Ezra 2:39), we note that **Rehum** corresponds to "Harim" in v. 15, Jedaiah appears in vv. 6 and 7 (and also in vv. 19 and 21), and Immer (in the form Amariah) appears in vv. 2 and 13. Pashhur, however, does not appear in ch. 12. **Meremoth** corresponds to Meraioth (v. 15 mg.; NRSV).

**12:2** / The family name **Hattush** is lacking in v. 14; compare 10:4.

**12:7** / It is not clear who **their associates** were. Kellermann, *Nehemia*, p. 106, suggested that a new heading began here: "Their associates . . . , namely the Levites, were . . ."

**12:8** / **Judah** seems to correspond to Hodaviah in 7:43 (= Ezra 2:40) and Hodiah in 9:5; 10:12–13. It has no counterpart in vv. 24–25.

**12:9** / **Unni** takes the place of Obadiah in v. 25; the name reappears for a singer in 1 Chr. 15:18.

**12:10–11** / The list of six names probably has some missing links, as is common in ancient genealogies, which over a long period were representative rather than exhaustive. For a comprehensive discussion of chronological problems associated with the postexilic high priesthood, see J. C. VanderKam, "Jewish High Priests of the Persian Period: Is the List Complete?" *Priesthood and Cult in Ancient Israel* (ed. G. A. Anderson and S. M. Olyan; JSOTSup 125; Sheffield: Sheffield Academic Press, 1991), pp. 67–91. Beginning about the year 520, the list goes down to

**Jaddua,** who may be the high priest of that name who met Alexander the Great in 332 according to Josephus, *Ant.* 11.326–331. The listing runs via **Eliashib,** the high priest in Nehemiah's period in 445. The corresponding name for **Jonathan** in v. 22 is Johanan, who is not necessarily the same person—perhaps a brother. Jonathan is known from the Elephantine papyri to have been in office in the years 411 and 408.

**12:12** / The list of twenty-one families was achieved by adding the six in vv. 19–21. It attests the gradual evolution to the eventual fixed twenty-four divisions of priests named in 1 Chr. 24:1–19, which grew from the basic four families in Neh. 7:39–42 (= Ezra 2:36–39). These divisions were maintained for centuries of temple worship (see Luke 1:5).

**12:17** / **Of Miniamin's and of Moadiah's:** Contrast the NRSV "of Miniamin, of Moadiah." The name of the current representative of the Miniamin family was lost, as the three dots in NJPS and NJB acknowledge.

**12:22** / **Darius the Persian:** It is difficult to say which of the three kings named Darius is meant, especially since the adjacent text is uncertain (contrast the NRSV). It may be Darius III, who reigned 336–330, which would fit the reference to **Jaddua** according to Josephus' dating. If Jaddua is a later addition to the list, as the form of the Heb. may suggest, the reference could be to Darius II (423–404). Then vv. 22–23 refer to the same closing period.

**12:23** / The **descendants of Levi** could refer to both priests and Levites, but here it seems to relate to Levites, as the same Heb. phrase does in Ezra 8:15.

**12:24** / Here and in vv. 8–9 singers are classified among Levites, as in 11:15–18, but not in the earlier 7:43–44 (= Ezra 2:40–41). The gatekeepers of v. 25 are also classified as Levites—a phenomenon that parallels the full development reflected in Chronicles and indicates the relative lateness of this list. The Heb. *ben,* **son of,** appears to be a corruption of "Binnui" (REB, NJB), which appears in v. 8. See *BHS* and the note on Ezra 2:40. **Who stood opposite them** appears to take the first named Levites as singers, which is not in accord with 11:16 or 7:43. Verses 8–9 avoid this implication. **One section responding to the other** should be, rather, "in shifts" (NJPS) or "turn by turn" (REB). For the traditional attribution to **David,** compare v. 36 and also Ezra 3:10. The Chronicler developed it: see 1 Chr. 16; 25.

**12:25** / **Mattaniah, Bakbukiah, Obadiah:** The verse division in the MT is faulty (see the NJB). These are the names of the singing "associates" in v. 24, as 11:17 confirms. "Mattaniah" is placed three generations earlier in 11:22 and 12:35. "Obadiah," replaced by Unni in v. 9, corresponds to a singer Abda in 11:17. **Meshullam** corresponds to Shallum in 7:45 (= Ezra 2:42) and 1 Chr. 9:17, 19.

**12:26** / **In the days of … and in the days of:** The overall context suggests that only one general period is in view. The epithets **governor … priest and scribe** depend respectively on 5:14 and 8:1, 2, 9 (the Heb. term for "governor" in 8:9 is different).

## §13 The Grand Finale (Neh. 12:27–43)

It was time for a celebration. We need to remember that the edited account continues from 11:1–20, and what intervenes is a compilation of supplementary material. The first half of chapter 11 briefly told the story of the repopulation of Jerusalem and enumerated the families who were involved in it. It used a source other than Nehemiah's memoirs—one that focused on the role of the people and their leaders, not Nehemiah. The editor used this same source from 12:27 to 12:30. In verse 31 we return to the memoirs, although the lists of priests and Levites in verses 33–36 and 41–42 reflect the other source or independent archival information available to the editor. The ceremony of **the dedication of the wall of Jerusalem** marks the climax of Nehemiah's two-part mission, just as the dedication of the completed temple in Ezra 6:16–17 signaled the climax of the first mission in Ezra 1–6. The ceremony seems to have involved only the people who had moved to the capital and the leaders who already lived there (11:1). It is significant that only extra Levites, not the whole people of Judah, were summoned from outside the city (vv. 27–29). The ceremony celebrated not just the completion of the wall but also the program to repopulate "the holy city" (11:1, 18). That is why this ceremony could not have been placed immediately after chapter 6. It had to be placed after the second part of Nehemiah's mission in chapters 7 and 11 had been accomplished.

**12:27–30** / We were told in 11:20 that (apart from those who moved to Jerusalem) the rest of the community, including priests and Levites, lived in their own towns. These temple personnel evidently lived there when they were not on duty. **Levites** who were musicians and **singers** and not currently on duty were required as extra staff for this special ceremony, the latter for the "large choirs" of verse 31. The ceremony was to take the form of two separate processions on the wall, dedicating it foot by foot, and then a joint service of sacrifice at the temple. Its keynote was to be joy, which the account highlights at the beginning and end (vv. 27, 43). The vocal and musical contributions of the Levites were to express and stimulate that joy by praising God. This group of Levites had settled locally in **villages** south, east, and north of the city.

Rites of purification were required, initially by **the priests and Levites** on their own behalf and then for **the people,** the old and new citizens of Jerusalem, and for **the gates and the wall** they were dedicating to the glory of God. To purify means to prepare for a sacred purpose. Such rites preceded approaching something holy. In this case it was for the holy city of Jerusalem that the tasks of rebuilding gates and walls and of importing representative citizens had been accomplished. This ceremony put these new elements before God in order to integrate them into the sacred space that spread out from the temple to the entire city.

**12:31–39** / These verses slot an extract from Nehemiah's memoirs into place, reverting to the **I** of 7:5. The account of the sacred processions, mainly on top of the city wall, serves as a triumphant counterpoint to Nehemiah's solitary walk around the ruined wall in 2:12–15 and to the communal repair of the wall in chapter 3. The two processions are symmetrical in composition: a Levitical choir, a leading layman (**Hoshaiah** in v. 32 and Nehemiah in v. 38) accompanied by **half** the civil **leaders,** and then seven priestly trumpeters, and eight Levitical musicians led by a conductor. The focus of the present account is on the music and song provided by the priestly trumpeters and (especially) the Levites. Linking the Levitical musicians with the inspired **David** (v. 36) emphasizes their traditional, authentic role. Similarly the first conductor, **Zechariah** (v. 35), is graced with a pedigree traced back to **Asaph** in David's era. The very arrangement of the processions to the temple, with singers in front, musicians in the rear, and lay leaders in between, reflects the preexilic processional order given in Psalm 68:25–28.

We can trace most of the routes taken by the two processions by comparing them with the places mentioned in chapter 3. Apparently they both started at the Valley Gate in the western stretch of wall, where Nehemiah had set out in 2:13, and then went different ways. The first procession went south and followed the wall around to **the Fountain Gate** on the southeast side of the city. It evidently left the top of the wall at that point because it was at too steep an angle to walk on, but had rejoined it by the time they passed two landmarks, **the house of David** (or at least its site) on the left and **the Water Gate** on their right. From that point they evidently went straight through the city to the temple area. The other procession, in which Nehemiah walked behind the choir, went north along the wall as far as **the Sheep Gate** on the northern stretch of wall and then proceeded away from the wall to the temple area.

**12:40–43** / The rest of the service took place in the temple area **(the house of God)**, in its courts (see 8:16; 13:7). The **choirs,** now in their customary antiphonal role, although much larger than usual in honor of the special occasion, took their places in the inner court east of the huge altar of burnt offering where 2 Chronicles 5:12 places them, probably on the temple steps. They accompanied the offering of multiple **sacrifices,** whose role in the worship service is left undeveloped. Instead, the focus remains on Levitical music and song in expressing the joy of the sacred occasion. The descriptions of "great" **choirs** (v. 31, NRSV), **great sacrifices, great joy** make the magnificence of the ceremony exuberantly evident, but the greatest of these was joy. Like the festive joy of Ezra 6:22, it is traced back to the providence of **God** in bringing Israel to this high point in its history. The men of the families who now lived in the city, and also their wives and **children,** all echoed this joy. Here was the spirit of Psalm 147:12–13:

> Extol the LORD, O Jerusalem;
> praise your God, O Zion,
> for he strengthens the bars of your gates
> and blesses your people within you.

The mountains of Judah reverberated with the joyful **sound** on this day to remember, this milestone gratefully reached in Israel's postexilic pilgrimage toward renewal.

---

### Additional Notes §13

**12:27** / Musicians and singers are here included among **the Levites,** as in 11:15–18. This reflects a development from the earliest postexilic period, when they were differentiated (7:43–44 = Ezra 2:40–41). The 284 Levites resident in Jerusalem (11:18) evidently did not include enough members of this group. **Were sought out . . . and were brought** is lit. "they sought out . . . to bring them" (NRSV). The subject is presumably "the leaders of the people settled in Jerusalem" (11:1).

**12:28–29** / For these places, which feature as early settlements of the returning exiles in 7:26–30 (= Ezra 2:21–26), apart from **(Beth) Gilgal** near Jericho, see *Macmillan Bible Atlas*, p. 129, map 170.

**12:30** / **Purified:** For the particular purificatory rites, see Williamson, *Ezra, Nehemiah*, p. 373.

**12:31** / **On top of the wall:** The mg. "alongside" here and in v. 38 reflects the ambiguity of the Heb. prepositional phrase, but the verb **go up** clearly points to the meaning. The new eastern wall was eight feet across, archaeologists have discovered, wide enough to walk along the top. **Right:** The situation of the Dung Gate in 2:13; 3:14 shows that, as often in the OT, the meaning is "south" (NJPS).

**12:35** / **As well as . . . and also:** The NIV has rightly restored "and also." In the MT, an incorrect sentence division led to having the priests enumerated in the following list of names, **Zechariah . . . and his associates** (see the NRSV, REB, and NJPS). But these are clearly Levitical musicians, as the name of Asaph shows by comparison with 11:17. The mistake in the MT was not only to omit "and" before "Zechariah," but also to put the conjunction before the priests whose names have been given in vv. 33–34; see *BHS* and the NJB. The parallel grouping in v. 41 leads us to the same conclusion. **Some priests** is lit. "sons of the priests," not here meaning "young priests" (NRSV, NJPS), but in the idiomatic sense of members of the priestly caste (BDB, p. 121). The phrase also occurs in this sense in Ezra 2:61, although not in the parallel Neh. 7:63, where the absence of "sons" shows that the meaning there is simply "priests." **Trumpets:** Priests would sound trumpet blasts to announce the beginning of the processional part of the service and its constituent parts (see Num. 10:8, 10; 1 Chr. 16:6). "Zechariah" . . . **Mattaniah:** For another great-grandson of Mattaniah in Nehemiah's period, see 11:22 and contrast 11:17.

**12:36** / **Ezra the scribe led the procession:** This statement does not accord with the symmetry of the two processions. Nor is it likely that "Ezra" in v. 33, among priestly trumpeters, is evidence of his real presence. "Ezra" was evidently added to the text at some stage as seemingly appropriate, especially after v. 26. As in v. 26, v. 36 reflects the presence of Neh. 8 in the final form of the book and so the role of the Torah as an indispensable aid to success in God's work.

**12:37** / The phrase **on the ascent to the wall** should be, rather, "at the ascent of the wall" (NRSV). Since the top of the wall was too steep, they climbed **the steps** and returned to the wall when it was more level.

**12:38** / **Half the people** refers to the other half of a particular group, the leaders of Judah cited in v. 31—the half mentioned in v. 40 (Barthélemy, *Critique textuelle*, vol. 1, p. 574).

**12:39** / **Over**, or "past" (Williamson, *Ezra, Nehemiah*, pp. 367, 375), see the note on 8:16. **The Gate of the Guard** was presumably a temple gate. It might have been an entry point to "the court of the guard" in 3:25, although that lies more to the south than we expect. It may be another name for "the Inspection Gate" of 3:31. The northeastern stretch of wall, from the Water Gate to the Sheep Gate, was apparently not traversed; we do not know why.

**12:40** / For the performance of music and song during the sacrificial service, see Kleinig, *The Lord's Song*, ch. 3.

**12:41–42** / One would expect the information about participating priests and Levites to appear in v. 38, with reference to the second procession. The editor inserted it here instead in order to illustrate the rejoicing at the service. **The choirs sang** should be, rather, "the musicians played loudly," especially on cymbals (Clines, *Ezra, Nehemiah, Esther,* p. 233). The Heb. noun may refer to singers or musicians according to the context. The Heb. verb is used as in 1 Chr. 15:19 (NIV "sound"). Here the second processional group of musicians is in view, parallel with the first group in vv. 35b–36a.

Was there anything else left to do after the grand finale of the wall dedication ceremony? Indeed there was, according to the editor. At the close of Ezra 1–6 the narrator recognized in the dedication of the rebuilt temple an opportunity to put into place normative guidelines that echoed the Torah concerning the regular staffing of the temple. Similarly here, the editor supplements the wall dedication story with the enactment of two guidelines that brought the community into line with religious tradition in 12:44–47 and 13:1–3. Each of these passages begins with the same Hebrew phrase, "On that day" (NRSV) in 12:44 and **On that day** in 13:1, echoing that very phrase in verse 43. However, a note of discord is struck in 13:4, where a time reference to a flashback, **Before this,** qualifies the second passage. This is the editor's introduction to the following passage about Nehemiah's reforms during his second administration. This all takes place after his first term as governor, with which chapters 2–12 are concerned. The timing of the guidelines in 12:44 and 13:1 is at odds with the real chronology— one would expect "After this" in 13:4. As we have observed before in Ezra-Nehemiah, there is an audacious clash between the literary composition and the historical timetable in the interests of a spiritual lesson taught by the editor. Joyful celebration must be responsibly matched by reform that bolsters sacred tradition, as in Ezra 6:16–18. After worship should come the adoption of a way of life that equally honors God by reaffirming God's revealed will. The day of worship must be a day to institute changes in the communal lifestyle.

A long extract from Nehemiah's memoirs about his religious reforms backs the editorial guidelines (13:4–31). Parallelism marks the block of four main reforms: Nehemiah discovers and describes a problem, reacts strongly, and introduces measures to rectify the problem. A formula for God's remembrance rounds off the second reform (13:14), which is closely related to the first. The third and fourth reforms also end with this formula (13:22b, 29), while a fourth instance of the formula comes after a survey of Nehemiah's reforms at the close (13:31b). Rhetorical questions are a feature of his verbal reactions to those responsible for the problems in the second and subsequent reforms. An introductory **In those days** (13:15) marks the transition to the third and fourth reforms. This general time marker and the remembrance formula indicate that 13:4–31 falls into four sections: verses 4–14; 15–22; 23–29, and the concluding verses 30–31. While not all of the material thematically fits the guidelines from chapter 13, most of it does. In general, the extract's purpose is to show that vigilance was necessary to maintain the guidelines. We noted in chapter 10 that the community's pledge was a measured adaptation of the ad hoc measures of Nehemiah, set mostly in his second administration in chapter 13. The introductory "Before this" in 13:4 admits that 13:4–31 also preceded the guidelines of 12:44–13:3 or at least the second one in 13:1–3. But that is not the point the editor wished to make. Rather, the guidelines are the crowning climax to the pledge of chapter 10, turning communal promise into performance. The guidelines build a bridge between the pledge and the reforms. These guidelines are monitored by Nehemiah's reforms, which have become responses to them in the years after they were laid down. The insights and achievements of the past do not automatically carry over into the present. Instead, deliberate and vigorous reimplementation is required. Nehemiah is the servant of the community as he seeks to help them maintain the values they affirmed, intervening vigorously whenever he saw them threatened. The editor envisioned him as a model of vigilance to succeeding generations. "Stand at the crossroads and look," God had once said; "ask for the ancient paths, ask where the good way is, and walk in it" (Jer. 6:16). The guidelines correspond to those ancient paths, rediscovered by the postexilic community. In turn, each generation had to strenuously seek out that good way for itself and walk in it.

**12:44–47** / These verses return to the theme of one of the stipulations in 10:35–39, the supply of food for the temple personnel, which required the provision of storage space in the temple and of staff to administer the arrangements. It was a principle of the Torah that temple worship required backing from material and human resources. Paul reiterated this principle before hermeneutically applying it: "Those who serve at the altar share in what is offered on the altar" (1 Cor. 9:13). Here the editor assures us that proper arrangements were made for feeding **priests and Levites** on duty, as **required by the Law.** The community at large willingly supported the temple staff by giving the required dues because they were **pleased with** them or, more literally, "rejoiced over" them (NRSV). The joy of worship (v. 43) shifted to the joy of giving to maintain the infrastructure of worship. As a result, the temple staff could do their work for **God.** This meant, too, that **singers and gatekeepers** could continue a tradition that went back to **David** and **Solomon,** founders of the temple. So two traditions could be honored—that of the Torah and that of the first temple. The editor expands the latter theme in verse 46, with the same pride in religious origins that traced Zechariah's origins back to **Asaph** in verse 35 (compare 7:44). Members of each generation were stewards responsible for keeping up this spiritual heritage. The survival of temple worship in the editor's day was taken as evidence that the postexilic generations—stretching from the governorship of **Zerubbabel** (7:7), when the temple was rebuilt, to that of **Nehemiah**—honored this heritage by supplying the **daily** needs of those who served in the temple. In Nehemiah's case, 13:10–14 will bear witness to such faithfulness.

**13:1–3** / The second guideline to be established will be formulated in verse 3. The setting is a public service at which the Torah was read. Evidently hermeneutical application was also given on which the people were to act. The editor apparently knew of a tradition of commitment in response to the Torah. **The people** here are not the residents of Jerusalem, as in 12:30, but a full gathering of **Israel,** which was no less than **the assembly of God**—a Torah description of the authentic, contemporary representatives of the covenant people. The reading was Deuteronomy 23:3–5a, which is echoed in verses 1b–2. This text, along with the related Deuteronomy 7:1–6, featured in the teaching of Ezra (Ezra 9:1), while Ezra 9:12 referred to Deuteronomy 23:6. As there, mention of particular neighboring peoples was interpreted in terms of a blanket ruling against admitting members of any such group to the community. Here the interpretation of the Torah was made the basis of a guideline for the expulsion of aliens from the religious community. This guideline was intended as the fulfillment of the pledge against intermarriage, itself based on Deuteronomy

7:3, in 10:30. The mixed marriages in 13:23–27 and the Tobiah story in 13:4–9 will illustrate this further.

**13:4–9** / Here Nehemiah carries out the first of a series of religious reforms during his second administration. The issue for the editor was not that the guidelines were broken, but that they needed to be rigorously reinstated. The general structure that shapes each reform, noted above, is amplified here by introductory material to give the background of the problem. This introduction also explains Nehemiah's enforced absence from Judah—the reason he had not been able to stop it from happening. Like the final reform measure in verse 28, it concerns a political enemy who had featured in the earlier stories of opposition to the wall project in chapters 2, 4, and 6. In the context of the memoirs, the idea of one so hostile to the work of God occupying a room in the temple precincts was obviously abhorrent. But how did the editor relate it to the established guidelines? To a certain degree the problem illustrates the first one, since a room dedicated to contributions for the temple staff was misused. But it was mainly regarded as impinging on the second guideline. The Hebrew term rendered **closely associated** can mean "connected by marriage" (REB), and mention of that very connection in the memoirs in 6:18 suggests this meaning here. For Nehemiah himself there was less focus on the factor of intermarriage. Eliashib would have been targeted as the chief offender otherwise, like the offenders in verses 23 and 28. The main concern for Nehemiah was to decontaminate the room inside the temple area, as verse 14 indicates. The editor, however, at this point has the guideline of 13:1–3 in view. He doubtless wanted readers to recall that Tobiah had regularly been called the "Ammonite" in earlier narratives, and so qualified literally for the Torah prohibition in verse 1. If Tobiah was not a bona fide member of the religious community, he could not dwell in the temple in the metaphorical sense of worshiping there at festival times (Ps. 15:1), let alone blatantly occupy a temple storeroom as his Jerusalem lodging. The governor personally **threw** Tobiah's furniture **out** and had the room cleansed and restored to its proper use. As governor, he had official authority in religious matters.

**13:10–14** / The resolution of the first problem disclosed a second—infringement of the first guideline. The storeroom was embarrassingly empty of part of its intended contents, the Levitical tithes (v. 5). Consequently, the posts of **the Levites and singers**

were also empty. Although they received a duty assignment, they had no food and returned to their off-duty quarters around Jerusalem (12:27–29) and elsewhere. Nehemiah blamed the civil leaders for letting this happen, presumably by not enforcing the collection of tithes along with other provincial taxes. His indignant question echoed on the literary level—and inspired on the chronological level—the summarizing statement of intent in 10:39, "We will not neglect the house of our God." He took affairs into his own hands by recalling the missing temple staff, ordering the payment of tithes, and setting up a distribution department. The first of a series of refrains follows in verse 14, a petition to **God** to **Remember** his loyal acts on behalf of the temple (vv. 4–9) and its **services** (vv. 10–13). In position and content it is parallel to the petition in 5:19. The writer to the Hebrews could give assurance that "God is not unjust; he will not forget your work and the love you have shown him" (Heb. 6:10).

**13:15–22** / This next problem of Sabbath breaking has little to do with the guidelines. It was included here because of the mention of **Men from Tyre** in verse 16 as another case of foreign influence. From a wider perspective it echoes the stipulation not to buy from foreign traders on the Sabbath (10:31), which in fact Nehemiah's reform inspired. The nub of the problem was a Sabbath market in Jerusalem, though grape treading was also involved. They were breaking the traditional injunction against work on the Sabbath, including selling (see Amos 8:5) and the associated conveyance of goods for sale (see Jer. 17:21, 27). Nehemiah blamed the Judean **nobles,** who doubtless resided in Jerusalem and formed a council of elders, for not exercising their authority. His speech has Jeremiah 17:19–23, 27 in view, which closes with a threat to destroy the capital. With hindsight, the governor thought of what had happened in the year 587 and the disastrous aftermath that dogged Judah thereafter. Like Ezra in Ezra 9:14 (also compare 10:14), he warned of a fresh outbreak of divine **wrath.** Again he took matters into his own hands. He closed the city gates near the market on Friday evening when the Sabbath began and took the extra precaution of temporarily manning them with his own staff. He warned traders who lingered hopefully outside, scaring them off. Then he put **Levites** in charge of **the gates** on the Sabbath, regarding maintenance of its holiness as an extension of their religious duties.

**13:23–29** / The two incidents in these verses connect with the second guideline in 13:1–3 and its prohibition against mixed marriages. The reference to **Ammon and Moab,** perhaps editorially inserted along with the matching reference to other peoples in verse 24, clinches the connection, although Nehemiah's report concentrates on cases of intermarriage with women from the province of **Ashdod.** He heard, rather than saw, evidence of the problem in the children's speech learned at their mothers' knee. Language is an emotive indicator of cultural identity. Welsh, Catalan, and Canadian French are modern instances. Hebrew had religious importance because it was the language of Torah and prayer. Nehemiah accosted the children's fathers and physically attacked them in his anger. His vehemence anticipates that of Jesus in driving out the temple traders, especially in the Johannine account (John 2:14–16). The oath Nehemiah made them take (v. 25) is couched in the language of Deuteronomy 7:3. It links with the similarly worded stipulation of 10:30. His ad hoc reaction apparently leaves the matter unresolved. Missing are the divorce proceedings of Ezra 10. Nehemiah was evidently concerned with preventing such marriages in the future and did not make his ruling retroactive. It thus falls short of the guideline in 13:3. The governor based his tirade on 1 Kings 11, contrasting it with the positive account of Solomon's reign in 1 Kings 2–10, especially 3:12–13 and 10:23. Nehemiah denounced these husbands as a pernicious influence on other Judeans. Whereas in the literal KJV the Tobiah affair had been called an "evil" (v. 7) and the breach of the Sabbath an "evil thing" (v. 17), this problem is branded a "great evil" (v. 27). It was a cardinal sin, and so Nehemiah's reaction was more physically vehement than in the other cases. This sin undermined the essence of the community, just as the pernicious wrong of verse 2 had struck at the very existence of Israel.

Nehemiah took a still more rigorous line in the case of a member of the high priestly family who had married a daughter of **Sanballat.** Beyond natural enmity, the editor probably wanted his readers to remember that the Samarians were one of the "surrounding nations" (6:16) and so featured in the stipulation forbidding intermarriage with "peoples of the land" (10:30, NRSV). There were special rulings for marriage in the case of the high priest's family (Lev. 21:13–15; contrast 21:7), which Nehemiah had in view in the negative petition of verse 29, with which 6:14 may be compared. Infringement deserved punishment beyond Nehemiah's own measures.

**13:30–31** / In verse 30, the more literal NRSV is to be followed, which reverses **the priests and the Levites** and **them.** "Them" probably refers to the people. The second clause seems to allude to the regular supply of food that in turn made possible the regular execution of temple duties. This brief summary of Nehemiah's reforms neatly parallels the two guidelines and shows why the editor used this long extract from the memoirs. There is also a brief reference to further religious reforms that correspond to the stipulations of 10:34–35. Then Nehemiah committed himself to God's good providence, praying in effect that "the Lord" would "reward" him "for whatever good" he had done (Eph. 6:8).

---

## Additional Notes §14

---

**12:44** / The vocabulary is close enough to that of 10:37–39 to establish that these verses are echoing that particular stipulation.

**12:45** / **The service of purification** presumably involved the rites carried out in the wall dedication ceremony (12:30); there may also be a glance ahead to 13:9. Mention of **singers and gatekeepers** recalls the inverse mention in 10:39, while v. 47b, though it uses different vocabulary, recalls the Levites' tithing of their tithes in 10:38.

**12:47** / **The other Levites:** The NIV has inserted "other," as comparison with the NRSV and MT shows. As in 10:37–39, they seem to be distinguished from the two lower orders, as they are also in the memoirs in 13:5, although there the singers and gatekeepers were evidently meant to receive the Levitical tithes as well, so that the old distinctions were breaking down in certain respects.

**13:1** / **The Book of Moses was read aloud** is lit. "there was a reading in the book of Moses." The impersonal passive parallels the indefinite passive at the beginning of v. 44. **Ever** is an interpretation of "even down to the tenth generation" in Deut. 23:3, and **the assembly of God** corresponds to "the assembly of the LORD" in Deut. 23:3.

**13:2** / The verb **had hired** is actually sg., as in the MT of Deut. 23:4 (MT v. 5), with reference to King Balak of Moab (see Num. 22:1–21). Fishbane, *Biblical Interpretation*, pp. 126f., finds a link with Tobiah and Sanballat's hiring prophets in 6:12–14.

**13:3** / **Who were of foreign descent** is lit. "admixture" (NJPS). The use of the related verb in Ezra 9:2 ("mingled") in connection with intermarriage is significant.

**13:4** / In view of his job, **Eliashib** was probably a different person from the high priest of 3:1.

**13:5** / **Incense** was an ingredient of **grain offerings,** most of which were eaten by priests (Lev. 2:1–2; 6:15–18).

**13:6** / The unusual title **king of Babylon** may have been used here because the king was residing in Babylon at the time. In Ezra 5:13, Cyrus was so called because of the dating of his reign from the conquest of Babylon.

**13:10** / There seems to be an allusion here to the tradition of Levitical cities (see Num. 35: 2–5; Josh. 21; 1 Chr. 6:54–80; 2 Chr. 11:14; 23:2).

**13:11** / **Them** refers to the Levites and singers of v. 10. The gatekeepers (v. 5) may be omitted because they customarily resided in Jerusalem (see 11:19).

**13:14** / **Blot out:** from the book of human deeds recorded by God. See Ps. 56:8; Isa. 65:6; Dan. 7:10. The Heb. term for **what I have so faithfully done** refers to acts inspired by covenant loyalty or love; the reiterated **my God** reinforces it. Nehemiah's acts were a response to God's covenant love (v. 22).

**13:15–16** / The market was probably held north of the temple near the Fish Gate (see 3:3; 12:39).

**13:22** / **Levites:** Gatekeepers are not specified; compare 7:1.

**13:24** / We do not know what **language** the people of **Ashdod** spoke at this time, whether it was the old Philistine language, Aramaic, or Nabataean. The Ammonites and Moabites would have used different Semitic dialects.

**13:25** / **Pulled out their hair:** Nehemiah's treatment of the men of Judah may be contrasted with Ezra's (Ezra 9:3), where he pulled out his own hair. It was perhaps the leadership tactics of an extrovert (Nehemiah) in contrast to those of an introvert (Ezra).

**13:26** / **Marriages like these:** The exegetical link with Deut. 23:3 was Solomon marrying Moabite and Ammonite women in 1 Kgs. 11:1. **Loved by his God** reflects Solomon's other name, Jedidiah, which means "loved by the LORD" (2 Sam. 12:24–25).

**13:27** / The precise force of the verb **Must we hear now** is uncertain, probably "Shall we then listen to you (and do . . . )" (NRSV); compare the REB, "Are we then to follow your example." Another option is to take the verb as passive, comparing Deut. 4:32, with the sense that they had never heard of such a thing being done by others in the community.

**13:28** / The reference to **the high priest** could qualify either **Joiada** or **Eliashib. Drove him away** refers to expulsion to Samaria.

**13:29** / **Them** refers to members of the high priestly family mentioned in v. 28, those responsible for the marriage.

# *Esther*

Timothy S. Laniak

# Introduction

## The Story of Esther

Biblical stories are in only one sense "contained" in biblical books. They are literary creations that set and keep in motion the paradigms of the communities of faith by whom and for whom they are created.[1] A biblical story calls its readers to enter its world, to be captivated by its characters, intrigued by its plot, and affectively engaged through suspense and complication till its final denouement. Biblical stories invite us into a world contoured by ancient conventions, yet pulsing with continuous relevance.

Commentaries are bound by their own conventions to read books of the Bible chapter-by-chapter, verse-by-verse, and word-by-word. This is an important ancient form of interpretation, but one that often leads to an atomization of "the text." It tends toward what has been called "excavative scholarship." But a story is a *whole* that conveys meaning through its totality, through the choice and placement of its parts, *and through the sum of its parts.* Therefore, a primary challenge of "commenting" on biblical narrative is tracking the larger story within its constituent elements, allowing the analytical to serve the aesthetic.

Biblical historiography has three dimensions: the literary, the historical, and the theological (or ideological). Much of modern critical scholarship has focused on the historicity of biblical narratives, asking "What happened?" The more recent interests of contemporary readers prefer the literary question, "How does the story work?" Theological meaning emerges out of the interaction between the artistic (literary) world of ancient authors and their referential (historical) world.[2] Reading biblical narrative without considering all of these three dimensions skews one's interpretation.

One more general word about biblical stories is in order. Two elements, in dynamic tension, distinguish historical narrative.[3] On one hand, there is a concrete, natural, historical *realism.* On the other hand, there is a proclivity for *romance:* serendipity, irony, and miracle. For biblical writers, the romantic impulse is not simply a function of literary artistry; it is also a feature of their referential world. As David Carr insists, "narrative is not merely a possibly successful way of describing events; its structure inheres in the events themselves."[4] The narrator locates and re-presents the order and meaning and transcendence in historical events. The narrator finds *kairos* (critical moment) in the *chronos* (sequential time).

With these introductory comments in mind, it will serve us well to consider briefly the following literary elements that contribute to the story of Esther: *point of view, setting, plot, themes, characterization, intertextuality,* and *genre.* The aim is better to appreciate the much-loved story of Esther in its wholeness by discerning its rudiments. The historical events of the book will be discussed further below.

The *point of view* of the narrator is important as the frame within which the meanings of the story emerge. To discern point of view, the reader pays attention to the choices, emphases, and silences of a story. In Esther, the narrator is omniscient, privy not only to conversations in highly restricted areas of the Persian palace but also to the private thoughts and feelings of certain individuals. Through these vignettes, the reader catches glimpses of a fickle king and a sinister prime minister, a Jewish exile with unshakable convictions, and his younger, adopted cousin who is swept by destiny into a crisis of genocidal proportions. With a sardonic point of view, the author of Esther presents a satire on the Persian king and his nobles. The story is clearly written from the perspective of the Jews in Diaspora.

Esther is more than a window into the fictive world of a creative author; it has an external referent with a well-defined *setting.* This setting is the Persian court of the historical King Xerxes, a court that Esther 1 elaborately details. Readers witness the extravagance of the Persian palace and the extent of its empire, the significant role of lavish banquets, the potent sensitivities to status and gender, and the consequence of violating social roles and rules. In short, we are introduced to the world Esther must master for the salvation of her people. The story will end with the Jews securely positioned in this world—a world all the better for their place in it.

Authors construct a setting with details pertinent to the story's *plot.* The plot in Esther follows the familiar U-shape development of a comic design: setting, conflict, response, resolution. It has many of the traditional elements of a story with universal appeal: a beautiful heroine, a strong hero; an evil villain, a powerful king; opulence and decadence; ethnic rivalry and civil war. Conflict (and subsequent "complication") is an essential ingredient for this type of plot. Esther has sustained conflict, the kind that tests the protagonist's character and maintains the story's suspense. Chance, or fate, takes a central role. There is surprise and irony. And there are many unanswered questions that keep the imagination of the reader active throughout.

The plot is managed through graphic descriptions (e.g., of the palace in chapter 1 or of Haman's interior world in chapter 6), action (e.g., the handling of Esther in chapter 2 or the king's return from the garden in chapter 7), and discourse (e.g., between Mordecai and Esther in chapter 4).

It is instructive to compare the structure and plot of Esther with the four "movements" of biblical laments. While laments are not written as narratives, they echo the realities of individuals and communities in crisis. First, a crisis challenges one's favored position. A period of abandonment and isolation follows this threat. An anticipated reversal eventually takes place, followed by a state of renewed and enhanced favor. This pattern is repeated more than once in the stories of Joseph and David, and it is also found in the narrative portions of Job and Daniel.[5]

There are two *themes* that also function as patterning devices in the story: reversals and banquets. J. Levenson has organized the fifteen reversals of the story in a chiastic structure as follows:[6]

A[1] Greatness of Ahasuerus (1:1–8)
    B[1] Two Banquets of the Persians (1:1–8)
        C[1] Esther Identifies as a Gentile (2:10–20)
            D[1] Elevation of Haman (3:1)
                E[1] Anti-Jewish Edict (3:12–15)
                    F[1] Fateful Exchange of Mordecai and Esther (ch. 4)
                        G[1] First Banquet of Threesome (5:5–8)

A[2] Greatness of Ahasuerus and Mordecai (10:1–3)
    B[2] Two Banquets of the Jews (9:17–19)
        C[2] Gentiles Identify as Jews (8:17)
            D[2] Elevation of Mordecai (8:15)
                E[2] Pro-Jewish Edict (8:9–14)
                    F[2] Fateful Exchange of Xerxes and Esther (7:1–6)
                        G[2] Second Banquet of Threesome (7:1–6)

                            H Royal Procession (ch. 6)

The feasts (Heb. *mishtot*) of the story punctuate this chiastic organization.[7] The two banquets of the Jews in chapter 9 echo the king's two banquets in chapter 1. Esther's enthronement banquet in 2:18 matches the celebration of Mordecai's elevation in 8:17. Esther's two banquets with the king and Haman (in chapters 5 and 7) sit at the center of the plot, following the fast (anti-banquet) of the Jews in chapter 4.

*Characterization* is also an important feature of the story of Esther.[8] The narrator portrays the king's dependence on his advisers by repeated descriptions of his malleable behavior in moments of crisis. A glimpse into Haman's reeling mind in chapter 6 exposes his narcissism. The story provides a satire on the foreign king and the villain, "the enemy Haman." Like wisdom literature, the book of Esther describes its primary characters in binary categories: the foolish and the wise, the righteous and the wicked.

The two heroes have less in common with each other than do the king and Haman. Mordecai is a static, unchanging character who is known most fully through his deeds of loyalty and conviction. The young Esther begins compliantly, subtly characterized as such by a string of Hebrew passives in chapter 2. What happens in her life, happens *to her*. She is a pawn in a game played by powerful men. However, she is transformed through the ordeal Haman's edict forces on her. Remarkable changes take place in the heart of this once young, dependent orphan who finally becomes a confident, assertive, and competent leader. In the final chapters, she speaks in imperatives and authorizes edicts.

The result of this skillfully crafted narrative is a story that conveys meaning on many levels and, one might say, in concentric circles. What is Esther "about"? The book of Esther is about a young girl who becomes queen. It is about the minority Jewish community in the dependent state of Diaspora (represented by Esther), navigating a precarious existence in two worlds. Esther is about the perseverance and loyalty of Esther and Mordecai and the Jewish community in Diaspora. It is about the salvation of the Jewish community at one moment in time. It is about their salvation at any time. Esther is about the origins of Purim, the annual celebration of their salvation from fools and villains. Esther is about the triumph of right over wrong, of God's people over their enemies. Esther also hints that God has once again saved this people through an unlikely vessel.

The author of Esther employs many conventions, themes, motifs, and terms borrowed from other stories in the Hebrew Bible. Esther is a thoroughly "biblical" book in this sense. In its *intertextuality*,[9] it provides an *interbiblical* dialog, making allusions to other heroes and incidents throughout. The naming of God in these other stories makes his presence all the more implicit in Esther.

The stories of Joseph and Esther share many different elements.[10] Phrases and motifs in common include the motif of "favor" in the eyes of the human lord (Esth. 2:8–20; Gen. 39:4); the questioning "day after day" (Esth 3:4; Gen. 39:10); the enemies who sit down to eat or drink when the hero is formally dispensed with (Esth. 3:15; Gen. 37:25); the "anger" of the king regarding his two ministers' "sins," followed by "hanging" and indifference to the forgotten, loyal Jew—forgotten, that is, until a sleepless night (Esth. 2:21–23; Gen. 40:1, 19, 22–23); the ritual mourning that precedes the surprise of new life (Esth. 4:1–3; Gen. 37:34); the promotion to prime minister with signet ring given to the loyal Jew, and a recognition parade (Esth. 6:8–11; Gen. 41:37–43); "pleading" for one's life (Esth. 8:3; Gen. 42:21); and prosperity for the Gentile kingdom as well as the Jews (Esth 10:1–3; Gen. 47:13–26). Both stories end with personal vindication and an obvious impression of a divinely superintended providential salvation of God's people.

The account of Moses also has much in common with Esther.[11] Shared elements include the threat to the Jews (Esth. 3; Exod. 1:9–10); the hesitant response to the call (Esth. 4:11; Exod. 3:11; 4:10, 13; 6:12, 30); confrontation with ("entreating") the Gentile king (Esth. 4:8; Exod. 7:1–2); the (supernatural) "changes" (see commentary, below, on 9:1–19); favor with the Gentiles (Esth. 5:2; Exod. 12:36); the growing reputations of Mordecai and Moses (Esth. 9:3–4; Exod. 11:3); the enemies' fear of God in the context of military victory (Esth. 9:2–3; Exod. 15:14–16); the institution of a sacred festival (Esth. 9:18–32; Exod. 12–13). To these we must add the confluence of dates between the two accounts: Haman rolled the *pur* on the eve of Passover. Esther commenced her fast when the feast was supposed to begin.

Another narrative to which Esther alludes is the account of King Saul in 1 Samuel. Mordecai's genealogy in 2:5 points the reader back to the tribe of Benjamin and the family of Kish, from which Saul comes. There is an unmistakable correspondence between his introduction and that of Saul in 1 Samuel 9:1. Behind the conflict with Haman lies Saul's confrontation with Agag, king of the Amalekites (1 Samuel 15). The critical issue in that episode was Saul's unwillingness to completely annihilate the Amalekites and to abstain from taking booty. He did not follow the strict laws of holy war prescribed in Deuteronomy 20 (esp. vv. 16–17). The ancient rivalry (evident in laws recorded in Exod. 22:21–23; Deut. 20:16–19) appears to be rekindled when Mordecai refuses to bow to Haman—*because he was a Jew* (Esth. 3:4). Haman's efforts to destroy the Jews mirror the corporate behavior of one of Israel's archetypal enemies, the Amalekites. In Esther, there are no compromises. All of the enemies associated with Haman are completely destroyed. The author of Esther is at pains to point out that, although the Jews were allowed to take spoils, they did not (9:10, 15, 16). The contrast between the endings of these stories is instructive. As a result of disobedience and self-interest, Saul lost the kingship. The prophet explained, "The LORD has torn the kingdom of Israel from you today and has given it to one of your neighbors—to one better than you" (1 Sam. 15:28). In Esther 1:19, the king is encouraged to "give [Vashti's] royal position to some-one else who is better than she." Saul eventually dies, reportedly at the hands of an Amalekite (2 Sam. 1:8–10). The irony in his death is matched by the irony of Agag's (1 Sam. 15:33). Haman's death is equally fitting (Esth. 7:9–10). His body is hung out in pub-lic, as was Saul's (1 Sam. 31:10). Mordecai, on the other hand, as-cends to a secure position, serving his community well as their faithful representative (Esth. 10:3).

Theoretically, our discussion about the literary elements in Esther would have brought us to some obvious conclusions regarding its genre. However, such is not the case. Numerous des-ignations have been proposed, including Persian chronicle, his-toricized wisdom, oriental tale, court conflict tale, court legend, novella, *Diasporanovella*, novel, festal legend, historicized myth, folklore, and romance.[12] These labels represent attempts to de-scribe its content and/or form, to take into account its length, and to assess its historical authenticity. Consequently, they represent different understandings of genre and occasionally complemen-tary categorizations and perceptions of the book.

The U-shaped plot underlies many of the conflict stories and myths of the ancient world. On this basic structure, Esther builds its account with an eye toward its readership, the Jews in the Dias-pora. It has much in common with the stories of Joseph and Daniel, other heroes living in "exile," or, more specifically, in the foreign court. From these stories Jews gained hope and models for a life-style living away from their homeland.[13] This use granted, the story in its present form is most clearly constructed to provide the his-torical background (and therefore legitimization) for the feast of Purim. Esther is thus a festival etiology (that is, an explanation of the origin of Purim) that follows the conflict story pattern.

## The Stories of Esther

The ambiguities of genre designation are perhaps the result of the history of the story and the modifications it underwent prior to (or after) its final form in the Hebrew Bible. Until recently, it was generally believed that there was a single, evolving textual tradition of the Esther story: the original Hebrew preserved well in the Masoretic text (MT) and the free Greek translations of it, preserved in both the Septuagint (LXX) and an alternative Alpha Text (AT). Carey A. Moore was the first to discern that the AT was not, however, simply another Greek translation of Esther from the MT.[14] Rather, it was an early translation of a separate Hebrew *Vorlage,* an original source other than the MT. Moore has been followed in this assessment by Clines, Fox, Bush, and Levenson.[15]

The AT story differs from its MT counterpart in significant ways.[16] Most significantly in terms of the plot, it does not refer to the unalterable laws of the Persians. There is, therefore, no counteredict by Mordecai at the end of the story, but simply a new edict by the king to punish the enemies of the Jews. As significantly, the AT does not refer to the lots by the name *pur,* nor does it end with legislation for Purim. There is no reference to two days of fighting or two days of celebration. It describes a one-time celebration of victory. There is no notice at the end about Mordecai's fame and support for the Jews. Clearly, the AT is not an etiology for Purim. The AT does mention God and it includes the LXX "additions" (discussed below), but these are probably later editorial layers to an authentic, early version of the story of Esther.[17]

The search for early Esther stories has reached back even further.[18] Several commentators are persuaded that original Esther and Mordecai stories were merged and then combined with the Purim legislation in chapter 9 to form an etiology of the festival.[19] However, if there were two original stories, the final author has done such a fine job transforming them into a literary whole that recreating them is needless.[20] The Hebrew (MT) tradition, then, ought to be considered a primary source.

The *Vorlage* of the AT is also a primary source, however. Since this other "original" story of Esther does not mention Purim, the MT represents only one version and is, perhaps, as a later version, the result of redactional activity. Different endings appear to have been added, one beginning at least by 8:17 (the point after which the AT has no correspondence), another beginning with 9:20. Most agree that the story is tightly constructed only through chapter 8, and after that it appears to reveal the work of editors. The confluence of evidence suggests that an original story has been adapted to become a festival lection.[21]

Our commentary on the story of Esther interprets the story in its final form—as the historical basis for Purim. However, the evidence that other versions of this story circulated without Purim should encourage us to consider literary patterns and genre designations that explain the plot of the core story apart from the endings in the MT. As noted above, Esther is both a court conflict story and a festival etiology.

The MT version of Esther is a well-preserved Hebrew text, probably written in the Persian period itself. It contains many features typical of late biblical Hebrew[22] and it exhibits an amazing acquaintance with Persian terms and specific conventions in the court setting. There are no Greek words or references that suggest a date in the Hellenistic period that followed. The ninth chapter reflects a certain distance from the events as it exposes the need to regulate the observance of Purim in Susa and in outlying areas of the empire. Thus the final form of the book is dated toward the end of the fifth century B.C.[23]

The Septuagint (which translates the MT, not the AT) is periphrastic. It is a more religious rendering of the story, with explicit references to God.[24] The LXX accumulated several additions over a period of time. These additions are considered canonical within Roman Catholic and Orthodox traditions. They clearly exonerate the heroes as pious Jews.[25] The Aramaic Targums, of which there are two, are also expansionistic—especially with regard to religious themes.

The *stories* of Esther, then, are as follows: The AT reflects the first stage of the story, told without any association with Purim. The MT represents the next stage, with the story written as a basis for festival observance. The LXX and additions represent a third stage, adding a religious color to the whole narrative. This way of retelling the story—by making explicit its theological character—has continued to the present day, as we will see in the commentary that follows.

## The Story of Esther and History

Having explored the book of Esther as *story*, we must now decide if we are to read Esther as *history*. It presents itself as a historical account. But is it, as many would suggest, "fictionalized history" or "historicized fiction"?

To determine if a biblical story reports historical events accurately, scholars generally refer to the accounts of other ancient historians that either corroborate or contradict the biblical writer. Genre is another indicator—especially when, as is often the case, there is no extrabiblical data to consult. Some genres, such as romance, tend to be less concerned with historical accuracy than do others, such as court annal. It is also typically assumed that an inverse relationship exists between literary art and historical authenticity: the more artistic an account, the less historical it is. A third, more subjective, criterion is "likelihood." The assumption in most mainstream scholarship is that the romantic dimension of the literature (i.e., the presence of miracle) represents wishful thinking rather than fact. The modern historian is expected to sift through the fanciful, looking for some evidence out of which to create a realistic reconstruction of ancient events.

Esther has been weighed in the historian's balance and found wanting on all three counts.[26] There are no extrabiblical sources that mention either queen (Vashti or Esther) or vizier (Haman or Mordecai) during the reign of Xerxes. What is clear in the Greek histories of Persia is that Xerxes' queen at this time was Amestris, a non-Jew (Herodotus, *Hist.* 7.14, 61; 9.112). Herodotus (*Hist.* 3.84) explains the Persian restriction of royal marriages to members of seven aristocratic families.

There are other discrepancies: Esther 1:1 begins with a reference to 127 satrapies in the Persian empire; Herodotus (*Hist.* 3.89) mentions only 20. One of the major complicating factors in the plot of MT Esther is the irrevocable nature of the laws of Persia (Esth. 1:19; 8:8; see also Dan. 6:8, 12). However, there is no extrabiblical reference to confirm this convention. There is likewise no confirmation of a law that uninvited guests approaching the king would be slain without the king raising his scepter (Esth. 4:11). There is no evidence of laws promulgated in languages other than Aramaic. There is no mention of a civil war between Jews and their enemies. The list goes on.

There are also historical problems that emerge when Esther is read in the light of other biblical/Jewish histories. Mordecai was taken captive with Jehoiachin (596 B.C.; Esth. 2:6) but became prime minister during the twelfth year of Xerxes (474 B.C.; Esth. 3:7; 8:2)—122 years later! Purim, if established by name during the time of Xerxes, would likely have been mentioned by name in 2 Maccabees 15:36 (rather than "Mordecai's Day"), a text from the first century B.C. Also, neither Esther nor Mordecai are mentioned in the list of heroes in Ecclesiasticus 44–49.

Paton[27] notes other improbabilities that discount the book's historical value. Among these he mentions the unlikeliness of the following: a six-month feast for the nobles of every province (1:1–4); Vashti's refusal to come before the king (1:12); the perceived threat to *every* man in his own home (1:16–22); the gathering of virgins (2:1–4); the four-year wait for Esther's turn (2:16); the lineages of Mordecai (2:5) and Haman (3:1); the long toleration of Mordecai by Haman (3:6); the 10,000 talents (3:9); and the year-long wait for the attack on the Jews (3:8–15).

Paton's lists are sufficient to cast considerable doubt on the historicity of the account. He reports that the "conclusions seem inevitable that the Book of Esther is not historical, and that it is doubtful whether even an historical kernel underlies its narrative."[28] Paton's analysis leads him to the conclusion that Esther is a legend set in the court of an ancient king, much like the stories of Daniel, Judith, and Ahiqar.

Generally, Esther scholarship in the century since Paton's commentary (1908) has maintained his assessment of the book's historical value. The lack of external corroboration for its events and its consistent use of hyperbole constitute evidence of a story without more than a kernel of historical fact. Many have suggested genre designations more specific than legend, but virtually always with the assumption that the events of the story are fictitious.

The commentary that follows will suggest that, for two reasons, the historicity of the book of Esther ought to be reconsidered. The first reason is that research on a number of the discrepancies mentioned above should qualify considerably their impact on our assessment. Second, because it is characteristic for biblical narrative to anchor hope for present and future readers in stories of God's deliverance in the past (hence, "salvation history"), its intentions ought to be taken seriously. Its "message" depends on having historical referents in time and space.

The author of Esther surely intends to have the book read as history.[29] The conventions of biblical historiography are evident as the book begins (with the phrases *vayhi bimey* in v. 1 and *bayyamim hahem* in v. 2) and at its close ("are they not written in the book of the annals of the kings of Media and Persia?" in 10:2).[30] Just as importantly, the basis for the celebration of Purim is the historic(al) moment (i.e., the two days in Adar) during which the Jews were delivered from their enemies. If the story does not report this historical incident with a certain measure of accuracy, then Purim is only a celebration of a legendary victory.[31]

With Esther as a historical resource by its own characterization, we are left to compare it with extrabiblical sources from the same period. We must also be mindful of the level of historical veracity each of these ancient writers, according to literary conventions, expected to convey.

Modern historians of ancient Persia lament the lack of sources. There are only self-aggrandizing inscriptions about King Xerxes' reign, and even these are few. The Greek historians Herodotus and Ctesias are more useful, although Ctesias is criticized for occasional inaccuracies.[32] They preserved records primarily of Xerxes' infamous encounter with the Greeks (480–479 B.C.). There is little information on the period between 479 and the end of Xerxes' reign in 465.

The most significant historical problem in Esther is the absence of the names of the four main characters (other than Xerxes) from extrabiblical records. The queen at the time of Xerxes, according to both Greek historians, was Amestris. This queen is described as strong-willed and brutal, once ordering eighteen noble Persian youths to be buried alive as a thank offering (Herodotus, *Hist.* 7.113, 114). On the way back from the Greek campaign, Amestris gave Xerxes a robe she had personally woven. Xerxes was tricked into giving this robe to his niece, Artaynte, with whom he was seeking to have an affair. In fact, he had attempted also to have an affair with her mother, his brother Masistes' wife. Once Amestris found out about the affairs, she had the sister-in-law mutilated. Amestris is not mentioned after this event during Xerxes' reign—apparently suffering the consequences of her own vindictiveness. She reappears as a strong figure later, after Xerxes was assassinated, during the reign of her son, Artaxerxes I. As queen mother, according to Ctesias, she pressured the king to behead fifty Greek prisoners and crucify another.

To make a connection between Vashti and Amestris would require a linguistic explanation of the different spellings for the queen's original Persian name, as well as a historical explanation of Amestris' presence in later Persian history. Two scholars have provided plausible reconstructions to equate these names and events.[33]

Using the accounts of both Greek and biblical historians, the following is what apparently took place in ancient Persia. The grand vision of Cyrus for a diverse but unified empire living in peace had been shattered in the last years of Darius' reign by revolts in Egypt (485–84) and Babylon (the first one in 484). After quelling these revolts, Darius' son Xerxes held a banquet in his third regnal year, 483 (the year of the banquets in Esther 1 during which Vashti was deposed)[34] to hold council to plan the invasion of Greece (Herodotus, *Hist.* 7.7–19). The war (which explains the time lag between Esther 1 and 2) began well but ended with a major naval defeat at Salamis in 480. While away, the king had his final rift with Amestris/Vashti. Masistes almost succeeded in a coup following the ordeal. The king returned home in his seventh year, 479, seeking comfort among members of his harem (Herodotus, *Hist.* 9.108). This was the year of Esther's marriage to the king.

On a second look at the biblical story, one finds that Vashti was not banished but lost access to the king's presence and to her royal powers (2:4, 17).[35] Esther was Xerxes' favored among women in 2:17. However, she fears coming before the king after an absence of thirty days in 4:11. The fact that Esther did not come from one of the seven select families is no more an anomaly than Xerxes' own mother, one of several wives of Darius from outside these seven (Herodotus, *Hist.* 3.87) or Xerxes' wife Amestris, the daughter of Otanes, the son of Sisamnes (Herodotus, *Hist.* 7.61).

Another potential problem concerns the prime ministers. Though once doubted, Mordecai's name is a well-attested personal name in this period, derived as it is from the name of the principal Babylonian deity, Marduk.[36] Now, amid thirty texts from Persepolis with the names Marduka or Marduku (referring possibly to four separate officials), there are several candidates that could match the male hero in Esther. The problem with Mordecai's age in Esther 2:5 is resolved simply by reading the relative pronoun in that verse in relation to Kish, the great-grandfather of Mordecai (see commentary and note on 2:5, below). Although there is no record of Haman the Agagite, there is an inscription of Sargon that mentions the district of Agag in the Persian empire.[37]

Other historical problems are less than troubling. The 127 satrapies *(medinot)* of Esther 1:1 are apparently smaller units than those of Herodotus' record. The term *medinah* is used in Ezra 2:1 and Nehemiah 1:3; 7:6 for the province of Judah, a subcategory of the larger satrapy. It is also noteworthy that the empire was categorized into language/ethnic groupings when described in royal inscriptions. The total number of groupings varies among (and within!) these inscriptions.

The irrevocable law convention need not be relegated to a literary device for Jewish writers in the postexilic period. Diodorus Siculus records the words of Darius III, remorseful over his ordering of the execution of Charidemus: "When the king's anger abated, he at once repented and blamed himself for having made the greatest mistake, but what was done could not be undone by the royal authority."[38] "What was done" is a reference to what earlier is called the "law of the Persians." Perhaps even more pertinent to our story is the account in Herodotus of the king's gift of Amestris' robe to Artaynte, because he couldn't go back on his word. Xerxes offered whole cities, gold, and even his army to get the cloak back—but to no avail. Then, at his own birthday party, Amestris holds him to his word again, gaining the right to have his sister-in-law mutilated. This act was so odious to Xerxes' brother, Masistes, that a revolt was only barely avoided. There is certainly a precedent—at least as a matter of honor—that the king could not waffle on his decisions.

While uncertainty lingers over some of the identifications and historical events mentioned above, there is considerable accuracy in many of the story's details. The book of Esther exhibits such a thorough knowledge of Persian names and the details of the Persian court and palace that the book can be dated in the late Persian period.[39] Other particulars in the story match what we read in nonbiblical sources. The kingdom of Xerxes (486–65 B.C.) was known for extending from India to Cush. He was also known for his passion and hot temper (Herodotus, *Hist.* 7.3ff.; 9.108ff.). The architecture of the palace matches the excavated palace of Artaxerxes II at Susa, a palace modeled after the one built by Darius and used by Xerxes.[40] Mordecai appears to be one of the *orosanges*, or benefactors of the king, described by Herodotus (*Hist.* 3.138, 140; 5.11; 8.85, 88, 90; 9.109). The term *puru*, meaning "lot," is found in Old Assyrian inscriptions dating back into the early second millennium B.C. Persian "dice" were found by the excavator Dieulafoy at the site of ancient Shushan. Anti-Semitism is evident during this period, with the destruction of a Jewish temple at the other end of the kingdom in Egypt. The Persian postal system was famous for its global reach and efficiency.[41] Robert Gordis[42] describes the realistic, historical nature of delayed executions, attempted genocide (80,000 reported killed in one day in 88 B.C.), and the high degree of Jewish acculturation to Persian mores. Cyrus Gordon[43] has also provided light on the ancient Iranian practice of religious dissimulation, the choice to hide one's religious identity in contexts of mortal danger. Paton[44] himself provides a list of historically accurate motifs: "the seven princes who formed the council of state (1:14), obeisance before the King and his favourites (3:2), belief in lucky and unlucky days (3:7), exclusion of mourning garb from the palace (4:2), hanging as the death-penalty (5:14), dressing a royal benefactor in the King's robes (6:8), the dispatching of couriers with royal messages (3:13; 8:10)."

It seems inadvisable to disregard both the author's intentions and these historical details that speak together of actual events in the ancient world. Esther is not "history" as moderns would conceive of it. It is a great story with many traditional features, and it deserves merit as a historical source written close in time and space to the events it describes.

Esther is written not simply to record historical events, but also to articulate critical realities and hopes for the Jewish community of the Diaspora. The "plot" of the story begins with the Jews "minding their own business." Then the all too familiar threat appears. Haman and his scheme represent all forms of anti-Semitism, every form of discrimination, each attempt to restrict Jews from their cultural distinctiveness. The ending represents the ideal resolution: the world recognizes that Jews are good and loyal citizens and their enemies get what they deserve. It is a good story in part because it proves that the happy ending does happen—occasionally.

## The Story of Esther and Its Morality

Christian interpreters have avoided Esther because of its Jewishness (what Luther called excessive "Judaizing") and because of its perceived inferior morality. The episode most disturbing to modern readers is Esther's request for the hanging of Haman's sons and a second day of killing in Esther 9:13. Paton[45] comments, "For this horrible request no justification can be found. A second massacre was in no sense an act of self-defense, . . . This shows a malignant spirit of revenge more akin to the teaching of the Talmud." Of Esther's request for the hanging of Haman's (already dead) sons, Paton avers, "The vengeance of Esther pursues them even after they are dead."[46]

Criticism of the ethics represented in the Esther narrative is likely due to a misunderstanding of biblical ethics *and* biblical narrative. The moral code of the story is really a code of honor. Esther and Mordecai are champions of their people because they are loyal to them. They courageously resist an enemy who seeks their destruction, acting only in self-defense (as the author notes more than once). The Jews resist greed, refusing to take the spoils they deserve. The author insists that the Jews acted only within the boundaries of the law. Once every person in the empire was given the opportunity to take sides, the Jews were authorized to execute justice. The book of Esther portrays evil as a reckless reality successfully arrested by force and by law.[47]

The rest of the Hebrew Bible promotes these ethics, especially in the conquest traditions. Threatening God's chosen ones eventually and inevitably brings divine judgment. That judgment may take the shape of supernatural interventions, or it may be expressed through the armies of Israel.

Having made an apology for the morality in Esther, it is necessary to end with an important qualification. Biblical narratives rarely describe their heroes without an almost embarrassing transparency regarding their shortcomings, frailties, and moral failures. Yet rarely is there a moral commentary. As a result, we are left to decide for ourselves what matches the morality prescribed elsewhere in Scripture, and what does not.

An honest interpretation of the protagonists in our story is one that takes into account the possibility of ethnic pride in Mordecai and overzealous vengeance in Esther. They are not heroes because they were perfect. Rather, they fit into the larger scheme of salvation history in which they participate and to which they contribute—often *in spite of* their shortcomings. Biblical history celebrates the deliverance of God (named or not), generally accomplished with the most unlikely partners.

### The Story of Esther and Its Theology

While there have been some attempts[48] to leave God out of Esther (i.e., not to locate him in the story that fails to name him), it is a long-standing tradition to read the book as having constant, implicit references to the hand of God. This approach is evident in the earliest translations of the book of Esther into Greek and Aramaic (discussed above).

Some commentators have emphasized the allusion to God in the statement Mordecai makes in Esther 4:14: "For if you remain silent at this time, relief and deliverance for the Jews will arise from another place, but you and your father's family will perish. And who knows but that you have come to royal position for such a time as this?" "Another place" is, perhaps, a subtle reference to God, playing off the ancient designation for God's chosen place *(hammaqom)* in Deuteronomy. At the very least, there is a strong sense of confidence that deliverance will come. And why should Mordecai add to this a threat to Esther and her family unless he is thinking of the ancient consequences of disobedience to God's law? Finally, the phrase "for such a time as this" is certainly pregnant with the implication that there was some design in these events. Although these allusions are opaque, Esther seems to understand their implications. She calls for a fast in preparation for her visit to the king.

The most consistent "evidence" for divine presence in Esther is in the many instances of coincidence and peripety (unexpected reversals). Coincidences are clustered throughout the story, but they are most obvious during the episode of the king's sleepless night. He "just happens" to have insomnia the night before Haman's visit to request Mordecai's neck. Haman "just happens" to be in the court. The king "just happens" to choose an ambiguous form of question. Haman "just happens" to assume that he is the one to be honored. And so goes the story. The chain of events is beyond anyone's apparent control, but it heads so inexorably toward Haman's humiliation that it implies providential influence. And all of this follows Esther's fast.[49] Instead of constituting evidence against Esther's historicity, these events implicate God in history.

Peripety is similar to coincidence, but it tends to suggest divine justice more programmatically. The imposition in human experience of the lex talionis (law of retribution, such as an eye for an eye and a tooth for a tooth) principle of retribution is a fingerprint of God.[50] Haman will hang on the pole he erected for Mordecai. This is the inevitable consequence of malice in a sapiential worldview that sees a divinely ordered cosmos organized around God's righteousness. The structure of the book of Esther reflects this principle of reversal. The summarizing verse for the plot is found in 9:1: "On this day the enemies of the Jews had hoped to overpower them, *but now the tables were turned* and the Jews got the upper hand over those who hated them."

The most intriguing evidence for the hidden God in Esther is found in the intertextual links to other biblical stories that mention God. *God* blessed Joseph and gave him favor with Potiphar (Gen. 39:3–4). *God* gave the Israelites favor with the Egyptians (Exod. 12:36). Esther simply "gained favor." The Israelites cried out to God (Exod. 2:23). The Jews in Esther simply cry out (Esth. 4:3). God promised *personally* to put fear of the Jews among their enemies in the promised land (Deut. 2:25); in Esther, simply, the enemies of the Jews fear them (Esth. 8:17). In Genesis 50:20, Joseph explains that what his brothers intended for harm, *"God* intended . . . for good to accomplish what is now being done, the saving of many lives." In Esther we simply have a report of many lives being saved (see 3:14). Esther deserves a place among the great narratives of salvation history because of its continuous use of themes and motifs from the conquest account.

While it has seemed patent to most interpreters that God is virtually visible in Esther, we are right to ask, "If all of these allusions and coincidences point to the God of biblical history, why is he *not* named?" Is it just a literary maneuver to prompt the reader to fill in the obvious name? Perhaps it is not so much the *presence* of God but the *hiddenness* of God in human events that the story articulates. To be hidden is to be present yet unseen. What is visible is only the human side of the story. Perceiving something beyond or behind takes faith.

## The Story of Esther and Its Message

It is inappropriate to think of a story as having a single message. However, attention to the crafting of a narrative and an awareness of its likely intended readership leads us to some fairly obvious conclusions. Esther provides a message of hope to Jews in the Diaspora. If an orphaned, exiled, foreign woman could rise to royalty in the center of the world's greatest power, who couldn't take heart in the most marginal of circumstances? Who couldn't believe that the Jewish people (i.e., the people of YHWH) were still, even in the state of "exile," able to find protection and prosperity? This message of hope is close to the surface of the story.

When Esther is read in the context of other biblical exilic and postexilic literature, the subtle nature of the story's "message" becomes clearer. Like Esther, other stories and prophecies from this period are hopeful. However, the basis of hope in Esther is categorically different. For most of Israel's visionaries, hope for the exilic community is Zion-centered. While in exile, Daniel risks his life praying toward Jerusalem, the geographical center of his faith. Ezekiel predicts, "I will put my Spirit in you . . . and I will settle you *in your own land.* Then you will know that I the LORD have spoken" (Ezek. 37:14). Isaiah's promise that the Israelites ("Jacob") would "rule over their oppressors" (Isa. 14:2) is preceded by the expectation that the Lord would "settle them in *their own land*" (Isa. 14:1). He later promises a day when " . . . the ransomed of the LORD will return. They will enter *Zion* with singing; everlasting joy will crown their heads. Gladness and joy will overtake them, and sorrow and sighing will flee away (Isa. 35:10). Similarly, Jeremiah promises, "They will come and shout for joy on the heights of Zion; . . . I will turn their mourning into gladness; I will give them comfort and joy instead of sorrow" (Jer. 31:12–13). Many of these same terms are used in Esther 9 to describe Jewish experience, but *apart from* a return to Judah. Even the promise of proselytes who will join the Jews in their return to Zion (Zech. 8:23) is mirrored in Esther with the inclusion of proselytes *in Persia* (Esth. 8:17).

Esther, then, is an affirmation of Jewish hope apart from returning to Jerusalem. Exile is not just a temporary state of punishment; it is a legitimate place in which to anticipate prosperity and (divine) blessing. The precedent for this affirmation is found in the protection and provision of God for his people in the wilderness. Before there was a divine presence on Mt. Zion, he was among his people as they wandered.

Esther is also unique in its deemphasis on cultic observance. The prophets of this period imagined a day when the temple would be rebuilt and the Torah would be fully obeyed. Ezekiel (chs. 43–44) pictured the return to Zion as a time for a rebuilt temple filled with holy worshipers. In exile, Daniel risks his life by keeping a kosher diet. Haggai (1:4–11) and Malachi (3:8–12) each call those who did return to Zion to reengage formal worship as the only means to experience God's blessings. But Esther engages in no formal religious observance. There is fasting, but this is all. She eats the king's food and sleeps in the king's bed.

The message of hope in Esther is rooted not in cultic observance but in loyalty to the Jewish people. Esther is a paragon of virtue in this sense. She risks everything to save her kin. Her courage and sagacity are the virtues of the wisdom tradition more than Torah. Mordecai, like Esther, is an emblem of honor (note the last two verses of the book) rather than an example of religious purity. The Jews in the Diaspora needed to know that commitment to the community was itself a religious value. Contributing to the history of salvation was a religious act. Through its many allusions to the Exodus account and through the actual dates recorded in Esther, it becomes clear that Purim is a valid counterpart to Passover.

The story of Esther, as mentioned above, uses an orphaned, female exile as its heroine. Thus the book qualifies the traditional Jewish hope for deliverance and leadership in the lines of Aaron and David. Ezekiel describes another David in Ezekiel 34 (compare Jer. 22:30) and a purified Zadokite priesthood in chapters 40–48. Hope for Zechariah was inextricably tied to Zerubbabel, a Davidic ruler (Zech. 4; so also Hag. 1; Ezra 3:2–6; Neh. 12:1). The postexilic Chronicler will emphasize the traditional royal and priestly lineages of Israel's golden age as a way of inspiring hope for the despondent community.

In contrast, Esther places hope in a "nobody" or, more accurately, an "anybody." This story taps the traditional biblical theme of the unexpected and unlikely deliverer. There are the second-born children who are chosen in Genesis. There is Gideon, who is from the least of Israel's tribes and clans (Judg. 6:15). There are Deborah and Jael, defeating the Midianites. This is the perspective Esther brings back into Diaspora consciousness. Jews did not need to be in Zion to have hope. Jews did not need to be fully observant of the cultic law to have hope. Jews did not need to wait for a priestly or royal figure to have hope. With a distinct yet "biblical" hermeneutic, the book of Esther invites its readers to find hope anywhere, any time, and through anyone.

Perhaps these novel emphases in Esther make it possible to understand why the author does not name the God of the Jews. This story assumes that there are two dimensions of reality—one seen and the other unseen. Esther is herself a person with two identities; she has two names, one of which means "hidden." On the surface, to be a faithful Jew would require return to Zion, cultic observance, and a legitimate pedigree. But being a faithful Jew means more than that. Ultimately, being a Jew means being the presence of YHWH in the world. We look in vain to find his name in Esther because his identity is joined to that of his people. There is a divine hand present in serendipitous circumstance beyond their control—but salvation, in the end, comes most directly through human saviors.

---

## Notes

---

1. Several books written during the 1980s provided a rationale and tools for the study of biblical narrative *as literature*. Primary contributions include R. Alter, *The Art of Biblical Narrative* (New York: Basic, 1981); M. Sternberg, *The Poetics of Biblical Narrative* (Bloomington: Indiana University, 1985); A. Berlin, *Poetics and Interpretation of Biblical*

*Narrative* (Sheffield: Almond, 1983); L. Ryken, *How to Read the Bible as Literature* (Grand Rapids: Zondervan, 1984); and T. Longman, *Literary Approaches to Biblical Interpretation* (Grand Rapids: Zondervan, 1987).

2. A wonderful discussion of these three features of biblical narrative is V. P. Long, *The Art of Biblical History* (Grand Rapids: Zondervan, 1994).

3. On these elements, see L. Ryken, *Words of Delight* (2d ed.; Grand Rapids: Baker, 1992), pp. 36–39.

4. From "Narrative and the Real World: An Argument for Continuity," *HTh* 25 (1986), p. 118, as quoted by Long (*Art*, p. 70).

5. For more on "narratized laments," see C. Westermann, "The Role of the Lament in the Theology of the Old Testament," *Int* 28.1 (1974), pp. 20–38; *The Structure of the Book of Job* (Philadelphia: Fortress, 1981); and T. Laniak, *Shame and Honor in the Book of Esther* (SBLDS 165; Atlanta: Scholars Press, 1998), pp. 7–17.

6. *Esther: A Commentary* (OTL; Louisville: Westminster John Knox, 1997), p. 8.

7. There are ten feasts in Esther. Apart from these mentioned, there is the feast that Vashti prepares in chapter 1 and the private drinking party of Haman and the king in chapter 3.

8. M. Fox provides an engaging treatment of characterization in Esther in *Character and Ideology in the Book of Esther* (Columbia, S.C.: University of South Carolina, 1991).

9. Intertextuality refers to intentional connections made to other texts.

10. These have been noted and analyzed especially by Rosenthal, Gan, and Berg. L. A. Rosenthal, "Die Josephgeschichte mit den Buchern Ester und Daniel verglichen," *ZAW* 15 (1895), pp. 278–85; Rosenthal, "Nochmals der Vergleich Ester, Joseph, Daniel," *ZAW* 17 (1897), pp. 125–28; M. Gan, "The Book of Esther in the Light of the Story of Joseph in Egypt" (in Hebrew), *Tarbiz* 61 (1961), pp. 144–49; and S. B. Berg, *The Book of Esther: Motifs, Themes, and Structures* (Chico, Calif.: Scholars Press, 1979).

11. These are explored in G. Gerleman, *Esther* (Neukirchen-Vluyn: Neukirchener Verlag, 1973).

12. The different genres have been discussed by the following: Persian chronicle, R. Gordis, "Religion, Wisdom and History in the Book of Esther: A New Solution to an Ancient Crux," *JBL* 100 (1981), pp. 359–88; historicized wisdom, S. Talmon, "Wisdom in the Book of Esther," *VT* 13 (1963), pp. 419–55; oriental tale, E. Bickerman, *Four Strange Books of the Bible* (New York: Schocken, 1967); court conflict tale, W. L. Humphreys, "A Life-Style for Diaspora: A Study of the Tales of Esther and Daniel," *CBQ* 92 (1973), pp. 211–23; court legend, L. Wills, *The Jew in the Court of the Foreign King: Ancient Jewish Court Legends* (HDR 26; Minneapolis: Fortress, 1986); novella, M. Siegel, "Book of Esther: A Novelle," *Dor Le Dor* 14.3 (1984), pp. 142–51; *Diasporanovella*, A. Meinhold, "Die

Gattung der Josephsgeschichte und des Estherbuches: and Diaspora-novelle, I, II," *ZAW* 87 (1975), pp. 306–24; 88 (1976), pp. 79–93; novel, J. A. Loader, "Esther as a Novel with Different Levels of Meaning," *ZAW* 90.3 (1974), pp. 417–21; festal legend, Gerleman, *Esther;* historicized myth, H. Gunkel, *Esther* (Tübingen: Mohr, 1916); folklore, S. Niditch and R. Doran, "Esther: Folklore, Wisdom, Feminism and Authority," in *A Feminist Companion to Esther, Judith and Susanna* (ed. A. Brenner; Sheffield: Sheffield Academic Press, 1987), pp. 26–46; and romance, Ryken, *Words.* Fox (*Character,* pp. 148–50) suggests that Esther is "history." This designation represents the author's intention to account for the events leading up to Purim but sidesteps the issue of structure that other designations represent more precisely.

13. This point has been articulated fully by Humphreys ("Life-Style") and S. A. White, "Esther: A Feminine Model for Jewish Diaspora," in *Gender and Difference in Ancient Israel* (ed. P. L. Day; Minneapolis: Fortress, 1988), pp. 161–77.

14. *The Greek Text of Esther* (Ann Arbor, Mich.: University Microfilms, 1965), pp. 133–39.

15. D. J. A. Clines, *The Esther Scroll: The Story of the Story* (JSOTSup 30; Sheffield: JSOT, 1987); M. V. Fox, *The Redaction of the Books of Esther: On Reading Composite Texts* (SBLMS 40; Atlanta: Scholars Press, 1991); F. W. Bush, *Ruth, Esther* (WBC 9; Dallas: Word, 1996); and Levenson, *Esther.*

16. For a detailed comparison of the "proto-AT" and MT, see Clines, *Esther Scroll,* pp. 93–114; Fox, *Redaction,* pp. 96–126.

17. If the references to God in the AT are original, then another question about the final form of the MT emerges: Why would its author *remove* the name of God?

18. In the search for ancient parallels to the stories of Esther and Mordecai, some Aramaic fragments from Qumran have come to light. These contain portions of stories about Jews in the Persian court who suffer and experience vindication. J. T. Milik ("Les modèles araméens du livre d'Esther dans la grotte 4 de Qumrân," *RevQ* 15–16 [1992/3], pp. 321–99) pressed these much too far as references to Mordecai, but they do attest to certain motifs in the story that must have had a common currency. For translation and comment, see W. G. E. Watson, "Aramaic Proto-Esther," in *Dead Sea Scrolls Translated* (Brill: Leiden, 1991), pp. 291–92; and R. Eisenmann and M. Wise, "Stories from the Persian Court," in *The Dead Sea Scrolls Uncovered* (Rockport, Me.: Element, 1992), pp. 99–103.

19. H. Cazelles ("Note sur la composition du rouleau d'Esther," in *Lex Tua Veritas* [ed. H. Gross and F. Mussner; Trier: Paulinus-Verlag, 1961], pp. 17–30) provides the most detailed reconstruction of this textual history, although for him the Esther story was liturgical and included Purim while the Mordecai story was political. Clines (*Esther Scroll,* pp. 130–38) summarizes completely the history of these efforts.

20. For more, see Fox, *Redaction,* pp. 97–99.

21. For a good summary of this position, see Bush, *Ruth, Esther,* p. 305.

22. R. L. Bergey ("Late Linguistic Features in Esther," *JQR* 75 [1984], pp. 66–78; and "Post-exilic Hebrew Linguistic Developments in Esther: A Diachronic Approach," *JETS* 31 [1988], pp. 161–68) locates the language of Esther at the end of the postexilic literary spectrum. At least the ending of the book is written from a Susan perspective (Fox, *Character,* p. 140). And there is a generally favorable view of the Gentile king throughout (not what one would expect in a later period).

23. See the remarks of S. Talmon ("Wisdom," p. 449), who notes that Judith, written in the Hellenistic period, is patterned after Esther.

24. For example, a periphrastic addition (in italics) in Esth. 2:20 reads, "Now Esther had not discovered her kindred; for so Mardochaeus commanded her, *to fear God, and perform his commandments,* as when she was with him: and Esther changed not her manner of life." Or, in 6:13, Haman's wife confesses, "thou wilt assuredly fall, and thou wilt not be able to withstand him, *for the living God is with him.*"

25. The content of the LXX additions (designated A–F) is as follows: (A) At the beginning of the story is Mordecai's dream of combat between two dragons and his fear of the annihilation of the just. A river rises, the sun comes out, and the just are saved. This vision prefigures the conflict about to ensue in the court. (B) Between Esth. 3:13 and 3:14 there is an account of the king (understood to be Artaxerxes) following Haman's warning about the race that threatens the empire. The king orders their annihilation (on Adar 14). (C) After Esth. 4:17, prayers of both Mordecai and Esther show their sincerity and innocence before God. Mordecai even prays for Haman's descendants. (D) follows directly after C with a description of Esther before the king that supplements the MT account. Esther faints before Artaxerxes, whose angry appearance intimidates her. As he consoles her, he makes his generous promise. (E) is an account of the king's edict between Esth. 8:12 and 8:13. He accuses Haman of treachery and vows to protect the Jews. He proclaims Adar 13 a holiday. (F) After the end of the story, Mordecai interprets his original dream and honors God for their deliverance.

26. Paton catalogues most of the problems. L. B. Paton, *A Critical and Exegetical Commentary on the Book of Esther* (ICC; Edinburgh: T&T Clark, 1908), pp. 65–77.

27. Paton, *Esther,* pp. 73–75.

28. Paton, *Esther,* p. 75.

29. M. Fox (*Character,* p. 138) considers Esther fictional yet categorizes it as history (pp. 148–50) because the author's intention is clearly to have the account read as such.

30. Compare 1 Kgs. 14:19, 29; 15:23.

31. Purim would be like our Fourth of July without a historical basis. History books would report only legends "set" in our world two hundred years ago.

32. See E. M. Yamauchi, "The Archaeological Background of Esther," *BSac* 137 (1980), pp. 99–117, p. 102.

33. J. S. Wright ("The Historicity of the Book of Esther," in *New Perspectives on the Old Testament* [ed. J. B. Payne; Waco, Tex.: Word, 1970]: pp. 41–43) reminds us that both Jewish and Greek historians were transliterating Persian names, often with different results. (For example, the Persian Khshayarsha became *Xerxes* in Greek but *Akhashwerosh* in Hebrew.) Ancient Greek had no equivalent for "w" or "sh," both of which were sounds in the original Hebrew name, Vashti. On the other hand, as W. H. Shea ("Esther and History," *AUSS* 14 [1976], pp. 227–46, pp. 236–37) observes, Hebrew (and several other Near Eastern languages including Persian) does not pronounce the "r" found in the Greek pronunciation of Artaxerxes (Xerxes' son). Therefore, it is likely that Amestris' proper Persian pronunciation did not have that sound. Shea ("Esther and History," p. 237) states that "m" is one of two typical Greek replacements for "w" as is "s" for "sh." The conclusion of the matter is that Amestris and Vashti are plausible renderings of the same Persian name.

34. Based on dating inferred from Ctesias (13.51), Amestris bore no children after 483 (Wright, "Historicity," p. 43). The episode during the Greek campaign (481–79) suggests that Amestris was at that time a person with influence in the king's retinue, but perhaps the unusual, handmade gift was an attempt to regain some lost favor. Her marginalization would have begun with the events described in Esther 1 and was complete after the fateful transaction with Xerxes' mistresses. She is not mentioned after 479 during the reign of Xerxes (who died in 465), but appears later only in the context of her role as queen mother with her last child, Artaxerxes I (until her death in 424). This would make sense in light of both accounts.

35. In Esth. 2:4 and 2:17, the Hebrew uses a verb *(m-l-k)* to describe Esther's new role. Literally, she "ruled" (or "became queen") instead of Vashti. This replacement signaled Vashti's demotion in status and authority.

36. Arthur Ungnad ("Keilinschriftliche Beiträge zum Buch Ezra und Esther," *ZAW* 59 [1942–43], p. 219) equates biblical Mordecai with an official accountant under Xerxes named Marduka, mentioned in a tablet from Borsippa.

37. J. Urquhart, "Esther," pp. 1006–09 in vol. 2 of *ISBE*, p. 1008.

38. Quoted and analyzed by Wright, "Historicity," pp. 39–40.

39. A. R. Millard ("Persian Names in Esther and the Reliability of the Hebrew Text," *JBL* 96 [1977]: 481–88) demonstrates the reliability of the Hebrew transcriptions of many Persian names over their rendering

in the Septuagint. E. M. Yamauchi (*Persia and the Bible* [Grand Rapids: Baker, 1990], p. 108) reports over thirty personal names of Persian or Elamite origin and twelve Persian loanwords in the text of Esther. Michael Heltzer ("The Book of Esther," *BA* 81 [1992], pp. 25–30, 41, pp. 26–27) demonstrates that certain Old Persian terms for officials and architecture used in Esther 1 went out of use before the Hellenistic period. An inscription of Artaxerxes II states that the palace of Xerxes was burned by fire during the reign of Artaxerxes I, less than thirty years after the time of Esther.

40. The detailed correspondence to the descriptions in Esther is remarkable. For more, see the comments of Urquhart ("Esther"), p. 1009.

41. Herodotus, *Hist.* 5:52–53; 8.98; Yamauchi, *Persia*, pp. 174–78.

42. "Religion, Wisdom," pp. 383–88.

43. *Riddles in History* (New York: Crown, 1974), pp. 88–89.

44. *Esther*, p. 65.

45. *Esther*, p. 287.

46. Fox (*Character*, p. 221) quotes the following commentators: The Jewish heroes authorize "a massacre of defenseless Gentiles on a given day, within a great peaceful empire, with the connivance of the central government" (R. Pfeiffer). The book is "inspired by a fierce nationalism and an unblushing vindictiveness which stand in glaring contradiction to the Sermon on the Mount . . . The Jews, in their actions, are not essentially different from the heathen. Mordecai and Esther merely put Haman's plan into reverse" (B. Anderson). Fox exposes Anderson's implicit charge that the Jews were attempting to exterminate Gentiles.

47. Readers with personal experience of the Holocaust understand all too well what state-supported violence against a race can entail. Certainly the persistent, comprehensive rooting out of their enemies provided the only assurance of protection for Jews in Esther's day.

48. Fox (*Character*, pp. 235–47) has made the strongest and most recent case for a secular Jewish vision in Esther.

49. Another allusion to providence follows Haman's "fate-full" excursion with Mordecai through the city streets. His wife and friends discern that he is beginning to fall irretrievably before Mordecai because he is a Jew (Esth. 6:13). These sentiments echo the prophecies of Balaam, who also realizes that no one can stand against the people of YHWH (Num. 23).

50. For example, the Canaanite king Adoni-Bezek admits, "Seventy kings with their thumbs and big toes cut off have picked up scraps under my table. Now God has paid me back for what I did to them" (Judg. 1:7). His punishment was having his own toes and thumbs cut off.

## §1 Three Royal Banquets (Esth. 1:1–9)

The book of Esther opens with an extended description of a royal banquet in the Persian court of Xerxes I. More precisely, there are descriptions of three banquets: one for the noblemen and other male dignitaries, one for the male commoners, and one for the women.

Banqueting is a central motif in Esther. There are feasts (*mishtot*) at the beginning and end of Esther, and the same root (*sh-t-h*) is used at crucial turning points throughout the story. In chapter 1, the celebrations for the men provide an opportunity for the king to display his enormous wealth and power and to provide generously for his subjects. In response to this display and provision, the royal host anticipates gratitude, respect, and loyalty. He is threatened when the unanticipated happens.

Many other motifs and themes in the book are introduced in this opening "scene." Status is explicit as it is on other official occasions throughout the story. Status and honor are defined by proximity to or possession by royalty (*malkut*). There is excessive pomp and an obsession with protocol. For instance, a royal command is necessary so that a guest can drink "in his own way" (1:8)—a law to drink without a law! Finally, separation of the sexes during the banquets indicates gender conventions that must be observed in this particular royal setting.

**1:1–2** / The story begins with Hebrew phraseology typical of historical narrative in the Bible: **This is what happened . . .** The king is Xerxes I, who ruled in 486–465 B.C., following his father, Darius I. Darius had organized the Persian empire into satrapies that extended **from India to Cush** (Ethiopia). Identifying the geographical extent of Xerxes' reign was a standard means of honoring an ancient monarch (Herodotus, *Hist.* 1.134). With his power, Xerxes was known to be tyrannical and unpredictably brutal—as the story of Esther will confirm.

Xerxes had four capitals. Susa was his primary one, and its citadel served as his winter/spring palace. The statement that **King Xerxes reigned from his royal throne in the citadel of Susa** suggests a certain newly won stability for the empire. His **third year** (v. 3; 483/82 B.C.) marked the end of serious revolts in Egypt (485 B.C.) and the containment of upheavals in Babylon (484 and 482 B.C.). Xerxes now sat securely on his throne, and it was time to celebrate with members of his renowned armed forces and the nobles and commoners in the capital. Feasting on such occasions was a typical Near Eastern expression of confidence that all threats were under control. This was also the occasion for Xerxes' war council to prepare for their historic invasion of Greece.

**1:3–9** / The first nine verses of Esther are unusually descriptive. Hebrew narrative is typically more conservative with such details. The story begins without any dialogue, merging the impressive images of the first and second parties.

The list of visitors for the king's six-month banquet included all of his officials from across the empire. There was a display of military might **(military leaders)**, aristocratic prestige **(nobles** and **princes)**, and tangible evidence of the king's **vast wealth** (vv. 3, 4). The respective ranks of the officials were evident in dress, seating, and gesture (Strabo, *Geogr.* 15.3.20). For those who didn't count in the social ranking of the first party—**all the people from the least to the greatest**—the king arranged a seven-day follow-up feast (v. 5).

The narrator emphasizes the extravagance and overwhelming opulence of **the enclosed garden of the king's palace** (v. 5). Persian kings were known for their impressive gardens and parks. Here guests walked among Xerxes' private planting beds, columns, and mosaics. The banquets provided the opportunity to show off his extraordinary wealth and splendor. The visual impact of this display was impressive. The Hebrew syntax in verse 6 reads like the words of breathless guests who, on entering the king's garden, can only stutter a litany of colors and materials that fill their gaze. Many of the items in the list—**hangings of white and blue linen ... purple material ... marble pillars ... gold and silver ... porphyry, marble, mother-of-pearl and other costly stones**—are also found in descriptions of the tabernacle and/or the temple (Exod. 26–27; 1 Kgs. 7; 1 Chr. 29:2).

The royal gala did not just provide an opportunity for extravagant exhibition; it was also a time for generous hospitality.

The royal host welcomed everyone in the kingdom (at least in representative form) into his home. The guests sat down to a virtually continuous meal with an endless supply of drinks, **in keeping with the king's liberality** (v. 7). They, as his guests and patrons, were expected only to enjoy the banquet as a form of royal provision. A description of the first Persian king could easily apply to Xerxes: "And although [the empire] was of such magnitude, it was governed by the single will of Cyrus; and he honored his subjects and cared for them as if they were his own children; and they, on their part, reverenced Cyrus as a father" (Xenophon, *Cyropaedia* 8.1).

As patron, the king established the conventions for drinking. According to his determination, everyone was **to drink in his own way** (v. 8). The Hebrew word for law *(dat)* is introduced here to refer to the king's ruling. This is our first clue that Persian life is governed by laws that originate in the palace. It is highly ironic that the only law in this story that the king puts into effect without the counsel of his advisers is one that lets others do as they please. This foreshadows Haman's abuse of *dat.*

The double feast of verses 3–8 is, at first glance, an image of the empire as "one big, happy family." Such grand events should denote peace and prosperity. However, this scene is also, from a literary point of view, *so* bloated with excess as to suggest that something is awry.

A brief and strictly factual notice follows the lavishly detailed description of the king's raucous parties: **Queen Vashti also gave a banquet for the women in the royal palace of King Xerxes** (v. 9). The contrast seems intentional, as the narrator juxtaposes the impulsiveness of the former host with the modesty of the latter. The stage is set for the unexpected (and unwanted) invitation of the eunuchs for Vashti to join the king's party.

## Additional Notes §1

**1:1** / **This is what happened:** The Hebrew phrase that begins the account of Esther (*vayhi bimey* . . . ) is typical of historical narrative (Gen. 14:1; Ruth 1:1; Isa. 7:1; Jer. 1:3).
**Xerxes:** The Masoretic rendering of the Persian king's name is *ʾAkhashverosh,* the Hebrew equivalent of the Old Persian name *Xshayarshan* (transliterated by the Greeks as *Xerxes*). The Septuagint and Josephus

misidentified this king as *Artaxerxes*. There are about twenty inscriptions associated with Xerxes. The Greek historians Herodotus and Ctesias provide most of the history from this period.

**127 provinces:** Herodotus (*Hist.* 3.89) indicates that Darius I (522–486 B.C.) had organized the Persian empire into twenty satrapies. Old Persian sources from the reigns of Darius and Xerxes identify as many as eighty different ethnic groups. The 127 *medinot* in Esther (or the districts of the 120 satraps [governors] in Dan. 6:1) may refer to the number of organized nationalities in the empire (E. Herzfeld, *The Persian Empire: Studies in the Geography and Ethnography of the Ancient Near East* [Wiesbaden: Steiner, 1968], p. 288, quoted in Yamauchi, *Persia,* p. 179). The Old Persian lists, according to G. Cameron ("The Persian Satrapies and Related Matters," *JNES* 32 [1973], pp. 47–56), were not district lists for tax purposes but propaganda for the great Persian experiment in pluralism. Certainly this purpose fits the story of Esther, which highlights not only the splendor of the Persian empire but also its ethnic tensions. On the use of *medinah* as a subunit of a satrapy, see Ezra 2:1 and Neh. 1:3.

**1:2** / **At that time,** *bayyamim hahem,* is also characteristic terminology of historical narrative, used more than thirty times in the Heb. Bible (Gen. 6:4; Exod. 2:11, etc.).

**1:3** / Ancient historians noted that Persian kings were great **banquet** givers (Xenophon, *Cyr.* 8.4.1–27). Wine was an important feature of royal banquets, esp. as it was served in special goblets (Herodotus, *Hist.* 1.126, 9.80; Xenophon, *Cyr.* 8.8.10, 18; Strabo, *Geogr.* 15.3.20).

**For all his nobles and officials:** Extremely large banquets had a long-standing precedent in the ancient world. The Assyrian king Assurnasirpal hosted a feast with 69,574 guests (H. Bardtke, *Das Buch Esther* [Gütersloh: KAT, 1963], p. 279, quoted in Levenson, *Esther,* p. 45).

**1:4** / **For a full 180 days:** Compare the 120-day victory celebration of Nebuchadnezzar recorded in Judith 1:16.

**He displayed the vast wealth of his kingdom:** In Esther, as in wisdom literature, wealth and power are suspect when arrogantly accumulated, trusted, and displayed excessively (Ps. 49:6–7, 13; Eccl. 2:1–11; compare Esth. 5:11). The hubris of ANE kings is, from a biblical point of view, an invitation for humiliation (see also Dan. 3 and 5). See further Levenson, *Esther,* p. 45.

**1:6** / **Hangings of white and blue linen . . . on marble pillars.** The king's banquets were held in his winter palace on the ten-acre citadel in Susa. The palace was a square building with walls on each side over 350 feet long. There were seventy-two stone columns between sixty-five and eighty feet tall. Persia's royal colors were blue and white.

**1:7** / **The king's liberality:** Literally, the wine was served "according to the hand of the king." Compare the use of this phrase in Esth. 2:18 and in the description of Solomon's generosity with the queen of Sheba in 1 Kgs. 10:13. In Neh. 2:8, the expression describes God's generosity through the Persian king.

**1:8** / **By the king's command:** The royal host determined the conventions of drinking. (See the references to Herodotus, Xenophon, and Strabo on 1:3, above.)

**1:9** / **Queen Vashti also gave a banquet for the women in the royal palace:** The Septuagint understands the banquets in this chapter as wedding celebrations for Xerxes and Vashti. There is no external corroboration for this assessment. The "women" are probably the harem, including the king's more than 360 concubines. Xerxes adds the unsuccessful contestants of chapter 2 to this group.

## §2 Vashti's Refusal and Its Fallout (Esth. 1:10–22)

All of the king's efforts to make a good impression with his lavish banquets are wasted when he decides to exhibit his queen as the epitome of his possessions. Months of feasting and laughter instantly turn to consternation and anger when Queen Vashti refuses the request of the king's eunuchs to go on display (like some concubine or dancer) before his male guests. When Xerxes seeks counsel from his leading advisers, they propose an empire-wide sanction against insubordination on the part of wives. The king must discipline Vashti, they say, so that her action will not set a precedent for widespread domestic disrespect.

Another isolated individual event will escalate to global proportions later in the story. Haman universalizes Mordecai's indifference in chapter 3 and plots the destruction of all the Jews. He also enlists the Persian communication system to publish his decree in every language and province (3:13).

This section introduces the reader to the role of royal decrees in the Persian empire. Formal, written edict *(dat)* is the preferred mechanism for those in power to control subordinates (1:15, 19; 2:8; 3:14–15; 4:11, 16; 8:13–14, 17; 9:13–14). The king looks to his legal experts to know how to deal with Vashti according to *dat* (vv. 13–15). As in the stories of Daniel (6:8, 12, 15), the Persian laws are irrevocable and may therefore effectively restrict even the power of the king. *Dat* also refers to protocol—of which there is an abundance in this chapter.

A key term throughout this scene is *malkut,* an adjective translated "royal" six times (1:2, 7, 9, 11, 19 [2x]) and a noun translated "kingdom/realm" three times (1:4, 14, 20). The emphasis on things and persons that are royal reflects the values of the Persian court. Vashti had forgotten that her royalty was a contingent status. Her only claims in this environment were in relationship with the king. The party she gave in verse 9 was held in "the royal palace of King Xerxes," literally, "the royal house that *belonged to* King Xerxes." She forgot the source and owner of her possessions and status. In response, the king strips her of these prerogatives (v. 19).

Chapter 1 is full of references to royal honor, a concern central to the plot. Rank and status are highlighted throughout the banquets and the Vashti ordeal. The king indulges himself in self-honoring, only to have it backfire when he pushes too far. The visible distinctions among persons surrounding Xerxes—and the need to preserve them through appropriate gestures of submission—give an insight into the highly stratified community of leaders out of which Haman will emerge. Xerxes provides a character template for Haman as he shamelessly seeks public honor. In contrast to both of these men, we will find two young exiles—one from nobility who is indifferent to the rules of the court and one without any inherited status who moves into the queen's place.

Once the king's honor is challenged, the full weight of the bureaucratic mechanism is called into action to erase the defiance and snuff out any residual traces of insubordination in the kingdom. The plot then returns to the opening vista: a vast kingdom ruled by an absolutely powerful king (compare 1:20 with v. 1).

**1:10–12** / A sense of foreboding is in the air when the king is described as **in high spirits from wine** (v. 10). Readers familiar with biblical narrative will anticipate some expression of poor judgment, usually at the expense of someone else's status. The scene recalls the Philistines in such a state who publicly dishonored Samson in Judges 16:25: "Bring out Samson to entertain us" (see also 1 Sam. 25:36; 2 Sam. 13:28). Daniel 5:2–4, where a drunken Belshazzar called for the vessels from the Jerusalem temple and thereby dishonored YHWH, presents an even closer parallel.

Xerxes wants **to display [Vashti's] beauty to the people and nobles** (v. 11). Xerxes was known for his good looks (Herodotus, *Hist.* 7.187). The verb "to display" *(lehar'ot)*, which referred to the king's material possessions in verse 4, now refers to the king's wife. In this lavish pageant of the king's wealth, Vashti is his greatest treasure. She was to come **wearing her royal crown** (better, "turban"; v. 11). This impromptu request was to bring the parade of goods to a grand climax with the queen. Her beauty was only one aspect of the royal display in this finale. Her immediate response to such a command was even more significant (perhaps more than the king consciously realized).

The royal banquets were subtly self-centered and self-serving affairs. Two similar court conflict stories from the book of Daniel also illustrate royal self-absorption (Dan. 3 and 6). In these cases, royalty is too easily confused with deity.

Vashti's refusal shook the palace and brought the celebration to a premature close. After this unprecedented display of wealth and power, Vashti "ruin[s] at one stroke the effect of the whole ostentatious exhibition" (T. H. Gaster, "Esther 1:22," *JBL* 69.4 [1950], p. 381). The king's honor, so thoroughly reinforced during his lengthy banquet, was brought into contempt because a simple request was denied. Xerxes' celebration of his control over "127 provinces stretching from India to Cush" (1:1) paled when he could not demonstrate control over the will of one woman.

The reaction of the king was expected but excessive: **Then the king became furious and burned with anger** (v. 12). Though Xerxes, like other Persian kings, boasted, "I am not hot-tempered . . . I hold firmly under control by my will" (B. Gharib, "A Newly Found Old Persian Inscription," *Iranica Antiqua* 8 [1968], pp. 54–69, p. 60), he was known for his unpredictable temper. The Persian king had become a public spectacle as a spurned lord. (His anger will again flare when he finds Haman on the couch with Esther in 7:8.) The fact that the king resorts to legal counsel is humorous but also explainable. He is drunk and enraged, but his impulses must not overstep the boundaries of the legal system. Persians were known for making decisions while drinking but confirming them while sober. As the biblical sage warns, "It is not for kings, O Lemuel—not for kings to drink wine, not for rulers to crave beer, lest they drink and forget what the law decrees, and deprive all the oppressed of their rights" (Prov. 31:4, 5).

**1:13–22** / Whatever prompted Vashti's refusal (and there are many ancient and modern speculations), she certainly had **not obeyed the command of King Xerxes** (v. 15) and had **done wrong . . . against the king** (v. 16). She dishonored her master in public by disobeying him. In verse 17, Memucan reasons that unless Vashti is banished, other women will similarly **despise their husbands.** Their specific concern is that word will spread among those closest to the incident, **the Persian and Median women of the nobility** (v. 18).

The nobles overreact when they presume that Vashti's behavior will automatically become commonplace throughout the empire, that it will sow the seeds for a state of chaos described as

**no end of disrespect and discord** (v. 18). Such a decree could just as easily *empower* the single act of Vashti to become such a precedent for widespread insurrection! But such is the narrator's parody of the Persian court.

Chapter 1 contributes a great deal to our understanding of the story's main characters—even those who have not yet appeared. In her independence and disregard for protocol (albeit justified), Vashti becomes a foil for Esther. The king will search for **someone else who is better than she** (v. 19). Esther will be measured against the former queen. Ironically, while treating the king with unequivocal deference, Esther will prove to be *more* independent than Vashti.

Xerxes is the king of a vast realm, unprecedented in scope and power. He is also, we learn, a king with a "dangerously tender ego" (Fox, *Character*, p. 26). This enormously powerful Gentile monarch is a weak man. He is quickly enraged and easily consoled. He seems unable to make decisions without his band of advisers, who provide just-in-time solutions for his dilemmas, and he is **pleased with this advice** (v. 21). He proves to be consistently blind to anything beneath the surface in human relations. Xerxes and all of his men set a pattern for Haman, who desperately desires the royal honor to which his detractor, Mordecai, is indifferent.

Most commentators find in this chapter a sardonic parody on the Persian monarchy, a satire laced with irony. There is an exaggerated sense of pomp and protocol as the seven eunuchs carry the king's request to the queen, as another seven nobles discuss how he should solve his personal problem through legislation, and as a major law is written in every language and delivered in haste to decree that **every man should be ruler over his own household** (v. 22). The raw power and efficiency of the Persian legal system is put to work in the most delicate and domestic of affairs. Ironically, what the king (and his male advisers) wants most is not available by fiat, written or otherwise.

---

### Additional Notes §2

**1:10** / **The seven eunuchs who served him:** Ancient sources refer to the royal counselors of Xerxes (Herodotus, *Hist.* 3.31, 84, 118;

Xenophon, *Anab.* 1.6.4). Ezra 7:14 mentions the seven counselors of Artaxerxes.

**1:12 / Queen Vashti refused to come:** The narrator does not explain the basis for Vashti's refusal. Josephus (*Ant.* XI.6.1) records her reticence to break protocol. Women were present at royal Persian banquets, but typically the sexes were separated once the drinking began. Only the concubines were left for entertainment (see also Dan. 5:2). To ask Vashti to appear with her royal turban would have insulted the queen's appearance as mere entertainment at the all-male party. See further Bickerman, *Four Strange Books*, pp. 185–86, and Fox, *Character*, pp. 167–69.

**1:13 / The wise men who understood the times:** The "wise men" may be those who understand (1) the law, (2) the "times" in the sense of how people were thinking, or (3) astrology. Ancient Babylonians and Persians loked for signs from the heavens. Haman will seek a date for destroying the Jews by casting a lot in chapter 3. Interestingly, when Haman's family and friends see a bad omen in Mordecai's parade in 6:13, they are referred to as "wise men" (NIV: "advisers"). In 1:13, however, the use of *dat* (law) and *din* (legal judgment) imply expertise in the affairs of the court (meaning these wise men understood the law).

**1:16 / Done wrong . . . against the king:** This particular Hebrew word for doing wrong (*'avah*) is used elsewhere to describe showing disrespect for one's superior. For example, in 2 Sam. 19:19, David was wronged by Shimei who, like Vashti, took advantage of the king's vulnerability on an occasion when loyalty was expected.

**1:17 / So they will despise their husbands:** To assume that disobeying is despising is a traditional biblical equation found in Prov. 14:2 and 15:20. To assume that the behavior of the royal family is precedent setting was axiomatic as well (e.g., 1 Kgs. 16:31).

**1:19 / Which cannot be repealed:** For traces of the unalterable law tradition in extrabiblical sources, see the introduction, "The Story of Esther and History."

**Vashti is never again to enter the presence of King Xerxes:** Ironically, Vashti got what she wanted (*not* to be in the king's presence). Yet having access to the king was highly significant. The book of Esther frequently uses the common Hebrew idioms for presence, each of which employs the plural form of the word "face" (*panim*). All of the princes and nobles "were present" before the king (lit., "to his face") in v. 3. The seven eunuchs "who served him" (literally, "with the face of him") in v. 10 have similar prerogatives to the seven nobles "who had special access to the king" (lit., "see the face of" the king) in v. 14. Queen Vashti had been called "before him" ("to his face") in v. 11. The most common form of the idiom is *lifney* (the construct form with the preposition *le*). It describes the legal experts in v. 13 and Memucan in v. 16, who is "in the presence of the king." When Vashti is forbidden here in v. 19 to come again "before [the king]," it is clear that her status is permanently damaged. On the future of Vashti (as Amestris), see the introduction, "The Story of Esther and History."

**Let the king give her royal position to someone else who is better than she:** Intertextual connections are beginning to take shape in Esther, many of which will continue throughout the story. The narrator suggests parallels between Vashti/Esther and Saul/David with this phrase (1 Sam. 15:28). A royal figure who proved unworthy is about to be replaced by a historic person who will please the Lord.

**1:20** / **Vast realm:** Literally the verse reads, "When the decree the king has made is heard in all his kingdom, *for it is great*, . . ." This is another indication of the feigning and flattering of the king that was expected in the court. Esther (in contrast to Vashti) will master these conventions well.

**1:22** / **That every man should be ruler over his own household:** Verse 22 literally reads: " . . . each man to be ruler over his house and to speak in the tongue of his people." The NIV transposes the two phrases, assuming that one's native tongue refers to the proclamation. Although this translation flows from the description that precedes it, it is not necessary. Mixed marriages created the challenge of various languages and religions in the home, as Nehemiah (another fifth-century figure) points out (Neh. 13:23–28).

## §3 Esther's Rise to Royalty (Esth. 2:1–18)

The first chapter/scene closes with a sense of comedy, as well as an alarming revelation of fragile emotions at the highest levels of decision making. The Persian court is not a safe place. It is a place of power and intrigue (as is clear also in 2:19–23); a place with unstable relationships and fragile egos; a place with unresolved crisis. Vashti must be replaced by a "better" queen—one who must prove herself as beautiful, but more diplomatic, in this vortex of circumstances and emotions. The two Jewish heroes of the story enter into a world rich with power and pomp, obsessive about physical beauty, and bound by written law.

Historically, the time between the Vashti affair and the choice of a new queen is the four years Xerxes was fighting a series of ultimately disappointing battles with the Greeks. He returned to Susa from a humiliating (and unnecessary) defeat, facing the unwanted consequences of the queen's banishment (his own loneliness). It was the task of the court officials to redirect the emotionally vulnerable sovereign.

**2:1–4** / In the wake of an irrational reaction, the king now has to reconstruct his personal world—a world that is also necessarily public. The scene begins, **Later when the anger of King Xerxes had subsided, he remembered Vashti . . .** (2:1). Grief and a sense of remorse follow his anger. The verb translated "subsided" *(shakak)* occurs infrequently in the Bible and conjures up images of the great flood (an expression of God's anger) as it began to recede (Gen. 8:1). Here royal anger had, likewise, covered the entire known world (through the edict), and now the process of recreation had to begin. Interestingly, the same verb "remembered" is also used in both accounts (Gen. 8:1; Esth. 2:1).

Xerxes is immediately aided by **personal attendants** who take responsibility for helping the king out of a situation they (royal advisers in general) had helped create. The king is melancholy about **what [Vashti] had done** and what, literally, *"had been* *decreed* concerning her" (v. 1). He is willing to let others make decisions about laws promulgated in his name, as we shall see later in the story. The approach of the attendants is characteristically cumbersome and comprehensive: **Let the king appoint commissioners in *every* province of his realm to bring *all* these beautiful girls into the harem . . .** (2:3).

The **beautiful young virgins** (i.e., marriageable maidens; vv. 2–3) were corralled to begin preparing for a night with the king. Apparently, while the king was anxious to find a more compliant replacement queen, he also wanted one who was at least as attractive. Before Xerxes would see any of the candidates, they had to spend twelve months enhancing their appearance with special **beauty treatments** (2:3, 9). The particular phrase for "beautiful" used in verses 2 and 3 *(tobat mar'eh)* is used elsewhere of women whom men find irresistibly attractive (Rebekah in Gen. 26:7 and Bathsheba in 2 Sam. 11:2).

**2:5–7** / In verse 5, the focus shifts to the two central Jewish characters. **Now there was in the citadel of Susa a Jew . . .** The principal character is Mordecai, whose introduction emphasizes his ethnic identity, literally: "A Jewish man was in Susa . . ." This identity lies at the heart of the story's plot.

The vision has shifted (literally, "after these things," in 2:1) from the "frilly burlesque" (Fox, *Character*, p. 28) of the Persian king, his court, and his recent empire-wide edict to a rather terse identification of two displaced (exiled) Jews and their genealogies. As Levenson (*Esther*, pp. 55–56) describes it,

> The contrast between the situation of Mordecai and Esther and that of Ahasuerus and Vashti could not be bolder. While the Persians are aristocrats living amid legendary opulence, exercising power worldwide, and partying with abandon, the Jews are kingless and in exile, where they have been driven by a foreign conqueror. In fact, v. 6 employs the root for exile *(glh)* in four distinct constructions, lest the full measure of the Jewish plight be overlooked.

Like the Jews without king and land, Esther is without parents, living in a foreign land and hiding under a foreign name.

There is another contrast in these biographies. Within the context of the Jewish community, Mordecai's genealogy is impressive while Esther's is marginal. The exiled Jews in 597 B.C., **with Jehoiachin** (v. 6), were from the upper classes. Mordecai had an inherited status in his own culture that was, perhaps, the basis for a measure of status in the Diaspora: **Mordecai [sat] at the king's gate**—that is, he was a royal official (vv. 19, 21).

Mordecai's "bio" contains other useful information for the plot at hand. He is from the family line of the first king of Israel, Saul. The introduction of Mordecai in 2:5 echoes the introduction of Saul in 1 Samuel 9:1, with references to Kish, Shimei (2 Samuel 16), and the tribe of Benjamin. This biographical information helps explain the tension between Mordecai and Haman, *the Agagite,* in chapter 3 and following. The conflict that is about to unfold is framed as a new chapter in an ancient conflict—between Israel and the Amalekites, between Saul and Agag. Perhaps, even centuries later, there is a chance to rectify Saul's failure.

Esther is then introduced as a dependent of Mordecai. She was his **cousin,** whom he **had taken . . . as his own daughter** when she was orphaned (v. 7). Mordecai had become a father to Esther (*ʾomen,* literally, "one who nurses"), the patriarchal figure whom she dutifully obeys (vv. 10, 20). While Esther will eventually take on a leading role in the story, her dependency is evident at the beginning and at the end. (Esther is completely absent from the last chapter.)

Esther is also introduced by her Jewish name, **Hadassah** ("myrtle," v. 7), although she is never called Hadassah in the story. This signals that Esther has a dual identity. Only the reader will know about her Jewishness until later in the story. Mordecai explicitly asks her to keep it a secret (v. 10). Interestingly, the name Esther comes from the verbal root in Hebrew *str,* meaning "to conceal."

The final detail we learn about Esther in this introduction concerns her beauty. She was **lovely in form and features.** This phrase is important to the plot because, as we have seen, the king is intent on replacing Vashti, the "beautiful" queen whose beauty he tried to exploit (1:11). Esther's attractiveness is also serendipitous. Here is Esther, in the home of a relative, in a foreign land, at a time when the king happens to be looking for pretty girls to replace his banished queen. This Cinderella quality of the story creates a sense of anticipation for the most unlikely thing to become irresistibly likely: "Many girls were brought to the citadel of Susa . . . [and] Esther also was taken . . ." (v. 8).

**2:8–11** / The serendipity continues as Esther attracts substantial support from Hegai: **The girl pleased him and won his favor. Immediately he provided her with her beauty treatments**

and special food. He assigned to her seven maids selected from the king's palace and moved her and her maids into the best place in the harem (v. 9). "Favor" is the concrete expression of the actions of others on her behalf. Esther benefited from a select group of palace maids as she began her preparation.

Passive (Niphal) verbs reinforce the sense that Esther is not in control of her fate but is being specially cared for by others. She is **taken** and **entrusted** (v. 8), "provided" for, with maids "assigned to her," and she is "moved" to the "best place in the harem" (v. 9). Mordecai is concerned in verse 11 about **what was** *happening to* **her.** Hegai shares Mordecai's paternal role, providing for Esther with an eye toward her best interests.

*Khen* and *khesed,* words typically translated "favor" and "kindness" respectively, are important terms in the book of Esther (see *khesed* in 2:9, 17 and *khen* in 2:15, 17; 5:2, 8; 7:3; 8:5) and in biblical narrative in general. Because the Lord was with him (Gen. 39:3), Joseph found *khen* in the eyes of Potiphar (Gen. 39:4), *khen* and *khesed* in the eyes of the prison warden (Gen. 39:21), and *khen* in the eyes of Pharaoh himself (Gen. 50:4). God gave Daniel *khesed* among the eunuchs in Nebuchadnezzar's court (Dan. 1:9) and Nehemiah *khen* before the Persian king (Neh. 2:8, 18). In all of these accounts, finding favor is equated with material benefits bestowed on the subordinate by his or her superior. It is also noteworthy that in each of these accounts God is the ultimate source of this favor. In Esther, ultimate causality is only implied.

The expression "won his favor" conveys a unique emphasis in Esther 2. The Hebrew *(vattissaʾ)* suggests that Esther adopted a more active role than "finding" favor (the typical expression); Esther *takes* it. She **won [the] favor** of Hegai in verse 9, of **everyone who saw her** in verse 15, and of **the king** himself in verse 17. The subtle indication is that while Esther is formally passive with respect to the process, she is somehow actively attracting and engaging those around her in ways that bring her benefit. This ability contrasts with the behavior of Vashti, whose overt assertiveness cost her royal status.

Esther's relationship with Mordecai now takes a different shape, but the substance of it is the same. He forbids her to reveal **her nationality and family background** (v. 10). This "background" may include her familial ties with Mordecai—ties that are unknown to Haman (and the king) until later in the story. Presumably Mordecai wants her "nationality" secret to protect her from the anti-Semitism in the empire. Mordecai reveals his ongoing concern for Esther's well-being by pacing outside her quarters: **Every day he walked back and forth near the courtyard of the harem to find out how Esther was and what was happening to her** (v. 11). The secret bond of loyalty between these two Jews, as well as Mordecai's paternal influence in Esther's life, remain intact throughout this remarkable transition.

**2:12–14** / Verses 12–14 describe the logistics of the contest. Still under the care of Hegai, the girls followed a twelve-month regime of beauty treatments, **six months with oil of myrrh and six with perfumes and cosmetics.** The Hebrew word *dat* recurs here with reference to the prescribed time of preparation—another reminder that everything in the court must be done according to proper protocol. Each girl, in **turn** (*dat*, v. 12), would go to the king with **anything she wanted . . . to take with her from the harem** (v. 13). After her single night with the king she would become an official concubine, thereafter assigned to the care of a different eunuch, **Shaashgaz.** Eunuchs are considered "safe" guardians of royal "property."

This is clearly a sex contest as much as a beauty contest. The virgins were physically prepared and coached for a night with the king. They were encouraged to take something of their own choosing with them to the king, presumably something for erotic entertainment. The verb "to go to" (*bvʾ*), used four times in this short three-verse summary, has a double entendre—it is a common idiom for sexual relations. All of the girls except the one chosen would live the life of a concubine, returning to the king's bed only if **he was pleased with her and summoned her by name** (v. 14).

**2:15–18** / When Esther's **turn** comes, she decides not to exercise the one opportunity for independence given the maidens: **she asked for nothing other than what Hegai, the king's eunuch who was in charge of the harem, suggested** (v. 15). The narrator immediately adds the comment, **And Esther won the favor of everyone who saw her.** This young Jewish girl is obedient to her foster father and submissive to her Persian caretaker. She wins favor not by threatening the structures of leadership (as Vashti had), but by compliance, by listening to and pleasing those under whose care she finds herself. However, the word "won" is a subtle hint that Esther is more independent than she might appear to be.

In the royal palace where Vashti challenged the king four years earlier, Esther now wins the heart of the king, and as a result she is named Vashti's successor and wears her **crown**. The verse literally reads, "And the king loved Esther more than all the women and she took favor and kindness before him more than all the virgins." Esther stands out among all women, not just among the virgin contestants. She won his favor *(khen)* and kindness *(khesed)*—both of which signal betterment for her as a subordinate.

The king crowns Esther in a ceremony that marks the end of a bad memory for the king. To celebrate, Xerxes holds **a great banquet, Esther's banquet, for all his nobles and officials. He proclaimed a holiday throughout the provinces and distributed gifts with royal liberality.** For Esther, this is the culmination of a series of unanticipated events that has thrust her into the public arena, the court, and, now, into the king's immediate family. For the king, this is an opportunity to celebrate a new love and a return to the way things were before the trouble began: a big banquet and a beautiful queen.

## Additional Notes §3

**2:1** / **What she had done:** For the purposes of this narrative, Vashti's misdeed was her refusal to come before Xerxes during his party. In Herodotus' account of this period, Amestris (probably the Greek name for Vashti; see "The Story of Esther and History" in the introduction) had committed a heinous crime against one of Xerxes' mistresses on the way back from the failed Greek campaign. Xerxes came home seeking comfort in his harem. It is possible that Xerxes set in place the plan to replace Vashti before he arrived home in Susa.

**2:3** / **To bring all these beautiful girls:** Herodotus reports that queens in ancient Persia were exclusively chosen from seven noble families who had helped Darius overthrow a usurper to the throne (*Hist.* 1.135; 3.84; 7.61). However, Amestris (the queen identified at this time by Herodotus) was the daughter of Otanes, son of Sisamnes—not from one of the seven families named. Darius also married outside these families. For more detail, see "The Story of Esther and History" in the introduction.

**2:5–6** / **Among those taken captive with Jehoiachin king of Judah:** The most straightforward reading of v. 5 is that Mordecai was taken into exile in 597 B.C. This would make him about 120 years old when Xerxes begins to rule. For this reason, some have suggested that the relative clauses in v. 6 refer to a different Kish—not the one of King Saul's period—and that this other Kish was **among those taken captive.** Such a reading would do justice to established dates and standard Hebrew syntax and would leave intact the associations with the Saulide line that the narrator suggests here and below. Mordecai does not need to be identified with the exile named in Ezra 2:2 and Neh. 7:7.

**Named Mordecai:** Mordecai's name is a variation of the name for the Babylonian deity Marduk. Esther has a Jewish name, Hadassah, but her common name in this story is a variation on the name for Ishtar, the goddess of eroticism and love (!). Some scholars have supposed that the entire story was originally a myth about these two principal deities. (The name Haman may also be related to the name of an Elamite deity.) However, the story's attention to historical detail and its links with known historical events and personages suggest otherwise. It is more likely that these were common Persian names, taken by Jews living as expatriates. For example, although Daniel is referred to primarily by his Jewish name, his three friends retain their Babylonian names throughout that narrative (beginning with Dan. 1:7). For more on the occurrences of the name Mordecai in extrabiblical texts of this period, consult the list and bibliography in Bush (*Ruth, Esther*, pp. 361–62).

**2:7** / **Who was also known as Esther:** The theme of hiddenness may go beyond the explicit concealing of Esther's ethnic identity. The rabbis related Esther's name to the hiddenness of *God* in Deut. 31:18: "And I will certainly hide (*'astir*) my face on that day because of all their wickedness in turning to other gods." The exile was typically viewed as a time of God's punitive absence. In Esther, however, exilic life is presented in a more positive way (see "The Story of Esther and Its Message" in the introduction).

**2:12** / **Twelve months of beauty treatments:** Archaeologists have found incense burners like the ones that Esther and the other contestants might have used. See W. F. Albright, "The Lachish Cosmetic Burner and Esther 2:12," in *A Light unto My Path* (ed. H. N. Bream et al.; Philadelphia: Temple University, 1974), pp. 25–32; and H. Shanks, "Albright, the Beautician Reveals Secrets of Queen Esther's Cosmetic Aids," *BAR* 2 (1976), pp. 1, 5–6. There is, however, no literary corroboration of this practice in the Persian context.

**2:16** / **In the tenth month, the month of Tebeth:** The narrator uses the Babylonian name for the tenth month ("Tebeth"), one of the winter months corresponding to December-January.

**In the seventh year of his reign:** While the author gives no explanation for the four-year time lapse between Vashti's unseating and Esther's "turn" in the contest, there is extrabiblical evidence that Xerxes was fighting the Greeks during the first three of these years. The twelve-month period of preparation for the maidens may have begun before he returned.

## §4 The Attempted Coup and the Loyal Jew (Esth. 2:19–23)

Chapter 2 introduces both of the Jewish characters, first with a biographical note and then with episodes that distinguish their respective personalities. Esther is the compliant dependent of Mordecai who finds herself in unexpected glory. She uses her physical attractiveness and dutifully respects male superiors. Mordecai is introduced as a strong Jewish man with a royal lineage and a place in the Persian court, a man personally providing for his kin in need. In this episode, he also distinguishes himself (together with Esther) as a loyal servant of the king.

**2:19–20** / Banquets and holidays provide opportunities for clarifying status in the book of Esther. The wedding banquet in verse 18 formally installs Esther as queen. It is also a time for the narrator to comment on her cousin's position in the capital: **Mordecai was sitting at the king's gate** (v. 19). This expression identifies Mordecai as an official (see 2:21; 3:2, 3; 5:9, 13). Although the nature of a second gathering of the virgins in verse 19 is unexplained (and the whole phrase is missing in the Septuagint), it is an occasion to note that Esther's secret relative has a position in the court irrespective of her own.

It is important to the narrator that Esther conceals her identity (and her relationship with Mordecai)—even in this sudden transition to notoriety. She did this **just as Mordecai had told her to do, for she continued to follow Mordecai's instructions as she had done when he was bringing her up** (v. 20). Had the reader missed the comment in verse 10 that Esther was submissive to Mordecai, the point would certainly register here. Esther was obedient to Mordecai in this case because she *always* obeyed him. This point is significant because Esther has moved out from under the direct supervision of her adopted father and into the care of a foreigner with great power. Mordecai, apparently looking out for her best interests, still exercises control over her will. Later, in chapter

4, Mordecai will appeal to her against her own instincts. She will ultimately agree with him, but the nature of their relationship will change from that moment forward.

**2:21–23**  /  While Mordecai was in his position at the gate, **two of the king's officers . . . became angry and conspired to assassinate King Xerxes** (v. 21). This conspiracy is the basis for the first collaborative effort between the two Jewish heroes. Once Mordecai found out about it, he relayed the information to Esther in the palace. She in turn relayed the information to the king, **giving credit to Mordecai** (literally, "in his name," v. 22). The case was investigated and the conspirators were executed.

The reference to naming Mordecai is important from both a historical and a literary point of view. Herodotus remarks that the Persian rulers were well-known for rewarding benefactors (*Hist.* 3.139–141, 153; 5.11; 9.107). For such an act of bravery and loyalty, one could expect any number of benefits—including a significant promotion and tax exemption. *Orosangai,* as these heroes were called, were often exempted from bowing to other nobles! Although **all this was recorded . . . in the presence of the king** (v. 23), the king failed to reward him. For no apparent reason—and to the king's embarrassment in chapter 6—Mordecai was passed over. Chapter 3 begins with awkward unfairness as the king promotes a rival of Mordecai's (and the king's!) instead of his true benefactor.

Linguistic subtleties reveal the character of the Jews in the court. Esther (literally) "sought" *(bqsh)* nothing when she went to the king in 2:15. But the conspirators "sought" (NIV "conspired") to assassinate the king in 2:21 (see 6:2). Haman will "seek" the lives of all the Jews in 3:6, as do their enemies in 9:2. Esther follows Mordecai's direction in 4:8 to "seek" the protection of those lives. Unlike the conspirators (and Haman who "seeks" his own life in 7:7), the text portrays Esther and Mordecai as persons intent on serving others.

The scene ends with a recording of these events **in the book of the annals in the presence of the king** (v. 23). One of the motifs in Esther is writing. Usually it is law that is written (as it has been in 1:19 and will be throughout chapters 3, 8, and 9), but here (and in chapter 10) it is history that is written. Law, in Esther, is written to (dis)empower certain persons (based on gender or race), while history is written to preserve certain persons (based on their actions). In the case of the officers, their evil deeds are forever sealed in the book. For Mordecai, this written record guarantees eventual reward.

---

## Additional Notes §4

---

**2:19** / **Sitting at the king's gate:** Although the meaning of this phrase has been debated, archaeological evidence suggests what chapter 3 implies—that Mordecai was a palace official of some sort. This is to be expected of a person who was brought to Persia along with the other nobles from Judah. It is possible that, in light of his access to Esther in the harem, Mordecai was a eunuch. For bibliography and comments on the meaning of the phrase, see Bush, *Ruth, Esther,* pp. 372–73.

**2:23** / **The two officials:** There are many intertextual connections between the plot and execution of Bigthana and Teresh and the two ministers of Pharaoh in the Joseph narrative (Genesis 40–41; see Levenson, *Esther,* p. 65). In both cases, anger (*qtsf* in Gen. 40:2; Esth. 2:21) serves as the catalyst for the rise of the Jewish protagonist to prominence (although for both it is delayed). In both situations, impalement (*talah ʾal-ʿets,* see below) awaits the enemies of the king (Gen. 40:19, 22; Esth. 2:23) and indifference awaits the loyal Jew (Gen. 40:23; Esth. 6:3b).

**Hanged on a gallows:** In Esther, the phrase, lit. "hung on a tree" (used here and in the account of the hanging of Haman [7:9, 10] and his sons [9:13, 14]), refers to the ancient custom of impalement, not the later Roman practice of crucifixion (assumed by the Septuagint translators). Note that Haman's sons were hung *after* they were dead. The "tree" (*ʾets*) is a beam used for impaling persons dead or alive (Herodotus, *Hist.* 3.125, 129; 4.43). This kind of display would humiliate as well as terrify the victim.

## §5 Haman's Promotion and Plot against the Jews (Esth. 3:1–15)

Esther 1–2 describes the splendors of the Persian court as well as its dangers. One queen was banished and her replacement installed. An assassination attempt by two officials was uncovered and executions followed. Chapter 3 begins with echoes of these earlier chapters. Like the king, Haman is a person with great honor (and wealth, 5:11). He also has a very sensitive ego. Mordecai, like Vashti, refuses to comply with a simple command to perform a gesture of deference. Thus, both challenge the honor of the one to whom all others pay their respects. Both Mordecai and Vashti provoke empire-wide efforts to punish not only themselves but also those associated with them by deed or race. Retaliation escalates to dramatic proportions, forcing what is a personal (though not private) affront into a global affair. As both scenes come to a close with a feast in the palace, a host of Persia's famous riders speed in every direction with the script of an edict which, it is assumed, will settle the case with finality.

Chapter 3 begins disjunctively, with the promotion of a person as yet unknown to the reader. This promotion follows immediately after the account of the miscarried coup and the official recording of the hero in the whole affair, Mordecai the Jew. This disconnection prompts the reader to ask, Who is this Haman? and Why was *he* promoted *and not Mordecai?*

Without answering these questions, the author moves on to describe a series of events that bring this loyal Jew and this recently honored Haman into direct conflict. Before the third chapter is over, Haman will have a plot in place that is nothing short of genocide.

**3:1–6** / Although the narrator provides no historical information on Haman's history in the court up to this point, his identity is provided by way of a brief (but provocative) genealogy. Haman was the **son of Hammedatha, the Agagite.** As we shall see, this designation is as significant as the biographical note on Mordecai in 2:5 for the plot.

Haman's promotion places him in a visibly superior role to his peers. The verb *gdl* in the Piel (literally, "to make great") implies the *public* nature of the promotion (compare Josh. 3:7; 4:14; 1 Chr. 29:25). The NIV appropriately translates this term as "honor." Elevation over others is explicit in what follows: **King Xerxes honored Haman . . . elevating him and giving him a seat of honor higher than that of all the other nobles** (v. 1). Honor is a limited commodity, and Haman's promotion forces a new pecking order in the court. The king commanded the other officials to acknowledge Haman's new superiority by kneeling down before him. Herodotus reports (*Hist.* 1. 134) that such bowing was done extensively in the Persian court, since it marked social ranking. Haman's substantial promotion (i.e., over *all* the other nobles) raises questions for the reader. Why was he held in such high regard by the king?

Mordecai refuses to bow and prostrate himself: **Mordecai would not . . . pay him honor** (v. 2). By his refusal, Mordecai was also challenging the king whose command it was to bow. And why doesn't Mordecai bow? This is precisely the question of the other officials—a question they ask repeatedly. Was it something implied by the gesture of respect? Was it something personal?

While the story does not provide unequivocal answers to the many questions of its readers (ancient and modern), there are some hints that Mordecai is justified in withholding honor from Haman. First, Mordecai has just exposed an assassination attempt by two angry conspirators. Now the king has promoted a person who is prone to anger and to royal aspirations, as we shall see. Perhaps Mordecai cannot bow to one whom he "knows" to be other than he appears. Perhaps Mordecai refuses to acquiesce to the injustice of a bypassed promotion. After all, chapter 6 will make it clear that the king was remiss in not rewarding Mordecai at this time. When he does honor him, it is with a great deal of royal honor. When Haman dies, Mordecai is the natural successor. But these are not the motives stated in chapter 3.

The narrator makes it clear that ethnicity is the basis for Mordecai's refusal. The servants point out Mordecai's behavior to Haman to see if he could get away with it (literally, "to see if Mordecai's words would stand," compare Deut. 19:15) **for he had told them he was a Jew** (v. 4). The primary emphasis in Mordecai's genealogy is on his identity as "a Jew" (2:5). Mordecai's refusal to bow to an Amalekite flows from his historical Jewish loyalties (see Deut. 25:17–19). This is part of the "family background" that is to be scrupulously hidden (2:10, 20). It is "Mordecai's people, the Jews," that Haman seeks to annihilate completely, once he identifies them (3:6). It is "that Jew Mordecai" who infuriates Haman later in 5:13. The king requires Haman to lead "Mordecai the Jew" through the streets in 6:10. Although Haman's wife encourages him to get rid of his personal nemesis, she will confess that because Mordecai is "of Jewish origin," no plan against him can succeed (6:13). Once the king realizes the significance of this origin, he supports the efforts of those who help the Jews (8:7; 9:3, etc.). In the end, it is "Mordecai the Jew" who emerges as the king's official prime minister—replacing Haman in 8:7, authorized to enact law in 9:29, 31, and ruling for the good of all Jews in 10:3.

Note that Mordecai is not just any Jew. His lineage, as already noted, had obvious links to the first (Saulide) monarchy in Israel. Haman is identified as "the Agagite" (3:1), an intertextual link to the Amalekite king who proved to be the downfall of Saul's hoped-for dynasty (1 Sam. 15; Num. 24:7). Saul was reportedly killed by an Amalekite in his final battle with the Philistines (2 Sam. 1:1–16). Esther 3, then, presents a pitting of ancient rivals against each other. It is clear that the conflict that is about to erupt is one rooted in ethnic rivalry—a rivalry that is understood biblically to date back to the earliest days of the conquest (Exod. 17:8–16). That passage ends ominously: "The LORD will be at war against the Amalekites from generation to generation" (Exod. 17:16). The two rivals in Esther represent their respective communities as federal heads. Ethnic hostilities begin to boil in ways that the other members of the court half expect (3:4). Mordecai has explained his behavior in terms of his Jewishness.

The effect of Mordecai's refusal to bow is dramatic. Haman was **enraged** enough to begin plotting **to destroy all Mordecai's people, the Jews, throughout the whole kingdom of Xerxes** (3:6). This statement confirms that an ethnic rivalry is underfoot. Haman's anger *(qtsf)* is reminiscent of the king's anger over Vashti's insubordination (1:12; 2:1). In that case, the king resorted to publishing an edict to prohibit such misbehavior among "the peoples of all the provinces" and thereby limit resultant anger (1:16–20). Haman also resorts to an empire-wide edict to purge the Jews who live "in all the provinces" (3:8) to satisfy his personal anger. Retribution, in both cases, is massively disproportionate. The term **scorned** *(bzh)* in 3:6, the same anticipated response of all women in 1:17 ("despise"), underscores the parallels here. Haman barely controls his own anger by inventing a scheme that will eliminate Mordecai (and his people) without ever responding directly to Mordecai's insubordination. The lack of conscience and the excess of ego are appalling.

Haman's emotions and behavior reflect those of the king, as well as the king's would-be assassins in chapter 2. They, too, were described in terms of their anger *(qtsf)*. In their anger, they "conspired" (literally "sought," *bqsh*) to "assassinate" (literally "lay hands on," *lishloakh yad*) the king (2:21). These same phrases are used in 3:6 to describe Haman's conspiracy against the king's loyal minister.

A careful reader should wonder about the motives of the other **royal officials** at this point. **Day after day** they were asking Mordecai why he refused to bow to Haman (3:4). Although (literally) "he did not listen to them" (NIV **refused to comply,** 3:4), they eventually got the information that proved to be inflammatory. Haman hatches his plot after **having learned who Mordecai's people were** (3:6). He had not noticed Mordecai's behavior, nor did he know his ethnic identity, until they pointed it out. The other officials appeared interested in precipitating just such court intrigue.

**3:7–11** / Haman's plot involves employing *pur* (a clay die the Persians used to invite fate) to determine the date of Jewish annihilation. They cast the *pur* for each of the months and each of the days to discern the auspicious date. Haman seeks the cooperation of cosmic forces in what he intends to be the destruction of his personal enemies. The *pur* is cast in the month of **Nisan**—the month of the Passover. The author has now switched from the name of the months in the Persian calendar (2:16) to the names in the Hebrew calendar ("Nisan" and "Adar"). Haman is unaware that he is setting cosmic forces into motion that will seal his own destruction and annihilate his own kin. Even Persian sensibilities would have been aroused with the announcement of the unlucky "thirteenth day of the twelfth month" (v. 13).

Having received providential direction, Haman approaches Xerxes with a plan to rid the king of people who threaten the empire. His accusation is slick: **There is a certain people dispersed and scattered among the peoples in all the provinces of your kingdom whose customs are different from those of all other people and who do not obey the king's laws** (3:8). Without naming this people, he successfully characterizes them as being everywhere but not clearly visible, insidiously contaminating the empire. Like Vashti's rebellion, the deeds of this people cannot be overlooked. Only a comprehensive plan can free the empire from this menacing hazard.

The contrast between the ways of this "certain (or particular) people" (*ʿam ʾekhad*) and those of the rest of "the peoples" is drawn through parallelism. Literally, "their laws are different from all other people's and the laws of the king they do not do." Israel's distinct laws (intended to attract the world's admiration, according to Deut. 4:5–8) were in the Diaspora the basis of mistrust and hatred (so also in Dan. 6:5).

The two verbs Haman uses to refer to the Jews emphasize the nature of the threat they supposedly present. Although they are "one" (*ʾekhad*), they are "dispersed" (*pzr*), that is, they are not a clear, physically visible constituency. They are not an obvious target. In Israel's tradition, this verb describes "scattered" Israel in the punitive state of exile (Jer. 50:17). Haman also describes them as "scattered" (*prd*), a term better translated "isolated," "separated," or "divided" from the rest of the nations. They are not mixing well, not assimilated in the grand scheme of Persian pluralism. The accusation (and solution) of Haman sounds very much like the one presented to Xerxes against the inhabitants of Yehud (the Persian name for the province of Judah) in Ezra 4:12–16.

The only conclusion can be that **it is not in the king's best interest to tolerate them** (v. 8). Haman never explains that a personal feud with Mordecai is at the root of his plan. It is in *Haman's* best interest to convince Xerxes that it is in the *king's* best interest to destroy the Jews. How ironic that he enlists the king's support to annihilate an ethnic group that includes a man who saved the king's life and a woman who shares the king's bed! The Hebrew root translated "tolerate" means "to leave alone" (*nvh*). This verb is a variation of the root translated "holiday" in 2:18 and the word for the "relief" and "rest" that the Jews were finally able to achieve in chapter 9 (mentioned four times in vv. 16–22).

Attached to Haman's plan is an offer to pay for the entire operation. Rather than open himself up to questions from the king regarding the cost (or the identity of this threatening people), Haman offers the sum of **ten thousand talents of silver** from his own treasuries (v. 9). Haman may be motivating the king to act by suggesting that, if money were a problem, he himself would provide it. Perhaps Haman is aware that the king might consider the loss of any group as a loss of revenue. More likely, the money is required for carrying out the annihilation (see v. 11), although it is an exorbitant amount. Esther, after hearing the amount from Mordecai (4:7), refers to this transaction as being "sold" (7:4). This may be a way of referring to money used for the operation, in the worst (and most realistic) terms, as a bribe to get rid of the Jews. One way or the other, the whole proposal has an economic appeal.

The king seems perfectly taken in by official counsel (as he was in chapter 1) and, without further questioning, offers **his signet ring** to his overly trusted premier (v. 10; compare Gen. 41:42). The narrator highlights that the king is blind to this personal vendetta of **Haman . . . the Agagite, the enemy of the Jews** (v. 10; see 8:1; 9:10, 24). With blatant disregard for the whole affair (and a segment of his population), the king tells him to **"Keep the money** (literally, "the money is given to you") **. . . and do with the people as you please"** (v. 11). The king may be accepting the bribe (with typical Near Eastern rhetoric) or granting Haman the right to execute his plan without using his own money. Whatever the case, the people whose lives are targeted are never consulted. They are the silent victims of the negotiation. The indifference and insensitivity of the king, coupled with the malice of his chief officer, merge to endanger all of the Jews in the empire. While, to all appearances, decisions seem to be guided by court protocol and written law, the forces at work under the surface are the angry reflexes and capricious whims of those in power.

**3:12–15** / Once Haman holds the authority of the king's ring, he puts into unalterable script all that he planned to do. The language of verse 12 clearly echoes the description of the first edict that was put in place to solve the problem of Vashti (1:22). Haman, like the king, assumes that his personal problems will be solved once he removes all real and potential threats to his honor. While the scene at the end of chapter 1 was humorous, this scene is not. Haman is overreacting at the expense of the lives of large numbers of real people. As we shall see, many others were willing to comply with his desire to exterminate the Jews in Persia.

On the eve of the Passover, a massacre is authorized in which a new generation of enemies is encouraged to **destroy, kill and annihilate all the Jews** (v. 13). The word for "destroy" *(shmd)* represents the original intention of Haman in 3:6. The three terms together indicate the escalation of emotion and the totality of the destruction. The phrase that follows details this totality: **young**

**and old, women and little children** (v. 13). To complete the defeat
of the Jews, they were also **to plunder their goods** (v. 13). The nature of this devious and violent plan justifies the Jewish actions
later as self-defense, although they will resist taking plunder
(9:10, 15–16).

As already noted, Haman is ironically writing the prescription for his own demise (Prov. 26:27; Ps. 7:15–16). It is also ironic
that the impressive mechanism in place for establishing edicts be-
speaks an effective pluralism in the Persian empire that should be
*protecting* the various ethnic groups: **They wrote out in the script
of each province and in the language of each people . . .** (v. 12).
Unfortunately, Cyrus' grand vision for unity with diversity had
deteriorated by the time of his great-grandson. Now the means of
mass communication and transportation are marshaled against
diversity. Haman knows the king is in no mood for rebellion. The
two edicts that are sent to the edges of the empire suggest a reign
of intimidation and terror.

Verse 15 dramatically illustrates the effect of this pronounce-
ment on its authors and its objects. Haman and the king **sat down
to drink** (note the banquet motif) with an obvious sense of satisfaction that yet another vexing problem had been solved (so also
in Gen. 37:25). In contrast to the callous calmness in the court, **the
city of Susa was bewildered** (anxious and agitated). This is a very
alarming edict in the capital, for apparently relatively few of its inhabitants share the anti-Semitism that the edict calls for (9:15).
How easy it is for those in power to make a decision in a moment
that permanently alters the lives of those in their control.

The inhabitants of the capital do not understand the meaning or context of this new edict. Neither does the king. Even
Haman does not realize what he has just done. The next time he
sits with the king to drink, it will be at a feast prepared by Esther—
a feast that will begin to overturn his wicked plans.

---

### Additional Notes §5

**3:1** / **The Agagite:** While it seems clear that the author intends
to make associations between Saul/Agag and Mordecai/Haman, Agag is
also the name of a Persian province. Superficially this reference may
simply be identifying Haman in terms of his home state.

**Giving him a seat of honor higher than that of all the other nobles:** Haman became the top official in the court, taking a position regularly referred to as "prime minister" or "vizier." In Persian reliefs, the leading official in charge of the royal guard was called the *hazarapatish* (chiliarch). Another was called the "king's eye." It is possible that Haman functioned in the latter category, reporting potential threats in the provinces to the king.

**3:2** / **Knelt down and paid honor to:** The Greek historians report that Persians greeted social equals with a kiss on the mouth, those of slightly higher status with a kiss on the cheek, and those of much higher status with complete prostration.

**But Mordecai would not kneel down or pay him honor.** By not bowing, Mordecai is refusing to acknowledge that Haman's status is significantly higher than his. There are many explanations for this resistance to the king's command. In the Alpha Text of Esther (a Greek text other than the Septuagint), Haman is linked with the conspirators of chapter 2. As suggested above, Mordecai is thus distancing himself from another of the king's enemies. Some suggest that he, as a Jew, could not *worship* another human. Such an explanation appealed to early translators (LXX Addition C; Targum Rishon), and the terms used here typically demonstrate reverence for God. Certainly this is the challenge Daniel's friends face in Dan. 3. But there is ample evidence that ancient Jews bowed to other humans (Gen. 23:7; 27:29; 1 Sam. 24:8; 1 Kgs. 1:31; and, most pertinently, Esth. 8:3), and there is no indication that Mordecai's religious sensibilities are at stake in this account (or even that he had strong religious sensibilities).

**3:4** / **Day after day:** There are some instructive links between this opening scene of chapter 3 and Gen. 39. Potiphar's wife "spoke to Joseph day after day" (Gen. 39:10), obviously tempting him to give in to her. But "he refused" (lit., "he did not listen"). The same phraseology describes Mordecai and the royal officials who likewise question him "day after day" but he "refused" (lit., "did not listen"). Such a parallel would suggest that Mordecai was standing firm in his Jewish convictions *against* their questioning. In both stories, this resolve results in an angry false accusation that places the previously trusted Jewish exile in danger of death. Against all odds, both of these endangered Jews become agents of Jewish salvation and are promoted to higher positions when they are made second to the king. (See Levenson, *Esther*, p. 68.)

**3:5** / **Mordecai would not kneel down or pay him honor:** There are similarities between the court conflict stories of Daniel and the story of Esther. Daniel 2–3 also presents faithful, loyal Jews in the foreign court and those in the court who seek to impugn them; the motifs of bowing and pomp and royal honor; the significance of anger; the misplaced honor to an extension of the king—the image to which the king required all to bow; and the sentence of death for noncompliance. In both stories, the action of *not* bowing precipitated the danger to the Jewish protagonist. The accusation that follows characterizes the Jews as disregarding the commands of the king. In Daniel, exoneration comes rapidly. In Esther, it will take a much more complicated route.

**3:7 / They cast the *pur*:** Herodotus (*Hist.* 3.128) mentions the casting of lots among the Persians, as does Xenophon (*Cyr.* 1.6.46; 4.5.55). For general background on the use of lots in the ancient Near East, see W. W. Hallo, "The First Purim," *BA* 46 (1986), pp. 19–26. On the historical background for the term *pur*(im) used in the second millennium B.C. and following, see J. Lewy, "Old Assyrian *puru'um* and *purum*," *RHA* 5 (1939), pp. 116–24.

**3:8 / Who do not obey the king's laws:** Xerxes had faced rebellions in Egypt and (twice) in Babylon. He knew what tensions local loyalties could fuel. Any hint that another uprising was afoot therefore triggered the king's action.

**3:9 / Ten thousand talents of silver:** This sum is exorbitant from any perspective and likely hyperbolic. The highest tribute paid by any satrapy was 1,000 talents (Babylon). According to Herodotus (*Hist.* 3.89–95), the total revenue for the Persian empire was 14,560 Euboeic talents, or about 17,000 Babylonian talents. Whichever of these two designations was current at this time would make Haman's offer more than half the empire's economy. For these figures, see Fox, *Character*, p. 51. It is unclear if Haman is offering his own funds or those at his disposal (i.e., in the provincial treasuries).

**3:11 / Do with the people as you please:** The king's unhesitating response to Haman's accusation and proposal betrays a flaw that Xerxes did not admit. A portion of one of his inscriptions describes just the kind of king he *isn't* in the story of Esther: "What a man says against a man, that does not convince me, until I hear the solemn testimony of both" (Gharib, "Old Persian Inscription," p. 60).

**3:13 / With the order to destroy, kill and annihilate all the Jews:** This edict represented legalized genocide. Each province was ordered to engage its troops in a military confrontation with Jews regardless of age or gender.

## §6 The Jewish Response I: Mordecai's Plan for Esther (Esth. 4:1–17)

There are now two royal documents that refer directly or indirectly to Mordecai. His protection of the king in chapter 2, recorded in the royal annals, would typically guarantee him a place of protection and prestige among the king's benefactors. He is also a Jew and therefore a target of Haman's edict in chapter 3. In fact, he is Haman's primary target. Which of these two documents will determine the future of Mordecai and the Jews? Over the next two chapters, it appears that Haman's edict will have more to say about the destiny of the Jews than a forgotten deed of loyalty.

While the citizens of Susa were bewildered over Haman's decree, the Jews were devastated. The chapter begins with Mordecai, the representative Jew in mourning, reflecting the empire-wide lamentation of the whole Jewish people. Knowing the gravity of the decree, he led them in their rituals of grief. He also knew that their best hope lived in the palace. Mordecai would now challenge the young queen, whose Jewishness he had insisted she keep secret, to consider her providential placement to perform acts of loyalty and courage she could hardly imagine. With some coaxing on his part, the scene ends with Esther joining the rest of the Jewish community in their fast. With the risk of death in full view, she will take up their cause in the inner circle of power to which she alone has access.

The series of conversations in this chapter, though brief, trace a significant development in Esther's character. We know that Mordecai is a strong, principled person who deliberately defied the king's order in chapter 3. Esther has hitherto been passive, compliant and obedient to whatever Mordecai "commanded." What he has asked of her thus far served to protect her. When he asks her to defy the king's laws at great personal risk, however, she resists. When she does finally agree to go to the king, she owns the decision as her own and emerges as a leader in her own right. It is she who "commands" Mordecai and the Jews how to prepare for a counter-scheme that only she knows (vv. 16–17).

Esther's Jewishness has been a secret, and she will continue to keep this identity secret. In this chapter, though, she resolves to be an active, loyal Jew. Her first responses to Mordecai indicate that she has not yet fully identified with her people. When she hears of the plot, she apparently assumes that she will be exempt from the attack. Persuaded by Mordecai's reasoning, Esther eventually acknowledges solidarity with her people. From this point on, she will consider herself their agent in the court.

There is a strong consciousness in this scene of boundaries and spatial distance. Because Mordecai's attire prohibits him from passing through the palace gate, the cousins converse through an intermediary, Hathach, one of her trusted eunuchs. This distance reinforces Esther's sense of isolation. She is in the center of the capital, yet she does not know the news that is spreading from one end of the empire to the other. This seclusion is a kind of false sheltering for, as Mordecai points out, she is not safe from the edict. Esther is also distanced from Mordecai, and their relationship is markedly different with her new position (compare 2:11). Perhaps most importantly, she is isolated in her decision making. Whatever she hears from Mordecai is quoted by someone else, and she can decide what to do with it. Mordecai has provided her with a challenge and a rationale, but she must choose her course. Her resolve is formed in solitude, within the palace walls, where she must devise and execute her own plan. Esther decides to take advantage of the unique position destiny has granted her.

There are some unanswered questions in this scene. How does Mordecai know of Haman's plot when Esther doesn't? Why do the attendants know that Esther is related to Mordecai when neither the king nor Haman do? Why would Esther necessarily be in danger? (Wouldn't her status as queen provide immunity?) From what other "place" could deliverance come?

**4:1–4** / Mordecai is the first to "know" what Haman had decreed. The same verb (*yd$^c$*) is used of the experts who "know" (NIV "understood") in 1:13. Mordecai is deeply concerned with Esther's welfare in 2:11, walking back and forth to "find out (literally, to "know") how Esther was." The same verb is used when he "found out" the plot in 2:22. Mordecai is one who has access to important information, and he uses it to help people at risk.

Mordecai's response is dramatic and public: **he tore his clothes, put on sackcloth and ashes, and went out into the city, wailing loudly and bitterly** (v. 1). These behaviors in the ancient world are stereotypical expressions of grief and anguish over a loss or in the face of a grave threat (e.g., Gen. 37:29; 2 Sam. 1:2; 2 Sam. 13:19). Taking on these symbols of death also conveys shame and humiliation. Doing so in the city square underscores the public nature of the calamity (see Isa. 15:3; Jer. 48:38). Although there is no direct mention of prayer (the book contains no direct reference to anything "religious"), the reader's correct assumption is that this lamentation would have constituted a supplication for divine deliverance (2 Sam. 12:22; Jonah 3:5–9). One sees in the Jewish response the postures associated with laments: "I put on sackcloth and humbled myself with fasting" (Ps. 35:13).

Mordecai was leading a community ritual that extended to **every province** (v. 3). Jews everywhere were apparently informed of the threat quite quickly. There was **fasting, weeping and wailing** among all of **the Jews** (v. 3), except in the palace. There is a striking contrast between Mordecai, the representative leader of the Jews, and Esther, insulated from the news but the one on whom their hopes depend.

Between descriptions of mourning by Mordecai and the Jews, verse 2 depicts Mordecai's efforts to communicate with Esther: **he went only as far as the king's gate, because no one clothed in sackcloth was allowed to enter it.** While some speculate that Mordecai might have been trying to get the *king's* attention, it is obvious to those in the story that he needs Esther's. The one who is the cause of the problem is also the source of information, the gravity of which Esther needs to understand.

Esther is terrified **(in great distress)** when she hears about Mordecai's appearance (v. 4). Without knowing the cause of his predicament (and without asking why), she sends **clothes** to cover his self-imposed state of ritual humiliation. Her intention may have been to give him access into the palace compound to talk face to face. If so, Mordecai refuses to give up his provocative appearance for such an important conversation: **he would not accept them** (v. 4).

**4:5–9** / The next verses detail the indirect communication between the cousins through one of the eunuchs who is under orders with the queen. Intermediaries are apparently trusted in this environment (2:3, 8, 15; 7:9). Esther wanted **to find out what was troubling Mordecai and why** (v. 5).

Mordecai sends back a message regarding **everything that had happened to him** (v. 7), acknowledging thereby that this tragedy was a result of his behavior. He does not use first-person plural pronouns ("us" or "our") yet. Mordecai's message also included **the exact amount of money Haman had promised to pay** (v. 7). The mention of the money had been, for the king, a sign of loyalty and generosity. For Esther, however, it is a signal of the alarming scope of Haman's plan and the depth of his resolve.

Mordecai **gave him a copy of the text of the edict for their annihilation** (v. 8), asking the eunuch to explain the details and ramifications of it to the queen. He also tells Hathach to "command" (NIV **urge**) Esther **to go into the king's presence to beg for mercy** (v. 8). This is an important emphasis in this narrative for, even after Esther became queen, she had "continued to follow Mordecai's instructions as she had done when he was bringing her up" (2:20). Now Mordecai was asking her to do something much more dangerous than keep her nationality secret; he was asking her to make it public.

Mordecai makes Esther's relationship with her kin foundational to his command: he asks her to **plead with [Xerxes] for** *her people* (v. 8). It will take some persuasion for Esther to see herself as an integral part of the dispersed Jewish community with whom she no longer has ongoing contact.

**4:10–17** / This section begins with Esther commanding Hathach to respond to Mordecai's incredible request with certain things that she thinks *Mordecai* should know. *All* **the king's officials and the people of the royal provinces know** that the king has **but one law** for those who approach him unbidden: **death** (v. 11; Herodotus, *Hist.* 3.72, 77, 84, 118, 140). Esther is not simply protecting herself. She has not been **called to go to the king** for **thirty days** and cannot presume to hold any special favor with him.

Mordecai has a sense of urgency that supersedes any of Esther's concerns. If she *doesn't* go to the king, she will not **escape** (v. 13). She may have had grounds for thinking that some Jews in the extremities of the empire would be harmed, but those in the palace would be safe. (Esther will tell the king in 7:4 that she would have kept silent if the threat were less grave.)

Mordecai's comments become even more pointed. If she does not respond to this call, he expresses hope that the Jews will be delivered somehow. But in that case, **you and your father's family will perish** (v. 14). Perhaps Mordecai is suggesting that both of them will perish (at the hands of other Jews? or God?), and that this would end the family line he had preserved by adopting her. Maybe he is insinuating that he would disown her and that she would suffer the consequences of this choice as a member of the family to which she was born.

The use of "holy war" terms and themes in other portions of Esther would encourage us to read this phrase in light of the stories of Korah, Dathan, and Abiram (Num. 16) and Achan (Josh. 7). These individuals stepped outside of God's will and brought about the destruction of their families. Mordecai is pronouncing a warning of judgment on one who is on the verge of abandoning her people.

Verse 14 contains one of the most memorable lines in the story of Esther. At the height of this intense interchange, Mordecai persuades Esther with words of hope and threat. The hope is found in an unexplained assurance that **relief and deliverance for the Jews will arise from another place.** Esther must decide whether or not she will accept her appointed role in their deliverance. "Relief" *(revakh)* and "deliverance" *(hatsalah)* are rare words in the Hebrew Bible, but they represent important themes in Esther. The goal of the fighting in the later chapters will be "rest" and "relief," translations of a similar Hebrew verb *nukh* (Esth. 9:16, 17, 18, 22).

Many find in Mordecai's reference to "another place" the book's clearest allusion to God. If this is religious language, it is veiled. The term "place" in Hebrew *(maqom)* functions in the Bible (and in later rabbinic literature) as a veiled reference to Zion, God's dwelling place (Deut. 12:5, etc.). However, in Deuteronomy it is the definite form of the word, *hammaqom* ("the place"), that refers to the dwelling place, not "another place." It would be very unexpected for a subtle reference to Zion to surface in this story that otherwise has such an exclusively Diaspora perspective.

It is still likely that Mordecai is expressing his belief that God will deliver through some means, whether through Esther or not. The whole Jewish community has been fasting and mourning, presumably in prayer for deliverance. Esther fasts for three days in preparation for her role as the chosen deliverer. It is hard to imagine that ancient Jewish readers had anything other than God in mind when they read Mordecai's words. Both Josephus and the Targums make this association.

Mordecai finishes his appeal with a muted reference to providence: **who knows but that you have come to royal position for such a time as this?** (v. 14). The phrase "who knows?" recalls the hopes of those who are in distress elsewhere in the Hebrew Bible (2 Sam. 12:22; Joel 2:14; Jonah 3:9). In this case, it is a way of suggesting a destiny for Esther. Haven't all of the serendipitous events in the last four years put her in this position for this very moment? Mordecai uses the word "time" (*ʿet*) twice in this verse. The Septuagint translators appropriately use the Greek term *kairos* here. This is indeed Esther's "moment."

Esther resolves to defy the king's law (*dat*) in verse 16, even at the risk of perishing (sooner rather than later). Like Shadrach, Meshach, and Abednego, she will be faithful whatever the results (Dan. 3:16–18). She accepts her providential role. This includes more than risk taking; she also assumes the new role of leadership over her own people, and even over Mordecai himself. She now commands (by the use of imperatives) Mordecai and the rest of the Jews along with her coterie (v. 16). And **Mordecai went away and carried out all** that she "commanded" (v. 17, NIV **Esther's instructions**).

Esther requires the Susan Jews and her maids to participate in a severe fast (no water or food). Fasts in the Bible were typically from morning until night (Judg. 20:26; 2 Sam. 1:12), involving abstinence from certain foods. Esther's fast effectively overturns or overrules Passover, which began that night. It also, perhaps, demonstrates that her trust is not in her beauty alone (her previous source of favor with the king), but in the providence of God. Her final, haunting words, **if I perish, I perish,** suggest a resignation to fate (compare Gen. 43:14).

This whole chapter finds the Jews filled with apprehension and disquiet while maintaining a ritual state of supplication and hope. In marked contrast is the "drinking" of Haman and the king in 3:15. In fact, the fasting in chapter 4 is situated in the center of all of the "feasts" in the book and sets the stage for the reversals that ultimately lead to Purim.

---

### Additional Notes §6

---

**4:1–3** / **Sackcloth and ashes:** Biblical instances of ritual mourning using many of these terms are found in Gen. 37:34; 2 Sam. 13:19; Job

2:12. For a fuller understanding of these rituals of mourning and humiliation in their ancient Near Eastern context, see DeVaux, *Ancient Israel* (vol. 1; New York: McGraw Hill, 1965), p. 59; G. A. Anderson, *A Time to Mourn, A Time to Dance: The Expression of Grief and Joy in Israelite Religion* (University Park, Pa.: Pennsylvania State University, 1991), pp. 87–89; and M. Gruber, *Aspects of Nonverbal Communication in the Ancient Near East* (Rome: Pontifical Biblical Institute, 1979), pp. 412, 417–18, 446, 457, 460; or the summary in Laniak, *Shame,* pp. 91–95.

There are some parallels in this account to the fasting of the Ninevites in Jonah 3. Both stories feature the reversal of an irreversible (!) edict after widespread fasting in sackcloth and ashes. As noted above, the "who knows?" of Jonah 3:9 echoes in the words of Mordecai in 4:14.

**4:4** / **Instead of his sackcloth:** The only times the verb *svr* is used in Esther are in this phrase (lit., *"to turn aside* his sackcloth from him"), when the ring of the king was *turned over* to Haman in 3:10, and then when it is *turned over* to Mordecai in 8:2. Change in dress is an important indication of status change in the book, esp. in this chapter. Turning and (ex)changing are hints of reversals in Esther, marked in subtle ways throughout and eventually summarized in 9:1.

**4:5–9** / The verb "to know" (*yd*ᶜ) continues to be important in chapter 4, although it is partially lost in translation. In verse 5 Esther sends the eunuch "to know" (NIV "to find out") what is wrong with Mordecai. He tells Hathach exactly what had happened, including how much money Haman had offered. In verse 11 she tells Mordecai, **All the king's officials and the people of the royal provinces** *know . . .* that she could not go to the king without his summons. Mordecai has the last use of the verb in verse 14 when he asks her rhetorically, **And who** *knows* **but that you have come to royal position for such a time as this?**

**4:11** / **Any man or woman who approaches the king . . . without being summoned:** Josephus (*Ant.* 11.205 note), quoting Herodotus, describes the throne of Xerxes surrounded by men with axes ready to execute those who approach the throne unsummoned. A relief found in Persepolis shows the king guarded by a Median soldier with an ax in hand (for a picture see Yamauchi, *Persia,* p. 360). There is evidence that the king's chiliarch (see note on 3:1) was in charge of the guests whom the king would see. If this is the position that Haman held, Esther was in a precarious position indeed.

**4:14** / **If you remain silent at this time:** There are some parallels between Esther, a Jewess in the Persian court, and Moses, a Jew in the Egyptian court. Both enjoyed the privileges of nobility without being born into them. Both gave up the comforts of their unusual positions when they began to identify with their own people over those with whom they resided. When God called Moses to rescue his people, it involved interceding with the king. Moses' response, like Esther's, was hesitant (Exod. 3:11; 4:10, 13; 6:12, 30). Esther considers "remaining silent"; Moses declares he is unable to speak eloquently (Exod. 4:10). The encounter for both was life threatening (Exod. 10:28). In both accounts there is a complication (increased threat) before the people of God are rescued and find rest. God promises Moses "favor" with the Egyptians (Exod. 3:21), just as Esther will find favor with the king. Ultimately, both will risk their favored status before the Gentile king as they seek the deliverance of their people (compare Heb. 11:24–25).

**Deliverance for the Jews will arise:** J. M. Wiebe ("Esther 4:14: 'Will Relief and Deliverance Arise for the Jews from Another Place?'" *CBQ* 53 (1991), pp. 409–15, followed by Bush, *Ruth, Esther*, pp. 395–97) argues that Mordecai's words should be understood as a rhetorical question, Will relief and deliverance arise . . . ? This is a legitimate rendering of the Hebrew that communicates a stronger sense of urgency and hopelessness and that fits with a nontheological meaning of "another place." It seems more likely, however, that the theological suggestiveness seen throughout the book of Esther (and implicit in the rituals of this chapter) is also present here. Conquest motifs include the theme of family punishment ("perishing," from *ʾbd*) prominent in Num. 16:27–33 and Josh. 7:24–26.

**And who knows?:** A prophetic passage that may be in the background of Esth. 4 is Joel 2. The exact phraseology translated as "fasting and weeping and mourning" in Joel 2:12 is found elsewhere only in Esth. 4:3. The prophet expresses hope in God's deliverance as a response to these gestures with the same question, "*Who knows?* He may turn and have pity and leave behind a blessing . . ." (Joel 2:14). The next verse in Joel encourages the people to "declare a holy fast." Esther does just that in Esth. 4:16. This kind of intertextual linkage reinforces a tacit theological meaning for the Jewish fasting and hope in Esther. It suggests that hope for the Jews can be found apart from Zion. For reflections on the relation between these two passages, see K. H. Jobes, *Esther: NIV Application Commentary* (Grand Rapids: Zondervan, 1999), pp. 135–36.

**4:17** / **Mordecai went away:** Mordecai (lit.) "crossed over." That is, he crossed a bridge or causeway over the Ab-Kharkha River, which separated Susa from the fortress.

## §7 The Jewish Response II: Esther's Plan for Haman (Esth. 5:1–14)

As we have seen, banquets (feasting/drinking) occur at pivotal moments in the book of Esther and they regularly mask deeper realities. Vashti was deposed as a result of her insubordination during the public banquets of chapter 1. Esther is crowned as Vashti's replacement during a banquet in chapter 2, but her identity is kept secret throughout (2:18–20). Haman dined with the king in a sinister, private banquet after making the king an (unknowing) accomplice in his plot against the Jews in chapter 3. Now a series of equally portentous private banquets is under way. Esther is plotting to undo what Haman had put into effect when the king last "sat down to drink" (3:15). She will not reveal herself or her request to the king (and Haman) until she determines the right time to strike.

Suspense fills the air at this halfway point in the story as Haman prepares to celebrate his presumably enhanced status and Esther prepares for a decisive confrontation with him before the king. The queen is clearly "fattening him for the kill," at the risk of her own life. Before any resolution takes place, Haman's anger at Mordecai will deepen. Ironically, Mordecai's own status will begin to rise before the final banquet ever takes place.

**5:1–5a** / **On the third day,** prior to the completion of her privately decreed fast, Esther literally "puts on royalty" (NIV **her royal robes,** v. 1). Having identified herself with the Jews (and YHWH) in relative secrecy, she now returns to her public role as Persian queen. This is a dramatic moment that signals an invisible change in Esther. Underneath the garments of Persian royalty is a true Jew, a determined advocate for her people. She will now use the accoutrements of her role for larger purposes. While the other Jews continue to fast, she will bear their cause under the disguise of a feast. Like Moses, she will return to the court as a deliverer—and during the specified time for Passover. After reclothing herself, she takes her stand **in the inner court of the palace,** facing the king and awaiting his response.

There are three references to royal(ty) *(malkut)* in verse 1. It is used adjectivally to describe Esther's "royal robes," the king's **royal throne,** and the **king's hall.** This emphasis underscores the power of the office—a power that Mordecai points out in 4:14 when he challenges Esther to use it. The narrator refers to Esther simply by name in chapter 4, but it is *Queen (hammalkah)* **Esther** whom the king sees in verse 2. This emphasis foreshadows Esther's increasing acceptance and use of royal authority. Never unconscious that her own status is contingent upon the king's, she begins to construct a setting in which she and the king will face and immobilize Haman together.

Although the king had not sent for her in "thirty days" (4:11), Esther clearly regained her position of favor once the king *saw* his queen. Literally, she "gained favor *in his eyes*" (**was pleased with her,** v. 2). Appearances are very important in Esther. "Seeing" is a key theme in the banquets of chapter 1, during which the king sought to "display" (literally, "make others *see*") his wealth and his queen. Because Esther was "good in [Hegai's] eyes," (2:9) she "gained kindness." Esther 2:15 summarizes Esther's impact on the whole court by emphasizing her appearance: "Esther won the favor of *everyone who saw her.*"

Seeing is also important in the tension between Mordecai and Haman. The newly appointed prime minister was enraged when he *saw* that Mordecai would not bow to him (3:5). The other officials had been anxious to *see* (literally) if this "behavior would be tolerated" (3:4). Chapter 5 ends by noting twice that Haman was enraged again when he *saw* that Mordecai refused to bow before him (vv. 9, 13). The emphasis on what people see underscores the importance of protocol in the Persian court—protocol that Mordecai deliberately ignores but Esther skillfully exploits.

After a ritual of acceptance in which Esther **touched** the extended **scepter** (v. 2), the king offers his kindness in a standard formula of generosity: **"What is it, Queen Esther? What is your request? Even up to half the kingdom, it will be given you"** (5:3). Such an offer has precedents in Persian histories (Herodotus, *Hist.* 9.109–111). The king understands that she has presented herself for some purpose. Esther's response is simple and endearing. She asks him to come to a banquet she has already prepared for the king and Haman (v. 4). Xerxes agrees. He instructs his attendants to literally "rush" Haman to do what Esther had requested (compare

6:10). This haste is a subtle hint that Esther is taking charge, albeit within the prescribed boundaries of Persian protocol.

**5:5b–8** / Toward the end of the banquet, literally, "during the wine course," the king renews and intensifies his congenial interrogation of Esther: **"Now what is your petition? . . . what is your request?"** (v. 6). Her answer (like his question) is more involved, repeating her original request with a double statement of formal deference: **"If the king regards me with favor and if it pleases the king to grant my petition and fulfill my request, . . ."** Although the *narrator* points out that Esther actively *gains* favor from those around her, *she* always uses the passive verb, "to *find* favor," when she refers to herself. When Esther first came to the court, she "asked for nothing" except what was recommended (2:15).

Her invitation to a second banquet is now all the more intriguing: **". . . let the king and Haman come tomorrow to the banquet I will prepare for them. Then I will answer the king's question"** (v. 8). The king responded to the "word" *(debar)* of Esther (v. 5); now Esther promises to respond to the "word" *(debar)* of the king, cleverly framing the second banquet as a form of her compliance to him. Through a skillful use of language, the queen persuades the king to agree to her ultimate request *by accepting her invitation to the second banquet.* Although risky, this strategy may best explain her motive for another banquet. Esther's response most likely piques the king's curiosity and most definitely arouses the prime minister's arrogance. Both agree to a simple, seemingly playful request that has ominous implications.

Esther is aware that her whole plan depends on the king's favor and his oversight (pun intended). Her obsequiousness is in marked contrast to Vashti's obstinacy in chapter 1, although, interestingly, Esther is reversing the roles of that opening scene by inviting the king to *her* banquet. This scene is subtly reminiscent of Haman's request to the king in 3:8–9. Haman had suggested a plan to eradicate people who were "not in the king's best interest to tolerate," that is, "if it pleases the king." Esther is also taking advantage of the conventions of the court to promote her own cause without the king's awareness but with his formal approval.

**5:9–14** / Haman left **happy and in high spirits** (v. 9) after the first banquet with the good news that he was included in this private banquet with the royal couple. Yet seeing Mordecai's insolence once again at the gate triggers his anger toward the Jew.

Mordecai **neither rose nor showed fear in his presence** (v. 9; see also Dan. 5:19). Mordecai is not intimidated by the edict or by its architect and does not show any affective response. Haman is probably able to restrain his rage (v. 10) only with the thought that his well-crafted edict will unleash a widespread genocide of the Jews that Mordecai himself cannot escape. Presumably, Haman will never have to make his personal animosity public if he just waits for the edict to have its way. Patience, patience . . .

Haman comes home drunk (NIV **in high spirits**, v. 9; see also 1:10; Judg. 16:25; 1 Sam. 25:36; 2 Sam. 13:28), with his ego in an excited and unstable state. After calling his family and friends together, he reports the recent events that have brought him both joy and anger. The queen singled him out for special attention in the court, but Mordecai dishonored him in the gate. How ironic that the queen's flattering invitation was in reality a greater threat than Mordecai's indifference.

Haman's boasting in verse 11 reveals a man obsessing in his conceit. He recounts to his family the things that they, of all people, know well: **his vast wealth, his many sons, and all the ways the king had honored him.** Haman had every form of honor a Persian man could want (wealth, children, and public recognition). However, one person, a subordinate, withheld his formal respect and yet remained in the king's service. Haman's experience with Mordecai and his emotional reaction mirror those of the king with Vashti in chapter 1.

Haman reports that **all this gives me no satisfaction as long as I see that Jew Mordecai sitting at the king's gate** (v. 13). The verb for giving satisfaction *(shvh)* means "to agree with" or "to be(come) like." Though difficult to translate, this word typically implies a comparison. It is used in Esther three times—twice with reference to the king's interest. Haman told Xerxes it was "not in his best interest" to keep the Jews in his empire (3:8). Esther will tell the king that the affliction of the Jews would not have "justified" disturbing the king in 7:4. In 5:13, the interests of Haman are adversely affected. There is a loss to his honor.

Haman's wife and friends (like Xerxes' counselors) are ready with a straightforward solution: have Mordecai executed *now,* thereby removing the threat from his presence (as the king had done with Vashti). If Haman could win royal support for an edict to annihilate an entire ethnic population, surely he could ask the king's permission to rid himself of one individual. Haman's superficial "happiness" returns with the thought that he will be rid of his nemesis on the next day. Haman agrees to his wife's advice to build a tall post **(seventy-five feet high)** on which to hang his enemy. This was certainly an attempt to make a public spectacle of Mordecai's private insurrection (see also Esth. 2:23). The fact that Haman is **delighted** (v. 14) with this idea is as premature and presumptuous as his gloating over the original plan in 3:15. This sort of sadistic joy in the downfall of an enemy is the joy of triumph often feared in the psalms of lament (Ps. 35:19, 24, 26).

Haman has now twice concocted plans that will backfire on him. The date that was set to witness the widespread destruction of the Jews will become the day for executing those who hate the Jews. This gallows, intended to single out Mordecai as first among those executed for *being* Jews, will make Haman first among those executed for *opposing* Jews. Before either of these reversals takes place, however, Haman will fall prey once again to his self-centered intentions as he leads Mordecai in a procession of honor that he intended for himself.

This scene in Haman's home is the first of three scenes that provide the details of what transpired between the banquet invitation and the banquet itself the next day (chapter 7). The reader will be invited to listen to Haman's musings among family and friends once again (in chapter 6), but then he will have no cause for happiness.

### Additional Notes §7

**5:2** / **When he saw Queen Esther:** The careful reader will note that the title "Queen" was used of Esther's predecessor, but only until her judgment was prescribed (1:9, 11–12, 15–18). Then she became simply Vashti (1:19). Vashti's replacement is referred to as "Esther" nine times in chapter 2 but as "Queen Esther" in the context of exposing the suspected plot (2:22). She is "Esther" seven times in her dialogue with Mordecai in chapter 4, but she is "Queen Esther" as she reemerges in 5:2.

**5:3** / **What is your request? Even up to half the kingdom:** Ironically, it was by this same open-ended request that Xerxes had set in motion a previous scandal. His (would-be) mistress, Artaynte, took him at his word and requested the robe Amestris had made for him. Compelled to keep his promise, he gave the robe to her. Once Amestris found out about the transaction, she had Artaynte's mother (the sister-in-law and other mistress of Xerxes) mutilated—again, by forcing the king to honor the same open-ended promise (made at his birthday party). This story incidentally illustrates the way in which the royal word (be it promise or edict) can bind even the king (Herodotus, *Hist.* 9.109–111; cf. Mark 6:23).

**5:8** / **Come tomorrow to the banquet:** The rationale for Esther's decision to ask for a second banquet has given rise to a great deal of speculation. It is possible that the syntax of v. 7 reflects hesitancy and indeterminacy on Esther's part. Some commentators follow the Masoretic division, assuming that the sentence intentionally breaks off after "My petition and my request is . . ." Esther does not, with this reading, state that her request is for him to come to another banquet. Rather, she is saying that at the next banquet she will answer the king's question. Bush (*Ruth, Esther*, p. 405) sees the sentence as broken but quite plausibly suggests that, rather than hesitating, Esther is skillfully gaining the king's support prior to articulating her request. However, the parallel structure of this passage, which Bush himself recognizes (p. 403), does not support this suggestion. There are two questions/offers by the king and two answers/offers by the queen. In both answers Esther invites the king to another banquet at which she will state her request. Whichever the nuance, Esther is acting cleverly and intentionally. Certainly the rest of the story will prove her wisdom in keeping the king and his prime minister together over this two-day period.

**5:14** / **His wife Zeresh and all his friends said to him:** Zeresh consoles her pouting husband in much the same way that Jezebel comforts Ahab in 1 Kgs. 21:7. Both devise a scheme to use the law (grounded in a false accusation) to satisfy the sulking ruler and get him what he wants. However, pride goes before a downfall, not permanent happiness. For this insight, see Jobes (*Esther*, p. 145).

## §8 *Haman Honors Mordecai (Esth. 6:1–14)*

Chapter 6 recounts a series of ironic coincidences that provide just deserts for the antagonist of the story. The coincidences include the king's insomnia on a particular night; the reading of the annals at just the point where Mordecai had uncovered the plot; Haman's appearance in the court at this moment; the king's choice of a riddle-like question; and Haman's choice to assume that this riddle was an invitation for him to authorize his own honor!

These coincidences highlight the story's important reversals and constitute the hinge for the whole narrative. Mordecai will move up the social escalator as Haman moves down. He will begin to assume some of the royal prerogatives that were reserved for Haman. This status reversal suggests that the prospects for the Jewish community are also hopeful. What has been threatened will be secured once again. And the perpetrators of evil will taste the punishment they themselves designed. From a biblical perspective these reversals signal the involvement of providence, expressed through the principle of retribution (see Hos. 10:13–14) and the wondrous protection of God's people. Although these changes presage hope, Esther has yet to present the king with her request. And the parade for Mordecai is more symbol than substance.

The emerging "theology" in Esther takes *together* the initiatives of Mordecai and Esther *and* these [divinely] orchestrated coincidences. There is an implied confluence of human and divine activity, with causality located in both spheres.

**6:1–9** / Verse 1 in the Hebrew version begins, literally, "That night the sleep of the king *fled*." (The Septuagint translators of 6:1 take any guesswork out of the agency by stating, "*the Lord* kept sleep away from the king.") To pass away the sleepless hours, the king asks for **the book of the chronicles, the record of his reign** to be read to him. This reading would likely help the king review recent history with himself cast in the best possible light. When he heard the section regarding the attempted assassination by **Bigthana and Teresh** (v. 2), he asked what **honor and recognition** Mordecai had received for uncovering the plot (v. 3). The answer, to the king's own shame, was **"Nothing."**

To rectify this oversight, the king decides to solicit a remedy from any person who might be in the court. This would have been an official of some rank, for we know that Esther feared appearing in that very place without a formal invitation (5:1). Xerxes consistently looks to his official council for direction. Haman arrived early that day to ask for Mordecai's neck, but he obviously had no knowledge of the king's present concerns (v. 4). The young men say to the king, "Look!" or "Behold!" *(hinneh)*, **"Haman is standing in the court"** (v. 5). Perhaps they considered it serendipitous that the highest-ranking officer was available for consultation. Before asking Haman why he had come, the king asked him, **What should be done for the man the king delights to honor?** (v. 6). Literally, he asked, "What should be done for the man in whose honor(ing) the king delights?"

The king's indirect question would not have been an unusual way to communicate in the court (2 Sam. 12:1–12; 14:1–24). Haman, unable to imagine that the king would consider anyone other than (literally, "more" than) himself, responded in terms of his own fantasies. Had not the line between his own wishes and the king's command become quite permeable in chapter 3? Wasn't the king, of late, quite magnanimous when the queen had approached unbidden? Didn't the *exclusive* guest list for the queen's banquets suggest a shared admiration for him by the royal couple? And now he finds the king waiting for him early in the morning with what appears to be a blank check! Haman has arrived at the crack of dawn eager for revenge, but he is also obviously eager (as always) for his own honor.

The prime minister begins his answer by savoring a direct quote (which he repeats three times) from the king's unexpected request: **[T]he man the king delights to honor . . .** (The Hebrew text of v. 7 does not have the word "For.") There is a pause (signaled by the disjunctive syntax, as in 5:7) while Haman's imagination catches up with his narcissism: **". . . have them bring a royal robe the king has worn and a horse the king has ridden, one with a royal crest placed on its head. Then let the robe and horse be entrusted to one of the king's most noble princes. Let them robe the man the king delights to honor, and lead him on the horse** through the city streets, proclaiming before him, 'This is what is done for the man the king delights to honor!'" (vv. 7–9). Surely, "A fool's mouth is his undoing" (Prov. 18:7a). The prayer of many a lament is, "for the words of their lips, let them be caught in their pride" (Ps. 59:12).

Haman has made the equation between honor and royalty. His description of this ceremony uses the terms "king" *(melek)* or "royal" *(malkut)* eight times. Haman is so consumed with *royal* honor that some ancient commentators connect him with the attempted coup in chapter 2. It is also possible that such an extravagant parade was intended to be a succession ceremony (1 Kgs. 1:33–40). Apart from any conjecture, Haman's loyalty to the king is suspect. From a wisdom perspective, Haman is playing the part of the conceited fool whose blind ambition knows no boundaries.

**6:10–11** / The king approves of Haman's prescription and, without questioning any details, directs him to lead the procession for **Mordecai** (v. 10)! "Hurry" (NIV **Go at once**), he says, using the same verb he did when issuing his last order to Haman at Esther's request. Haman is losing control to the people he thought he could eliminate. The king identifies Mordecai in terms of what Haman hates most: *the Jew, who sits at the king's gate.* Recall that Haman's anger extended beyond Mordecai to the whole Jewish community, and seeing "Mordecai sitting at the king's gate" (5:13) inflamed his rage. He had come to the palace this morning to seek the removal of Mordecai from his position in the court, only to be placed in charge of enhancing Mordecai's honor throughout the capital! With words that have the effect of "rubbing it in," the king reminds him to **do just as** *you* **have suggested . . . Do not neglect anything** *you* **have recommended** (v. 10). Haman unwittingly continues to design his own demise.

The king, albeit unknowingly, has taken his turn at seeking commitment without offering details. Haman obtained the king's approval for his edict without ever mentioning the Jews by name. Esther moved the king into compliance for a request she has yet to define. Now the king has put a question to Haman that did not include Mordecai's name, his deed of loyalty, or the missed "promotion" ("recognition," v. 3). Any one of these pieces of information would have kept Haman from his mistaken assumption. Instead, these ambiguities set up Haman for his self-initiated humiliation, one of many examples of the principle of retribution.

Haman had to clothe Mordecai with royal garments, fore-shadowing the passing of the mantle of power in 8:2, 15. What Haman desired, Mordecai deserved—by true acts of loyalty to the king.

**6:12–14** / Mordecai returned to his place at the gate when the parade was over, but Haman **rushed home, with his head covered in grief** (literally, "hurried to his house grieving and his head was covered," v. 12; see also 2 Sam. 15:30; Jer 14:3). The last mention of "grief" (*'abel*) was in 4:3, describing the Jewish grief over Haman's edict. Jews also were "covered"—with sack-cloth and dust. Mordecai led them in this act of ritual humiliation, and Esther followed. The first hint of the story's great reversals is Esther's act of clothing herself with royalty in 5:1. Haman is now covered with shame and Mordecai is clothed with the garments of royal honor. The shifting currents are hard to miss.

At home with his wife and friends again (as in 5:9–14), Haman recounts what has transpired since their last meeting. This time, **his advisers and his wife** are not forthcoming with encouraging advice. Rather, they see in these events an omen: **"Since Mordecai, before whom your downfall has started, is of Jewish origin, you cannot stand against him—you will surely come to ruin!"** (v. 13). There is little doubt that an ethnic rivalry was at the root of Haman's enmity with Mordecai; now it is clear to those closest to Haman that the Jewish side will win. What capricious superstition had once supported (with the casting of the *pur*), it now denies. Zeresh speaks with the wisdom perceived by Gentiles when God is present among his people (Num. 22–24; Dan. 2:46–47; 3:28–29). Haman's friends are referred to ironically as "wise men" (NIV **advisers**). They offer no hope to a man who is marked by fate to fall. Like Balaam, they recognize the futility of trying to curse God's chosen people and bless Israel's enemies—especially when they are Amalekites (Num. 24:20; Jdt. 5:21).

Notice that Haman is not simply "falling"; he is falling *before* Mordecai. Haman's "rise" to power in 3:1 was "over" the other officials. Mordecai's rise to power will be at the expense of Haman's. Power is a limited commodity in the Persian court.

In Haman's earlier meeting with his family and friends, there was a shared sense of happiness over what would take place before the queen's banquet. The events of the day destabilized Haman's position and shook any merriment out of him. Before he could absorb the impact of the day's events and their meaning,

**the king's eunuchs arrived and hurried Haman away to the banquet Esther had prepared** (v. 14). Once more Haman is hurried (as in 5:5a; 6:10) to an activity that puts him further out of control and makes him more vulnerable to the queen's plans. Esther has moved from passive object to active subject; Haman is moving from active subject to passive object.

---

### Additional Notes §8

---

**6:1  /  That night the king could not sleep:** The motif of sleep fleeing a king is also found in Dan. 6:18. The reversal of fortunes for the Jewish protagonist also comes with the break of dawn in that story (Dan. 6:19), as does the downfall of the antagonist (Dan. 6:24). Like Mordecai, Daniel's objective innocence and loyalty to the king led to his exoneration (Dan. 6:22).

**6:3  /  Nothing has been done for him:** The king had certainly been lax in neglecting a reward for Mordecai. Persian rulers regularly singled out "benefactors" *(orosaggai)* to the king, as Mordecai had become, for a variety of privileges, including royal estates (or minor kingdoms), tax exemption, and money. One could say that being denied a reward constituted an injustice. (For more on the rewards for benefactors, see Herodotus, *Hist.* 3.138ff.; 5.11; 9.107; Xenophon, *Hell.* 3.1.6.; Thucydides 1.137ff.). These rewards also served the king's honor, for they gave him an opportunity to demonstrate his generosity as the grand patron. Josephus' version of this encounter frames the question legitimately, "How may I honor one . . . after a manner suitable to *my* magnificence?" (*Ant.* 11.1). In essence, the *king's* honor was at stake in this affair (see further Laniak, *Shame*, pp. 104–107).

**6:7  /  For the man the king delights to honor:** Haman describes a public recognition parade that resembles the account of Joseph's promotion in Gen. 41:39–45 (see also Dan. 2:48–49; 3:30; 5:29). The differences are important, however. Haman seeks more than the usual level of royalty in each request. Clines (*Ezra, Nehemiah, Esther* [NCB; Grand Rapids: Eerdmans, 1984], p. 308) and Fox (*Character*, pp. 76–77) note that whereas Joseph receives a linen garment and gold necklace, Haman seeks a garment the king has worn. Ancient historians comment on the great social (and near magical) significance of the king's robe. (Herodotus, *Hist.* 3.84; 9.110, 111; Plutarch, *Art.* 5, describes the gift of a royal robe, but with the condition that it must not be worn.) Joseph rides in the chariot of the second in command; Haman wants to ride on the king's own steed, with the horse itself dressed in royal splendor. A simple call before Joseph ("Make way") is replaced by the full statement, "This is what is done for the man the king delights to honor!" Clines (ibid.) also notes the difference between honor by the people (for Joseph in Gen.

41:43; compare Esth. 3:2) and honor by the king (in the explicit statement prescribed in Esth. 6:9). In short, Haman wants to be honored *like* a king, *by* the king. It is likely that by so doing, he is seeking royal validation for succession to the throne.

The significance of these differences is twofold. First, Haman has indirectly asked for the very things that must come as gifts. This difference is part of the contrast between the two rivals in the story of Esther. When Mordecai is honored in chapters 6 and 8, it is not the result of personal ambition but royal recognition of his loyalty (so also in Gen. 41:38). Of all people, Mordecai could have sought recognition for this act but had not. Second, as noted above, Haman's royal ambitions for himself are at the expense of true loyalty to the king. In contrast, Mordecai and Joseph (and Daniel) are presented as paragons of loyalty to their sovereigns. Their other loyalties (to God, kin, and custom) are perfectly complementary to their loyalties to the foreign king.

**6:8** / **Have them bring a royal robe:** Haman's answer shares the sentiments of an exiled Spartan king: "When Demaratus was commanded to choose a gift for himself, he asked to be permitted to ride in state through Sardis, wearing his tiara upright just like the Persian Kings" (Plutarch, *Them.* 29).

**A royal crest placed on its head:** Persian reliefs at Persepolis depict a horse with a crest on its head.

**6:13** / **Before whom your downfall has started:** The verb "to fall" *(nfl)* is a motif in this chapter (and in the book as a whole) that underscores certain elements in the plot. The lot "fell" on the month chosen for Jewish destruction in 3:7. The final use of the term in Esther also refers to the role of chance (providence) in the falling of the lots (9:24). The king told Haman, literally, not to let anything he had prescribed "fall" (6:10). Already providence was beginning to work against Haman. Zeresh consequently uses the verb three times in her prediction: literally, "Since Mordecai, before whom you have begun to 'fall' before him, is of the seed of the Jews, you will not prevail over him but will 'surely fall' before him." (The Hebrew construction uses the verb in two different forms to provide emphasis in the phrase "surely fall.") Haman's fate is complete in the next chapter once he "falls" on the couch before Esther (7:8). From that point on, it is fear that "falls" on those who oppose the Jews (8:17; 9:2–3).

## §9 Esther Accuses Haman (Esth. 7:1–10)

While the events of the preceding chapter mark the beginning of reversals in Esther, there is plenty of suspense as Esther begins to put her plan into action. Although the king has shown favor to Esther and Mordecai, he has given them nothing substantive to save their lives. Haman's head is covered in grief at the end of chapter 6; it will come under a death sentence in chapter 7. Mordecai was dressed with royal honor in chapter 6; he will be promoted in rank in chapter 8.

**7:1–6a** / **As they were drinking wine:** The king reassures the queen that his generous offer (stated here for the third time) is still available. She is now ready to explain her **petition** and **request** (v. 2). She does so with standard formalities of deference, adding, **"If I have found favor with you, O king, . . ."** (v. 3). This is the "favor" that Esther was said to have "won" earlier in the story. It is now the basis of her supplication (see also Exod. 33:12–13). The use of the second-person personal pronoun ("you") emphasizes her intimacy with the king.

Esther has not gone to the king to seek an exception for herself; nor is she only the spokesperson for her people. She has merged her identity—and destiny—with theirs. **"I and my people have been sold for destruction,"** she says, and then continues by using the word "we." Mordecai's questions in 4:13–14 appear to have brought about some soul-searching in the young Jewess. Courage and loyalty have replaced timidity and self-protection.

Before she finishes describing the threat, she adds another statement of deference to the king: **"If we had merely been sold as male and female slaves, I would have kept quiet, because no such distress would justify disturbing the king"** (v. 4). This disclaimer effectively underscores the gravity of her request. It is also a subtle way of recalling for the king the monetary transaction that took place at their expense. The word "sold" is used twice in this verse, referring to the money that Haman offered to the king in 3:9. The phrase translated "would [not] justify disturbing" likely means "it would not be *worth* it" to the king (using a rare word, *shoveh,* to connote monetary loss). Esther also quotes the terms of the edict, **"destruction and slaughter and annihilation."**

Esther articulates her request with clear resolve. She is asking the king to make a critical choice between his queen and his prime minister. Her request is crisp, and she delivers an accusation without so much as hinting at the king's complicity. Like Nathan with David, she elicits the king's anger before identifying the culprit (2 Sam. 12:1–6). Once Xerxes hears of this unnamed threat to herself and her people (compare 3:8), he is agitated (indicated by the Hebrew syntax) into demanding details: **"Who is he? Where is the man who has dared to do such a thing?"** Without hesitation, she answers (with similar staccato in Hebrew), **"The adversary and enemy is this vile Haman"** (v. 6). *Her* enemy is now *his* enemy and thus *The Enemy.*

Esther's extreme deference to the gracious Xerxes is matched by her open spite for the "wicked" Haman. The Hebrew adjective is the simple term for evil, the opposite of the Hebrew term for good used of Esther (1:19) and Mordecai (7:9) and the king's choices (i.e., "if it seems *good* . . ." translated "if it pleases the king . . ." in 3:9, etc.).

**7:6b–8a** / Esther's accusation triggers the kind of anger to be expected from those in power who are threatened. The king was enraged over Vashti's insubordination, as was Haman over Mordecai's indifference. The king's agitated questions in verse 5 reveal his readiness to protect his queen. Esther's appeal was based not only on the king's favor with her but perhaps even more on the king's own honor. Someone close to the king was plotting the destruction of his queen! Had the king been "taken for a ride," bribed unwittingly into giving up his wife? Once Haman was identified as the culprit who had, literally, "filled his heart with this thing" (v. 5), **The king got up in a rage . . .** (v. 7).

As this scene unfolds, Haman's demise becomes increasingly inevitable. The narrator refers to Esther as "queen" six times (vv. 1, 2, 5, 6, 7, 8). Although Haman is number two in the kingdom, Esther trumps him in her unique role as queen. When the power shifts visibly within this triangle, **Haman [became] terrified *before the king and queen*** (v. 6). How ironic that Haman had been so disturbed when Mordecai had not "showed fear in his presence" (5:9). Now Haman, like Saul before God, is terrorized by his own doom (1 Sam. 16:14). Fear characterizes others who sense the invincibility of the Jews (8:17; 9:2–3).

The king goes out to the **garden** in a rage, leaving Haman painfully aware **that the king had already decided his fate** (v. 7, literally, "his ruin"). Perhaps his ruin was not as certain as he thought at this moment, for it was the *king's* ring that had sealed the original edict. But circumstances will help isolate Haman in his culpability. Haman "falls" before Esther, begging for his life, in verse 7. How the tables have turned! Esther was "seeking" *(bqsh)* her life as a result of his edict in 7:3; now he is seeking *(bqsh)* his life from her. The verb for Haman **falling on the couch** *(nfl)* in verse 8a is the one Haman's wife used in her prediction, perhaps less than an hour earlier.

**7:8b–10** / Irony gives way to slapstick when the king returns to find what he identifies (perhaps conveniently) as attempted rape. The term **molest** refers to either sexual or military assault and subjugation. A sexual advance on the wife or concubine of an ancient king was tantamount to a run on the throne (2 Sam. 16:21–22). Persian protocol dictated that no man (non-eunuch male) be alone with one of the king's wives or within seven paces (Yamauchi, *Persia,* p. 262). If the king had been perplexed over what to do with Haman while in the garden, he has no doubt once he views Haman with Esther. How ironic, and just, that Haman will suffer the consequences of a false accusation!

As soon as the king makes his allegation, **they** (the attendants) **covered Haman's face.** Although we cannot be sure of the actual procedure, this appears to be an automatic response to cover the guilty. Harbona immediately points out the stake that Haman had prepared for Mordecai, providing the king (as the eunuchs do in the book of Esther) with a plan to rectify a problem and ease his anger. Harbona helps the king further with evidence against Haman by identifying Mordecai as the one **who spoke up to help the king** (v. 9; compare 2:22). Without hesitation, the king pronounces the sentence, "**Hang** (impale) **him on it!**" (v. 9; compare Gen. 40:19–22). Haman is suffering the punishment for treason shared by the conspirators of 2:23, and he is receiving the ill he had designed for others (Judg. 1:6–7; 1 Sam. 15:33). This is his second (and final) time trading places unintentionally with Mordecai.

Once Haman is impaled, **the king's fury subsided** (v. 10). This is precisely the phrase used of the king in 2:1 after Vashti was deposed and an edict was issued to control insubordination in the empire. Haman, like Vashti, was not only a personal threat to the king, but also a symbolic or symptomatic problem. The next chapters will take us again into edicts and countermeasures to control those related to Haman, both by blood and by intention.

---

### Additional Notes §9

---

**7:4** / **No such distress would justify disturbing the king:** This is the most difficult phrase to translate in the book of Esther, as there are three ambiguous terms in it. The word translated "distress" (*tsar*) can also mean "adversary." The word translated "justify" (*shoveh*) means "to be commensurate with." The word "disturbing" (*nzq*) typically implies (financial) loss (Fox, *Character*, p. 282). Levenson (*Esther*, pp. 99–100) rightly translates the first term personally: "the *adversary* would not have been worth the king's loss." Support for this translation comes from the king's question, "Who is *he*? Where is *the man* . . ." (v. 5) and the use of *tsar* in Esther's answer: "The *adversary* . . . is this vile Haman" (v. 6). The "loss" is perhaps Haman himself or, more likely, the monetary value of the Jews as slaves (a concern Esther is accepting as legitimate). Esther was an exile, and ethnic populations were bought and sold in the ancient world. Possibly Haman's bribe was compensation for not selling the Jews as slaves or for the loss of Jewish taxes to the king's treasury. In any case, Esther is expressing her concern for the king's monetary interests up to the point of her life. In so doing, she shames the king into action.

**7:8** / **They covered Haman's face:** Clothing and covering are important indices of status and status change in Esther. In chapter 4, the Jews in sackcloth and Esther's removal of her royal garb (implied by the fact that she has to put her royal robes back on in 5:1) marked their low status. The procession in chapter 6 marks Mordecai's rise to power, as he wears one of the king's robes. Haman covers his own head in shame as he hurries home. Now, as Haman's fate is sealed, his face is covered for him. In the next chapter, Mordecai takes over Haman's position and emerges from the palace with royal robes and a crown (8:15). For more on the anthropology of clothing as it relates to these scenes, see Laniak, *Shame*, pp. 116–21.

**7:9** / **A gallows:** Harbona (one of the advisers from 1:10) points out a tree (*ʿets*) in front of Haman's house. The *ʿets* is an important image in Esther. It is first mentioned in 2:23 in relation to the would-be assassins; and then in 5:14 and 6:4 for the seventy-five-foot post Haman builds for Mordecai. In 7:9–10, Haman is hanged on this very tree; and in 9:13, 25, his "ten sons" are hanged on it as well.

Chapter 8 begins with the king's personal fury abating, but Esther and her people still have a problem. The architect of the edict against them is dead but the edict itself—the unalterable edict—is still alive.

This chapter continues the reversals begun with the parade in chapter 6. Many elements from chapters 2–3 are now taken up in the movement toward resolution. Haman's edict from 3:12–15 will be reversed by the edict that allows the Jews to protect themselves in 8:9–16. Mordecai is honored in the capital in 8:15 as Haman had been in 3:1. Gentiles will "become Jews" in 8:17, signaling new safety and value in that identity, in contrast to the choice to keep it secret in 2:10, 20.

**8:1–2** / The reversals under way are both symbolic and substantial. Haman's execution is the first of many concrete measures that will bring security and honor to the Jews. The second comes later that day when **King Xerxes gave Queen Esther the estate of Haman** (v. 1). The property of a traitor, now owned by the state (Herodotus, *Hist.* 3.128–129), is given to the victim. Haman was a person of considerable means (3:9; 5:11) and his "estate" would have brought significant resources to the queen—including land, money, servants, and perhaps even family members. The irony is that money once earmarked for the destruction of the Jews is now given to them, along with everything else Haman possessed. It is a maxim in the biblical wisdom tradition that the object of a person's trust (if it is not YHWH) will eventually be taken away (Ps. 49).

Mordecai now joins the royal couple, sharing in the king's favor, **for Esther had told how he was related to her** (v. 1). Being in **the presence of the king** is to be in a dangerous (and powerful) situation, as we have seen (1:11, 14, 16, 19; 2:23; 4:2, 11; 5:2; 6:1; 7:9; 8:1, 3–5; 9:11, 25). However, this is an occasion for promotion, not fear. Once the king realizes the connection between his beloved queen and his loyal minister, he presents Mordecai with **his signet ring, which he had reclaimed from Haman.** This ring symbolizes royal authority as well as implicit trust (Gen. 41:42). The ring is a chilling reminder of the abuses of power in chapter 3, and it signifies the authority that Mordecai and Esther are about to use (vv. 2, 8, 10).

Esther, with newly established authority (and means) as queen, **appointed** Mordecai **over Haman's estate** (v. 2). The Hebrew word for "appointed" is the one used to refer to the king's promotion of Haman in 3:1. How things have changed since the days when the young Jewess did all that *Mordecai* commanded (2:10, 20). He is now the steward of her estate. Things have also changed dramatically for Mordecai, who oversees the house of his former nemesis—presently hanging outside the front door.

**8:3–8** / Although the two Jewish heroes might have savored these moments in the presence of the consoling king, Esther pleads with Xerxes again, this time with more deference— and urgency—than before: **falling at his feet and weeping. She begged him to put an end to the evil plan of Haman the Agagite** (v. 3). Like Haman, who fell on the couch before Esther, she now falls, begging for mercy from the one who has yet to decide definitively the fate of her people. Her pleading *(tithkhannen)* is precisely what Mordecai had challenged her to do in 4:8 (see also Gen. 42:21). In chapter 4 Esther had no tears for her people and told Mordecai that she could not go to the king unbidden. But, having succeeded in that first breach of protocol, she is about to ask the king to do the "impossible," to change unchangeable law (e.g., 1:19). The king **extended the gold scepter** (v. 4), a sign of his continued favor on her behalf.

Esther increases her deference toward her king and husband: **"If it pleases the king,"** she said, **"and if he regards me with favor and thinks it the right thing to do, and if he is pleased with me, . . ."** The first phrase is a standard one used often in Esther (1:19; 3:9; 5:4, 8; 7:3; 8:5; 9:13); Esther uses the second phrase in 5:8 and 7:3 at each of her banquets. The phrase "[if he] thinks it the right thing to do" might appear to bring an ethical dimension to her request. However, the word *kasher* means, rather, if the king considers it "advantageous" or "appropriate." The fundamental ethic in the court turns on what is, literally, "good in the eyes of the king." She has shrewdly framed this, like her previous requests, in terms of the *king's* interests. Esther finishes with "and if

he is pleased with *me*," hoping, last of all, that her personal intimacy with him (emphasized in 7:3)—or, literally, her attractiveness—may ultimately prompt a positive response. Her rhetorical
strategy keeps the king close to his own concerns, of which she
is one.

Esther seeks to overturn (*lehashiv*, NIV "overrule") **"the dispatches that Haman son of Hammedatha, the Agagite, devised
and wrote . . ."** She acknowledges that these schemes were devised by Haman, not the king. But she needs more than Xerxes'
favorable disposition to secure her safety; she needs the law. Re-
voking (*lehashiv*) a law is not technically possible, as the king reminds them in 8:8. Perhaps this is the reason she needs to be so
deferential: she is asking the king to overturn a law by making another one that no one can change. Skillfully, she avoids using the
term law (*dat*), preferring "letters" (NIV "dispatches") "devised" by
Haman. She shifts the focus from their objective permanence to
their subjective illegitimacy.

Esther concludes with a passionate statement of identification with the Jewish people, signaling her solidarity with them in
parallelism: **"For how can I bear to see disaster fall on my people?
How can I bear to see the destruction of my family?"** (v. 6; compare Gen. 44:34). Using a form of the typical interrogative of laments, *ᵓekaka*, Esther is asking her patron to take responsibility for
her troubles. If you truly love me, if our relationship means something, demonstrate it now by not letting me suffer (i.e., by watching the genocide of my people). Esther realizes that the king could
protect her and Mordecai while leaving the Jewish community at
risk. Perhaps the only reason he would care about them is his love
for her. Esther continues to absolve the king of any culpability by
speaking passively of their impending fate (literally, "how can I
bear to have evil be found to my people?").

The king takes responsibility not for the original decree but
for ridding the kingdom of its wicked author. Xerxes identifies
himself as the protector of the Jews, announcing the gift of the estate and the execution of the criminal as *his* response to Haman's
plot (v. 7). It is certainly in the Jews' best interest to have the king
see Haman as an insurrectionist—one who, literally, "sent his
hand on the Jews" (the phrase also used of the conspirators
in 2:21).

The triangle of power is in place for the rest of this chapter
and the next. Xerxes addresses **Mordecai the Jew** and **Queen
Esther** (v. 7), the two persons authorized (in v. 8) to do **as seems**

**best to you** (plural). Xerxes is not interested in the details at this point. He has given them Haman's estate and the seal of authority that Haman abused. There is a hint of impatience that this is not enough to satisfy Esther. He grants them the prerogative to find a way out of the legal dilemma, but he reminds them that Persian law (i.e., Haman's edict) is unalterable. "Do whatever you can, *legally*, to please yourselves," he seems to be saying, thereby removing himself. Ironically, what he gives the Jews here (i.e., carte blanche) exceeds Esther's request.

**8:9–14** / Verses 8–10 convey a strong sense of *royal* authority with an emphasis on decrees that are "written in the king's name" (v. 8) by **royal secretaries** (v. 9), **sealed . . . with the king's signet ring** (v. 10), and sent by **fast horses especially bred for the king** (v. 10). Once Haman himself has fallen, the fate of his plan is determined swiftly and officially by the same authority that helped him create it.

As already noted, writing is an important motif in Esther. It is the decisive method of authorization. As was the case in chapter 1 (and chapter 3), the edict to rectify a perceived threat in the court is **written in the script of each province and the language of each people.** The Persians were known for their egalitarian rule and for an efficient communications system that linked the disparate parts of their empire. It is important for the narrator to report the characteristic concern that everyone be able to understand the king's orders (1:22; 3:12–15), especially **the Jews,** who receive the edict first (v. 9). The irony here is that the "political correctness" of the Persian system does not provide the safety for its minorities (and women) that it may purport to.

The new decree, which grants them **the right to assemble and protect themselves; to destroy, kill and annihilate any armed force of any nationality or province that might attack them and their women and children; and to plunder the property of their enemies** (v. 11), empowers the Jews. This edict was sent out with haste to give the Jews time to prepare for military combat. The language echoes that of 3:13, for Haman's original decree was also delivered with a sense of urgency.

The effect of the decree was to publicize the right of the Jews to defend (v. 11; **avenge,** v. 13) themselves and take plunder. Everyone in the empire is hereby alerted to the shift in royal support to the Jewish side in a scheduled civil war. This is the formal legitimization of a state-sponsored, Jewish military response—a sanctioned reaction to unwarranted aggression. Thus Haman's decree is overruled.

**8:15–17** / Mordecai's position of honor, destabilized in chapter 3 but foreshadowed afresh in chapter 6, is now an established fact. He **left the king's presence wearing royal garments of blue and white, a large crown of gold and a purple robe of fine linen** (v. 15). Reversals are apparent here on many levels. Haman's public promotion and the command to show him homage had put Mordecai on a path of resistance that removed him from the presence of the king (4:1). Now Haman's honor is displaced by Mordecai's promotion and the honor he received in the capital. In chapter 3, Haman had celebrated his edict against the Jews by drinking with the king as "the city of Susa was bewildered" (3:15). With a counteredict in place, it is now time for a **joyous celebration** in **Susa** (8:15) and **among the Jews** there was **feasting and celebrating** (8:17).

As noted above, the narrator is intent on demonstrating more than a pattern of reversals. The tendency is to move beyond vindication and beyond return to the status quo to an *enhanced* state of honor. Mordecai receives the ring Haman had worn *but also* symbols of royalty (seen here in 8:15 and first in 1:6) that Haman had only dreamed of (see these terms also in Gen. 41:42 and Dan. 5:7, 29). Members of the court had bowed to Haman; now the whole city acclaims Mordecai. Haman's edict had been sent out by "couriers"; Mordecai's was sent by "couriers [on] royal horses." Haman had built a stake for Mordecai, but it was used for Haman *and* his ten sons. Haman's private celebration with the king is "replaced" with the Jewish festivities in this chapter but also, more significantly, with the permanent celebration of Purim. The city that was once bewildered with Haman's decree (3:15) is visibly delighted with Mordecai's.

**For the Jews it was a time of happiness** (literally, "light") **and joy, gladness and honor** (v. 16). There were two primary responses to Mordecai's edict and his promotion: happiness and honor. "Light" is synonymous here with "honor"; "joy" *(sason)* is synonymous with "gladness" (Jer. 31:13). These terms are arranged in chiasm. The happiness of the Jews replaces the happiness of Haman when he was honored (by the queen's invitation in 5:9) and when a plan was in place to eliminate his enemy (5:14). Jewish "feasting and celebrating" (v. 17) mark the reversal of the fasting and mourning of 4:2–3 (both being the response to

Mordecai's appearance). Mordecai is the barometer for the security and status of the Jewish people.

Many of those who witnessed this great turnabout joined
the Jews: **And many people of other nationalities became Jews
because fear** *(pakhad)* **of the Jews had seized them** (v. 17). Verses
16–17 share the sentiments and language of Jeremiah 33:9: "Then
this city will bring me renown, joy *(sason)*, praise and honor
*(tip'eret,* brightness) before all nations on earth that hear of all the
good things I do for it; and they will be in awe *(pakhad)* and will
tremble at the abundant prosperity and peace *(shalom)* I provide
for it" (see note below; see 9:30 for the use of *shalom*). This is one of
many prophecies about Zion that is made relevant to Diaspora realities in Esther.

The translation "some became Jews," is a legitimate rendering of a denominative verb form *(mityahadim* from *yehudim* [Jews];
see also Jdt. 14:10), although full conversion to Judaism is not necessarily in view. This is more likely a reference to joining ranks, to
*identifying themselves with* (or *as*) the Jews. (Perhaps this balances
the choice Esther once made to identify herself with the Persians.)
There is growing evidence that the Jews were destined to win.
Power has shifted in the empire. The *pakhad* mentioned here (and
in 9:2–3) recalls the awe other Gentile nations and persons felt in
the presence of Israel when YHWH was at work in a military context (Exod. 15:16; Ps. 105:38; Deut. 11:25; Josh. 2:9). Even the Persian king believes it is in his best interest to honor Jewish interests.

---

### Additional Notes §10

---

**8:9** / **On the twenty-third day of the third month:** This date
signals the end of a seventy-day interval between the decree of Haman
and the counterdecree. Clines *(Ezra, Nehemiah, Esther,* p. 316), like atten-
tive ancient readers, recognizes the symbolic equivalence between this
period and the seventy years of exile.

**8:11** / **That might attack them and their women and children:**
The NIV translators have understood the clause "women and children" as
those who were under attack. While this offers a less offensive reading of
the somewhat ambiguous Hebrew syntax, a straightforward reading of
the text reports the right of the Jews to destroy all those who might attack
them, *including* women and children. The law that legitimates Jewish

self-defense is framed as a complete reversal of the original edict (including the mention of plunder).

There is also a hint here of the requirements of holy war explicitly stated in the Amalekite episode (1 Sam. 15:3). The Jewish community is mobilizing as an agent of divine justice, finishing the task left unfinished during the reign of Saul.

**8:13 / So that the Jews would be ready on that day to avenge themselves:** Justice is served when persons suffer not only for what they have done to others, but also for what they have planned to do. Intent itself is grounds for judgment in Israel's legal code. The case of false accusation is esp. significant because, by its very nature, it impugns the character of another person or group. On the principle of retribution and the dynamics of shame in false accusations, see the article by T. Frymer-Kensky ("Tit for Tat: The Principle of Equal Retribution in Near Eastern and Biblical Law," *BA* 43 [1980], pp. 230–34), the response to it by L. G. Herr ("Retribution and Personal Honor: A Response to T. Frymer-Kensky (1980)," *BA* 44 [1981], p. 135), and the comments and references in Laniak, *Shame*, pp. 140–42.

**8:15 / Royal garments of blue and white, a large crown of gold:** These symbols of royalty designate royal favor but not royalty itself.

**8:16 / Honor:** Hebrew words for honor often have a broader range of meanings than comparable words in English. Certain words reflect concerns of status; others, substance (i.e., wealth); others, honorable character; and others, splendor. The simple word for light here (*ʾorah*) is an example of the last category. The book of Esther also uses the term *tipʾeret* for splendor or radiance (1:4) found in Jer. 33:9. For more on the semantics of honor, see Laniak, *Shame*, pp. 17–23.

## §11 The Victory of the Jews (Esth. 9:1–19)

The ninth chapter of Esther recounts the events that ensured Jewish victory. It begins with an emphasis on a particular day: **On the thirteenth day of the twelfth month, the month of Adar**—a date that chillingly recalls the events in chapter 3 that led to this crisis. This chapter is about this day (and the next), about the victory the Jews achieved over those who hated them, and about the *rest* that followed. These events provide the etiology of the Jewish festival of Purim. Much of chapter 9 is devoted to explaining, in annalistic fashion, the origin of the *two* days that constitute the holiday and the authorization to continue its observance. It is apparent that this material has been edited. The perspective now betrays some temporal distance; the narrator relates a condensed version of the story to varying traditions of Purim ritual in practice between "rural" and "urban" Jews (vv. 19, 26a, 31). The narrator brings the story to its climax with festival legislation for the Diaspora community (v. 28).

This chapter distills the meaning of these events (and of the whole story), stating that **On this day the enemies of the Jews had hoped to overpower them, but now the tables were turned and the Jews got the upper hand over those who hated them** (v. 1). The turning of tables is an apt picture of what has taken place throughout this story. Now the turning, or more literally, the *overturning*, is complete. **Their sorrow was turned into joy and their mourning into a day of celebration** (v. 22). Having happily made this "exchange," Mordecai and Esther authorize a holiday of remembrance and the "exchange" of gifts.

The narrator is not simply describing a reversal of events, righting of wrongs, or simple restitution. The Jews in this chapter (through 10:3) will experience *more* prosperity and honor than they had at the beginning. This is the objective toward which the story moves.

**9:1–5** / The king's capricious decision making offered much less security to the Jews than the elimination of their enemies. Verse 1 uses the verb **overpower** *(shlt)* to underscore what was at stake in this conflict. People in the empire were taking sides, and either the Jews or their enemies would emerge from the day's clash alive. Although Haman was dead, there was still concern regarding the many who were poised to annihilate the Jewish community—who apparently needed little prodding to murder the Jews of Persia.

The following verses explain the Jews' military success in terms of the recent power shift with Mordecai as the new prime minister. Now **the enemies of the Jews . . . who hated them** (vv. 1, 5) would receive their just deserts. Overturning (from the verb *hfk*) is a motif in this story that recalls Baalam's curse, which was *turned* into a blessing (Deut. 23:5; Neh. 13:2). This verb is used frequently in the exodus account to underscore the *changes* wrought by God on behalf of his people (Exod. 7:15, 17, 20; 10:19; 14:5). While God is *turning* Haman's plans against him, he is *turning* the Jews' experience of mourning into gladness (9:22).

The fact that the Jews **assembled** in their cities (v. 2 and vv. 15–16, 18) is an important right, established in 8:11. It is the right to self-defense. They gather to protect themselves from (literally, "to send a hand against") those **seeking their destruction** (or harm). The Jews were assembling to execute with legitimacy—and thereby to dishonor—those who sought to exterminate them.

The response to the Jewish mobilization marks a profound change in the empire: **No one could stand against them, because the people of all the other nationalities were afraid of them** (v. 2; on the "fear" of the Gentiles, see above at 8:17). In 8:11, the Jews are given the right to assemble, literally, "to *stand* for their souls" (NIV "protect themselves"; also in 9:16). When the fighting begins, "No one could *stand* against them" (see also Josh. 23:9). Esther is a story about falling and standing—the Jews' enemies fall, and the Jewish people stand.

Verse 3 continues the summary by noting that support for the Jews came from **all the nobles of the provinces, the satraps, the governors and the king's administrators** . . . because the **fear of Mordecai** had, literally, "fallen" on them. Three of these four groups were mentioned in 3:12 and 8:9, but the fourth group, "the king's administrators," hints at a more substantial level of royal support **(helped)** than the previous edicts enjoyed. This same verb (*ns'* in the Piel stem) was used in 3:1 and 5:11 to explain

Haman's *promotion* over all the other ministers (translated in both passages as "honored"). Now the king's officials are *promoting* the welfare of the Jews, the new object of their honor. The Greek versions of Esther translate the verb accordingly. The reversal in this chapter is not simply military; the fundamental issue is Jewish status and power in the Diaspora.

The obvious basis for their fear is given in the following verse: **Mordecai was prominent in the palace; his reputation spread throughout the provinces, and he became more and more powerful** (v. 4; compare Exod. 11:3). Mordecai (not Haman, and even more than Esther) was the new force to be reckoned with in the Persian empire. "A Jew" in 2:5 is now, literally, "the man Mordecai." The root *gdl* is used twice in this verse (translated "prominent" and "powerful") to emphasize Mordecai's newly established and widely recognized power. Those who had sought to "overpower" the Jews (v. 1) misunderstood the new political landscape. Haman's former promotion (*gdl* in the Piel stem) had been nullified, along with his edict.

Mordecai's "reputation" refers to what people *heard* about him (from *shmʾ*). Hearing is important in Esther, especially when it is related to what is written. Since what Vashti had done was *heard*, it was predicted that social chaos would ensue (1:18). Once the first edict was *heard*, there would be respect (1:20). Because Mordecai did not *listen* to the other officials' insistence that he obey the king's commands (3:4), he put his own life and the lives of the Jews at great risk. Now, as Mordecai's power is consolidated in Susa, everyone in the empire *hears* about it. Support for Jews and Mordecai's growing reputation characterize the period of nearly nine months between the second edict and Adar 13.

Esther 9:5 summarizes the battle in terse language, reminiscent of Haman's decree (3:13) and of biblical conquest accounts: **The Jews struck down all their enemies with the sword, killing and destroying them, and they did what they pleased to those who hated them.** The phrase *kiretson*, "as one pleases," is used in another postexilic text, Nehemiah 9:24, to describe the conquest of Canaan (see also Dan. 11:16). Interestingly, this phrase is used in Esther only in one other context—referring to the king's law regarding drinking at his first banquet (1:8). The Jews were now following the *king's* law to do as *they* pleased with their enemies. They won the battle of the wills with their enemies (v. 1), but within the boundaries of royal law.

**9:6–19** / Verse 6 provides detail on the slaughter summarized in verse 5: **In the citadel of Susa, the Jews killed and destroyed five hundred men.** This figure reflects a substantial number of enemies in the citadel, which is surprising in light of the general sense of favor that the Jews seemed to have had there all along (3:15; 8:15) and the rising support for Mordecai (9:4). Verses 7–10 list the names of Haman's ten sons who were also killed. They were likely coconspirators who were now deprived of their father and their estate. Thus Haman receives poetic justice: "not only is he killed, but his honor, his position, his wealth, and now his sons—all his boasts from his days of glory (5:11)—are stripped away" (Fox, *Character*, p. 110).

The names of Haman's sons attract attention for two reasons. Some appear to be *daiva* names—Old Persian names of pagan gods or demons. This may underscore their evil nature or cultic affiliation. The names are also singled out in an unusual way in the Hebrew text, with two names per line, margin justified. Despite substantial speculation, there is no clear explanation for this arrangement, which is found only here and in Joshua 12:9–24, a text which lists the names of the conquered Canaanite kings. Perhaps the Masoretes who copied and preserved the Hebrew text recognized this (and other) intertextual links between Esther and conquest traditions. Certainly such a layout graphically represents the execution of Israel's enemies.

"Holy war" in Old Testament narrative is often understood against the backdrop of the passage that institutionalizes it, Deuteronomy 20. Plunder was allowed generally, but all people (men, women, and children) were exterminated and all goods were burned in wars involving enemies who inhabited Canaan (Deut. 20:14–17). While very few wars were fought strictly according to these terms, the standard is clearly apparent in the battles against Jericho and against the Amalekites (see also 2 Chr. 20).

In 1 Samuel 15, the prophet insisted on a literal extermination of every breathing Amalekite, along with the destruction of all of their possessions. This group was the first to oppose the Israelites on their way into Canaan, thereby becoming paradigmatic enemies of God's people (Exod. 17:8, 14–16; Deut. 25:17–19). The Israelites were not to take plunder from this enemy (even though it was acceptable in the battle with the Philistines in 1 Sam. 14:30, 32). Esther 9:10 states that after the battles, **[the Jews] did not lay their hands on the plunder.** This phrase is repeated again in verses 15–16, when casualties are mentioned. The thrice-repeated statement helps characterize the Jews as controlled and not motivated by greed. However, it also recalls the historic occasion when the Jews were *not* faithful to YHWH's prescriptions for wars against this very people. Plunder was precisely the problem in 1 Samuel 15:19, 21 (see also Josh. 7:21; but compare Josh. 8:2 and 2 Chr. 20:25). Saul's decision to spare some lives cost him the kingship. From a biblical point of view, the Jews in the story of Esther are completing a task left unfinished since the early days of the monarchy.

The focus of verses 6–10 is on the location where killing is taking place: **the citadel of Susa.** Xerxes reports back to Esther on the death toll in Susa and asks her, **"What have they done in the rest of the king's provinces?"** (v. 12). Knowing that two opposing edicts are in action and knowing Esther's intense resolve (8:3–6), he asks what other **petition** and **request** she may have, attaching the stereotypic promise that **"It will also be granted"** (9:12).

Esther, that is *Queen* **Esther,** is the commander in chief of the operation and the king is asking her what she needs! Without hesitation, she articulates two specific requests, one of substance and one of symbol: **"If it pleases the king,"** Esther answered, **"give the Jews in Susa permission to carry out this day's edict tomorrow also, and let Haman's ten sons be hanged on gallows"** (v. 13). Although five hundred had been killed "in the citadel," there were apparently more enemies at large throughout the capital city. Haman's sons were guilty by association, and apparently they were among those actively opposing the Jews. The king's agreement on both counts provides a legal basis for continued operations.

While modern readers may question the desire to "hang" (impale) Haman's dead sons, it is an attested ancient convention that humiliates enemy leaders (Josh. 8:29; 10:26; 1 Sam. 31:10; Herodotus, *Hist.* 3.125; 6.30). Esther is relentless in her efforts to root out every enemy of the Jews and ensure that opposition will become unthinkable.

Another day of fighting yielded **three hundred** more executions in Susa (v. 15). The Jews in the provinces acted in self-defense **to protect themselves and get relief from their enemies** (v. 16). The casualties throughout the empire numbered **seventy-five thousand.** Whether in city or countryside, the Jews did not **lay their hands on the plunder** (vv. 15–16; see above on 9:10). As is the case in holy war when properly executed, there are no Jewish casualties.

"Relief" is a word that becomes important in Esther 9. The festival of Purim is a celebration of the *rest* (not the battles) the

Jews enjoyed on Adar 14, or Adar 15 for those who fought two days in Susa (vv. 17–18). The root for these words *(nvkh)* was introduced with the "holiday" *(hanakhah)* proclaimed when Esther became queen in 2:18. In 3:8, Haman informed the king that it was not in his interest to "tolerate" *(lehannikham)* this certain people (literally, to let them *rest,* or remain). Now, with a touch of irony, the Jews celebrate *rest* repeatedly (9:16–18, 22). *Rest* is also a leitmotif in conquest narratives (Deut. 3:20; 12:9–10; 25:19; Josh. 1:13, 15; 21:44; 22:4; 23:1; 2 Sam. 7:11). In fact, rest is the *goal* of holy war. The distinction in Esther is, of course, that YHWH is not named as the source of rest. An ancient Jewish reader would have made the theological connection but would also have appreciated the human means through whom it was accomplished.

Rest was accompanied by **feasting and joy** throughout the land. The "joy" of 8:16, 17 is now secured. This holiday was, from the beginning, **a day for giving presents to each other** (vv. 19, 22). Presents, or portions *(manot),* were a natural expression of joy on a sacred day, as was the case also in Nehemiah 8:10, 12. Within the narrative itself, this term is a reminder of the *manot* that Esther received at the beginning of the story when she first experienced the favor of the king (2:17) prior to the wedding festivities (2:18). Gift giving is a symptom, so to speak, of good times. From a literary point of view, Purim is the climax of all of the feasting *(mishtot)* in the book of Esther—feasting that began with the king's generous feast in chapter 1.

A two-day holiday is established that reflects the events of both urban and **rural** Jews. Technically, the distinction in this passage is the one initially evident between Jews living in Susa and those living in cities elsewhere in the empire. Over time, the holiday apparently followed the more traditional distinction outlined in Deuteronomy 3:5 (between inhabitants of walled and unwalled cities, thus urban and rural) which is present in LXX Esther. How long it took for these issues to require an official rendering of the original Purim legislation is hard to say. Perhaps it was within a generation (see the introduction to Esther for more).

## Additional Notes §11

**9:1** / **Hoped to overpower them:** These same dynamics are in place when Daniel is accused falsely and sentenced to death in the lion's pit. In the end, the lions "overpowered" *(shlt)* Daniel's accusers (Dan. 6:24 [MT v. 25]).

**9:2** / **To attack:** In the book of Esther no ethical distinction is made between preemptive strikes and simple self-defense. The Jewish engagement is considered reactive and therefore legitimate.

The phrase "seekers of harm" is used elsewhere in the Bible to describe persons with malevolent intentions (1 Sam. 24:9; Ps. 71:13, 24). The phrase "to send a hand against" is used only in Esther, twice describing the assassins (2:21; 6:2) and once describing Haman's intent to destroy Mordecai and his people (3:6).

**No one could stand against them:** *Standing (ʾmd)* is a recurring motif in Esther. It begins with the unlikelihood that Mordecai's refusal to bow to Haman would *stand* (NIV "be tolerated"; 3:4). Mordecai later reprimanded Esther with certainty that relief and deliverance would *stand* (NIV "arise"; 4:14). The story began its reversals when Esther was willing to *stand* before the king (5:1, 2). Haman unwittingly contributed to Mordecai's honor when he *stood* in the court one fateful morning (6:5). His fate was confirmed in 7:7 when he *stood* ("stayed behind") to beg for his life from the queen. With irony, Harbona points out to the king that a gallows "*stands* by Haman's house" (7:9). As Esther continues to execute her plan, she is beckoned to *stand* before the king (8:4).

**9:6** / **They also killed Parshandatha, . . . :** For more background on *daiva* and other Old Persian names, see Yamauchi, *Persia,* pp. 237–38.

**9:10** / **They did not lay their hands on the plunder:** One explanation for the prohibition against taking plunder in Israel's conquest traditions is the general rule that the spoils go to the victor. Since YHWH was fighting for Israel in the campaigns in Canaan, he alone deserved the booty. To convey this perspective, Israel was to burn the plunder as an offering *(kherem)*. For the narrator to imply that the Jews in Esther were following regulations for holy war is to affirm that (1) God was fighting for them and that (2) this was a case of divine justice (not simply personal revenge).

**9:13** / **Let Haman's ten sons be hanged on gallows:** Impaling is not only a literary motif in Esther, it was a harsh reality in Persian experience. Darius impaled three thousand Babylonians when he took the city of Babylon. This is recorded not only by the Greek historian Herodotus (*Hist.* 3.159), but also, proudly, by Darius himself on his Behistun Inscription (R. G. Kent, *Old Persian* [2d ed.; New Haven: American Oriental Society, 1953], pp. 127–28).

It is difficult for many modern readers to appreciate the "need" to publicly extinguish the lives of Haman's sons. Having a "punishment that fits the crime" was an axiom of ancient law. The lex talionis principle required and limited retribution and revenge to "eye for eye" and "life for life." The principle was applied to intent as well as action (see Frymer-Kensky, "Tit for Tat"). Haman deliberately designated all Jews as fair targets for legalized genocide. For justice to be served, Haman's family and all those willingly associated with him in this plot would face death. This account reflects the same perspective on justice exhibited in the stories of Achan (Josh. 7) and Korah, Dathan, and Abiram (Num. 16).

**9:15** / **Put to death in Susa three hundred men:** The Jews engage in self-defense, and they also execute their enemies legally. Since the Jews had been granted the authority to eliminate all of their enemies, there is no ethical concern in the narrative concerning what the Jews did this second day. While modern readers may wince at the vengeance implied, the author makes no apologies for what is plainly portrayed as a narrative of vindication. The book of Esther assumes that people can be evil ("vile"; Esth. 7:6), and that when such people are removed from the larger community, rejoicing follows. True "rest" comes only after certain threats are removed.

## §12 The Authorization of Purim (Esth. 9:20–32)

Having explained current practice (v. 19), the narrator turns his attention to the events that led to the establishment of Purim as a permanent, regularized institution. Though the festival legislation may be historically secondary to the Esther/Mordecai story, the book in its totality appears to follow deliberately the pattern found in Exodus. First, there is a story of threat and deliverance featuring a Jew with unlikely royal connections and a precedent-setting ritual (Exod. 1–12:42; Esth. 1–9:19). Formal legislation regarding perpetual festival observance follows (Exod 12:43–13:16; Esth. 9:20–32). Note that foreigners are included in each account as well (Exod. 12:48, 49; Esth. 8:17; 9:27).

**9:20–32 / Mordecai recorded these events,** presumably for Persian records (v. 20). We have seen how important writing is in the book of Esther—not only for law but also for history. We do not know exactly what Mordecai included in his recording—at least the battle report and probably a summary of the events recorded in chapters 1–8 (though not necessarily in the form we now have it). In the background here is the unusual command to the ancient Israelites to record in writing their defeat of the Amalekites, their first and prototypical enemy in the conquest (Exod. 17:14). This command included a divine oath to completely annihilate the Amalekites. Although Saul failed to complete the divine mission, Esther and Mordecai achieve the desired results. They put the final chapter of the Amalekite affair into writing.

Mordecai also **sent letters to all the Jews throughout the provinces** (v. 20) *to require (leqayyem ʿal)* them to observe the new holiday (v. 21). This is an audacious decision but one prompted in part by the spontaneous celebrations that followed the conflict. There are echoes of the community's acceptance of new obligations following its miraculous deliverance from Egypt (Exod. 12:50; 19:8).

It is possible that Mordecai is authorizing both days, the **fifteenth** for those in Susa and the **fourteenth** for those outside the city. In that case, he would be legitimizing *variant* traditions. The NIV, probably correctly, instead understands the legislation as a compromise solution: Purim will be a *two*-day celebration for *all* Jews everywhere. Mordecai thereby regularizes and consolidates the observance of festivities (already under way) with the authority of his office. Again, a certain distance from the first Purim is evident.

Mordecai's letters include a brief theological summary of the foundational events that led to the institution of Purim: **the time when the Jews got relief from their enemies, and as the month when their sorrow was turned into joy and their mourning into a day of celebration** (v. 22). "Relief" (rest) is a theme already analyzed within the tradition of holy war. It is also a theme in prophetic literature reflecting on exilic realities. In Jeremiah's vision of exiles returning to Zion, he predicts that "maidens will dance and be glad, young men and old as well. I will *turn* their *mourning* into *gladness;* I will give them comfort and *joy* instead of *sorrow*" (31:13; compare Isa. 35:10; 51:11; 61:3; Lam. 5:15). The use of these same (italicized) terms in Esther suggests that Mordecai was framing this event in terms of God's covenant faithfulness to the postexilic community (note also the use of "near and far" in Isa. 57:19 and Esth. 9:20). To see such promises fulfilled *apart from a return to Zion* is a shift in traditional Jewish thinking. Esther provides an unexpected affirmation of God's blessing on Jews *in the Diaspora,* a state typically understood as punishment.

After stating that the Jewish community agreed to Mordecai's letter (v. 23), the narrator provides a second, more detailed summary of the events in verses 24–25. In this passage Xerxes is completely exonerated; he is given credit for **[issuing] written orders** to bring Haman's scheme **back onto his own head** once he became aware of the plot, and for ordering the execution of Haman and his sons. The king is not held responsible for Haman's edict but is given full credit for Mordecai's, although both documents were sealed with the same (i.e., his) ring. Such a view of the king (as protector of the Jews and prosecutor of Haman) represents a politically adjusted "spin" that suits the official history in Persia well, with its newly sanctioned Jewish leadership. It may also reflect the hand of a later editor.

This historical summary (with its explanation of the origin of the name "Purim") also includes a theological interpretation. It

names **Haman son of Hammedatha, the Agagite, the enemy of all
the Jews,** as the one who **had plotted against the Jews to destroy
them** (v. 24; compare 3:13; 8:11). Haman is now fully appreciated
as the enemy of *all* Jews. His full title reminds those with intertextual sensitivities of the *Agag*/Saul backdrop for the story and of
the stereotypical role Haman plays as the *enemy* in the laments,
scheming and plotting (8:3, 5) against God's chosen. Trusting fate,
Haman **cast the** *pur.* As fate would have it, Haman's plot was
found out and **the evil scheme Haman had devised against the
Jews** [came] "back onto his own head" (v. 25). This is the clearest
statement (along with 9:1) of the proverbial maxim that the story
illustrates: people are caught in the traps they set for others (Pss.
33:10; 94:11; Prov. 19:21). As already noted, this is not simply an
empirical observation but a principle of a *divinely* ordered history.

The Jews accepted Mordecai's letter and **the Jews took it
upon themselves** to keep the new custom **in the way prescribed
and at the time appointed** (v. 27). Verse 27 emphasizes the seriousness of this self-imposed commitment. The Jews **and their descendants and all who join them should** *without fail* **observe these
two days every year.** Verse 28 legislates (for the reader) that the
holiday should be **remembered and observed in** *every* **generation
by** *every* **family, and in** *every* **province and in** *every* **city** (see also
v. 31). Clearly the Jews were law-abiding citizens, contrary to
Haman's caricature (3:8). It is also noteworthy that the holiday,
as it is prescribed in this chapter, does not have any explicitly religious content; it is a legal *Persian* holiday for Jews to feast and
give gifts. Presumably the original audience of this book lived in
the Persian period when such an insistence would have had
significance.

It is of consequence that "all who *join* them" *(hannilvim)*—
presumably those who had identified themselves with the Jews—
were considered part of the community henceforth. They will be
bound to keep this new custom "without fail" *(lo' ya'abor)*, a verb
that in the book of Esther refers to the irrevocability of Persian law
(1:19; 8:8). The term *hannilvim* refers to proselytes in Isaiah 14:1
and 56:3, 6 (see the use of the root also in Jer. 50:5). Here is another
link with prophetic expectations for God's renewed blessing on
his community when they return from exile. In Esther the unexpected element is blessing apart from returning to Zion. Diaspora has become a theologically legitimate, *post*exilic status. God's
faithfulness can be expected wherever his people are.

Verse 29 begins the conclusion of this scene, emphasizing the **full authority** with which **Queen Esther, daughter of Abihail,** and **Mordecai the Jew** wrote their letters. Both Esther and Mordecai are recognized in terms of their Jewish identities within the Persian context. Esther is understood as the coauthor of (and the ultimate authority behind) the earlier letter Mordecai had composed obligating the community to continue the holiday (vv. 20–22). Copies of a follow-up letter were sent to confirm the observance of Purim (v. 29). These letters go out as **words of goodwill** *(shalom)* **and assurance** (*'emet,* v. 30). This pair of terms and others from this passage are found in Zechariah 8:19, where the *voluntary fasts* of a distressed Israel are to become the *regular feasts* of a redeemed Israel. They will be *joined* by Gentiles who respond to the irresistible presence of God in their midst (Zech. 8:20–23).

The reference to **this** *second* **letter** (in v. 29) is confusing and may not reflect the original text. (The Septuagint and Syriac versions do not include the phrase.) The sentence apparently means that Esther and Mordecai wrote a second letter to confirm authoritatively the observance of Purim, which was initiated spontaneously and regulated by Mordecai's first letter. It is important to appreciate the fragility of a newly established holiday and the need for reconfirmation in its first years of observance (1 Macc. 4:56–59; 7:49; 13:49–52; 2 Macc. 10:1–8; 3 Macc. 6:30–36). **Esther's decree** is a formal public declaration (1:15), now **written down in the records** (v. 32). This may be another reference to the second letter itself, or at least to its content.

Purim has the official backing of Esther and Mordecai and the Persian legal system. With the narrator's emphasis on festival authorization, one might anticipate a reference to the Jewish God. In this story, the Jews themselves are the only visible evidence of YHWH, and the laws they initiate from Susa correspond to laws that God initiates from Sinai.

The **fasting and lamentation** of verse 31 refers either to other Jewish holidays (perhaps those in Zech. 8:19) or to self-imposed rituals associated with the mourning in 4:1–3 (where "lamentation" is used of Mordecai and "fasting" took place "in every province"; see also 4:16). Mordecai is not legislating a fast for all Jews during Purim but is referring to these rituals as a precedent for communal self-imposition of holiday observance.

---

**Additional Notes §12**

---

**9:22** / **Gifts to the poor:** Gifts are not for fellow Jews only but also, without explanation, for the poor (compare Tob. 2:1–2). This may be an intertextual allusion to the legislation for each seventh year in Deut. 15. The Israelites were commanded to take care of the poor once they settled in the land of promise (Deut. 15:4, 7, 11). From a literary point of view, this may serve as a reversal of the intended harm to innocent people (in Haman's edict) and signal a return to the banquet in chapter 1 to which all were invited, "from the least to the greatest" (1:5).

**9:24** / **Their ruin:** Haman intended to destroy (*'bd*) the Jews, as well as confuse or discomfit (*hmm*, NIV "ruin") them. The second verb is often found in military accounts in the Bible referring to the terrified reaction of Israel's enemies when God gives his people victory (Exod. 14:24; 23:27; Josh. 10:10, etc.). This verb recalls holy war imagery and illustrates that Haman himself experienced what he had intended for the Jews to experience (see also Jer. 51:34).

**9:25** / **[Came] back onto his own head:** The ancient covenant with Abraham included the promise, "I will bless those who bless you, and whoever curses you I will curse; and all peoples on earth will be blessed through you" (Gen. 12:3). Haman's downfall is more than a wisdom story featuring the proverbial "fool." It is a historical account of an evil person who opposes God's chosen people without cause. Like Pharaoh in the exodus story, he learns the hard way that the Jewish people cannot be abused with impunity. What Xerxes and the rest of the Persians learn is that blessing the Jews brings blessing. This principle is evident as the book closes in chapter 10.

**9:26** / **Therefore these days were called Purim, from the word** *pur:* Although the name Purim is a plural noun, the "pur" that was cast is a singular form. (The term *pur* comes from the Old Babylonian word *puru*, meaning "fate" or "lot.") Some have suggested that it has a plural ending because it is a two-day holiday, or that Purim existed already (without clear etymology) and that this story is a later etiology to explain it. Probably the most ingenious explanation is that the term refers to the two layers of fate in the book—the fate of the Jews according to the lot Haman cast and the divine will which was expressed through the miraculous turn of events (Clines, *Esther Scroll*, p. 164). Less fascinating (but more likely) is the explanation that Purim has taken on the plural ending typical of other Jewish festivals (*Shabu'ot, Sukkot, Matsot;* see also the alternative name for the latter festival of Hanukkah, *'Urim).*

## §13 Epilogue: Mordecai's Greatness (Esth. 10:1–3)

The final chapter of Esther, which says nothing about Esther, is a tribute to the leadership of Mordecai. It begins with an image of the vast empire under Xerxes' control. The second in command of this imposing realm is "Mordecai the Jew." He has proven that a Jew in the Diaspora can serve his king and his people well.

The book of Esther closes with a triumphant note of public vindication for the Jews and personal exoneration for Mordecai, their representative leader. If we read Esther as a lament in the form of a narrative, we have come to the moment in the psalm when "those who wanted to harm me have been put to shame" (Ps. 71:24). The prayer that God would "increase my honor" (Ps. 71:21) has been answered.

**10:1–3** / The first verse mentions the imposition of **tribute** (tax or forced labor) **throughout the empire, to its distant shores**—a somewhat unexpected statement following the authorization of Purim. It returns our attention, as a kind of inclusio, to the description of the great King Xerxes in 1:1 who "ruled over 127 provinces stretching from India to Cush." The capacity to impose taxes (or forced labor) reflects the power of the Persian monarch. The "distant shores" (literally, "islands and coastlands") represent the western limits of the known world (Herodotus, *Hist.* 3.96) to which the Jews were scattered (Isa. 11:11; 24:15–16; 41:5). There may be a subtle reference to the tax relief offered when Esther became queen (2:18; NIV "holiday") or to the missed bribe from Haman in 3:9. The Jews, in essence, constituted only gain to the king. The king himself had been the source of generous giving throughout chapters 1–2. Now, with the threat to the Jews gone, it is time for him to receive.

The story began with an image of a vast, wealthy, well-controlled empire that was threatened openly by a queen's insubordination. It was then undermined more subtly by a prime minister, whose personal animosity toward one of the king's loyal subjects led to (costly?) civil war. As the story draws to a close, the empire is now at peace, the treasuries of the king are being replenished, and the king's **acts** (accomplishments) **of power and might** are celebrated in writing (v. 2). One is reminded of the wealth that accrued to Egypt under the rule of another Jew (Gen. 41:41–57; 47:13–26), evidence of the promised blessing for those who bless the seed of Abraham (Gen. 12:3).

The second part of verse 2 notes that the **full** ("exact"; found in the Bible only here and in 4:7) **account of the greatness of Mordecai** is recorded in **the book of the annals** alongside the record of Xerxes. This passage is reminiscent of the descriptions of Mordecai's greatness in 9:1–4. The rhetorical question, **Are they not written . . . ?** is patterned after statements about the kings of Judah (1 Kgs. 11:41; 14:29, etc.), thereby providing Mordecai with similar status (and perhaps enhancing the status of Purim as well). Writing down the account of Mordecai would presumably ensure Jewish interests in the future, just as such a written account had served him well in chapter 6. Unfortunately, the "book" in which all of this was recorded is lost.

While Mordecai has followed Esther's lead since the end of chapter 4, he is the one who becomes part of Persian history. Her leadership as queen in civic affairs is understood to be exceptional rather than normal. As the new status quo takes shape, the prime minister resumes the role of chief administrator in the empire.

Mordecai's "greatness" (*gedolah*) participates in the king's "glory" (*gedolah*), mentioned first in 1:4. This term also reminds the reader that Mordecai deserved greatness much sooner. When the king was reminded of Mordecai's act of loyalty in 6:1–3, he asked, "What honor and recognition (*gedolah*) has Mordecai received for this?" Mordecai eventually became *gadol* (NIV "prominent") in the palace (9:4). The narrator uses the same root (*gdl*) in 10:2 to refer to Mordecai's promotion: Mordecai's *gedolah* is a status **to which the king had raised him** (*giddelo*). This is precisely the terminology employed to describe Haman's promotion in 3:1 and 5:11. The Agagite, who had craved the king's honor so transparently, is now replaced by the Jew, who is known not for self-seeking but for service to the king and his fellow Jews.

The final verse of the chapter brings the book of Esther to a close with a eulogy about **Mordecai the Jew.** His greatness is a function of positional proximity to the Persian ruler, being **second** in rank to King Xerxes (see also Gen. 41:43). He was **preeminent** (*gadol*) **among the Jews,** his "brothers" among whom he was **held in high esteem.** Their regard for him was the result of his deeds and his words: he **worked for the good of his people and spoke up for the welfare** (*shalom*) **of all the Jews.** While Esther is responsible for courageous intervention during a *particular* moment of crisis, Mordecai is praised in the end for his *ongoing* intermediary role on behalf of the Jews. Continuous advocacy is the basis for Jewish security in the Diaspora.

Throughout the story, Mordecai is identified as "the Jew." He represents the Jews in what he does and in what he says. He "stands" for them. There is evidence that, until the turn of the era, the other name for Purim was "Mordecai's Day" (2 Macc. 15:36).

---

## Additional Note §13

**10:2** / **A full account of the greatness of Mordecai:** The displacement of Esther in the last chapter of the book serves the same narrative purposes that the displacement of Ruth does in the last scene of the book named after her. Ruth bears a child, thereby saving the family name that was put at risk by the deaths of Naomi's husband and sons in chapter 1. The story ends with the women in the village praising God for *Naomi's* kinsman-redeemer and son (Ruth 4:14–15). In both stories, the crisis begins with the character whose identity is more typical in the community. The "savior" is a marginal person—a woman in both stories—a Moabite in Ruth's case, an orphan in Esther's case. Neither woman has any acquired status by birth. Once the threat to the family is resolved, the focus shifts back to the original persons most immediately threatened. It is the threatened figures (Mordecai, Naomi) whose experience represents the plight of the whole community. The whole community, therefore, can vicariously celebrate their vindication in these characters while maintaining the highest regard for their extraordinary deliverers.

# For Further Reading

## Commentaries on Ezra, Nehemiah, and Esther

Ackroyd, P. R. *I & II Chronicles, Ezra, Nehemiah*. TBC. London: SCM, 1973.

Berg, S. B. *The Book of Esther: Motifs, Themes, and Structures*. Chico, Calif.: Scholars Press, 1979.

Blenkinsopp, J. *Ezra-Nehemiah: A Commentary*. OTL. Philadelphia: Westminster, 1988.

Brockington, L. H. *Ezra, Nehemiah and Esther*. NCB. London: Oliphants, 1969. Repr., Grand Rapids: Eerdmans, 1984.

Bush, F. W. *Ruth, Esther*. WBC 9; Dallas: Word, 1996.

Clines, D. J. A. *Ezra, Nehemiah, Esther*. NCB. Grand Rapids: Eerdmans, 1984.

Fensham, F. C. *The Books of Ezra and Nehemiah*. NICOT. Grand Rapids: Eerdmans, 1982.

Gerleman, G. *Esther*. Neukirchen–Vluyn: Neukirchener Verlag, 1973.

Holmgren, F. C. *Israel Alive Again: A Commentary on the Books of Ezra and Nehemiah*. ITC. Grand Rapids: Eerdmans, 1987.

Kidner, D. *Ezra and Nehemiah: An Introduction and Commentary*. TOTC. Downers Grove, Ill.: InterVarsity Press, 1979.

Levenson, J. D. *Esther: A Commentary*. OTL. Louisville: Westminster John Knox, 1997.

McConville, J. G. *Ezra, Nehemiah and Esther*. Daily Study Bible. Philadelphia: Westminster, 1985.

Moore, C. A. *Esther*. AB. Garden City, N.Y.: Doubleday, 1971.

Myers, J. M. *Ezra, Nehemiah*. AB 14. Garden City, N.Y.: Doubleday, 1965.

Paton, L. B. *A Critical and Exegetical Commentary on the Book of Esther*. ICC. Edinburgh: T&T Clark, 1908.

Ryle, H. E. *The Books of Ezra and Nehemiah*. Cambridge Bible for Schools and Colleges. Cambridge: Cambridge University Press, 1893.

Throntveit, M. A. *Ezra-Nehemiah*. IBC. Louisville: John Knox, 1992.

Williamson, H. G. M. *Ezra, Nehemiah*. WBC 16. Waco: Word Books, 1985.

———. *Ezra and Nehemiah*. OTG. Sheffield: Sheffield Academic Press, 1987.

## Special Studies on Ezra, Nehemiah, and Esther

Anderson, B. W. "The Place of the Book of Esther in the Christian Bible." *JR* 30 (1950), pp. 32–43.

Bergey, R. L. "Late Linguistic Features in Esther." *JQR* 75 (1984), pp. 66–78.

———. "Post-exilic Hebrew Linguistic Developments in Esther: A Diachronic Approach." *JETS* 31 (1988), pp. 161–68.

Bickerman, E. *Four Strange Books of the Bible.* New York: Schocken, 1967.

Bowman, R. A. "The Book of Ezra and the Book of Nehemiah." Pages 549–819 in vol. 3 of *The Interpreter's Bible.* Edited by G. A. Buttrick et al. 12 vols. Nashville: Abingdon, 1954.

Brockington, L. H. "The Nehemiah Memoir: The Perils of Autobiography," in *What Does Eve Do to Help and Other Readerly Questions to the Old Testament.* JSOTSup 94. Sheffield: JSOT Press, 1990, pp. 124–64.

Camp, C. V. "The Three Faces of Esther: Traditional Woman, Royal Diplomat, Authenticator of Tradition." *Academy* 38 (1–2) (1987), pp. 20–25.

Clines, D. J. A. *The Esther Scroll: The Story of the Story.* JSOTSup 30. Sheffield: JSOT, 1987.

———. "Nehemiah 10 as an Example of Early Jewish Biblical Exegesis." *JSOT* 21 (1981), pp. 111–17.

Craig, K. M. *Reading Esther: A Case for the Literary Carnivalesque.* Louisville, Ky.: Westminster John Knox, 1995.

Day, L. M. *Three Faces of a Queen: Characterization in the Books of Esther.* JSOTSup 186. Sheffield: JSOT, 1995.

Dorothy, C. V. *The Books of Esther: Structure, Genre, and Textual Integrity.* Sheffield: Sheffield Academic, 1997.

Eskenazi, T. C. *In an Age of Prose: A Literary Approach to Ezra-Nehemiah.* SBLMS 36. Atlanta: Scholars Press, 1988.

Fox, M. V. *Character and Ideology in the Book of Esther.* Columbia: University of South Carolina Press, 1991.

———. *The Redaction of the Books of Esther: On Reading Composite Texts.* SBLMS 40. Atlanta: Scholars, 1991.

Goldman, S. "Narrative and Ethical Ironies in Esther." *JSOT* 47 (1990), pp. 15–31.

Gordis, R. "Religion, Wisdom and History in the Book of Esther: A New Solution to an Ancient Crux." *JBL* 100 (1981), pp. 359–88.

———. "Studies in the Esther Narrative." *JBL* 95(1) (1976), pp. 43–58.

Halpern, B. "A Historiographic Commentary on Ezra 1–6: Achronological Narrative and Dual Chronology in Israelite Historiography." Pages 81–142 in *The Hebrew Bible and Its Interpreters.* Edited by W. H. Propp et al. Winona Lake, Ind.: Eisenbrauns, 1990.

Heltzer, M. "The Book of Esther." *BA* 81 (1992), pp. 25–30, 41.

Hoglund, K. G. *Achaemenid Imperial Administration in Syria-Palestine and the Missions of Ezra and Nehemiah.* SBLDS. Atlanta: Scholars Press, 1992.

Huey, F. B. "Irony as the Key to Understanding the Book of Esther." *SwJT* 32(3) (1989), pp. 36–39.

Humphreys, W. L. "A Life-Style for Diaspora: A Study of the Tales of Esther and Daniel." *CBQ* 92 (1973), pp. 211–23.

————. "Novella" and "The Story of Esther and Mordecai: An Early Jewish Novella." Pages 82–96 and 97–113 in *Saga, Legend, Tale, Novella, Fable: Narrative Forms in Old Testament Literature*. Edited by G. W. Coates. JSOTSup 35. Sheffield: JSOT, 1985.

Jones, B. W. "Two Misconceptions about the Book of Esther." *CBQ* 39 (1977), pp. 171–81.

Klein, L. R. "Honor and Shame in Esther." Pages 149–75 in *A Feminist Companion to Esther, Judith, Susanna*. Edited by A. Brenner. Sheffield: Sheffield Academic, 1987.

Laniak, T. *Shame and Honor in the Book of Esther*. SBLDS 165. Atlanta: Scholars, 1998.

Levenson, J. D. "The Scroll of Esther in Ecumenical Perspective." *JES* 13(3) (1976), pp. 440–52.

Loader, J. A. "Esther as a Novel with Different Levels of Meaning." *ZAW* 90(3) (1974), pp. 417–21.

McKane, W. "Note on Esther 9 and I Samuel 15." *JTS* 12 (1961), pp. 260–61.

Moore, C. A. *The Greek Text of Esther*. Ann Arbor, Mich.: University Microfilms, 1965.

Niditch, S., and R. Doran. "Esther: Folklore, Wisdom, Feminism and Authority." Pages 26–46 in *A Feminist Companion to Esther, Judith and Susanna*. Edited by A. Brenner. Sheffield: Sheffield Academic, 1987.

Radday, Y. T. "Esther with Humour." Pages 295–313 in *On Humour and the Comic in the Hebrew Bible*. Edited by Y. T. Radday and A. Brenner. Sheffield: Almond, 1989.

Shea, W. H. "Esther and History." *AUSS* 14 (1976), pp. 227–46.

Siegel, M. "Book of Esther: A Novelle." *Dor Le Dor* 14(3) (1984), pp. 142–51.

Talmon, S. "Wisdom in the Book of Esther." *VT* 13 (1963), pp. 419–55.

White, S. A. "Esther: A Feminine Model for Jewish Diaspora." Pages 161–77 in *Gender and Difference in Ancient Israel*. Edited by P. L. Day. Minneapolis: Fortress, 1988.

Wiebe, J. M. "Esther 4:14: 'Will Relief and Deliverance Arise for the Jews from Another Place?'" *CBQ* 53 (1991), pp. 409–15.

Williamson, H. G. M. "The Composition of Ezra i–vi." *JTS* NS 34 (1983), pp. 1–30.

Williamson, H. G. M., and K. D. Tollefson. "Nehemiah as Cultural Revitalization: An Anthropological Perspective." *JSOT* 56 (1992), pp. 41–68.

Wright, J. S. "The Historicity of the Book of Esther." Pages 37–47 in *New Perspectives on the Old Testament*. Edited by J. B. Payne. Waco, Tex.: Word, 1970.

Yamauchi, E. M. "The Archaeological Background of Esther." *BSac* 137 (1980), pp. 99–117.

### Other Works

Berquist, J. L. *Judaism in Persia's Shadow: A Social and Historical Approach*. Minneapolis: Fortress, 1995.

Day, P. L., ed. *Gender and Difference in Ancient Israel.* Minneapolis: Fortress, 1987.

Eisenmann, R., and M. Wise. "Stories from the Persian Court." Pages 99–103 in *The Dead Sea Scrolls Uncovered.* Rockport, Me.: Element, 1992.

*Esther Rabbah I: An Analytical Translation.* BJS 182. Atlanta: Scholars, 1989.

Fishbane, M. *Biblical Interpretation in Ancient Israel.* Oxford: Clarendon, 1985.

Fuchs, E. "Status and Role of Female Heroines in the Biblical Narrative." *Mankind Quarterly* 23 (1981), pp. 149–60.

Gordon, C. *Riddles in History.* New York: Crown, 1974.

Grottanelli, C. "Tricksters, Scapegoats, Champions, Saviors." *HR* 23(2) (1983), pp. 117–39.

Herr, L. G. "Retribution and Personal Honor: A Response to T. Frymer-Kensky (1980)." *BA* 44 (1981), p. 135.

Huber, L. B. "The Biblical Experience of Shame/Shaming." Ph.D. diss., Drew University, 1983.

Klinger, E. "Revenge and Retribution." Pages 362–68 in vol. 12 of *The Encyclopedia of Religion.* Edited by M. Eliade. New York: Macmillan, 1985.

LaCocque, A. *The Feminine Unconventional: Four Subversive Figures in Israel's Tradition.* Minneapolis: Fortress, 1990.

Long, V. P. *The Art of Biblical History.* Grand Rapids: Zondervan, 1994.

Smith, M. *Palestinian Parties and Politics That Shaped the Old Testament.* 2d ed. London: SCM, 1987.

*The Two Targums of Esther.* The Aramaic Bible, vol. 18. Minneapolis: Liturgical, 1992.

Watson, W. G. E. "Aramaic Proto-Esther." Pages 291–92 in *Dead Sea Scrolls Translated.* Edited by F. García Martínez. Translated by W. G. E. Watson. Brill: Leiden, 1991.

Westermann, C. "The Role of the Lament in the Theology of the Old Testament." *Int* 28(1) (1974), pp. 20–38.

———. *The Structure of the Book of Job.* Philadelphia: Fortress, 1981.

Widengren, G. "The Persian Period." Pages 489–538 in *Israelite and Judean History.* Edited by J. H. Hayes and J. M. Miller. OTL. Philadelphia: Westminster, 1977.

Wills, L. *The Jew in the Court of the Foreign King: Ancient Jewish Court Legends.* HDR 26. Minneapolis: Fortress, 1986.

———. *The Jewish Novel in the Ancient World.* Ithaca: Cornell University, 1995.

Yamauchi, E. M. *Persia and the Bible.* Grand Rapids: Baker, 1990.

# Subject Index

# Scripture Index

# —CONTENTS—

# Visitor's Guide to Korea

*This guide booklet has been prepared as an aid to foreign visitors in the Republic of Korea.*

*In brief form this booklet describes the most important tourist areas and sites along the route of approach in the Republic; provides a very brief survey of Korean history, legends, and culture covering thousands of years.*

*Also listed are the principal tourist hotels, travel agencies, air, car, rail and sea internal transportation facilities, together with external air and sea transport and much other informative material which will help our foreign guests enjoy their visit to the "Land of the Morning Calm."*

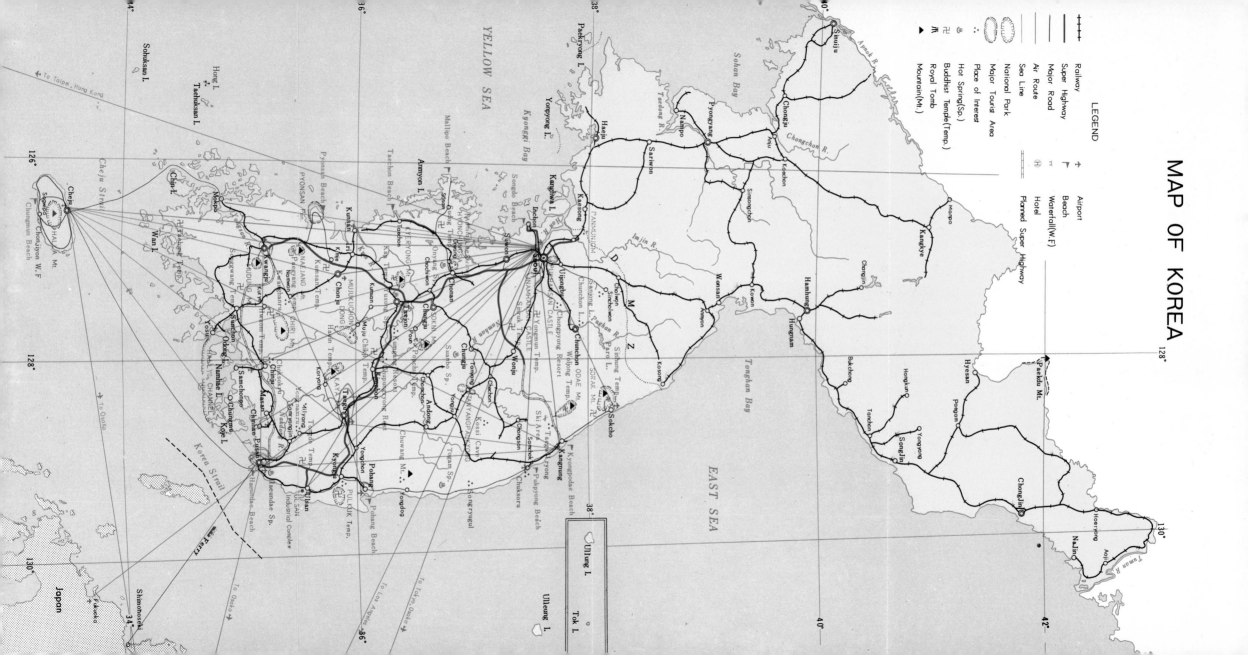

# MAP OF KOREA

## LEGEND

| | |
|---|---|
| +++++ | Railway |
| | Super Highway |
| | Major Road |
| | Sea Line |
| | Air Route |
| | National Park |
| | Major Tourist Area |
| ✈ | Airport |
| ⚓ | Beach |
| | Waterfall(W.F) |
| Ⓗ | Hotel |
| | Planned Super Highway |
| ∴ | Place of Interest |
| ♨ | Hot Spring(Sp.) |
| 卍 | Buddhist Temple(Temp.) |
| ⬟ | Royal Tomb |
| ▲ | Mountain(Mt.) |

YELLOW SEA

EAST SEA

Korea Strait

Cheju Strait

Japan

# How to Get to Korea

## INTERNATIONAL AIR ROUTE

In this jet age, Korea is located within 24 hours flying time from any part of the world, 13 hours from Los Angeles, 3 hours 30 minutes from Hong Kong and 100 minutes from Tokyo. Many international airlines depart from Europe and America daily. Some proceed directly to Seoul via Tokyo, others connect with Korea-bound flights from that city.

Airlines— *There are 228 flights weekly by international airlines including KAL and JAL's Jumbo 747, and NWA's DC-10 connecting Korea with Japan, Hong Kong, Thailand, and other world destinations.*

Ferry — *Pu-Kwan (Pusan-Shimonoseki) ferry provides service between Pusan, Korea and Shimonoseki, Japan with capacity for 620 passengers and 60 automobiles three times weekly.*
*Seoul  Office: 22–9716, 24–4194*
*Pusan  Office: 6–5372/6, 4–7344*
*Tokyo Office: (562)–0541*
*Osaka Office: (581)–7875*

# General Information

*According to mythology, a god-like person named Tangun founded Korea in the year 2333 B.C. From that time until the first century A.D. there are no written historical records. The first formal historical recordings begin with the "Three Kingdom Era" (Koguryo, Paekje, Silla Dynasties).*

*By 668 A.D. after a series of dynastic wars, the Silla Kingdom has conquered all opponents and for the first time unified the Korean people. The early years of the Silla Dynastic rule are known as "The Golden Age" because of the relatively enlightened rule of the Silla Kings. The remnants left behind by this ancient kingdom include remarkable jewelry, pottery, and Buddhist relics still to be seen around the ancient southern capital city, Kyongju. The Silla Dynasty was in turn overturned by Koryo, which ruled from 918 A.D. until 1392 A.D. During the Koryo Dynasty a system of civil service examination was instituted, laws were codified, and in 1234 A.D. movable metal type began to be used for printing long before Gutenberg's invention. The Koryo Dynasty was overthrown and replaced by Yi Dynasty in 1392. The enlightened rule of the early and middle Yi Dynasty monarchs was marked by the invention of Hangul (the Korean alphabet) by scholars especially appointed by the King. After World War II, the United States and Russia agreed that the U.S. would accept the surrender south of the 38th Parallel; the Russian above that line. Finally the United Nations in 1948 authorized national election in the southern half of Korea to establish the Republic of Korea and to elect national officials. The structure of government is based on the principle of insuring the independence of the three branches of government: the Executive, the Legislative, and*

*President Park Chung Hee greets villagers of
the New Community   Movement*

the Judiciary. The President is the chief executive of the administration. He represents the state in dealing with foreign countries, and also is the commander in chief of the armed forces.

Concurrently, Soviet Russia set up a communist regime in the north. The communist regime waited until all American troops had been withdrawn and then, in 1950, launched a massive invasion against the relatively undefended Republic. The United Nations reacted swiftly to this unprovoked naked aggression, and responding to resolutions passed by the U.N. General Assembly and Security Council, sixteen U.N. member countries sent troops, airplanes, warships, and supplies to the aid of the beleaguered nation. After three years of warfare the communists were defeated despite the intervention of huge Red Chinese Armies, and an Armistice was negotiated by the military commanders of both sides in 1953. But Korea is still divided. Since that time, overcoming various political and economic difficulties, the Republic of Korea has made enormous progress. Especially the Third Republic born in 1963 has marked great achievements in the economic area as well as in the field of social welfare through successful implementation of two consecutive 5 year economic development plans along with new community movement; a modern highway system has been constructed, railroad and internal air transportation facilities have been expanded and improved. New factories producing for internal consumption and export, are rising everywhere promising a brighter future.

## The Land and the People

The Korean peninsula is approximately 1,000 km in total north-south length, and 216 km wide at its narrowest point. It is separated from Manchuria and Siberia in the north by the Yalu and Tuman rivers and the Paektu mountain range; from mainland China in the west by the Yellow Sea; and from Japan to the east by the East Sea. Korea, in overall area is approximately equal to Great Britain or the State of New York.

The Korean people are the descendants of a number of migrating tribesmen originating in central Asia. These included the Paleo-Kelts, a white Aryan race who migrated through Korea to Japan about 8000 B.C. and are thought to be among the first inhabitants of the Japanese islands (A few remnants, the Ainu, still live in Hokkaido). They were followed by successive waves of Mins, Ugrians from Siberia, and Tungus from Mongolia among others. Of these, in their passage through or to Korea, a very considerable number settled in Korea and intermingled to form the very distinctive Korean people of today. Over the many thousands of years that have passed since the Neolithic stone age migrations the Korean people have evolved a most unique and homogeneous culture. Despite the terrific pressures exerted by China and Japan the Koreans have remained Korean, with a distinctive Korean culture, Korean language, Korean alphabet, Korean cuisine, and Korean arts.

Although Koreans cling tenaciously to their past they are also modern in outlook and this dichotomous attitude is perhaps best exemplified by the modern thirty and more story buildings which tower over the still standing city gates (construction of these began in 1392, one century before Columbus discovered America).

Although an oriental people, the Koreans, perhaps alone in Asia, are a charmingly gregarious people, and nowhere else in the world do foreign visitors find a more friendly and courteous welcome from all classes of the people.

## Language

The language itself is a member of the Ural-Altaic group, which also includes Hungarian and Finnish. It is emphasized that there is no similarity with either the Japanese or Chinese languages. The most logical speculation is that all three languages developed and spread from a single so far unidentified central Asian source in time.

During the enlightened reign •of King Sejong (1419–1450), a royal commission of linguists and philologists after years of study produced a Korean phonetic system, whose modern form consists of 24 letters, which is one of the simplest, most concise and efficient means of writing in the world.

좋은 일이다, 나라를 위한 일이다, 우리 민족에 도움이 되는 일이다, 우리 지방 발전을 위한 일이라고 생각하면 체면이나 위신 따위는 따지지 않고 나가서 실제로 행동을 하는 사람이 바로 애국자인 것이다.

— 대통령각하의 말씀 중에서 —

## Climate and Clothing

The climate is temperate, midway between the continental and marine types, but tending more toward the former than is usually the case of corresponding latitudes. The year is divided into four distinct seasons; spring, summer, autumn and winter. The rainy season and hottest months are July and August; the coldest and snowy months are December and January. The climate of Korea is comparable to that of Boston and northern parts of Italy.

The following graphical chart shows the average monthly temperature in Seoul:

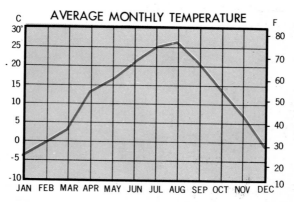

## Housing

The typical Korean house may be L-shaped, U-shaped, or even a three sided square. It is invariably one story, with walls of brick, clay wattle, earth, or red brick cement building blocks. The roof is tiled, metaled or straw thatched, according to the means of the family. The most distinctive aspect of a Korean house is its ages-old "Ondol" (hot floor) heating system. Under the floor run stone flues that carry heat from the kitchen fire or external ground-level grates. The hot floor warms the room as efficiently as a modern steam system if the house is well insulated. Shoes are never worn indoors, and with modern exceptions most houses have no chairs or bed-steads. People sit on the floor, eat from low tables, and sleep on soft, thick quilts or mattresses which are put away during the daytime.

## Entry Formalities

*Entry into Korea is simple. Travellers are required to present a current passport when applying for a visa. Tourist visas may be granted for thirty days which can be renewed for an additional 30 days at the Ministry of Justice in Seoul.*

*Tourists in transit may visit Korea for 120 hours (5 days) without visa, but proof of confirmed air reservation onward is required. Citizens of France, Norway, Sweden, Denmark, England, Iceland, Tunisia, Belgium, Luxemburg, Netherland, Lesotho, Spain, and Turkey, and only in case of possession of diplomatic and official passport, citizens of West Germany, Thailand, Switzerland, Austria and Philippines do not need a visa.*

## Currency

*The monetary unit in Korea is the Won. The basic rate of conversion, subject to change by fluctuations in the market, is about 400 Won for one US Dollar (as of June 1, 1973 ). Currency is easily exchanged at main banks and their branches as well as major tourist hotels.*

*Up to $200 of unused Won can be re-exchanged into foreign currency upon leaving the country at the authorized exchange offices in international air or seaports.*

*There are 10, 50, 100, 500 and 5,000 Won notes and coins of 1, 5, 10, 50 and 100 Won.*

## Customs and Tax Exemption

*Customs laws permit a visitor to bring in practically everything which is for personal use and is not for resale. Upon leaving the country all imported effects must be re-exported. Foreign visitors are allowed to take souvenir articles with them duty-free. Incoming passengers may bring in duty-free the following items: Wearing apparel, personal jewelry, toilet articles and other personal effects in reasonable quantities: 50 cigars, 400 cigarettes, 200 g of tobacco for pipe, two bottles of liquor, camera, movie camera, typewriter, portable phonograph, radio, tape recorder, etc.*

## Airport to Downtown Seoul

Airport Taxi Service: *Exclusive airport taxis are available from air terminal and charges are according to taxi meter. Tipping is not customary unless some extra service has been performed by the driver. Approximate fare from Kimpo International Airport to Seoul is* ₩ *800 ($2.00).*

Air Terminal Information:
  *KTB Information office: Tel. 8–6532*
  *KAL Information office: Tel: 8–7161/5*

## Tourist Aid Service

For assistance, advice, or complaint in any situation foreign visitors are invited to telephone 22–5685.

**Korea Tourist Association**

**Hours of Operation**
**09:00-19:00 (weekdays)**

## Business

### Federation of Korean Industries
*28th Floor Samilro Bldg.*
*10 Kwanchul-dong, Chung-ku*
*Tel: 75–8084, 72–5120*

### Korea Chamber of Commerce
*111, Sokong-dong, Chung-ku,*
*C.P.O. Box 25, Seoul*
*Tel: 22–3210, 22–5528*
*Cable: KOREA CHAMBER*

### Korea Trade Promotion Corporation (*KOTRA*)
*Head Office: 46, 4-ka, Namdaemunro, Chung-gu,*
*Seoul Korea*
*I.P.O. Box: 1621 Seoul, Korea*
*Cable: No. 2259     Tel. 23–4181/9*

### Korean Trade Association
*10-1, 2-ka, Hwehyon-dong, Chung-ku*
*I.P.O. Box: 1117*
*Tel: 28–8251. Telex: 2465S*

### American Chamber of Commerce in Korea
*Suite 529, Bando Bldg., 180, 1-ka*
*Ulchiro, Chung-ku*
*Tel: 23–6471. Cable: AMCHAMBER*

### Japanese Chamber of Commerce in Seoul
*Room 905, Kwangnam Bldg., 6 Mukyo-dong, Chung-ku*
*Tel: 23–7997*

# Tours

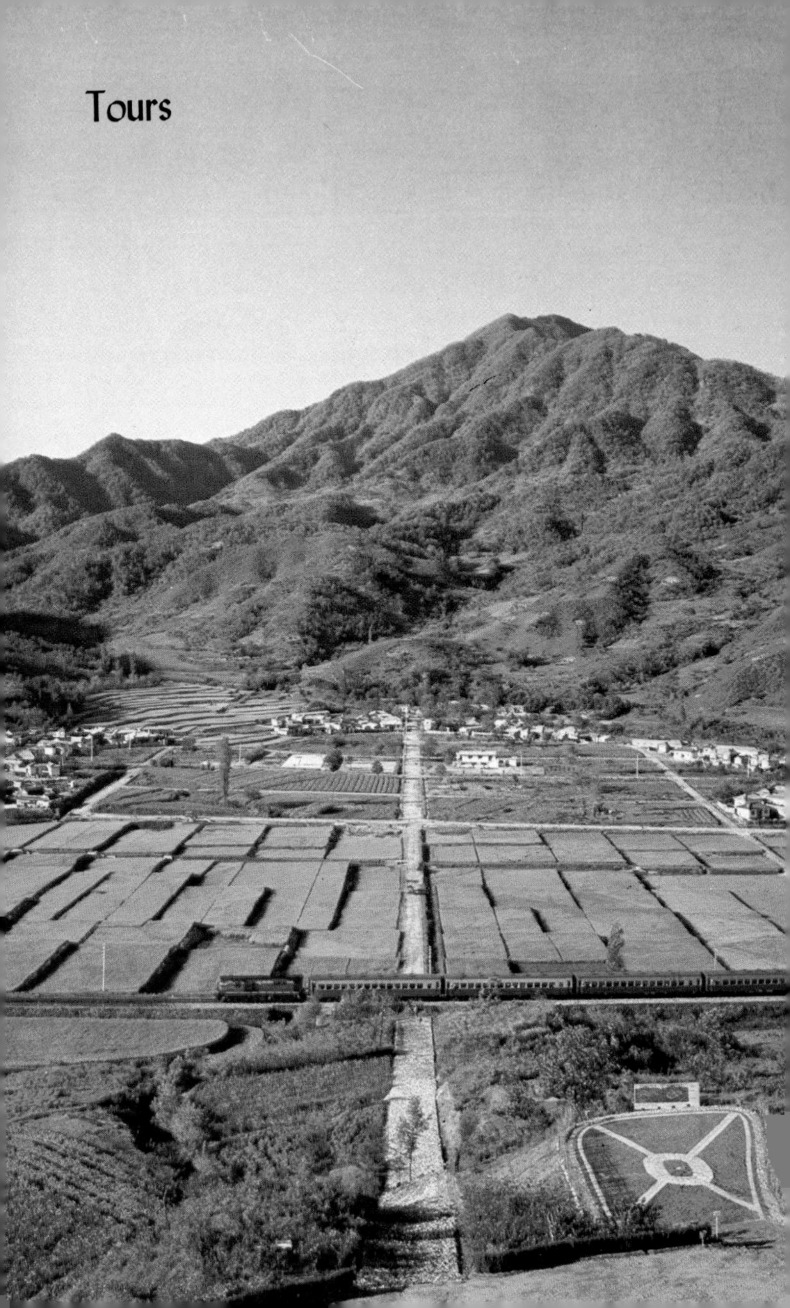

# Seoul

*What to do, where to go, what to see, in Seoul:*

*Seoul, the capital of Korea, has a population of more than 5,800, 000 people and covers an area of about 613 square kilometers. The city was founded by the first king of the Yi dynasty in 1392 A.D. In and near Seoul there are many hundreds of things to do and to see. These include well preserved ancient royal palaces, temples, tombs, museum, art galleries, etc.*

*There are excellent golf courses, sports stadiums, theaters, concert halls, nightclubs, restaurants....whatever a visitor may want, it is available. Seoul (like all Korea) is very photogenic and visitors are urged to keep cameras handy at all times.*

*For detailed information foreign visitors should consult the Korea Tourist Bureau, other local travel agencies, or the tourism office of the City of Seoul (72–5765).*

*A panoramic view of downtown Seoul*

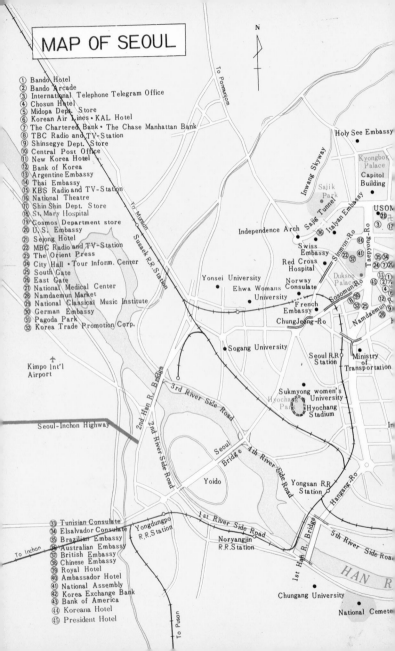

# MAP OF SEOUL

N

① Bando Hotel
② Bando Arcade
③ International Telephone Telegram Office
④ Chosun Hotel
⑤ Midopa Dept. Store
⑥ Korean Air Lines • KAL Hotel
⑦ The Chartered Bank • The Chase Manhattan Bank
⑧ TBC Radio and TV-Station
⑨ Shinsegye Dept. Store
⑩ Central Post Office
⑪ New Korea Hotel
⑫ Bank of Korea
⑬ Argentine Embassy
⑭ Thai Embassy
⑮ KBS Radio and TV-Station
⑯ National Theatre
⑰ Shin Shin Dept. Store
⑱ St. Mary Hospital
⑲ Cosmos Department store
⑳ U. S. Embassy
㉑ Sejong Hotel
㉒ MBC Radio and TV-Station
㉓ The Orient Press
㉔ City Hall • Tour Inform. Center
㉕ South Gate
㉖ East Gate
㉗ National Medical Center
㉘ Namdaemun Market
㉙ National Classical Music Institute
㉚ German Embassy
㉛ Pagoda Park
㉜ Korea Trade Promotion Corp.

Kimpo Int'l
Airport

㉝ Tunisian Consulate
㉞ Elsalvador Consulate
㉟ Brazilian Embassy
㊱ Australian Embassy
㊲ British Embassy
㊳ Chinese Embassy
㊴ Royal Hotel
㊵ Ambassador Hotel
㊶ National Assembly
㊷ Korea Exchange Bank
㊸ Bank of America
㊹ Koreana Hotel
㊺ President Hotel

To Pomunjom
To Munsan
Sussaek R.R.Station

Holy See Embassy

Kyongbok Palace
Capitol Building

Inwang Skyway
Sajik Park
Sajik Tunnel
Italyan Embassy
USOM

Independence Arch
Shinmun-Ro
Taepyong-Ro

Swiss Embassy
Red Cross Hospital

Yonsei University
Ehwa Womans University
Norway Consulate

Duksoo Palace
Sosomun-Ro

French Embassy
ChungJeong-Ro
Namdaemun

Sogang University

Seoul R.R Station
Ministry of Transportation

3rd Han R. Bridge
2nd Han R. Bridge
2nd River Side Road
3rd River Side Road

Seoul-Inchon Highway

Sukmyong women's University
Hyochang Park
Hyochang Stadium

Seoul Bridge
4th River Side Road

Yoido

Yongsan R.R Station
Hangang-Ro

Yongdungpo R.R.Station
To Inchon

1st River Side Road
Noryangjin R.R.Station

1st Han R. Bridge
5th River Side Road

To Pusan

HAN R.

Chungang University

National Cemetery

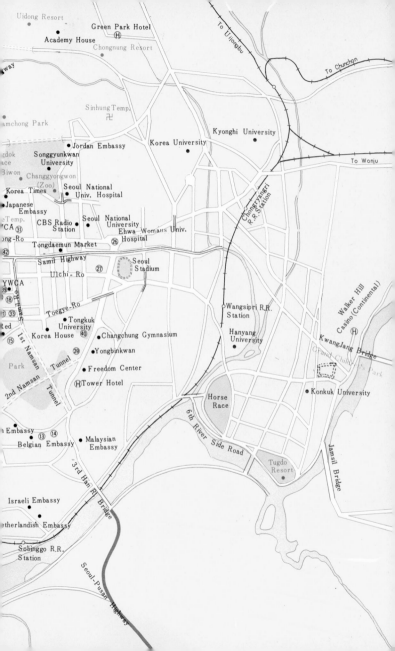

**Kyongbok Palace—**
*built in 1395 by King Taejo, the founder of the Yi dynasty once housed kings, queens, and their courtiers. Standing behind the Capitol, they are well preserved in their original condition. Particularly photogenic are the Royal Audience Hall and Kyonghweru Pavilion.*

**Kwanghwamun Gate—** *(Bottom Right)*
*the front gate leading to the Capitol and Kyongbok palace.*

**Specimen Tours**

1. Seoul City Morning Tour (3 hours)
*Hotel—Changdok Palace and Secret Garden—East Gate Market—*
*Namsan Mt.—South Gate—Hotel*

2. Seoul City Afternoon Tour (3 hours)
*Hotel—Pugak Skyway—Korea House—Kyongbok*
*Palace & National Museum—Hotel.*

3. Seoul City Night Tour (4 hours)
*Hotel—Dinner (Pulgogi)—Pugak Skyway—Nightclub—Hotel*

4. Seoul One Day Tour (7 hours)
*Hotel—Kumgok Royal Tombs—Oryong-dong Farm Village—*
*Korea House (Luncheon)—Kyongbok Palace, & National Museum*
*—Hotel*

## National Museum—

*located in Kyongbok palace grounds is
filled with ancient and modern works
of art and historical relics.*

**Biwon, Secret Garden—** *(Top Left)*
*studded with many charming pavilions is a masterpiece of the land-scape gardener's art—an island of sylvan beauty in the heart of the city.*

**Toksu Palace—** *(Bottom Left)*
*although the present palace is but one-third of the original palace in scale, there are many beautiful buildings scattered through the beautifully landscaped grounds.*

**A Night View of Namdaemun, South Gate—**
*in olden times this was the principal gateway through the defensive*
*wall which surrounded the city of Seoul, built in 1394.*

**Tongdaemun, East Gate—** *(Top Right)*
*the strong defensive point piercing the city wall and a wooden*
*super-structure  with various ornamental designs set on the high*
*stone foundation.*

**Changkyongwon Palace—** *(Bottom Right)*
*the zoo in the palace grounds has more than 800 specimens.*

24

**Snow-bedecked Namhansan-song Castle—**
*one hour by taxi from Seoul, is among the most popular hiking and picnic areas. The 24 feet high walls still encircle an area five miles in circumference bounding the ancient fortress.*

**Grand Children's Park—** *(Bottom Right)*
*built on the extensive grounds of the former Seoul Golf Club, one of the finest parks in Asia, extensive educational facilities designed especially for children.*

26

*Children's center at Namsan park*

## Korea House—

*the Korea House in Seoul presents live programs of traditional folk dancing and music and is supported by the government.*

*Visitors are the guests of the Korea House: everything is free except the traditional Korean food. The architecture and construction, uses no nails, bolts, or other metal fasteners.*

*Guests are welcome to view one or more of the many documentary films kept in the library.*

## Walker Hill Hotels—

*five beautiful hotels, many guest villas, a recreation building, Western, Chinese, Japanese, and Korean restaurants, cocktail lounges, Hill Top Bar, gambling casino, nightclub etc., cater to every taste. Swimming, boating, bowling, horseback riding.... nearly all sports are available.*

Seoul Vicinity

Suwon castle

*There lures plenty of tourist potentiality ranging from Cold War in Action, scenic beauty, beach, golf, water skiing, casino, to historical relics.*

*Suwon is an old, walled city located about 30 minutes by bus from Seoul and is the home of the Agricultural College of Seoul National University.   The city wall of Suwon was first built in 1796, and despite  heavy damage during the war is still largely intact.*

## Specimen Tours

### 1. Seoul-Panmunjom Tour  (7 hours)

*Bando Hotel—Unification Road—Freedom Bridge—Advance Camp (Luncheon)—Demilitarized Zone—Panmunjom Conference Site— Bando Hotel. (3 times a week; Mon. Wed. Fri.)*

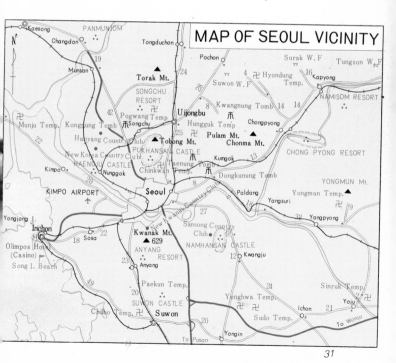

MAP OF SEOUL VICINITY

*United Nations Command and Communist delegates at the conference table*

## Panmunjom

A reminder of the tragic division of Korea is the truce village at Panmunjom. Here the truce that ended the fighting in the Korean War was signed, and here representatives of the U.N. and Communist sides still meet to haggle over alleged violations of the armistice. Panmunjom is 35 miles north of Seoul by bus. Applications to visit

*South-North Korean Red Cross Meeting held at Panmunjom*

*and observe an armistice commission meeting must be placed with the U.N. Command in Seoul 72 hours in advance to guarantee accommodations. Tours are limited to Monday, Wednesday and Friday, and the fare is  $9.00  per person including luncheon. For further information consult your travel agent or Rm. 100, Bando Hotel, Korea Tourist Bureau. Tel: 28–0207|9*

**Namisom Island —**
*one hour and 30 minutes by taxi or two hours by bus from Seoul,
is a summer resort for swimming, boating, fishing (Han River),
and relaxation.*

**Mankuk Park in Inchon City—**
*Statue of Gen. MacArthur in the park marks the site of the historic amphibious landing operation in 1950.*

# East Coast

*40 min. by plane from Seoul to Sokcho, Kangnung and Samchok cities. The northern stretch of Korea's eastern coast, which can be reached by air or rail from Seoul, is rugged and mountainous, with breathtaking scenery. Skiing and other winter sports help make the area an all-year-round resort, but the most popular recreations are swimming in summer and mountain-climbing in fall. The clean, gently shelving beaches are perhaps the finest in Korea.*

*The principal inland resort area is Sorak Mt., which boasts a western-style lodge with individual tourist cabins. There are also beachside tourist hotels outside the port of Kangnung. The entire coastline is dotted with ancient pavilions once used for moon-viewing and wine-sipping excursions by poet-scholars of past ages, located in all noted scenic areas.*

37

**Specimen Tours**

## 1. One Day Seoul—Sorak Mt. Tour

*Hotel—40 min. by plane—Sokcho Airport—Soraksan Tourist Hotel—Sinhung Temple—Cable Car—Soraksan Tourist Hotel (Luncheon)—Sightseeing along the coastline (Naksan Temple, Naksan Beach, Kyongpodae Beach)—Kangnung Airport—Seoul via air*

## 2. Three Day Seoul—East Coast Tour

*1st Day: Hotel—40 min. by plane—Sokcho Airport—Soraksan Tourist Hotel—Sinhung Temple—Kejoam Hermitage—Hotel.*

*2nd Day: Hotel—Bisondae—Hotel (Luncheon)—Biryong Waterfalls—Hotel*

*3rd Day: Hotel—Naksan Temple and Uisangdae—Chumunjin—Sachon—Kangnung—Kyongpodae Tourist Hotel—(Luncheon)—Seoul via air*

*Crimson foliage in November, Sorak mountain*

## Ulsanbawi Rock—

soaring into the sky north of the Sinhung temple, the rock is composed of four sheer peaks rising 650m above the sea level. Nearby Naksan temple, along with Uisangdae and Podok cave are ranked among the eight most scenic sites in the east coast area.

40

**Uisangdae Pavilion—**

*the Uisangdae offers a beautiful view of the east coast sea and the rugged coastline. It is near the Naksan temple about half way between Sokcho and Yangyang town.*

**Rocking Stone—** *one man can move the huge rock with a push.*

**Kyongpodae Beach—**

*attracts many thousands of people during the summer. It can be reached by a short 20 min. flight by jet from Seoul. Kyongpodae*

*Tourist and Kangnung Beach hotels provide up-to-date accommodations.*

The 428 kilometer super highway connects the port city of Pusan with Seoul in 4 hours 30 minutes driving time. Feeder highways along the route lead to various points of interest to tourists.

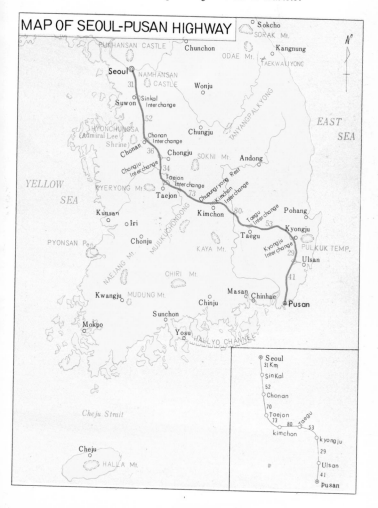

MAP OF SEOUL-PUSAN HIGHWAY

**Hyonchungsa Shrine—**

*one hour 30 minutes by bus from Seoul is located near the Onyang hot spring resort. This shrine was dedicated to Admiral Yi,*

46

*Sun Sin, Korea's greatest naval hero, who defeated a numerically vastly superior Japanese invasion fleet by the use of iron clad warships....the first in the history of the world.*

**Todam Sambong Peaks—**
*these picturesque islands in the Han river, are typical of the scenery in this area, which can be reached in 25 min. by bus from Tanyang town.*

*Songhwan ranch near Pyongtaek*

49

**Popchu Temple—**

*2 hours 10 minutes by bus from Seoul via Chongju city, is located at the foot of Sokni Mt., and boasts of its world famous 27 meter high Granite Buddha with a hat overlooking the temple. There are four stone lamps standing on the premises, the oldest of their kind in the nation.*

### Haein Temple—

*two hours by bus from Taegu city, is located deep in the Kaya Mt., area famed for its grotesque scenery of rocks and valley. Perhaps the most important intellectual accomplishment of the Koryo Dynasty was the publication of the Buddhist scriptures. The first 5,048 volumes of scriptures were placed at Haein temple in 1232, which were later burned by the invading Mongols. The massive task of reprinting was begun while the king was still in refuge from the Mongols. The resulting compilation was completed in 1252, after 16 years of work by scores of scholars and craftsmen: 80,000 wooden plates carved on both sides were prepared to print the 160,000 pages of Tripitaka Koreana, regarded as the best version among the twenty now existing. The original wooden blocks are still preserved at Haein temple.*

# Kyongju City

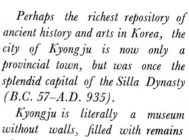

Perhaps the richest repository of ancient history and arts in Korea, the city of Kyongju is now only a provincial town, but was once the splendid capital of the Silla Dynasty (B.C. 57–A.D. 935).

Kyongju is literally a museum without walls, filled with remains of ancient Silla: temples, royal tombs, monuments, one of the earliest astronomical observatories in Asia, pagodas, the crumbling remains of palaces and fortresses. There is a branch of the National Museum in town where thousands of items are exhibited.

The two supreme treasures of Kyongju are the Pulkuk temple, one of the most beautiful in Korea (easily accessible, just outside the city) and the nearby mountaintop stone grotto, Sokguram, known throughout the world for its stone statues and carved friezes, considered pinnacles of Buddhist art. Kyongju is highly recommended to the tourist if he has time for only one trip outside Seoul. The journey can be made overnight on a train with sleeping cars or via the new expressway bus in 3 hrs. 30 min.

Pulkuk temple

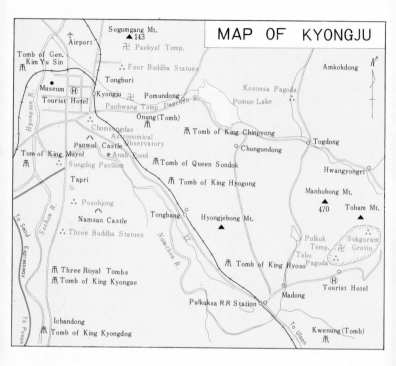

MAP OF KYONGJU

## Specimen Tours

### 1. Kyongju Morning Tour (3 hours)
*Hotel—Toham Mt.—Sokguram Grotto—Pulkuk Temple—Pulkuk Station—Kwenung Royal Tomb—Hotel*

### 2. Kyongju Afternoon Tour (3 hours)
*Hotel—Museum—Bunhwang Temple—Anapji Pond—Sokpinggo Ice Storage—Chomsongdae Astronomical Observatory—Posok Bower—Onung Royal Tomb—Hotel*

### 3. Kyongju Night Tour (4 hours)
*Hotel—Banwol (half moon) Castle—Kyerim Forest—Silla House—Hotel*

56

**Bronze Statue of Gen. Kim Yu Sin—**

*was commander in chief when Silla Kingdom unified Korea at the end of the "Three Kingdom Era". The statue stands in Hwangsong Park in Kyongju city.*

**Tabotap Pagoda—**
*this white granite pagoda has a height of 10.4m and stands in front of the main hall of Pulkuk temple.*

**Sokguram Grotto—**
*located about 4km from Pulkuk temple on the slope of Toham Mt.
This granite image of Buddha in the grotto and its surrounding
wall relief carvings are considered among the finest example of
Buddhist sculptural art.*

**Posokjong Pavilion—** *(Top Left)*
*during the Silla Kingdom this carved stone channel located in what
then was a dense forest, was a recreation place for the Kings who
enjoyed floating cups of wine along the channel to his favorites.*

**Kwenung Royal Tomb—** *(Bottom Left)*
*the mausoleum of an unidentified king during the golden age of
the Silla Kingdom after the unification of the three kingdoms on
the peninsula in 57 A.D. In front are stone images of civil and
military guardians of the tomb.*

59

**An Aerial View of the Under-
sea Tomb of King Munmu—**
*the tomb is enshrined about 100m
offshore on a rocky island in the depths of the East Coast... the first of its
kind in world history. King Munmu
(661–681) on his deathbed wished
to be buried at sea in an attempt to
protect the country from a Japanese
invasion fleet.*

# Ulsan Industrial Complex

*Hankuk Oil Refinery and the Taehan Steel Plant plus many more plants programed to be built in the area. International standard tourist hotel provides up-to-date facilities.*

## Pusan City

The second largest city and principal port of Korea lies on the southern tip of the peninsula, and thus enjoys somewhat milder weather than the capital. There are many beautiful beach resorts nearby. The beaches at Haeundae and Songdo are clean and sandy. Water is warm and the surf is mild. There are several hotels meeting international standards in each town. Tongnae is especially noted for its natural hot spring health baths. Just outside Pusan

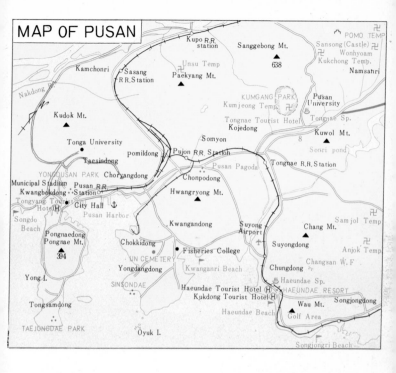

MAP OF PUSAN

is the impressive U.N. Cemetery, the only one of its kind in the world, where the dead from several of the 16 Korean War allies rest in honored serenity.

**Specimen Tours**

1. Pusan City Tour (3 hours)
*Hotel—Yongdusan Park—Kwangbok-dong Shopping Street—Fishery Market—U.N. Cemetery—Haeundae Resort—Hotel*

2. One Day Pusan City Tour
*Hotel—Songdo Resort—Tongnae Spa—Kumkang Park—Pomo Temple—Haeundae Resort—U.N. Cemetery—Hotel*

## Haeundae Beach—

*best beach on the south coast and one of the eight scenic wonders of Korea, is located 30 minutes by car from Pusan. Clean white sand, mild surf, crystal clear water, international standard accommodations, spa and casino. attract hundreds of thousands of summer vacationers.*

**United Nations Cemetery—**

*located about 8 km east of Pusan city hall, enshrines a total of 2,266 fallen soldiers from 16 allied countries who died during the Korean War.*

*A panoramic view of the channel connecting Pusan-Chungmu-Yosu*

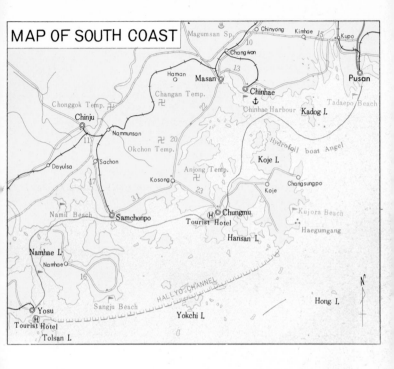

# MAP OF SOUTH COAST

Magumsan Sp.  Chinyong  Kimhae 15  Kupo
Changwon
13
Haman  Masan  Chinhae
Changan Temp.  Chinhae Harbour  Kadog I.  Tadaepo Beach
Chonggok Temp.
Chinju  Nammunsan  20  Pusan
11  Okchon Temp.  Koje I.  Hydrofoil boat Angel
Dayulsa  Sachon  Anjong Temp.
17  Kosong  23  Koje  Changsungpo
31  Kujora Beach
Namil Beach  Samchonpo  Chungmu  Haegumgang
Tourist Hotel
Hansan I.
Namhae I.
Namhae
16  HALLYO CHANNEL  Hong I.
Yosu  Sangju Beach  Yokchi I.
Tourist Hotel
Tolsan I.

## South Coast Tour

*The magnificent scenery along the southern sea coast has been designated one of the Eight Wonders of Korea, often called the Cote azur of Korea. Foreign tourists enjoy boating offshore by hydrofoil boat. Widely scattered tourist hotels serve travelers convenience.*

## Specimen Tours

### Three Day Pusan—Yosu Tour (hydrofoil)

1. *Hotel (in Yosu)—Odong Island—Namhae Sea—Kumsan—Hadong—Samchonpo—Chungmu(accommodation)—Hansan Island—Chesondang—Pusan*

2. *Hotel (in Yosu)—Odong Island—Namhae—Kumsan—Hadong—Samchonpo—Chungmu(accommodation)—Hansan Island—Chesongdang—Chungmu—Yonghwa Temple—Sub-marine Tunnel—Chungyol Temple—Chungmu (accommodation)-Chinju—Choksog Pavilion—Masan—Chinhae—Masan—Pusan*

*The Great Namhae Bridge — a suspension bridge connecting the island of Namhae to the mainland.*

**Hydrofoil "Angel"—**
*hydrofoil operates along the channel Pusan-Chung-mu-Yosu daily with capacity for 71 passengers and sail at 32 knots for sight-seeing tourists.*

**Sea Fishing—**

*fishing boats and tackle are available on a rental basis*

*Mai mountain*

The area offers a bounty of harmonious landscape: mountains with pristine forests and miles long spectacular narrow valleys of unsurpassed beauty. Naejang Mt. is a National Park, and Naejangsan Tourist Hotel provides modern accommodation.

## Mai Mountain—

4 km from Chinan-up. Two temples stand amidst the towering heights. A two storied inn accommodates tourists.

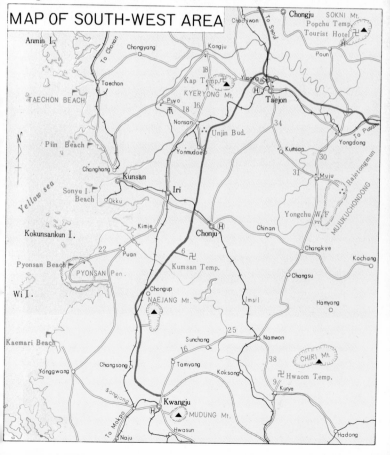

MAP OF SOUTH-WEST AREA

**Naejang Mountain—**

*10 km from Chong-up, is famous for magnificent scenery, particularly in the autumn months. Naejangsan Tourist Hotel provides up-to-date accommodation.*

### Nakhwaam Cliff—

*located in Puyo by the Paekma river. Puyo was the capital of the ancient kingdom of Paekje from 538 A.D. to 660 A.D. Thirteen hundred years have elasped since the Paekje power was ruined, but the magnificent remains of those glorious days are still well preserved in and around Puyo. When the Paekje Kingdom fell, some 3,000 court ladies plunged into the river from this cliff to avoid capture. In their honor a hexagonal pavilion on the top of the cliff is named Paekhwa-jong "White Flower Pavilion."*

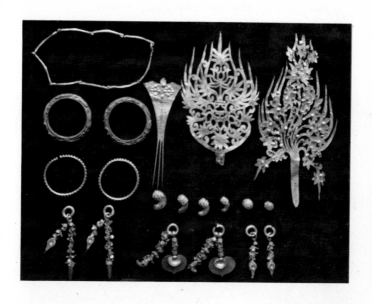

**Gold Crown of the Paekje Dynasty**— *the Paekje crowns are distinguished by their boldly stylized designs of flowers and flames, while contemporary crowns from the Silla kingdom to the south resemble tree forms or animal antlers. Over 500 relics were recovered from the tomb chamber near the old Paekje capital, Puyo in 1971.*

**Tomb Chamber of King Muryong (501–523 A.D.)**— *wall tiles with floral patterns, ornament the lotus-like designs and geometrical patterns also attest the surprising cultural and technological advancement of the ancient kingdom. Especially important are the carved burial inscriptions in Chinese giving historical information, the oldest such material ever unearthed in Korea, which have not yet been fully deciphered. (Left)*

## Entrance of Muju-kuchondong Valley—

*32 km from Muju-up, the long, spectacularly narrow valley of unsurpassed beauty is pierced by rapidly flowing streams.*

**Unjin Miruk—**

One of the largest stone statues of Maitreya in the Orient, stands at Kwanchock Temple near Puyo. This mammoth Buddhist statue with three-meter-long ears is 24.5 meters high.

# Cheju-do(Island)

Korea's only island province is one hour plane ride from Seoul, but it takes the traveler to a different world. Cheju-do, 60 miles off the southern port of Pusan enjoys a semi-tropical climate, with mild weather all year round. The plants and landscape are entirely distinct from those of the mainland, and are unique to Cheju-do. Oranges are the principal product.

The beauties of the island range from lofty Halla Mt., an extinct volcano and the highest mountain in Korea, to the famed diving women who make their living gathering seafood and other marine products from the depths of the ocean, even in winter. There are three modern hotels in Cheju-do, and a

new highway encircles the island for the convenience of sight-seers. The island province is also known by the name of "Samda-do", which means island abundant in three things, rocks, women and wind. It is also called "Sammu-do", or an island lacking in three things: thieves, beggars and gates.

There is a legend that approximately 2,650 years ago, 3 gods emerged from a cave located at the northern foot of Halla Mt.—Ko, Pu and Yang. Since then the cave, the original name of which was Mohung-hyol, has been called Samsong-hyol (the cave of three family names).

*Halla mountain*

## Samsonghyol Caves—

*according to legend, about 2,650 years ago, 3 gods emerged from a cave located at the northern foot of Halla Mt.— Ko, Yang and Pu to found the Korean people. Since then the caves are called Samsonghyol – the cave of the three family names. (Top Right)*

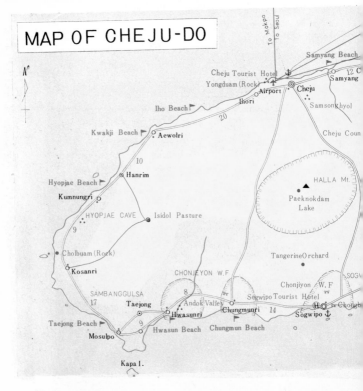

MAP OF CHEJU-DO

To Mokpo
To Seoul

Samyang Beach

Cheju Tourist Hotel
Yongduam (Rock)
Airport
Cheju
12 C
Samyang

N

Ihori

Samsonghyol

Iho Beach

20

Cheju Coun

Kwakji Beach
Aewolri

10

Hanrim

HALLA Mt.

Hyopjae Beach

Paeknokdam
Lake

Kumnungri

HYOPJAE CAVE
Isidol Pasture

9

Cholbuam (Rock)

Kosanri

CHONJEYON W.F.

TangerineOrchard

Chonjiyon W.F

SOGW

SAMBANGGULSA

8

Sogwipo Tourist Hotel

17

Taejong

Andok Valley

Chungmunri

14

Sogwipo

Chongb

Taejong Beach

9

Hwasunri

Chonge

Mosulpo

Hwasun Beach

Chungmun Beach

Kapa I.

82

*Tolharabang*

**Specimen Tours**

One Day Cheju-do Tour
*1. Hotel (Sogwipo)—Tangerine Orchard—Chongbang Falls
—Sinhyo Model Farm Village—Songsanilchulbong—Songdang
Ranch—Kumyong Snake Cave—Cheju Hotel.
2. Cheju Hotel—Hillside Forest—Paeknokdam Lake—Yongsil
Rocks—Mountain Cabin.*

**Women Divers—** *(Top Right)*
*work the year round, gathering all kinds of seaweeds, abalone,
top-shell, etc., without benefit of scuba aparatus or diving suits.*

**Hunting**
*Pheasant hunting is a popular sport on Cheju-do. Interested persons
must obtain a fire-arms permit from the Government.*

*Maid carrying water vase on her back drawn from nearby wells or streams (Bottom)*

**Jongbang falls—**
*drainage stream from the slopes of Halla Mt., plunges
into the ocean.*

**Chungmun Beach—**
*clean sands, crystal clear water, mild surf, and warm water
temperature make this one of the finest beaches in Korea.*

# Custom

**Greeting to Senior—** *(Left)*

*the first day of the first moon is celebrated at home with the offering of lunar Calendar new year greetings to senior members of the family and relatives.*

**Seesaw—**

*girls and women, clad in traditional costumes are catapulted high in the air from the "jumping seesaw". This is a feature of the lunar new year celebration. In recent years, seesaw play can be observed during new year's day by lunar calendar.*

*In the snugness of home, children play Yut game*

**Traditional Wedding Ceremony—** ( *Left* )
*old-fashioned wedding ceremonies, with the elaborately costumed groom riding in a sedan chair or palanquin to the house of the bride, there to share with her ceremonial sips of wine at their first meeting, are very rare now. Instead, an institution has grown up in cities called the wedding hall, where an auditorium...complete with music and flowers, and with "Western style" bridal gowns and dress suits..presided over by a family friend or an ex-teacher of the groom.*

91

**Songpyon (rice cakes)—**
*traditional cakes made of pounded rice flour*

*Typical Korean houses*

## Visiting a Korean Home

Foreign visitors who would like to see the Korean way of life in a friendly private home should apply at the Seoul City Tourist Information Center (72–5765) which will make all arrangements.

Visitors may include a simple family tea or perhaps an excellent home prepared typical Korean family dinner.

Hosts in all cases are volunteers who wish to welcome foreign visitors. The social status ranges from just ordinary citizens to highly placed businessmen and officials.

## Changdokdae, Earthen jars

*Kimchi, soy sauce, and hot sauce are stored in earthen jars.*

# Korean Food

The basic everyday meals are simple enough: each will include a bowl of boiled rice, a meat or fish soup, and a dish of kimchi, the peppery, fermented pickle stored underground in earthen jars all through the winter, or prepared daily in modified form during hot weather. Fresh vegetables are eaten in season.

But foods prepared for guests tend to be fancy. There is

*Pulgogi, strips of beef charcoal-roasted over a brazier at table after marinating in a complex mixture of soy sauce, sesame, and spices; sinsollo, a regal casserole of vegetables, and meats, also cooked at table; and numerous elaborate meat, fish and vegetable dishes, including delicate rice cakes and cookies for special occasions, whose preparation requires many stages and much labor.*

*A Korean dishes*　97

# Arts and Festivals

*Members of the Korean Classical Music Institute present a Kaya-kum concert*

## Arts

Tomb wall murals in fresco from the Koguryo Dynasty period ( 37 B.C.–668) are the earliest surviving examples of Korean painting. The mytholoigcal beasts depicted in some of these frescoes. show a fantastic imagination and wild abandon. Later, in Yi Dynasty days (1392–1910), there were two classes of artists: professionals employed by the court for portraits, decorative landscapes, and genre paintings; and amateurs who painted and practiced calligraphy. The latter were highly cultivated aristocratic scholar-poets. Western art trends which came to Korea early in the 20th century have influenced but not submerged the still-active tradition of Oriental style painting. A national gallery is sponsored by the government to promote the arts. Meanwhile, the number of private galleries is gradually increasing.

*A Korean Classic orchestra plays A-ak (court music)*

## Music and Dance

*If Koreans are known by one trait among foreigners, it is their love for and proficiency in the arts of music and dance.*

*Native Korean music divides into A-ak (Confucian ritual music), Tang-ak and Hyong-ak (Court ceremonial music of Chinese and local origin respectively), and several varieties of military, chamber, and vocal music. To these must be added Buddhist chants and the folk music and farmers' bands of the common people.*

*Korean's traditional fan dance*

The court music is slow, solemn, and complex in its intertwining of long, elaborately decorated melodic lines. Ancient instruments, many adapted from Chinese prototypes, include plucked-string zithers, double reeds and flutes, and a variety of percussion. The human voice is traditionally accompanied by drum only to mark the beat.

The dances that go with some of the court music are likewise stately, static and highly stylized.

Folk music, in contrast, is usually fast and lively, with vigorous, athletic dancing. Irregular rhythms in compound triple time predominate. Some of the same instruments are used, but folk music relies largely on metal gongs, the hour-glass shaped drum called the changgo and a loud, trumpet-like oboe.

Modern composers, including some foreign experts, have noted, adapted, and paraphrased portions of the old music.

*Various kinds of Masques*

*The spectacular drum dance performed by the world-famous "Little Angels." (Left)*

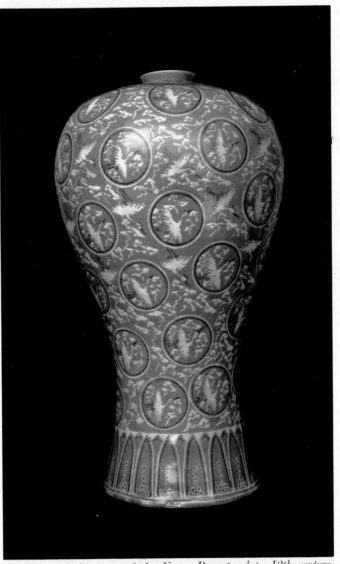

*Celadon vase of the Koryo Dynasty, late 12th century,*
104  *preserved in the Natianal Museum. (H: 41cm, D: 23cm)*

*King's Crown of the Old Silla Dynasty, (B.C 57–A.D 936), preserved in the National Museum. (H: 27Cm., D: 16.5Cm.)*

## Ceramic

Korean ceramics, especially the glazed celadon utensils of the Koryo Dynasty (918–1392), are by far the most famous single class of art objects the nation has produced. Long valued and sought after in the West (Madame Pompadour had a Korean vase in her collection), not only for their artistic beauty but for their high craftmanship, Koryo celadon like the Stradivarius violin—can be imitated but not duplicated today. Modern imitations of Koryo celadon are quite convincing to anyone but a specialist. They are cheap, too, and can of course be legally taken out of the country by travelers—something that cannot be done with the genuine antique Koryo ware.

*18th century genre painting titled "Custom" by Yoon-bok Shin on display in the National Museum.*

*Bronze image of Buddha, 80 cm high, a masterpiece of Buddhist art and craftsmanship of the Old Sila Dynasty, (B.C. 57–A.D. 936) is preserved in the National Museum.*

*Oriental painting of a tiger*

*Painting of a farm girl by Hyong-ku Sim (1937) pre-*
*served in the National Museum of Modern Art.*

**Kosam-nori—**
*a group game played in rural area, recalling ancient battles*

| Name of festival | Date | Location |
| --- | --- | --- |
| Admiral Yi's Commemoration | during Oct. | Chungmu city |
| Haengju Daechob festival | 14th Mar. | Koyang town |
| Chunhyang folk festival | 8th Apr. by the lunar calendar | Namwon town |
| Admiral Yi's birthday celebration | during Apr. | Onyang town |
| Yongnam art festival | during May | Miryang town |
| Honam art festival | during May | Kwangju city |
| Kaenari lake festival | during June | Chunchon city |
| Nanke art festival | during Sept. | Yongdong town |
| Sejong folk festival | during Oct. | Yoju town |
| Yulkok folk festival | during Oct. | Kangnung city |
| Sorak folk festival | during Oct. | Sokcho city |
| Chungbuk art festival | during Oct. | Chongju city |
| Paekje folk festival | during Oct. | Kongju & Puyo |
| Silla folk festival | during Oct. | Kyongju city |
| Halla folk festival | during Oct. | Cheju-do Island |
| Samsonghyol cave festival | twice a year, Spring & Autumn | Cheju-do Island |
| Kaechun art festival | during Nov. | Chinju city |

# Sports

*Koreans have always been an athletics-minded, competition-loving people. Games and sports, as well as physical culture, are taught in all schools, and intramural contests between traditional rivals attract fervent public attention and partisanship.*

*Archery*

There are many traditional folk games and contests still surviving, especially in the country among the rural populace. The government has taken steps to encourage preservation of these old customs by sponsoring an annual National Folk Arts Contest each autumn. These colorful events pit province against province, with individual and team winners sharing prizes and honors.

There is also a national athletic meet every year under government patronage, where international sports events are given, in part as a preparation of screening for the Korean Olympics team.

Korean athletes have participated in many international events, beginning in the 1930s, and have been especially outstanding in track events, as well as boxing, wrestling, weight lifting, basketball and volley ball.

Besides the international Olympics, Korean participants have been sent to the Asian Games, World Women's Basketball Matches, and many other such events.

Visiting foreign athletes and teams occasionally come to Seoul for exhibition events or to compete with Koreans.

**A demonstration of Taekwondo—**

*the deadly art of self-defense originating in Korea and spreading rapidly all over the world.*

# Religion

**A Buddhist Ceremony—**
*there are 2,397 Buddhist temples and shrines, and 15,320
priests in Korea.*

The early Koreans worshipped almost anything they could not understand or control. Heavenly bodies such as the sun and the moon, and in some cases the stars, were objects of veneration.

In ancient times, the dead were buried with their personal belongings, and family tombs were built underground for burial of all the members of one family. The burials of kings and royalty were naturally more elaborated. Constructed underground of stone or clay covered by a semispherical mound, the royal tombs contained

Myongdong Catholic Cathedral, Seoul

sealed halls where the king's possessions, ornaments and daily utensils were placed. Upon the walls were painted pictures of rituals, customs and other contemporary activities.

Major religions are Christianity and Buddhism. Christiainty has greatly influenced the nation. At the end of 1970, Protestant and Catholic Christians totaled 3,192,621 and 751,217 respectively. Institutional Buddhism claims about 90,000 lay members with some 2,397 temples and shrines throughout Korea.

# Education

The current system of school education in Korea is organized in accordance with the 6-3-3-4 pattern. The Ministry of Education organized the National Education Charter Commission and formally created the Charter of National Education, which was promulgated by President Park Chung Hee on Dec. 5, 1968.

In accordance with the Constitution, elementary education is compulsory for every child in the 6 to 11 years age group. There are a total of 51 two-year junior colleges and 85 four-year colleges and universities and 64 graduate schools in Korea.

*Junior sports*

*Girls relax on the campus at Ehwa Womans University, Seoul*

## Kisaeng House

*If tourists wish to sample the true exotic flavor of Korean entertainment, they should visit a Kisaeng house where graceful, English-speaking Kisaeng hostesses in bright traditional costumes will sing, dance and entertain you amidst lavish old-style surroundings. This graceful entertainment with its strictly Korean tradition and atmosphere delights every visitor from abroad.*

### Leading Kisaeng Houses Include:

| | |
|---|---|
| Chongpung | 99 Ikson-dong, Chongno-ku, Tel: 72-1511 |
| Chungun-gak | Chungun-dong, Chongno-ku, Tel: 73-3552/53 |
| Dobongsan-jang | 405, Dobong-dong, Songbuk-ku Tel: 99-3380 |
| Donghae-jang | 138 Hasu-dong, Mapo-ku, Tel: 32-2520 |
| Dorang | 34 Ikson-dong, Chongno-ku, Tel: 74-1214 |
| Haewoon-dae | 18, Mukjong-dong, Chung-ku, Tel: 54-3267 |
| Jindang | 42 Tangju-dong, Chongno-ku, Tel: 73-5709 |
| Mansudae | 9 Hyonjo-dong, Sodaemun-ku, Tel: 72-6550 |
| Ojin-am | 34-6 Ikson-dong, Chongno-ku, Tel: 72-3206/7 |
| Okryu-jang | Kongpyong-dong, Chongno-ku, Tel: 75-4621 |
| Pungrim | 57 Mukyo-dong, Chung-ku, Tel: 24-4801, 22-0145 |
| Samcheong-gak | 115-330, Songbuk-dong, Songbuk-ku, Tel: 94-7006 |
| Sonun-gak | Ui-dong, Songbuk-ku, Tel: 99-3986 |
| Daeha | 56 Ikson-dong, Chongno-ku, Tel: 72-3202 |
| Daewon-gak | 324 Songbuk-dong, Songbuk-ku, Tel: 93-0034 |

## Bars, Cabarets and Nightclubs—

*There are many night spots in Seoul which feature floor shows, dancing, music, and refreshments. . . . They range from the inexpensive beer halls to the elaborate shows presented on the top floors of downtown hotels. Hostesses, many of whom speak English and Japanese, will help to make your evening a delight.*

## Casinos—

*Government licensed casinos are operated at the Walker Hill Resort, Seoul; the Olympos Hotel, Inchon; Haeundae Tourist Hotel, Pusan; and Sogwipo Tourist Hotel, Cheju-do Island.*

## Golf —

*In recent years golf has become very popular in Korea. There are 14 golf clubs in the country.*

*Horse Racing at Tuksom Track, Seoul*

*Korea offers the following opportunities for golfing in and outside of Seoul :*

New *Korea Country Club in Seoul.*
*Taenung Country Club at Songdong-ku, Seoul*
*Kwanak Country Club at Osanri, Kyonggi-do*
*Anyang Country Club at Pukokri, Sihung-kun, Kyonggi-do*
*Hanyang Country Club at Wontangri, Koyang-kun, Kyonggi-do*
*Pupyong Country Club at Kyongso-dong, Inchon*
*Yongin Country Club at Yangjiri, Yongin-kun, Kyonggi-do*
*Osan Country Club at Pukri, Yongin-kun, Kyonggi-go*
*Sansong Country Club at Tamiri, Kwangju-kun, Kyonggi-do*
*Nam-Seoul Country Club at Paekhyonri, Kwangju-kun, Kyonggi-do*
*Yusong Country Club at Taedok-kun, Chungchong-nam do*
*Tongnae Country Club at Tongnae-ku, Pusan*
*Pusan Country Club in Pusan*
*Cheju Country Club in Cheju*

## Recommended Climbing Course

*Course A (Pukhan Mt., Seoul): Entrance Way—Manhwajang-Segumjong (Two hour course)*
*Course B (Sorak Mt., East Coast): Entrance Way—Sinhung Temple—Kyejoam—Pisondae. (One day course)*
*Course C (Halla Mt., Cheju-do): Entrance Way—Tamna Ravine—Kaemidong—Ongjin Pavilion—Wangkwan-nung (Crown tomb)—mountaintop (One day course)*

*A camping area*

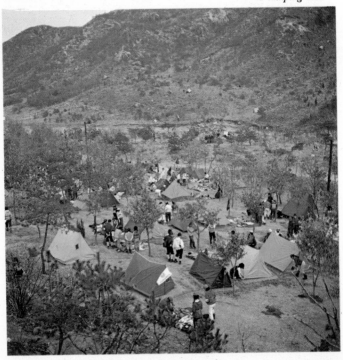

### Skiing at Taekwallryong Highland—

*alt. 870m, is situated 8km by bus from Kangnung Airport.
The sloping hillside around the pass provides the best place
for skiing in the country. Modern facilities, such as lifts,
and bungalows, have been installed in the area for the
convenience of skiers.*

129

### Water Skiing—

*in Korea, water skiing, like her delicious shrimps and crabs, comes in both the salt and fresh water varieties. Huge lakes accumulated behind multi-purpose dams, have become beautiful summer resorts and offer swimming, water skiing, fishing, etc.*

### Outdoor Swimming Pool at Walker Hill Hotels— *(Right)*

*there are many public swimming pools in Seoul both indoor and outdoor.*

# Beaches

| Beach | Location | Characteristics |
|---|---|---|
| Songdo | 6 km south of Inchon | Boating, cabaret, hotels, other entertainment facilities |
| Jagyak Island | 3km by boat from Inchon | Best sand beach in Inchon area |
| Palmi-do | 20km by boat from Inchon | Lovely landscape, no inhabitants |
| Taechon | 10km west of Taechon | 2.5km long and 30m wide sand beach, Numerous entertainment and accommodation facilities |
| Mallipo | 88km by boat from Inchon | Exceptionally lovely countryside, mild surf, good accommodations and entertainment facilities |
| Pyonsan | 23km by car from Kunsan | 6km long sand beach, points of interest, temples, inns, and entertainment facilities |
| Namildae | 35km by car or train from Chinju | best sand, mild surf, crystal clear water, warm temperature and accommodation in Samchonpo |
| Haeundae | 15km by car from Pusan | Best beach on the south coast, one of eight scenic wonders of Korea, spa, and international standard accommodation and casino |
| Tadaepo | 16km by car from Pusan | Clean sand, mild surf, crystal clear water, and lovely landscape |

| Beach | Location | Characteristics |
|-------|----------|-----------------|
| Mansongri | *Yosu* | *Black sand, crystal clear water, mild surf and lovely coastline. Accommodation in Yosu* |
| Chungmu-kongsol | *Chungmu* | *Points of interest, Hallyo Channel, warm temperature and good hotels and entertainment facilities* |
| Hwajinpo | *30min. by car from Sokcho* | *Eight scenic wonders of Hwajin, crystal clear water, clean sand and villas* |
| Naksan | *12km by car from Sokcho* | *Clean sand, lovely countryside, fishing snapper and inns* |
| Kyongpodae | *8km by car from Kangnung* | *Best beach on the east coast, fishing snapper, boating and good accommodation* |
| Pohang | *Pohang* | *4km long clean and beach, warm temperature, mild surf and numerous accommodations and entertainments facilities* |
| Eho | *Cheju-Do* | *White sand and best beach in Cheju Island* |
| Chungmun | *15km by car from Sogwipo* | *White sand, crystal clear water* |

# National Parks

| Park | Location | Characteristics |
|------|----------|-----------------|
| Sorak Mt. | *On the East Coast between Sokcho and Yangyang* | *Alt. 1,708m, rocky precipices, spectacular waterfalls; towering peaks, famous temples, beaches, crimson foliage and skiing* |
| Sokni Mt. | *South-west area between Chungju and Sangju* | *Alt. 1,057m, towering rocks, historical relics, such as Haein temple and Tripitaka Koreana Blocks, exceptionally beautiful landscape; Sujongam, Munjang-dae* |
| Kyeryong Mt. | *Kongju-gun, Chungchong-Namdo* | *Alt. 828m, natural beauties, waterfalls, valleys, Sampullpong, Kwanum-pong* |
| Kyongju | *Kyongju city, Kyongsang-Pukdo* | *Sun rise view from Sokguram Grotto, Pulkuk temple, Chomsongdae Astronomical observatory, Sokpinggo Ice storage, undersea tomb and National Museum* |
| Naejang Mt. | *Chongup-kun, Cholla-pukdo* | *Alt. 640m, natural beauties, temples, and towering peaks* |
| Chiri Mt. | *Between Kurye and Hamyang-kun, Cholla-Namdo* | *Alt. 1,915m, natural beauties, Nokodaṇ Mt., Hwaum temple, Saja-tap, Sonsankyo and dense forest* |

| Park | Location | Characteristics |
|------|----------|-----------------|
| Hallyo Channel | *South Coast connecting Pusan-Chungmu-Yosu* | *One of eight wonders of Korea, picturesque coastline, historical relics, temples, offshore tour by hydrofoil boat* |
| Halla Mt. | *Cheju-do Island* | *Alt. 1,950m, Paeknok lake in the crater of Halla Mt., strange-shaped rocks, waterfalls, beautiful volcanic tube, women divers, historical remains* |

*Hak-do (crane island) near Samchonpo*

# Shopping

Seoul is a paradise for shoppers. Visitors may shop in modern, fixed price department stores and shopping arcades or may haggle over prices in the fantastic East Gate Market, a typical Oriental bazaar.

What is there to buy in Seoul? You name it, Seoul has it. Perfectly fitted, hand-tailored suits made from first quality Korean cloth (including hand-loomed tweeds from Cheju Island) may be bought at prices far below those prevailing in the United States or Eruope. Sweaters, plain, embroidered and beaded, are now being exported in huge quantities all over the world. The exquisitely beautiful

A department st

Korean silks and brocades are among the finest in the world. Ladies handbags and leather work are popular. Locally manufactured transistor radios are exported world-wide. Jewelry, beautifully designed and fabricated, especially attracts the eyes of the ladies. Some like the heavy, hand-carved rings, necklaces, brooches, etc., made from pure 24kt. gold. Others prefer the artistically designed and painstakingly handicrafted jewelry items featuring smoky topaz, amethyst, fossil amber, jade, and other precious stones. Silver is an especially good bargain.

As to souvenirs, the range is endless... as is the price. There are Korean ginseng, paintings, the lovely costume dolls, some "weaving" on scale models of hand looms, others "playing" Korean musical instrument, etc. The white or yellow brassware has long been popular. So are the lacquerware, produced in many colors, and intricately inlaid with silver, brass, and or varicolored mother-

*Brassware*

of-pearl. Carved soapstone objects are popular, this is only a surface sampling... look around for yourself... and remember the prices are right.

Recommended to foreign shoppers are the following: Bando Arcade, Chosun Arcade, Midopa Dept. Store, Shinsegye Dept. Store, Sidae Dept. Store, Hwasin Dept. Store, Shin-Shin Dept. Store, Pagoda Park Arcade, Saewoon Arcade and East Gate Market.

There are tax-free commissaries for foreigners. The Korea Tourist Service, Inc. (KTS), operates a chain of Foreigners' Commissaries in major cities and you will find one on the 2nd floor of the Bando Arcade. All you need is a valid passport and foreign currency (Korean Won is not accepted). Also there are four privately operated commissaries. Two of these are the Ulchiro and Myongdong shops. Another is the Shinsegye Dept. Store and Saewoon Shop on the 3rd floor of the Nadong building.

It is recommended that anyone unfamiliar with Korea market ways should be accompanied by a guide to get the most out of shopping in this market.

Silk

## Wood Carvings—

*wood carving is a Korean traditional art. These examples of Korean handicraft make excellent gifts.*

*Toys*

## Tailor Shops—

*there are many excellent tailor shops where both men's and women's suits, coats, etc., will be tailored from the finest fabrics at low prices. Workmanship is excellent. Sample prices are:*
*3 piece suit for Winter and Fall: $80.00*
*2 piece suit for Summer and Spring: $50.00*

## Korean Ginseng

Ginseng is the mysterious herbal medicine which is highly valued throughout the world as a rejuvenator and an elixir of life and is reputed to have curative value in many disease such as nervous prostration, anemia, anorexia, asthenia, lack of vigour of male and female, for skin beauty and hypertension. There are two kinds of Ginseng; White Ginseng and Red Ginseng, the latter being the Government Monopoly product. Besides these two kinds of Ginseng, Ginseng exists also as tea, extract, powder and drink preparation.

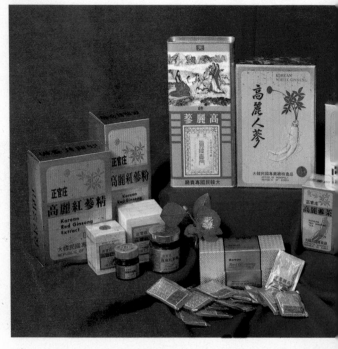

## Dosage:

### Red Ginseng & White Ginseng

*Average dose for adults—Put into earthenware 50~60g with 0.9 l of water, 5g of ginger, 3 jujubes, and boil slowly. When about 0.2 l of water remains, put it all into the ramie or cotton wrapper and squeeze. Drink the water squeezed from the wrapper everyday.*

*Average dose for children (7~15 age)—½ adult dosage.*

### Ginseng Tea

*One package contains 30 tea bags, each bag containing 3g. The usage is as same as with ordinary tea bags.*

### Ginseng Extract

*Adult—Mix 1~2g with warm water and drink 1~3 times daily.*

### Ginseng powder

*Same as Ginseng Extract. (Be careful of moisture while storing.)*

## Purchasing Center
### Red Ginseng

*Red Ginseng is sold at the Government designated Korea Ginseng Industrial Co., Ltd. whose sales office is situated at the west exit of Bando Arcade in Seoul (tel. 23—3445).*
*When you purchase the Ginseng, you should check for the Government guaranteed inspection seal on the package.*

### White Ginseng and Others

*are available at any foreigner's commissary, Bando Arcade etc.*

## Price:

| | | | |
|---|---|---|---|
| *Red Ginseng (High class)* | *150g* | | *US $30.90* |
| *Red Ginseng Extract* | *30g* | | *3.90* |
| *Red Ginseng Powder* | *60g* | | *3.90* |
| *Red Ginseng Tea* | *30 tea bags,* | *3g each* | *3.35* |
| *White Ginseng* | *300g* | | *₩ 5,000~10,000* |
| *White Ginseng Extract* | *25g* | | *₩ 1,200* |
| *White Ginseng Powder* | *50g* | | *₩ 1,000* |
| *White Ginseng tea* | *30 tea bags,* | *3g each* | *₩ 600* |

## Quantity Limit one can take out of Korea.

*Red and White Ginseng—3kg (by mail—1.2kg)*
*Ginseng powder & Ginseng tea bags—2kg*
*Ginseng extract—1kg*
*Drink preparation—2l*

## Tips to the Foreign Shoppers:

*Genuine antiques, such as handicrafts, paintings and documents are not authorized for export unless approved by the Bureau of Cultural Property along with a certificate issued by this office. Otherwise such antiques are subject to confiscation by officials of the Bureau.*

*The following items may not be removed from Korea:*

*a. Cultural assets designated as national treasure in accordance with the preservation act of the cultural assets.*

*b. Other cultural assets pending appreciation.*

*The format of certificate issued by Bureau of Cultural Property is as follows:*

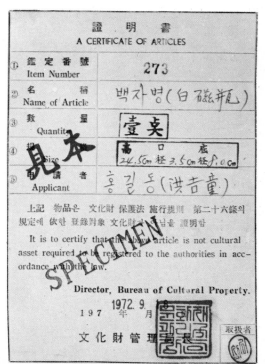

### 證 明 書
#### A CERTIFICATE OF ARTICLES

| | |
|---|---|
| ① 鑑 定 番 號<br>Item Number | 273 |
| ② 名 稱<br>Name of Article | 백자병（白磁瓶） |
| ③ 數 量<br>Quantity | 壹 箇 |
| ④ 規 格<br>Size | 高 口 底<br>24.5cm 徑 3.5cm 徑 5.0cm |
| ⑤ 申 請 者<br>Applicant | 홍길동（洪吉童） |

上記 物品은 文化財 保護法 施行規則 第二十六條의 規定에 依한 登錄對象 文化財가 아님을 證明함

It is to certify that the above article is not cultural asset required to be registered to the authorities in accordance with the law.

**Director, Bureau of Cultural Property.**

１９７２．9.
１９７ 年 月

文 化 財 管 理 局 長

取扱者

145

# Restaurants

There are innumerable restaurants in addition to those operated by hotels. Many serve "Western, Chinese and Japanese Style" food, but a real treat would be a typical Korean cuisine. Representative restaurants are as follows:

## Korean Restaurants

Baikkung: Myo-dong, Chongno-ku, Tel: 74–2389
Hanil-kwan: Myong-dong, Chung-ku, Tel: 28–1693
Keoku-jang: Sokong-dong, Chung-ku, Tel: 28–8011
Kukil-kwan: Kwansoo-dong, Chongno-ku, Tel: 73–5515
Uchon-kak: Sindang-dong, Songdong-ku, Tel: 54–2372

## Western Restaurants

Donghwa Grill: Sosomun-dong, Sodaemun-ku,
       Tel: 23–7555

Sky-park: Myong-dong, Chung-ku, Tel: 24–1091
World Cup (Theatre restaurant):
       Da-dong, Chung-ku, Tel: 28–0956

## Chinese Restaurants

Four Seasons: Sokong-dong, Chung-ku, Tel: 24–1841
Hongposok: Ichon-dong, Yongsan-ku, Tel: 43–8012

## Japanese Restaurants

Eunji: Kwanchol-dong, Chongno-ku, Tel: 73–3434
Mijori: Pukchang-dong, Chung-ku, Tel: 22–3966
Soorakwon: Ulchiro, Chung-ku, Tel: 28–3261

# Hotels

Here are recommended hotels suitable for foreign tourists in major cities and tourist areas. All of these are registered with the government. Most rooms have private baths, heating and cooling systems. Facilities in most hotels include dining rooms, convention halls, bars, souvenir shops, cocktail lounges, barber and beauty shops and recreation areas.

*Chosun hotel*

## Seoul

| Cl | Hotel | Location | Room | Telephone |
|----|-------|----------|------|-----------|
| B | Ambassador | *Mukchong-dong, Chung-ku* | *107* | *52–1151/9* |
| D | Academy house | *Suyu-dong, Songbuk-ku* | *40* | *99–1181/5* |
| D | Astoria | *Namhak-dong 13-2 Chung-ku* | *61* | *27–7121/5* |
| B | Bando | *Ulchiro 1-ka, Chung-ku* | *111* | *22–7151/9* |
| D | Central | *Changsa-dong, Chongno-ku* | *68* | *75–8057/9* |
| A | Chosun | *Sokong-dong, Chung-ku* | *504* | *24–3901/9* |
| D | Chunji | *Ulchiro 5-ka, Chung-ku* | *35* | *53–6131/3* |
| D | Grand | *Namdaemunro 4-ka, Chung-ku* | *35* | *23–4171/9* |
| C | Green park | *Suyu-dong, Songbuk-ku* | *80* | *99–2171/6* |
| D | International | *Sokong-dong, Chung-ku* | *41* | *24–2211/5* |
| B | KAL | *Namdaemunro 2-ka. Chung-ku* | *111* | *23–8401/5* |
| A | Koreana | *Taepyongro 1-ka Chung-ku* | *268* | *75–7591/9* |
| C | Lions | *Chungmuro 2-ka, Chung-ku* | *54* | *26–1110/4* |
| C | Metro | *Ulchiro 2-ka, Chung-ku* | *82* | *23–5131/4* |
| C | Munhwa | *Chon-dong, Sodaemun-ku* | *87* | *73–4712/3* |

| Cl | Hotel | Location | Room | Telephone |
|---|---|---|---|---|
| C | New Namsan | *Hwehyon-dong 1-ka, Chung-ku* | 103 | *22–3191/4* |
| B | New Korea | *Ulchiro 1-ka, Chung-ku* | 104 | *28–4221/9* |
| C | New Naeja | *Naeja-dong, Chongno-ku* | 61 | *73–9011/5* |
| B | New Seoul | *Taepyongro 1-ka, Chung-ku* | 147 | *75–9071/9* |
| C | New Sky | *Pyongchang-dong, Sodaemun-ku* | 51 | *75–5121/5* |
| C | New Yongsan | *Hannam-dong, Yongsan-ku* | 56 | *54–9181/5 1055/8* |
| D | Oriental | *Hwehyon-dong, Chung-ku* | 22 | *23–0700/6* |
| D | Palace | *Hwehyon-dong, Chung-ku* | 52 | *24–3111/7* |
| C | Poong Jun | *Inhyon-dong, Chung-ku* | 108 | *26–2151/9* |
| A | President | *Ulchiro 1-ka Chung-ku* | 201 | *23–3131/5* |
| C | Prince | *Namsan-dong, Chung-ku* | 60 | *22–7111/5* |
| A | Royal | *Myong-dong, Chung-ku* | 320 | *24–2681/9* |
| D | Sanda | *Da-dong, Chung-ku* | 70 | *24–3271/5* |
| B | Sejong | *Chungmuro 2-ka, Chung-ku* | 244 | *24–1811/9* |
| A | Seoulin | *149, Sorin-dong, Chongno-ku* | 228 | *75–9116/23* |
| A | Seoul Tokyu | *Yang-aong, Chung-ku* | 210 | *24–1626/9* |
| D | Star Dust | *Sorin-dong, Chongno-ku* | 38 | *73–7204/5* |

| Cl | Hotel | Location | Room | Telephone |
|----|-------|----------|------|-----------|
| C | Savoy | *Chungmuro 1-ka, Chung-ku* | *121* | *28–7281/5* |
| D | Daewon | *Chungmuro 3-ka, Chung-ku* | *50* | *26–7141/6* |
| B | Tower | *Changchun-dong, Chung-ku* | *91* | *53–9181/5* |
| B | Walker Hill | *Kwangjang-dong, Songdong-ku* | *263* | *55–0181/9* |
| D | YMCA | *Chongno 2-ka, Chongno-ku* | *43* | *72–8291/8* |

**Pusan area**

| Cl | Hotel | Location | Room | Telephone |
|----|-------|----------|------|-----------|
| C | Bando | *Chungang-dong,* | *52* | *6–7161/5* |
| D | Bay | *Chungang-dong,* | *24* | *4–0161/3* |
| C | Haeundae | *Chung-dong, Tongnae-ku,* | *45* | *7–1461/5* |
| B | Kukdong | *Chung-dong,* | *105* | *7–0081/8* |
| D | Mijinjang | *Chung-dong,* | *50* | *7–0191/5* |
| C | New Pusan | *Nampo-dong,* | *41* | *23–2353/7* |
| D | New Tongnae | *Onchun-dong,* | *49* | *5–1112/8* |
| C | Tongnae | *Onchun-dong,* | *52* | *5–1121/8* |
| C | Tongyang | *Kwangbok-dong,* | *48* | *22–1205/7* |
| C | Plaza | *Daechang-dong, Tong-ku* | *66* | *6–2281/5* |
| C | New Port | *Daechang-dong, Tong-ku,* | *50* | *6–2644* |
| D | UN | *Nampo-dong,* | *35* | *22–9933/4* |

**Kyonggi-do**

| Cl | Hotel | Location | Room | Telephone |
|----|-------|----------|------|-----------|
| C | Anyang | *Anyang-up, Sihung-gun* | *53* | |

| Cl | Hotel | Location | Room | Telephone |
|---|---|---|---|---|
| B | Olympos | Hang-dong, Inchon city | 250 | 2–0185/7 |
| E | Prince | Kwan-dong 3-ka, Inchon city | 20 | 3–0171/3 |
| D | Saemaeul | Paldallro 1-ka, Suwon city | 24 | |
| C | Yurimgak | Kumgokri, Hwasong-gun | 65 | |

### Kangwon-do

| | | | | |
|---|---|---|---|---|
| C | Chunchon Sejong | Pongi-dong, Chunchon city | 30 | 3191/3 |
| D | Kangnung Beach | Kangnung-dong, Kangnung city | 55 | |
| D | Kyongpodae | Kángmun-dong, Kangnung city | 42 | 2147/8 |
| E | Soraksan | Sorak-dong, Sokcho city | 27 | |

### Chungchong-pukdo

| | | | | |
|---|---|---|---|---|
| C | Soknisan | Sokni-myon, Poeun-gun | 35 | 21/5 |
| D | Suanbo | Sangmo-myon, Changwon-gun | 13 | 9, 19 |

### Chungchong-namdo

| | | | | |
|---|---|---|---|---|
| B | Mannyon-jang | Yusong-myon, Taedok-gun | 76 | 2–3197/8 |
| C | Mallipo | Sowon-myon Susan-gun | 37 | |
| B | Onyang | Onyang-up, Asan-gun | 54 | |

| Cl | Hotel | Location | Room | Telephone |
|---|---|---|---|---|
| C | Yusong | *Yusong-myon, Taedok-gun* | *57* | |
| D | Samhwa | *Won-dong, Taejon city* | *30* | *2–5711/5* |
| C | Taejon | *Won-dong, Taejon city* | *31* | *2–6640* |
| D | Onyang Kukje | *Onyang-up, Asan-gun* | *28* | *328* |

### Kyongsang-pukdo

| | | | | |
|---|---|---|---|---|
| B | Hanil | *Namil-dong, Taegu city* | *107* | *3–5111/9* |
| C | Kumho | *Haso-dong, Taegu* | *46* | *2–5012/6* |
| D | Kwankwang Center | *Puksongro 1-ka, Taegu city* | *50* | *3–2831/5* |
| C | Kyongju | *Songdong-dong,* | *61* | *1182/4* |
| C | Pulkuksa | *Chunhyon-dong, Kyongju city* | *35* | *6, 33* |
| C | Sangkum | *Dongsungro Taegu city* | *22* | |
| B | Taegu | *Tusan-dong, Taegu city* | *62* | *4–7311/3* |

### Kyongsang-namdo

| | | | | |
|---|---|---|---|---|
| C | Chungmu | *Tonam-dong, Chungmu city* | *32* | |
| D | Ulsan | *Yaeupri, Ulsan* | *22* | *7146/7* |

### Cholla-pukdo

| | | | | |
|---|---|---|---|---|
| D | Chonju | *Taga-dong,* | *46* | *5811* |
| D | Naejangsan | *Naejang-myon, Chongup-gun* | *30* | *9, 10* |

| Cl | Hotel | Location | Room | Telephone |
|----|-------|----------|------|-----------|
| D | Venus | *Youngwha-dong Kunsan City* | *18* | |

### Cholla-namdo

| Cl | Hotel | Location | Room | Telephone |
|----|-------|----------|------|-----------|
| C | Kwangju | *Keumnam-ro, Kwangju* | *70* | *2/6231* |
| D | Yosu | *Konghwa-dong* | *42* | *1491/5* |

### Cheju-do (Island)

| Cl | Hotel | Location | Room | Telephone |
|----|-------|----------|------|-----------|
| C | Cheju | *Cheju city* | *30* | *875/8* |
| C | Halla | *Sogwi-up, Namcheju-gun* | *44* | *·905, 906* |
| C | Sogwipo | *Sogwi-up, Namcheju-gun* | *70* | *116, 276* |

### Legend

| | |
|---|---|
| A: | Deluxe |
| B: | First Class |
| C: | Second Class |
| D: | Third Class |
| E: | Fourth Class |

# Travel agents

*Your travel agent offers you a wide range of services including air, surface, and sea travel, hotel reservations, etc. The travel agent is the accredited representative of scheduled air lines and of steamship lines, both domestic and foreign. He can advise you and issue your tickets.*

Railroad and Bus Travel: *Some travel agents represent bus companies for which they make reservations and issue tickets. Railroad reservations in connection with tour will be made by him and he will inform you of special discounts and bargain rates.*

Tours and Travel: *The travel agent represents all accredited tour operators, both foreign and domestic. He has a large stock of descriptive material which will aid you in selection of a tour and will make all arrangements for you. He will also provide full assistance on independent tours, conventions, group travel, and incentive tours such as those given by clubs and businesses.*

Hotel Reservations: *The travel agent will make your reservations and help you to obtain the best accommodations for the price you choose.*

Departure and Arrival of Foreigners: *The travel agent will make all arrangements and will help with permits, visas, etc. Whatever you need in travel: See your travel agent.*

| Travel Agencies | Address | Telephone |
|---|---|---|
| Aju Travel Service Co., Ltd. | *11, 1-ka, Tongkwang-dong, Chung-ku, Pusan* | *22–2222* |
| Bando Travel Service | *1st Floor, Saehan Bldg. 1, Bukchang-dong, Chung-ku, Seoul* | *24–1281/4* |
| Chunusa Travel (American Express) | *Rm. 401, Sokong Bldg. Seoul* | *23–3121/9* |
| Everett Air Korea, Ltd. | *Rm. 206, Tongmyong Bldg., Seoul* | *24–3411/5* |
| First Travel Service | *Rm. 203, Najon Bldg., Seoul* | *28–5504/5* |
| Global Tours of Korea | *8th Floor, Tonghwa Bldg., Seoul* | *22–9125/9* |
| Hana Tours, Inc. | *1st Floor, Kwangnam Bldg., Seoul* | *28–9863/5* |
| Hanjin Transportation Co.,Ltd. | *Rm. 2001, KAL Bldg., Seoul* | *23–0681/9* |
| International Air Travel Svc. | *3rd Floor, Center Bldg., Seoul* | *28–7803* |
| KODCO Travel Agency | *Rm. 501 ,Kong-dong, Bldg., Seoul* | *22–4271* |
| Korea Tour Center | *12-19, Kwanchul-dong, Chongno-ku, Seoul* | *74–8611/4* |
| Korea Tourist Bureau | *Rm. 100, Bando Hotel, Seoul* | *28–8697* |
| Korea Travel International | *Rm. 101, 201, Grand Hotel, Seoul* | *24–1291/5* |
| Korea Travel Service | *Rm. 201, Phoenix Bldg., Seoul* | *24–3151/5* |

| Travel Agencies | Address | Telephone |
|---|---|---|
| National Tours Agency | Rm. 501, Tongsin Bldg., Seoul | 54–0064 |
| Oriental Air Service | Rm. 302, Taipyong Bldg., Seoul | 23–3932 |
| Pana Korea Travel | Rm. 102, Kwanghak Bldg., Seoul | 28–5729 |
| Samyong Travel Service | Rm. 201/202, Samjong Bldg., Seoul | 24–2721/4 |
| Seoul Kyo-Tong Tour Service | 5th Floor, Sekwang Bldg., Seoul | 73–5202/3 |
| The Korea Express Co. Air & Tourist Office | 1st Floor, Tonga Bldg., Seoul | 22–2421 |
| Orient Express Co. | 101, 1-ka, Ulchi-ro, Chung-ku, Seoul | 24–3651/5 |
| Universal Travel Service | Rm. 234, Bando Hotel, Seoul | 24–1151/3 |
| World Travel Service Inc. | 51, Sokong-dong Chung-ku | 28–4322 |

## Banks

**The Bank of Korea**
*110, Namdaemunro, 3-ka, Chung-ku*
*Tel: SWB 22–9150/59*

**Korea Exchange Bank**
*7-3, Kwanchurl-dong, Chongno-ku*
*Tel: SWB 72–0041, 74–0051*
Bank of America N.T. and S.A.
*1st Floor, Ohyang Bldg.*
*199-63, 1-ka, Ulchiro, Chung-ku*

*I.P.O. Box 3026*
*Tel: 24–2641/4, 23–9236*

The Chartered Bank
*Rm. 108-110, Samsung Bldg.*
*50, 1-ka, Ulchiro, Chung-ku*
*I.P.O. Box 259*
*Tel: 23–3702/4, 22–0983, 28–3575*

Chase Manhattan Bank
*Rm. 208, Samsung Bldg.*
*50, 1-ka, Ulchiro, Chung-ku*
*Tel: 24–4251/5*

First National City Bank
*1st Floor, Taeyang Bldg.*
*28, Sokong-dong, Chung-ku*
*Tel: 28–4251/5*

## Airline Offices

| Airlines | Address | Telephone |
|---|---|---|
| Air France | *3rd Floor, Chosun Hotel* | *23–2524* |
| Air India | *Rm. 218, Bando Hotel* | *23–0557/9* |
| ALITALIA | *Rm. 207, New Korea Hotel* | *22–8454* |
| American Air Lines | *3rd, Floor, Chosun Hotel* | *23–5747* |
| British Overseas Airways Corps | *Rm. 218, Bando Hotel* | *23–0550* |
| Canadian Pacific Air | *Rm. 222, Bando Hotel* | *23–8271/5* |
| Cathay Pacific Airways | *Rm. 501, New Korea Hotel* | *23–0321/8* |
| China Air Lines | *Rm. 224, 226, Bando Hotel* | *28–3678* |
| Flying Tiger Line | *Rm. 306, Bando Hotel* | *22–6739* |

| Airlines | Address | Telephone |
|---|---|---|
| Japan Air Lines | 1st, 2nd Floor, Paknam Bldg. | 24-2081/4 |
| KLM Royal Dutch Air Lines | 2nd Floor, Chosun Hotel | 24-2495 |
| Korean Air Lines | KAL Bldg. | 28-2221 |
| Lufthansa German Air Lines | 2nd Floor, Chosun Hotel | 24-1655/6 |
| Northwest Air Lines | 2nd Floor, Chosun Hotel | 23-4191 |
| Pan American World Airways | Rm. 142, Bando Hotel | 24-1451/4 |
| Qantas Airways | Rm. 218, Bando Hotel | 23-0321 |
| Scandinavian Air Lines System | Sokong Bldg. | 22-1408 |
| Swiss Air Transport Co., Ltd. | Sokong Bldg. | 22-1408 |
| Thai Airways Int'I | Sokong Bldg. | 22-5641 |
| Varig Brazilian Air Lines | 2nd Floor, Chosun Hotel | 23-0244/6 |

## Medical Service

*Medical service in Korea is excellent. There are a number of hospitals staffed by professional doctors and nurses and the treatment is as good. In an emergency the hotel desk will call the house physician or ambulance as required.*

Korea National Medical Center
*18-70, Ulchiro, 6-ka*
*Tel: 52-2101/11, 52-6583*

Severance Hospital
*15, Sinchon, Sodaemun-ku   Tel: 32-0161/69, 32-0171/79*

Songshim Hospital
*82-1, Pildong, 2-ka, Chung-ku*
*Tel: 27-8111/19. 27-8200*
Koryo Hospital
*1, Chungjungro 1-ka, Chongno-ku*
*Tel: 75-8021/25, 75-8061/5*

Communications

*Ministry of Communications provides telegraph, telephone,*
*telex, and telephoto services for foreign visitors, and there are*
*overseas telephone and telegraph offices in Chosun and Bando*
*hotels.*
*Telephone rates as of September 1, 1972 are as follows:*

| Destination | Via | Basic Fare initial 3 Min. | Additional one Min. |
|---|---|---|---|
| Belgium | ATT | $12 | ₩ 1,484 |
| Denmark | ATT | $15 | ₩ 1,855 |
| France | ATT | $12 | ₩ 1,484 |
| Germany | ATT | $15 | ₩ 1,855 |
| Greece | ATT | $15 | ₩ 1,855 |
| Ireland | ATT | $15 | ₩ 1,855 |
| Italy | ATT | $12 | ₩ 1,484 |
| Luxemburg | ATT | $15 | ₩ 1,655 |
| Netherlands | ATT | $12 | ₩ 1,484 |
| Norway | ATT | $15 | ₩ 1,855 |
| Sweden | ATT | $12 | ₩ 1,484 |
| Switzerland | ATT | $12 | ₩ 1,521 |
| United Kingdom | ATT | $15 | ₩ 1,855 |
| Burma | KDD | GF 30 | ₩ 1,210 |
| Khmer | KDD | GF 30 | ₩ 1,210 |
| Hong Kong | C/W | GF 22.50 | ₩ 908 |

| Destination | Via | Basic Fare initial 3 Min. | Additional one Min. |
|---|---|---|---|
| India | C/W | GF 36 | ₩ 1,452 |
| Indonesia | KDD | GF 30 | ₩ 1,210 |
| Israel | ATT | $ 15 | ₩ 1,855 |
| Japan | KDD | GF 18 | ₩ 726 |
| Macao | C/W | GF 27 | ₩ 1,089 |
| Malaysia | KDDG/W | GF 36 | ₩ 1,452 |
| Philippines | RCA | $ 9 | ₩ 1,113 |
| Taiwan | KDDC/W | GF 18 | ₩ 726 |
| Thailand | KDDC/W | GF 36 | ₩ 1,452 |
| Turkey | ATT | $ 15 | ₩ 1,855 |
| Vietnam | KDD | 24 | ₩ 968 |
| Tunisia | ATT | $ 15 | ₩ 1,855 |
| Canada | ATT KDDC | $ 12 | ₩ 1,484 |
| | /W | $ 9 | ₩ 1,113 |
| Mexico | ATT | $ 15 | ₩ 1,855 |
| Alaska | ATT | $ 15 | ₩ 1,855 |
| U.S.A. | ATT | $ 12 | ₩ 1,484 |
| Brazil | ATT | $ 15 | ₩ 1,855 |
| Chile | ATT | $ 15 | ₩ 1,855 |
| Australia | ATTKDD | GF 36 | ₩ 1,452 |
| | C/W | GF 36 | |
| New Zealand | ATT | $ 12.84 | ₩ 1,584 |
| Okinawa | ATT KDD | GF 30 | ₩ 1,210 |
| | C/W | | |
| Hawaii | ATT | $ 12 | ₩ 1,484 |
| Puerto-Rico | ATT | $ 15 | ₩ 1,855 |
| El Salvador | ATT | $ 15 | ₩ 1,855 |
| Panama | ATT | $ 15 | ₩ 1,855 |

*For information concerning calls overseas, dial number
117 when overseas telephone and telegraph offices are not*

available. But you can request a call by dialing 72–2691, through 72–2694, and state the number you desire to call and give the operator your own number. As for telegrams, any of the major hotels in the cities will have cable forms and somebody to send out the telegrams for you. Telegram charges are always on a cash basis.

## Internal Transportation

### Domestic Air Flights:
Korean Airlines provides convenient flights connecting all major cities: Pusan, Taegu, Kwangju, Kunsan, Chonju, Mokpo, Yosu, Chinju, Chinhae, Cheju Island, Ulsan, Pohang, Samchok, Kangnung and Sokcho.
Passengers are not allowed to carry luggage or cameras on domestic flights.

### Railroad:
The Korean National Railroads provides deluxe express trains between Seoul-Pusan, and connects with lines to other cities.

### Highway Bus Lines:
There are many deluxe express bus lines connecting all major cities, and covering Seoul-Pusan in 4 hours 30 minutes.

### Taxi Service:
All taxis have meters. The fare is ₩90 for the first 2km (1.25miles) and ₩20 for each additional 500m. Advance negotiations with driver are advisable for long trips.

## Holidays and Gala Events
Numerous holidays and special events are observed in Korea throughout the year. Some are centuries old and others relatively new. Traditional festivals are based on the lunar calendar,

*while holidays of recent origin are set according to the solar almanac. Major holidays and gala events include:*

January 1: New Year's Day—
*Celebrated as in occidental countries. The first day of the first month by the lunar calendar is celebrated at home with the offering of new year greeting to senior members of the family. Many families also hold a memorial service for the spirits of their ancestors.*

March 1: Independence Movement Day—
*Koreans observe the anniversary of the March 1, 1919 Independence Movement against the Japanese rule.*

8th Day of the 4th Month by the Lunar Calendar
*Buddha's Birthday—Buddhists observe a "lantern festival". Solemn rituals are held at Buddhist temples, and the day's festival is climaxed by a lantern parade.*

5th Day of the 5th Month by the Lunar Calendar
*Tano Festival—Highlights of the day's festival are wrestling contests among young men and swinging for women.*

June 6: Memorial Day—
*On this day the nation pays tribute to the war dead, and memorial services are held at the National Cemetery in Seoul and at the United Nations Cemetery in Pusan.*

June 10: Farmers' Day—
*Farmers in colorful costume rejoice with age-old farmers' dances and music.*

July 17: Constitution Day—
*This day commemorates the adoption of the Republic of Korea Constitution in 1948.*

August 15: Liberation Day—
*On this day in 1945 Korea was liberated from Japan after 36 years of colonial rule.*

October 1: Armed Forces Day—
*The day is celebrated with colorful programs such as military parades, honor guard ceremonies, and air show.*

October 3: National Foundation Day—
*This day marks the traditional founding of Korea by Tangun 4304 (B.C. 2333) years ago.*

## 15th day of the 8th month by the Lunar Calender.

Chusok or Moon Festival Day—
*Viewing the full moon is a feature of the evening. It is one of the great national holidays of the year and is the Korean version of Thanksgiving Day.*

October 9: Hangul (Korean Alphabet) Day—
*This day celebrates the anniversary of the promulgation of Hangul by King Sejong of the Yi Dynasty in 1443.*

October 24: United Nations Day—
*At the U.N. Cemetery in Pusan, a memorial service is held in tribute to the war dead of the U.N. forces which took part in the Korean War.*

December 25: Christmas—
*Christians and other citizens celebrate this holiday as in the West.*

# The National Flag (Tae Geuk Ki)

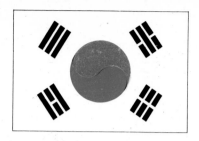

The Korean flag symbolizes much of the thought, philosophy and mysticism of the Orient. The symbol, and sometimes the flag itself, is called *Tae Geuk Ki*.

Depicted on the flag is a circle divided equally and locked in perfect balance. The upper (red) section represents the Yang and the lower (blue) section the Um, an ancient symbol of the universe originating in China. These two opposites express the dualism of the cosmos: fire and water, day and night, dark and light, construction and destruction, masculine and feminine, active and passive, heat and cold, plus and minus, and so on.

The central thought in the *Tae Geuk* indicates that while there is a constant movement within the sphere of infinity, there are also balance and harmony. As a simple example, kindness and cruelty may be taken into consideration. If parents are kind to a child, it is good, but they may spoil and weaken him and thus lead him to become a vicious man and a source of disgrace to his ancestors.

Three bars at each corner also carry the ideas of opposition and balance. The three unbroken lines stand for heaven: the opposite three broken lines represent the earth. At the lower left hand of the flag are two lines with a broken line in between. This symbolizes fire. The opposite is the symbol of water.

## ARIRANG

Korean Folk Song

A ri rang a ri rang a ra ri yo

A ri rang go gae ro no mo gan da

Na rul po ri go ga shi nun nim un

Shim ni do mot ga so pal byong nan da

## DORAJI TARYONG

Do ra ji do ra ji do ra ji

Shim shim san cheon ei paek do ra ji

Han tu bu ri man kae yo do

Tae pa ku ni ro pan shil man doe nu na.

E he ya E he ya E ha ya

E yo ro nan da chi hwa ja jo ta

jo ki jo san mi tei do ra ji ga han tul han tul

166

# Simple Phrases in Korean

| English | Korean |
|---|---|
| *How are you?* | An-nyeong hasim-nika? |
| *I am fine, thank you.* | Jotsum-nida gamsa-hamnida. |
| *Are you a Korean?* | Dangsin-eun hanguk saram imnika? |
| *Yes, I am.* | Ne, geu-reot seumnida. |
| *Are you an American?* | Dangsin-eun miguk saram imnika? |
| *Yes, I am.* | Ne, geu-reot seumnida. |
| *I am a Japanese* | Naneun illbon saram imnida. |
| *I am a Chinese* | Naneun jungguk saram imnida. |
| *Take me to the Bando Hotel.* *(to the taxi driver)* | Bando hotel ae gapsida. |
| *You are pretty.* | Dangsin eun ye-bbum-nida. |
| *I like you.* | Na-neun dangsin-eul jowa hamnida. |
| *I want to buy a doll.* | Naneun inhyong-eul sago sipseumnida. |
| *How much does it cost?* | Igeoseun eolma imnika? |
| *Show me another one, please.* | Dareun geoseul boyeo jusipsiyo. |
| *Thank you very much.* | Dae-danhi gamsa hamnida. |
| *I hope to see you again.* | Dasi bepget seumnida. |
| *Good bye* *(to the person leaving)* | An-nyeonghi gasipsiyo. |
| *(to the person staying)* | An-nyeonghi gesipsiyo |

# KOREAN MISSIONS ABROAD

## EMBASSIES

**ARGENTINA:** Juez Tedin 2722, Buenos Aires, Argentina *Tel:* 826548, 826704 *Cable Add:* GONGKWAN BUENOS AIRES/ARGENTINA

**AUSTRALIA:** 55, Muggaway, Red Hill, Canberra. A.C.,T., Australia *Tel:* 956995/6 *Cable Add:* GONGKWAN CANBERRA/AUSTRALIA

**AUSTRIA:** Reisnerstrasse 48, 1030, Wien, Austria *Tel:* 725811/2 *Cable Add:* GONGKWAN WIEN/AUSTRIA

**BELGIUM:** 9, Rue de Crayer, 1050. Brussels, Belgium *Tel:* 499065/6 *Cable Add:* GONGKWAN BRUSSELS/BELGIUM

**BRAZIL:** Edificio Central, 4-andar (floor), Sector Commercial Sul, Brasilia, D.F., Brazil *Tel:* 43–9827, 24–8173, 24–9173, *Cable Add:* GONGKWAN/BRASILIA/BRAZIL

**CAMEROON:** B.P. 301, Yaounde, Cameroon *Tel:* 22–3223 *Cable Add:* GONGKWAN RAOUNDE/CAMEROON

**CANADA:** 151 Slalor St., Room 608, Ottawa 4, Ontario, Canada *Tel:* 2359184, 2359439 *Cable Add:* GONGKWAN OTTAWA/CANADA

**CENTRAL AFRICA :** Villa Ministre ALAZOULA, Route de Colline Bangui Republique Centrafricaine *Post:* B.P., 841, Bangui Republique Centrafricaine (RCA) *Tel.:* 32–57, *Cable Add.:* GONGKWAN BANGUI

**CHILE:** Departamento 710, Mireflores 686, Santiago, Chile P.O. Box Casilla 1301, Correo Central, Santiago, Chile *Tel:* 32135, 32316 *Cable Add:* GONGKWAN SANTIAGO/CHILE

**CHINA:** 72, Fenai-Road, Section 3, Taipei, China *Tel:* 772463, 773108/9 *Cable Add:* GONGKWAN TALPEI/CHINA

**COLOMBIA:** Carrera 7a No. 37-21 Oficina 501 Edificio Lutaima, Bogota D.E. Colombia *Tel:* 32–76–63 *Cable Add:* GONGKWAN BOGOTA/COLOMBIA

**DENMARK:** Strandvejen 687, 2930 Klampenborg, Denmark *Tel:* (01)630297 *Cable Add:* GONGKWAN/COPENHAGEN

**ETHIOPIA:** P.O. Box 2047, Africa Road, Addis Ababa, Ethiopia *Tel:* 44490 *Cable Add:* GONGKWAN ADDIS ABABA/ETHIOPIA

**FRANCE:** 29, Avenue de Villiers, Paris 17, France *Tel:* 2270214 *Cable Add:* GONGKWAN PARIS/FRANCE

**GERMANY:** Adenaueralle 124, Bonn, Germany *Tel:* 226391/2 (Bonn) *Cable Add:* GONGKWAN BONN/GERMANY

**IRAN:** K.H. Kakh No. 427, Teheran Iran *Tel:* 662888 663913 *Cable Add:* GONGKWAN TEHERAN/IRAN

**ITALY:** Via Barnaba Oriani 30, Rome, Italy *Tel:* 878626, 805306, 805292 *Cable Add:* GONGKWAN ROME/ITALY

**IVORY COAST:** 3 eme etage, Immeuble Le General', Avenue du General de Gaulle, Abidjan, Cote d'Ivorie B.P. 21040 *Tel:* 25014 *Cable Add:* GONGKWAN ABIDJAN/IVORY COAST

**JAPAN:** 2-5, 1-Chome, Minami-Azabu, Minato-ku, Tokyo, Japan *Tel:* 452–7611/9, 453–7734 *Cable Add:* GONGKWAN TOKYO/

JAPAN

**KENYA:** P.O. Box 30455, 10th Floor, I.P.S. Bldg., Kimathi St., Nairobi, Kenya *Tel:* 28011/2 *Cable Add:* GONGKWAN MAIROBI/ KENYA

**KHMER:** 4 Boulevard, Monivong, Phnom Penh *Tel:* 22047, 24288 *Cable Add:* GONGKWAN PHNOM PENH/CAMBODIA

**MALAYSIA:** 422, Circular Road, Kuala Lumpur. Malaysia *Tel:* 21651/2 *Cable Add:* GONGKWAN KUALA LUMPUR/MALAYSIA

**MEXICO:** Paseo De Las Palmas No. 7552, Piso Lomas De Chapultepec Mexico, 10 D.F. *Tel:* 520–77–14, 540–33–02 *Cable Add:* GONGKWAN MEXICO/MEXICO

**MOROCCO:** 23, Avenue de France, Rabal, Morocco *Tel:* 702–98, 729–68, 728–28 *Cable Add:* GONGKWAN RABAT/MOROCCO

**THE NETHERLANDS:** 64 Nieuwe Parklaan, The Hague, Netherlands *Tel:* 550514, 549638 *Cable Add:* GONGKWAN HAGUE/NETHERLANDS

**NEW ZEALAND:** Embassy of the Republic of Korea, 7th Floor, Molesworth House, Molesworth Street, Wellington, P.O. Box 12115, Wellington North. *Tel:* 70216, 70217 *Cable Add:* GONGKWAN WELLINGTON

**NORWAY:** Hotel Continental Rm. 611, Stortingsgt, 24–26 OSLO Norway *Cable Add.:* GONGKWAN OSLO.

**PERU:** Embajada de La Republica de Core Avenida Arequipa 3362, San Isidro, Lima, Peru *Tel:* 40–3748, 40–4349 *Cable Add:* GONGKWAN LIMA

**THE PHILIPPINES:** Rm. 201-208, Rufino Bldg., 123 Ayala Avenue, Makati, Rizal, Philippines P.O. Box: Commercial Center P.O. Box 621, Makati, Rizal, D-708 *Tel:* 886423, 886897, 887712 *Cable Add:* GONGKWAN MANILA/PHILIPPINES

**RWANDA:** B.P. 1337, Kigali, Rwanda *Tel.:* 5112, 5583 *Cable Add.:* GONGKWAN, KIGALI/ RWANDA

**SPAIN:** Av. Generalisimo, No. 10. Madrid-16, Spain *Tel:* 2628504/6 2624560 *Cable Add:* GONGKWAN MADRID/SPAIN

**SWEDEN:** Strandvagen 80, 115-27, Stockholm, Sweden: *Tel:* 618650, 623000, 616826 *Cable Add:* GONGKWAN STOCKHOLM/SWEDEN

**SWITZERLAND:** Hallwylster 34, Bern Switzerland *Tel:* 431081/2 *Cable Add:* GONGKWAN BERN/ SWITZERLAND

**THAILAND :**Olympia Tai Building 956 Rama 4, Bangkok 5, Thailand *Tel:* 861074/7, 861663, 863771 *Cable Add:* GONGKWAN BANGKOK/THAILAND

**TUNISIA:** 85, Avenue de la Liberle, Tunis, Tunisia *Tel:* 282548, 286741 *Cable Add:* GONGKWAN TUNIS/ TUNISIA

**TURKEY:** Kavaklidere, Posta Caddest Alasam, Sokak 9, Ankara, Turkey *Tel:* 121793, 120489, 176870 *Cable Add:* GONGKWAN ANKARA/TURKEY

**UGANDA:** P.O. Box 3717, Bauman House, Kampala, Uganda *Tel:* 45312, 45336 *Cable Add:* GONGKWAN KAMPALA/UGANDA

**THE UNITED KINGDOM:** 36, Cadogan Square, London, S.W.I., United Kingdom *Tel:* 581–0247/9, 581–0250 *Cable Add:* GONGKWAN LONDON/ENGLAND/U.K. Postcode: 36, Cadogan Square, Landon Swix OJN

**THE UNITED STATES OF AMERICA:** 2320, Massachusetts Avenve, N.W., Washington D.C. 20008, U.S.A. *Tel:* 4837383 *Cable Add:* KORIC WASHINGTON D.C./ U.S.A.

**UPPER VOLTA:** B.P. 618, Ouagadougou, Haute Volta *Tel:* 2205 *Cable Add:* GONGKWAN OUAGADOUGOU/UPPER VOLTA

**URUGUAY:** P.O. Box 1678, Bulevard Artigas 26 Montevideo. Uruguay *Tel:* 703082 *Cable Add:* GONGKWAN MONTEVIDEO/ URUGUAY

**VIETNAM:** 107, Rue Nguyen Du Saigon, Viet Nam *Tel:* 23146 *Cable Add:* GONGKWAN SAIGON/ VIETNAM

**ZAIRE:** No. 147 Boulevard du 30 Juin, Kinshasa, B.P. 628, Kin-1 *Tel:* 31345 *Cable Add:* GONGKWAN KINSHASA/CONGO

## CONSULATE GENERAL

**CAIRO:** 6. Shaira Dr. Mohamed Sobhy. Guizea, Cairo, U.A.R. *Tel:* 842564, 846637 *Cable Add:* GONGKWAN GIZA CAIRO/U.A.R.

**KATH MANDU:** Anna Purna Hotel. Kathmandu, Nepal *Cable:* GONGKWAN KATH MANDU

**CHICAGO:** 500, North Michigan Avenue, Chicago, Illinois 60611, U.S.A., *Tel:* 822 9485/6 *Cable Add:* GONGKWAN CHICAGO/U.S.A.

**DJAKARTA:** Djalan Diponegoro 13. Djakarta. Indonesia *Tel:* 51972/3 *Cable Add:* GONGKWAN DJAKARTA INDONESIA

**FUKUOKA:** 10-20, 1-Chome, Akasaka, Fukuoka, Japan *Tel:* 77-0461/3 *Cable Add:* GONGKWAN FUKUOKA/JAPAN

**HAMBURG:** 2 Hamburg 13, Hagedornstr. 53, West Germany *Tel:* 4102031/2 *Cable Add:* GONGKWAN HAMBURG/GERMANY

**HONG KONG:** Korea Center Bldg., 3/F, 119-121 Connaught Rd., C., Hong Kong *Tel:* 430224/8 *Cable Add:* GONGKWAN HONG KONG/HONG KONG

**HONOLULU:** 2756 Pali highway, Honolulu, Hawaii 96817, U.S.A. *Tel:* 595-6274, 585-6109 *Cable Add:* GONGKWAN HONOLULU/U.S.A.

**HOUSTON:** 802, World Trade Bldg., 1520 Texas Avenue, Houston, Texas 77002, U.S.A. *Tel:* (713) 227-4205/7 *Cable Add:* GONGKWAN HOUSTON/U.S.A.

**ISLAMABAD:** 450, G6/4, Ramna 6 Islamabad, Pakistan *Tel:* 22305, 21092 *Cable Add:* GONGKWAN ISLAMABAD/PAKISTAN

**LOS ANGELES:** Iee Tower, Bldg., Suile 1101, 5455 Wilshire Blvd., Los Angeles, California 90036, U.S.A. *Tel:* Wel-1331/2 *Cable Add:* GONGKWAN LOS AVGELES/U.S.A.

**NEW DELHI:** 5, Mansingh Road New Delhi-11, India *Tel:* 384295/6 *Cable Add:* GONGKWAN NEW DELHI/INDIA

**NEW YORK:** 720 Fifth Aveneu, New Yrok. N.Y. 10019. *Tel:* (212) 586-5800 *Cable Add:* GONGKWAN NEW YORK/U.S.A.

**OSAKA:** 23-1, 4th St., Sueyoshi-bashi-dori Minami-ku, Osaka, Japan *Tel:* 2524251/4 *Cable Add:* GONGKWAN OSAKA/JAPAN

**RANGOON:** No. 591, Prome Road, Rangoon, Burma *Tel:* 30497, 30655 *Cable:* KONGKWAN RANGOON/ BURMA

**SAN FRANCISCO:** 3500, Clay St., San Francisco 18. California, U.S.A. *Tel:* 921-2252/3 *Cable Add.* GONGKWAN SAN FRANCISCO/U.S.A.

**SAO PAULO:** Av. Paulista 810 Conjunto 1, Paraiso, Soo Paulo,

Brazil *Tel:* 287–9332 *Cable Add:* GONGKWAN SAO PAULO/ BRAZIL

**SAPPORO:** Nisi 21-Chome, Gida-Sancho, Sapporo, Japan *Tel:* 62–0288/9 *Cable Add:* GONGKWAN/ SAPPORO/JAPAN

**SINGAPORE:** 5th Floor, phong Teck Bldg., 15 Scotts Rood. Singapore *Tel:* 376411, 376334, 376089 *Cable Add:* GONGKWAN SINGAPORE

**SYDNEY:** 91, Wolseley Road, Point Piper. Sydney, N.S.W. 2027. Australia *Tel:* 363753 *Cable Add:* GONGKWAN SYDENY/AUSTRALIA

**VANCOUVER:** 550, Guiness Tower, 1055 West Hastings St., Vancouver 1, B.C., Canada *Tel:* 681–9581/2 *Cable Add:* GONGKWAN VANCOURVER/ CANDA

## CONSULATE

**AGANA, GUAM:** Amistad Bldg. Room 5, Marine Drive Agana, Guam 96910 *Tel:* 7726488 *Cable Add:* GONGKWAN AGANA/ GUAM/U.S.

**KOBE:** 2-73, Nakayamate-dori, Ikuta-ku, Kobe, Japan, *Tel:* 22–5608, 22–4453/5 *Cable Add:* GONGKWAN KOBE/JAPAN

**MUENCHEN:** Graefelfingerstr. 138, 8, MUENCHEN 70, West Germany *Tel:* 707181, 707182

**NAGOYA:** 8, Higashi-Osone. Minami-1-Chome, Higashi-ku, Nagoya, Japan *Tel:* 961–9221 *Cable Add:* GONGKWAN NAGOYA/JAPAN

**SENDAI:** 5-22, Kamisugi 5-Chome, Sendai, Japan *Tel:* 21–2751/4 21–5030 *Cable Add:* GLANGKWAN SENDAI/JAPAN

**SHIMONOSEKI:** 13-10, Higashi Yamato-machi, Shimonoseki, Japan *Tel:* 66–5341/3 *Cable Add:* GONGKWAN SHIMONOSEKI/JAPAN

**YOKOHAMA:** 118, Yamatecho, Naka-ku, Yokohama, Japan *Tel:* 20–4531/3 *Cable Add:* GONGKWAN YOKOHAMA/JAPAN

## KOTRA'S OVERSEAS NETWORKS

**MONTREAL:** Floor "F" (Frontenac 30), International Trade Center, Place Bonaventure, Montreal 114, P.Q., Canada, P.O. Box: 646, *Cable:* MOOGONG, *Tel:* (514)878–3425/6

**NEW YORK:** Suite 4601, Empire State Bldg., 350, 5th Ave.. New York, N.Y. 10001, U.S.A. *Cable:* MOOGONG *Tel:* (212) 594–9464, Telex: 224957

**CHICAGO:** 111 East Wacker Drive, Chicago, Illinois 60601, U.S.A. *Cable:* MOOGONG, *Tel:* (312) 644–4323/4

**SAN FRANCISCO:** Rm. 250-C, World Trade Center, Ferry Bldg., San Francisco, Calif. 94111, U.S.A. *Cable:* MOOGONG, *Tel:* (415) 391–2637

**LOS ANGELES:** Occidental Center, 1149, South Hill St., Los Angeles, Calif. 90015, U.S.A. *Cable:* MOOGONG, *Tel:* (213) 748–5331/4

**VANCOUVER:** Suite 960, One Bentall Center, 505 Burrard St., Vancouver 1, B.C., Canada. *Cable:* MOOGONG, *Tel:* (604) 683–1820

**DALLAS:** 2001 Bryan Tower, Dallas, Texas 75201. U.S.A. *Cable:* MOOGONG, *Tel:* (214) 748–9341/2

**STOCHKHOLM:** Hamngatan 13, 11147. Stockholm. Sweden *Cable:* MOOGONG, *Tel:* (08) 217177. 113211, *Telex:* 10520 CEOFICES

**AMSTERDAM:** Van Baerlestraat 3, Amsterdam, Netherlands, *Cable:* MOOGONG, *Tel:* (020)730555/6, *Telex:* 16368 KOTRA NL

**LONDON:** 28 Charing Cross Road, London W.C., 2, United Kingdom, *Cable:* MOOGONG, *Tel:* (240) 3192, *Telex:* 22375 MOOGONG

**FRANKFURT:** 6 Frankfurt A.M., Seilerstrasse 16-18, Federal Republic of Germany *Cable:* MOOGONG, *Tel:* (0611) 287166/7, *Telex:* 416357 KOTRA D

**PARIS:** 49, Ave. Kleber, Paris 16-eme, France, *Cable:* MOOGONG, *Tel:* (704) 6639, 7177, *Telex:* ITESER 28823 Serv. 480

**MILAN:** Via Manfredo Comperio 1, 20123 Milano, Italy, *Cable:* MOONGNG, *Tel:* (876) 806

**TEHERAN:** 1st Floor, Shahriar Bldg., No. 52, Ave. Shah, Teheran, Iran, P.O. Box 3091 Teheran, *Cable:* MOOGONG *Tel:* (66) 4740

**TOKYO:** Yurakucho Bldg., No. 5, 1-chome, Yurakucho, Chiyoda-ku, Tokyo, Japan, *Cable:* DAEHAN-KOTRA, *Tel:* (03) 214-6951/3, *Telex:* TK 4393

**OSAKA:** 5th Floor, Shin Shibagawa Bldg., 6-1, 4-chome, Doshomachi, Higashi-ku, Osaka, Japan, *Cable:* MOOGONG, *Tel:* (06) 231-1026/8

**HONG KONG:** 2nd Floor, Korea Center Bldg., 119-121, Connaught Road, C., Hong Kong, C.P.O. Box; 15573, *Cable:* MOOGONG, *Tel:* H-448109, 448100, *Telex:* HX 3497 HONGKONG

**SAIGON:** 125A Tu-Do St., Saigon, Vietnam, P.O. Box: 1202 Saigon, *Cable:* MOOGONG, *Tel:* 23807, 91805

**BANGKOK:** 294/296, Roma 1 Road (Patumwan Square), Bangkok, Thailand, P.O. Box: 1896, *Cable:* MOOGONG, *Tel:* 58857

**SINGAPORE:** 6th Floor, Hong Leong Bldg., 144, Robinson Road, Singapore 1, Singapore. P.O. Box: 421, *Cable:* MOOGONG, *Tel:* 97267

**DJAKARTA:** Djlo Ir. H. Djuanda, No. 29, Djakarta, Indonesia, P.O. Box: 362/DKT, *Cable:* MOOGONG, *Tel:* 44823 *Telex:* MOOGONG DKT 6188

**SYDNEY:** Suite No. 2204, Australia Square, George St., Sydney N.S.W. Australia, G.P.O. Box: 2738 Sydney, N.S.W., *Cable:* MOOGONG, *Tel:* (27)3369, 2524

## TRADE OFFICES

**TORONTO:** Suite 805, Board of Trade Bldg., 11, Adelaide St., West Toronto, Ontario, Canada, *Cable:* MOOGONG, *Tel.* (864) 1076/7

**PANAMA:** Edificio 32, Local 1-2, Colon Free Zone, Rep. of Panama, P.O. Box: 2137, *Cable:* MOOGONG *Tel:* (47) 6177, *Telex:* 3482098 MOOGONG COLON

**CARACAS:** Torre Lincoln, Officina 10-B (10 Piso) Ave. Lincoln (Eqs. Ave., Las Acacial), Sabana Grand, Caracas, Venezuela, P.O. Box: Apartado 5368 Carmelias, *Cable:* MOOGONG, *Tel:* (72) 0293

**VIENNA:** 1010 Wien, Lugeck 1/v/ 17, Republik Österreich, *Tel:* (0222) 521475, *Cable:* MOOGONG

**BRUSSELS:** c/o Korean Embassy, 9, Rue De Crayer, 1050 Brussels, Belgium, *Cable:* MOOGONG, *Tel:* (49) 9065, 9066

**ZURICH:** Lowenstrasse 64, 8001, Zurich, Switzerland, *Cable:* MOOGONG, *Tel:* (01) 728244

**MADRID:** Jose Lazaro Galdiano 4-1 Madrid-16, Spain, *Cable:* MOOGONG MADRID, *Tel:* (457) 5929

**BEIRUT:** Rm. 209, Gefinor Center, Bloc D, Clemenceau St., Beirut, Lebanon, P.O. Box: 6176, *Cable:* MOOGONG, *Tel:* 344092

**KUWAIT:** Flat No. 17, 2nd Floor, AlSour Bldg., AlSour St., Kuwait, P.O. Box: 20771 Safat, *Cable:* MOOGONG, *Tel:* 422410

**LAGOS:** 82 Awolowo Road, Ikoyi Lagos, Nigeria, G.P.O. Box: 1019, *Cable:* MOOGONG, *Tel:* 24054

**NAIROBI:** Rm. No. 123, Uniafric House, Koinange St., Nairobi, Kenya, P.O. Box: 40569 Nairobi, *Cable:* MOOGONG. *Tel:* 28928

**JOHANNESBURG:** 8th Flo/, The Trust Bank Center, 56 Eloff St., Johannesburg, Republic of South Africa, P.O. Box: 9675 Johannesburg. *Tel:* (21) 1855, *Cable:* MOOGONG

**MANILA:** Rm. 802 Sikatuna Bldg., Ayala Ave., Makati, Rizal, Philippines, *Cable:* MOOGONG, *Tel:* (88) 4711, (87) 3244

**TAIPEI:** 3rd Floor, 52, Chungsan North Road, Section 2, Taipei, Taiwan, P.O. Box: 1555 Taipei, *Cable:* MOOGONG, *Tel:* 583030/1

**FUKUOKA:** Fukuoka Chamber of Commerce & Industry Bldg., 9-28, 2-cheme, Hokataekimae, Fukuoka, Japan, *Cable:* MOOCHONG, *Tel:* (44) 2358/9

**NAGOYA:** No. 301, Hakuzen Bldg., 13-21, 2-chome, Nishiki, Naka-ku, Nagoya, Japan, *Tel:* (052) 2116333/4, *Cable:* Nagoya, MOOGONG

## KOTRA REPRESENTATIVES TO KOREAN EMBASSIES AND MISSIONS

**MEXICO:** Korean Embassy in Mexico, Av., Palmas No. 755, Piso-2 Lomas De Chapultepec, Mexico 10, D.F. Mexico, *Cable:* GONGKWAN MEXICO, *Tel:* 520-77-14, 540-33-02

**BRAZIL:** Consulado Geral da Republica da Coreia, Av. Paulista 810 Conjunto 1, Sao Paulo, Brazil, *Cable:* GONGKWAN SAOPAULO, *Tel:* 287-9332

**ARGENTINA:** Korean Embassy in Argentina, Juez Tedin 2722, Buenos Aires, Argentina, *Cable:* GONGKWAN BUENOSAIRES, *Tel:*

(82) 6548, 6704

**GERMANY:** Korea-Europe Trade Information Center, 2 Hamburg 1, Steindamn 97, Federal Republic of Germany, *Tel:* 247657/9, *Telex:* 2162414 KOHA D

**ETHIOPIA:** Korean Embassy in Ethiopia, Africa Road, Addis Ababa, Ethiopia, P.O. Box: 2047 Addis Ababa, *Cable:* GONGKWAN, *Tel:* 44490

## CORRESPONDENT POSTS

**ECUADOR:** Mr. Bum Jae Lee, Correspondent, Korea Trade Promotion Corp., P.O. Box: 6680, Guayaguil, Ecuador, *Tel:* (250) 46-11

**CALCUTTA:** Mr. P.M. Singhui, Vice President, Century, Spinning and Manufacturing Co., 11 Owners Court Mayfair Road, Calcutta-19,, India

**BOMBAY:** Mr. T. J. Lalvani, President, East-West Trading Company, Advani Chambers: Sir P. Mehta Road, Bombay-1, India

## DIPLOMATIC AND CONSULAR MISSIONS IN KOREA

**AUSTRAILIA, Embassy**—*Tel:* 73-4330/73-4527/75-9958, *Address:* 58-1, 1-ka, Sinmun-ro, Chongro-ku, Seoul K.P.O. Box: 562

**BELGIUM, Embassy**—*Tel.* 43-5597/3514, *Address:* 258-25, Itaewon-dong, Yongsan-ku, Seoul.

**BRAZIL, Embassy**—*Tel.* 28-6379/28-6293, *Address:* 3rd Floor, New Korea Hotel Bldg., 192-11, 1-ka, Ulchiro, Chung-ku, Seoul.

**CHINA, Embassy**—*Tel.* 28-1216/9, *Address:* 2-83, Myung-dong, Chung-ku, Seoul.

**DENMARK, Consulate**—*Tel.* 22-9648/23-3121/6. *Address:* 81, Sokong-dong, Chung-ku, Seoul.

**FRANCE, Embassy**—

*Tel.* 72–5547/9. *Address:* 30, Hap-dong, Sudaemun-ku, Seoul.

**GERMANY, Embassy**—*Tel.* 22–4037/22–4237, *Address:* 9th Floor, Dae Han Bldg., 75, Susomun-dong, Sudaemun-ku, Seoul.

**GREECE, Consulate**—*Tel.* 22–6763/28–5221/9, *Address:* Duck Soo Bldg., 28, 2-ka, Taepyung-no, Chung-ku, Seoul.

**HOLY SEE, Embassy**—*Tel.* 72–5725, *Address:* 2, Kungjong-dong, Chungno-ku, Seoul. P.O. Box 393

**INDIA, Consulate**—*Tel.* 43–4142/3 *Address:* 258-6, Itaewon-dong, Yong-san-ku, Seoul.

**INDONESIA, Consulate**—*Tel:* 42–9107/43–2007. *Address:* 258-87, Itaewon-dong, Yongsan-ku, Seoul.

**ISRAEL, Embassy**—*Tel.* 43–3586/7. *Address:* 309-8, Dongbinggo-dong, Yongsan-ku, Seoul.

**ITALY, Embassy**—*Tel.* 74–7405, 72–6001. *Address:* 1-169, 2-ka, Shin Moon-ro, Chongro-ku, Seoul

**JAPAN, Embassy**—*Tel.* 73–5626/8 74–5378/9, *Address:* 18-11, Choong-hak-dong, Chongro-ku, Seoul.

**JAPAN ,Consulate**—*Tel.* 22–0267/0294 *Address:* 41, 1-ka, Kwangbok-dong, Chung-ku, Pusan.

**JORDAN, Consulate**—*Tel.* 75–5552 *Address:* 188-7, 4-ka, Myong-yun-dong, Chongro-ku, Seoul.

**KHMER Republic, Embassy**—*Tel.* 72–6152 (Chancery) 73–4819 (Residence) *Address:* 98-78, Wooni-dong, Chongro-ku, Seoul.

**MALAYSIA, Embassy**—*Tel.* 54–2203/5. *Address:* 726, Hannam-dong, Yongsan-ku, Seoul.

**NETHERLANDS, Consulate**—*Tel.* 43–0651 43–0652, *Address:* 1-85, Dongbinggo-dong, Yongsan-ku, Seoul.

**NORWAY, Consulate**—*Tel.* 28–3000. *Ahdress:* Rm. 1001. Dae Han Bldg., 75.Susomun-dong, Sudaemun ku, Seoul.

**PANAMA, Consulate**—*Tel.* 28–1434 *Address:* 133, 2-ka, Namdac-mun-ro, Chung-ku, Seoul.

**PERU, Consulate**—*Tel.* 28–8468. *Address:* 125, 4-ka, Chungmu-ro, Chung-ku, Seoul.

**PHILIPPINES, Embassy**—*Tel.* 43–8771/2 *Address:* 258-25, Itaewon-dong, Yongsan-ku, Seoul.

**SWEDISH EMBASSY, OFFICE OF COMMERCIAL ATTACHE** Room 1306, Tae Yang Bldg., No. 60, 1-ka, Myung-dong, Chung-ku, Seoul *Tel.* 24–4836, 22–7937

**SWITZERLAND, Embassy**—*Tel.* 73–7876 73–3861. *Address:* 32. Songwol-dong, Suhdaemun-ku, Seoul.

**THAILAND, Embassy**—*Tel.* 42–0197 *Address:* House No. 127, Nam-san Village, Itaewon-dong, Yongsan-ku, Seoul.

**TUNISIA, Consulate**—*Tel.* 22–1952 *Address:* Rm. 702, Hansin Bldg., 62-10, 2-ka, Chungmoo-ro, Chung-ku, Seoul.

**TURKEY, Embassy**—*Tel.* 52–2774/ 52–6485. *Address:* 248-2, Ssangrim-dong, Chung-ku, Seoul.

**UNITED KINGDOM, Embassy**—*Tel.* 75–7341/3. *Address:* 4, Chong-dong, Sudaemun-ku, Seoul.

**URUGUAY, Embassy**—*Tel.* 42–0131, Ext. 12, *Address:* C 12, Namsan Mansion Apartment, Itaewon-dong, Yongsan-ku, Seoul.

**U.S.A. Embassy**—*Tel.* 72–2601/19, *Address:* 82, Sejong-ro, Chongro-ku, Seoul.

**U.S.A.(Annex)**—*Tel.* 72–2601/9. Ext. 4479, *Address:* 63, 1-ka, Ulchiro, Chung-ku, Seoul.

**VIETNAM, Embassy**—*Tel.* 28–6127/9. *Address:* 24-31, 1-ka, Chung-mu-ro, Seoul.

# INDEX